First World War
and Army of Occupation
War Diary
France, Belgium and Germany

40 DIVISION
Headquarters, Branches and Services
Adjutant and Quarter-Master General
4 June 1916 - 28 February 1919

WO95/2594/2

The Naval & Military Press Ltd
www.nmarchive.com
Published in association with The National Archives

Published by

The Naval & Military Press Ltd

Unit 10 Ridgewood Industrial Park,

Uckfield, East Sussex,

TN22 5QE England

Tel: +44 (0) 1825 749494

www.naval-military-press.com

www.nmarchive.com

This diary has been reprinted in facsimile from the original. Any imperfections are inevitably reproduced and the quality may fall short of modern type and cartographic standards.

© **Crown Copyright**
Images reproduced by permission of The National Archives, London, England, 2015.

Contents

Document type	Place/Title	Date From	Date To
Heading	WO95/2594/2 Adjutant & Quartes-Mastes General		
Heading	40th Division 'A' & 'Q' Branch Jun 1916-Feb 1919		
Heading	War Diary Of Assistant Adjutant & Quarter Master General. 40th Division. From 4th to 30th June 1916		
War Diary	Norrent Fontes	04/06/1916	18/06/1916
War Diary	Bruay	19/06/1916	30/06/1916
Miscellaneous	Arrivals Sunday, 4th June, 1916		
Miscellaneous	Arrivals Monday, 5th June, 1916		
Miscellaneous	Arrivals Tuesday, 6th June, 1916		
Miscellaneous	Arrivals Wednesday, 7th June, 1916		
Miscellaneous	Arrivals Thursday, 8th June, 1916	09/06/1916	09/06/1916
Miscellaneous	Arrivals Friday, 9th June, 1916		
Miscellaneous	Billeting Scheme. 40th Division.		
Miscellaneous	Billets of 40th Division In Area of Concentration.		
Miscellaneous	40th Division.		
Miscellaneous	Details and dates have been arranged with the A.D.M.S. of Divisions concerned Programme of instructions of Field Ambulances	10/06/1916	10/06/1916
Heading	War Diary of A. & Q. Branch, 40th Division. Period-1st to 31st, July. 1916 Volume II.		
War Diary	Bruay	01/07/1917	04/07/1917
War Diary	Braquemont. Noeux Les Mines.	04/07/1916	31/07/1916
Miscellaneous	Billets of 40th Division On 24th June, 1916	24/06/1916	24/06/1916
Miscellaneous			
War Diary	Programme of relief of 1st Division by 40th Division.		
Miscellaneous	Billets Of 40th Division On 5th July, 1916	03/07/1916	03/07/1916
War Diary	Billets Of 40th Division On 8th July, 1916	07/07/1916	07/07/1916
Heading	War Diary of A & Q Branch 40th Division. From 1st. August 1916. To 31st. August 1916. Vol. III		
War Diary	Braquemont (Noeux Les Mines)	01/08/1916	31/08/1916
Heading	War Diary of "A" & "Q" Branch, 40th Division. For Period 1st to 30th September, 1916. Vol. IV.		
War Diary	Braquemont Near Noeux Les Mines	01/09/1916	30/09/1916
Miscellaneous	Billets of 40th Division On 26th August, 1916	26/08/1916	26/08/1916
Heading	War Diary of 'A' and 'Q' Branch. 40th Division. For Period 1st to 31st October, 1916. Vol. V.		
War Diary	Braquemont (Noeux Les Mines)	01/10/1916	29/10/1916
War Diary	Roellecourt	30/10/1916	31/10/1916
Miscellaneous	Billets Of 40th Division On 30th September, 1916	30/09/1916	30/09/1916
War Diary	Billets Of 40th Division On 28th October, 1916	28/10/1916	28/10/1916
Heading	War Diary of 'A' & 'Q' Branch, Headquarters, 40th Division For Period 1st to 30th November, 1916. Vol. VI.		
War Diary	Roellecourt	01/11/1916	04/11/1916
War Diary	Frohen Le Grand	05/11/1916	05/11/1916
War Diary	Bernaville	06/11/1916	13/11/1916
War Diary	Frohen Le Grand	14/11/1916	18/11/1916
War Diary	Bouquemaison	19/11/1916	21/11/1916
War Diary	Doullens	22/11/1916	22/11/1916
War Diary	Canaples	23/11/1916	23/11/1916

War Diary	Ailly Le	24/11/1916	24/11/1916
War Diary	Hautclocher	25/11/1916	30/11/1916
Miscellaneous	40th Division.		
War Diary	Billeting-Houvin Area.	02/11/1916	04/11/1916
War Diary	Refilling Points.		
War Diary	40th Division.		
War Diary	Location of Units.	12/11/1916	12/11/1916
War Diary	40th Division.		
War Diary	40th. Division.	23/11/1916	23/11/1916
Miscellaneous	40th. Division.	24/11/1916	24/11/1916
Miscellaneous	40th. Division.		
Heading	War Diary Of "A" And "Q" Branch 40th Division. From 1/12/1916 To 31/12/1916. Volume VII.		
War Diary	Ailly Le Haut	01/12/1916	02/12/1916
War Diary	Clocher	02/12/1916	13/12/1916
War Diary	Chipilly	14/12/1916	28/12/1916
War Diary	Maurepas	28/12/1916	31/12/1916
Miscellaneous	40th Division.	15/12/1916	15/12/1916
Miscellaneous	40th Division.	29/12/1916	29/12/1916
Heading	War Diary "A" And "Q" Branch 40th Division From 1st January To 31st January, 1917. Vol. VIII.		
War Diary	Near Maurepas	01/01/1917	25/01/1917
War Diary	Near Maurepas	26/12/1917	28/12/1917
War Diary	Corbie	29/12/1917	31/12/1917
Heading	War Diary of Q Branch 40th Division for. February 1917		
War Diary	Corbie	01/02/1917	11/02/1917
War Diary	Maurepas	12/02/1917	28/02/1917
Miscellaneous	40th Division.	02/02/1917	02/02/1917
Miscellaneous	40th Division.	12/02/1917	12/02/1917
Heading	War Diary of "A" And "Q" Branch. 40th Division. Vol. X. From 1st to 31st March, 1917		
War Diary	Maurepas (P.C. Bonnet)	01/03/1917	07/03/1917
War Diary	P.C. Chapeau (Near Curlu)	08/03/1917	18/03/1917
War Diary	P.C. Chapeau	18/03/1917	26/03/1917
War Diary	P.C. Jean Near Curlu	27/03/1917	31/03/1917
Miscellaneous	40th Division No. 505 (Q)	03/03/1917	03/03/1917
Miscellaneous	XV Corps Administrative Instruction No. 18	02/03/1917	02/03/1917
Miscellaneous	40th Division.	09/03/1917	09/03/1917
Miscellaneous	40th Division. Appendix C	28/03/1917	28/03/1917
Miscellaneous	Appendix 1		
Miscellaneous	Hd Qrs. 40th Divn. No. 12 (A). Appendix II	20/03/1917	20/03/1917
Map	Traffic Circuits		
Map			
Miscellaneous	40th Division. Appendix III	23/03/1917	23/03/1917
Miscellaneous	40th Division. Appendix IV	25/03/1917	25/03/1917
Heading	War Diary of "A. & Q". Branch, 40th Division. Period-1st to 30th April, 1917		
War Diary	PC Jean Near Curlu	01/04/1917	05/04/1917
War Diary	Manancourt	06/04/1917	30/04/1917
Miscellaneous	40th Division.	08/04/1917	08/04/1917
Miscellaneous	40th Division.	16/04/1917	16/04/1917
Miscellaneous	40th Division.	23/04/1917	23/04/1917
Miscellaneous	Summary Of Casualties From 21st to 27th April 1917		
Miscellaneous	40th Division.	29/04/1917	29/04/1917

Type	Description	Start	End
Heading	War Diary "A" and "Q" Branch, Headquarters, 40th Division May 1917		
War Diary	Manancourt	01/05/1917	31/05/1917
Miscellaneous	40th Division.	04/05/1917	04/05/1917
Heading	War Diary "A. & Q". Branch Headquarters 40th. Division. June 1917		
War Diary	Manancourt	01/06/1917	30/06/1917
Miscellaneous	40th Division.	20/06/1917	20/06/1917
Heading	War Diary A & Q Branch. Headquarters 40th. Division. July 1917		
War Diary	Manancourt	01/07/1917	06/07/1917
War Diary	Sorel Le Grand	07/07/1917	31/07/1917
Miscellaneous	40 Div. War Diary A & Q Appendix I	29/06/1917	29/06/1917
Miscellaneous	40th Division Horse Transport Show. Appendix II	10/07/1917	10/07/1917
Miscellaneous	40th Division. Appendix III	10/07/1917	10/07/1917
Heading	War Diary of "A" And "Q" Branch, 40th Division. Volume XV. From 1st to 31st August, 1917		
Miscellaneous	Cover for Documents. Nature of Enclosures		
War Diary	Sorel	01/08/1917	31/08/1917
Miscellaneous	40th Division. "A"	01/08/1917	01/08/1917
Heading	War Diary of "A" And "Q" Branch 40th Division From 1st To 30th September, 1917 Volume XVI.		
Miscellaneous	Cover for Documents. Nature of Enclosures		
War Diary	Sorel	01/09/1917	30/09/1917
Heading	War Diary A. & Q. Branch, Headquarters, 40th Division. for October 1917 Vol. XVII		
Miscellaneous	Cover for Documents. Nature of Enclosures		
War Diary	Sorel	01/10/1917	09/10/1917
War Diary	Fosseux	10/10/1917	28/10/1917
War Diary	Lucheux	29/10/1917	31/10/1917
Miscellaneous	40th Division.	13/04/1917	13/04/1917
Miscellaneous	40th Division.	29/10/1917	29/10/1917
Heading	War Diary of "A" And "Q" Branch 40th Division. For Period 1st to 30th November, 1917 Vol XVIII.		
War Diary	Lucheux	01/11/1917	15/11/1917
War Diary	Fosseux	16/11/1917	16/11/1917
War Diary	Achiet Le Petit	17/11/1917	20/11/1917
War Diary	Haplincourt	20/11/1917	21/11/1917
War Diary	Beaumetz	22/11/1917	22/11/1917
War Diary	Havrincourt	23/11/1917	26/11/1917
War Diary	Neuville	27/11/1917	27/11/1917
War Diary	Boursonval	27/11/1917	27/11/1917
War Diary	Basseux	28/11/1917	30/11/1917
Miscellaneous	40th Division.	04/11/1917	04/11/1917
Miscellaneous	40th Division.	16/11/1917	16/11/1917
Miscellaneous	40th Division-Location of Units.		
Miscellaneous	40th Division.	19/11/1917	19/11/1917
Miscellaneous	Location of Units of 40th Division on 26th November, 1917		
Miscellaneous	Location of Units of 40th Division on 28th November, 1917		
Heading	War Diary of 'A And Q' Branch 40th Division. Volume XIX. From 1st December, 1917 to 31st December, 1917		
Miscellaneous	Cover for Documents Nature of Enclosures		
War Diary	Basseux	01/12/1917	02/12/1917
War Diary	Bahagnies.	03/12/1917	13/12/1917

War Diary	Comiecourt	14/12/1917	31/12/1917
Miscellaneous	40th. Division.	01/12/1917	01/12/1917
Miscellaneous	Location of Units of 40th Division on 3rd December, 1917		
Miscellaneous	40th Division.	14/12/1917	14/12/1917
Miscellaneous	40th Division.	29/12/1917	29/12/1917
Heading	War Diary of 'A' And 'Q' Branch 40th Division. Volume XX. From 1st to 31st January, 1918		
War Diary	Gomiecourt	01/01/1918	06/01/1918
War Diary	Bahagnies	07/01/1918	31/01/1918
Miscellaneous	40th Division.	27/01/1918	27/01/1918
Heading	War Diary "A" & Q" Branch 40th Division. From 1st to 28th February, 1918 Volume XXI.		
War Diary	Behagnies	01/02/1918	12/02/1918
War Diary	Gomiecourt	13/02/1918	27/02/1918
War Diary	Basseux.	28/02/1918	28/02/1918
Miscellaneous	Allotment Of Accommodation To Units Of 40th Division Showing Not Referred To In 40th Division. O.O. No. 117		
Miscellaneous	40th Division. Appendix I	27/01/1918	27/01/1918
Miscellaneous	From To. Appendix II		
Miscellaneous	Headquarters, 40th Division. Appendix III	04/02/1918	04/02/1918
Miscellaneous	H.Q., 40th Division No. S/122/Q. Appendix IV	06/02/1918	06/02/1918
Miscellaneous	Units To Move By Lorry (a) Vide Relief Table.		
Miscellaneous	H.Q., 40th Division No. 327 (A). Appendix V	07/02/1918	07/02/1918
Miscellaneous	Postings To 40th Division Under Reorganization Scheme.		
Miscellaneous	40th Division. Appendix VII	13/01/1918	13/01/1918
Miscellaneous			
Miscellaneous	H.Q., 40th Division No. 139 (Q). Appendix 8	16/02/1918	16/02/1918
Miscellaneous	40th Division. Appendix IX		
Miscellaneous			
Heading	War Diary A & Q Branch, Headquarters, 40th. Division. March 1918		
War Diary	Bassuex.	01/03/1918	21/03/1918
War Diary	Hamelincourt	22/03/1918	22/03/1918
War Diary	Bucquoy	23/03/1918	23/03/1918
War Diary	Bucquoy Monchy Au Bois	24/03/1918	25/03/1918
War Diary	Habarcq	25/03/1918	25/03/1918
War Diary	Lucheux Warluzel	26/03/1918	26/03/1918
War Diary	Lucheux.	27/03/1918	28/03/1918
War Diary	Chelers	29/03/1918	30/03/1918
War Diary	Merville	31/03/1918	31/03/1918
Miscellaneous	40th Division.	01/03/1918	01/03/1918
Miscellaneous	40th Division.	12/03/1918	12/03/1918
Miscellaneous	Entraining Instructions for 20th Division While In G.H.Q. Reserve.	13/03/1918	13/03/1918
Miscellaneous	40th Division Adv. No. S/1/Q.	22/03/1918	22/03/1918
Miscellaneous	H.Q,, 40th Division No. C/131/A.	23/03/1918	23/03/1918
Miscellaneous	Location of Units.	28/03/1918	28/03/1918
Miscellaneous		30/03/1918	30/03/1918
Heading	War Diary A. & Q. 40th Division. April 1918 Appendices attached Location Returns. Battle Casualties 21st March-6th April Battle Casualties 9th-23rd April.		
Heading	War Diary 'A' And 'Q' Branch. 40th Division. Volume XXIII. From-1st to 30th April, 1918		

Type	Description	Start	End
War Diary	Croix Du Bac	01/04/1918	09/04/1918
War Diary	Vieux Berquin	10/04/1918	13/04/1918
War Diary	Renescure	14/04/1918	14/04/1918
War Diary	Longuenesse	15/04/1918	16/04/1918
War Diary	Wizernes	17/04/1918	29/04/1918
War Diary	St. Omer	30/04/1918	30/04/1918
Miscellaneous	40th Division.	17/04/1918	17/04/1918
Miscellaneous	H.Q., 40th Division No. 816 (A).	19/04/1918	19/04/1918
Miscellaneous	H.Q., 40th Division No. 271 (Q).	19/04/1918	19/04/1918
Miscellaneous	List of Total Casualties Incurred During Battle From 9-4-1918, Amended to Date.	23/04/1918	23/04/1918
Miscellaneous	Details of Casualties to Officers.		
Miscellaneous	List of Total Casualties Incurred During Battle From 21-3-18 Amended to Date.		
Miscellaneous	Names Of Officers.		
Miscellaneous	Order of Battle.	27/04/1918	27/04/1918
Miscellaneous	40th Division No. 822 (A).	27/04/1918	27/04/1918
Miscellaneous		23/04/1918	23/04/1918
Heading	War Diary. "A" And "Q" Branch. 40th Division. Vol. XXIV. From-1st May, 1918. To-31st May, 1918		
Miscellaneous	Cover for Documents Nature of Enclosures		
War Diary	St. Omer	01/05/1918	31/05/1918
Miscellaneous	40th Division.	05/05/1918	05/05/1918
Miscellaneous	40th Division.	11/05/1918	11/05/1918
Miscellaneous	40th Division.	15/05/1918	15/05/1918
Miscellaneous	40th Division.	18/05/1918	18/05/1918
Miscellaneous	40th Division.	28/05/1918	28/05/1918
Heading	War Diary. 40th Division. "A" & "Q" Branch. From-1st June, 1918. To-30th June, 1918. Volume XXV.		
Miscellaneous	Cover for Documents Nature of Enclosures		
War Diary	St. Omer	01/06/1918	02/06/1918
War Diary	Lederzeele	03/06/1918	22/06/1918
War Diary	Renescure	23/06/1918	30/06/1918
Miscellaneous	40th Division.	03/06/1918	03/06/1918
Miscellaneous	40th Division.		
Miscellaneous	40th Division.	08/06/1918	08/06/1918
Miscellaneous	40th Division.	10/06/1918	10/06/1918
Miscellaneous	40th Division.	17/06/1918	17/06/1918
Miscellaneous	40th Division.	23/06/1918	23/06/1918
Heading	War Diary of "A" And "Q" Branch. 40th Division. From-1st to 31st July, 1918. Volume XXVI.		
War Diary	Renescure	01/07/1918	31/07/1918
Miscellaneous	40th Division No. 866 (A).	30/06/1918	30/06/1918
Miscellaneous	Routine Orders by Major-General J. Ponsonby, C.B., C.I.G., D.S.O., Commanding 40th Division.	02/07/1918	02/07/1918
Miscellaneous	40th Division.	18/07/1918	18/07/1918
Heading	War Diary. 40th Division. A and Q Branch. Volume. XXVII. From-1st August, 1918. To 31st August, 1918		
War Diary	Renescure	01/08/1918	20/08/1918
War Diary	Walloncappel	21/08/1918	31/08/1918
Miscellaneous	40th Division.	05/08/1918	05/08/1918
Miscellaneous	40th Division.	23/08/1918	23/08/1918
Miscellaneous	40th Division.	31/08/1918	31/08/1918
Miscellaneous	40th Division.	04/08/1918	04/08/1918

Heading	War Diary. 40th Division. "A" And "Q" Branch. Vol. XXVIII. From-1st September, 1918, To-30th September, 1918		
War Diary	Walloncappell	01/09/1918	02/09/1918
War Diary	La Motte	02/09/1918	30/09/1918
Miscellaneous	40th Division.	04/09/1918	04/09/1918
Miscellaneous	40th Division.	17/09/1918	17/09/1918
Heading	War Diary. 40th Division. "A" And "Q" Branch. Vol. XXIX. From-1st October, 1918. To-31st October, 1918		
War Diary	Near Steenwerck	01/10/1918	17/10/1918
War Diary	Armentieres	18/10/1918	19/10/1918
War Diary	Mouvaux	20/10/1918	20/10/1918
War Diary	Mouvaux Near Roubaix	21/10/1918	25/10/1918
War Diary	Lennoy	26/10/1918	31/10/1918
Miscellaneous	40th Division.	01/10/1918	01/10/1918
Miscellaneous	Allotment Of Accommodation.		
Miscellaneous	40th Division.	21/10/1918	21/10/1918
Miscellaneous	40th Division.	28/10/1918	28/10/1918
Heading	War Diary "A" And "Q" Branch. 40th Division. Volume XXX From-1st November, 1918. To-30th November, 1918		
War Diary	Lannoy	01/11/1918	24/11/1918
War Diary	Roubaix	25/11/1918	30/11/1918
Heading	War Diary of 'A' and 'Q' Branch, 40th Division. Period-1st to 31st December, 1918. Volume XXXI.		
War Diary	Roubaix	01/12/1918	31/12/1918
Heading	40th Division. War Diary. "A. & Q". Branch. Vol. XXXII. 1st January, 1919 to 31st January, 1919		
War Diary	Roubaix	01/01/1919	31/01/1919
Heading	War Diary. 40th Division. "A" And "Q" Branch. Vol. XXVIII. From-1st February, 1919 To-28th February, 1919		
Miscellaneous	Cover for Documents.Nature of Enclosures.		
War Diary	Roubaix	01/02/1919	28/02/1919
Heading	Extract from Diary of Major General Ponsonby.		
Miscellaneous	List of Commands Held by Major-General J. Ponsonby Mentioned in this Diary		
Miscellaneous			

WO 95/2594/2
Adjutant & Quarter-Master General

40TH DIVISION

'A' & 'Q' BRANCH

JUN 1916-FEB 1919

Original

Secret

CONFIDENTIAL.

WAR DIARY

OF

ASSISTANT ADJUTANT & QUARTER MASTER GENERAL,

40th DIVISION.

FROM, 4th to 30th JUNe, 1916.

Army Form C. 2118

WAR DIARY
or
INTELLIGENCE SUMMARY
(Erase heading not required.)

Original A & Q 40 DIVL. H.Q.

Place	Date 1916	Hour	Summary of Events and Information	Remarks and references to Appendices
NORRENT FONTES	JUNE 4 to 9		Concentration of Division. Arrival of Units appendix A. Units quartered appendix B. Divl H.Q. established at NORRENT FONTES on 5 June.	A B
	10		Refilling point BOURECQ. Railhead CHOCQUES.	copy
	11		Divl. Fuel dump at Lillers. Washing of soldiers clothing under reg'tal arrangements - payments made through Impresl a/cs. 40 Divl Cyclist Coy leave division for Reserve Army.	copy
	12		Inspection of 20 Middx. 21 Middx & 13 Yorks Rgt. (121st Inf Bde) by 1 Army Cdr. at pt. N 20 C. North of LINGHEM. Divl. Coy Officer, Divn. Officers, Laundry Officer and Salvage Officer appointed.	copy
	13		Memorial service - Lord Kitchener at 11 A.M.	copy
	14		1/1 Sqdn. R. Wilts Yeomanry ordered to leave Division 18 June.	copy
	15		Instructions - Corps - for division concentration in area BARLIN, MAISNIL, BRUAY, DIVION, MARLES LES MINES, LA FEUBRIÈRE, LAPUGNOY, CHOCQUES.	copy
	16		Yorks and 12 Divn. Laundry South of BETHUNE. Divisional School of Instruction near FOUQUIÈRES, and Divisional Canteen LILLERS.	copy
	17		Move of Cav. Sqdn. postponed.	copy
	18		Billeting parties sent to new area of concentration.	copy
BRUAY	19		Concentration of division in area appendix C. Less recruits under instruction in front line appointed Bde Machine Gun companies from 119, 120th, 121st Inf Bdes. Divl Cavalry leave for ST JANS CAPPEL North of BATTLEUL from 2d Army. Divisional	copy C. D
	20		Baggage & ammunition shop established BRUAY.	copy
	21		Railhead still at CHOCQUES. BRUAY would be more suitable. 150 Tunnelling Coy RE at BEUVRY & 253 Coy RE at SAILLY LA BOURSE attd to division for maintenance of keep MT vehicles and for their Laundry both and upkeep of their horses.	copy copy

WAR DIARY
or
INTELLIGENCE SUMMARY

Army Form C. 2118

Place	Date 1916 JUNE	Hour	Summary of Events and Information	Remarks and references to Appendices
BRUAY	22	3 PM	Inspection of 119, 120 & 121st M.G. Bde Machine gun Companies by 1 Army Cdr. at place MARMOTTAN BRUAY.	Appx
	23		1 Officer 30 other ranks joined division from Cyclist Battalion at La Recque to act as divisional snipers. 1 Officer 20 other Ranks joined 12 S.W. Borderers (reinforcements). 1st Army decision that CHOCQUES was henceforward considered as of supply column & depot troops & lorries at 1st disposal. This will necessitate use of supply column at BRUAY being primarily effected. BARLIN group is primarily effected. 1 Officer & 30 other ranks rejoined division from cyclist coy. Held no divisional snipers and sent officer.	Appx Appx
	24			Appx
	25		Arrangements made for traffic for troops in each group of formations, clean down dry hutted from 3rd Laundry Bethune. Previously troops fetched under regtl arrangement & washing done by local inhabitants changed unrinsed accounts.	Appx
	26		Opened Divisional Canteen at Bruay. Class Canteen at LILLERS.	Appx
	27		Arrangements made to supply troops in Bruay & March battens by horsetransport from CHOCQUES. BARLIN group must continue to be fed by Supply Column, but as 2 Essentially 4/1 battalions will be found time from this group, use of supply the Column will be restricted accordingly.	Appx
	28		Railhead moves from CHOCQUES to LILLERS. Horse transport for supplies will be utilized as for CHOCQUES for the present – pending stands base of horses sufficient for any journeys.	Appx
	30		Total Casualties for the month of June Officers K 1. W. 2 M.Nil – Other Ranks K 46 W. 199 M.	Appx

C.J. Moore Lt. Col. A.A.Q.M.G.
HQ 1st Division
for Major Genl. Cdg 1st Div.

ARRIVALS

SUNDAY, 4TH JUNE, 1916.

UNIT	TIME	PLACE
19th (S) Bn. Royal Welsh Fusiliers	0.47	LILLERS.
"B" Battery, 181st Brigade, R.F.A.	3.07	BERGUETTE.
12th (S) Bn. S. Wales Borderers	3.47 x	LILLERS.
Brigade H.Q., 181st Brigade, R.F.A.) & "A" Battery, 181st Bde., R.F.A.)	6.47	BERGUETTE.
40th Divl. Signal Co. H.Q. & No. 1) Section; also H.Q. & H.Q.Coy. of) 40th Divisional Train)	9.07	LILLERS.
"C" Battery, 181st Brigade, R.F.A.	9.47 x	BERGUETTE.
Pioneer Battalion, 12th Yorks. Regt.	11.07	LILLERS.
"D" Battery, 181st Brigade, R.F.A.	12.37	BERGUETTE.
224th Field Company, R.E.	13.47 x	LILLERS.

    x May be late.

ARRIVALS

MONDAY, 5TH JUNE, 1916.

UNIT	TIME	PLACE.
17th Welsh Regiment	0.47	LILLERS.
"B" Battery, 178th Bde., R.F.A.	3.07	BERGUETTE.
18th Welsh Regiment	4.47	LILLERS.
178th Bde. H.Q.) "A" Battery, 178th Bde., R.F.A.)	5.47	BERGUETTE.
D.H.Q.) 135th Field Ambulance)	9.07	LILLERS.
H.Q. Divl. Artillery.) "C" Battery, 178th Bde, R.F.A.)	9.47	BERGUETTE.
No.2 Section Signal Coy.) "D" Battery, 178th Bde. R.F.A.)	13.47	LILLERS.
229th Field Coy., R.E.	15.07	BERGUETTE.
H.Q. 119th Infantry Brigade) No.2 Coy. 40th Divl. Train) 136th Field Ambulance)	15.47	LILLERS.

ARRIVALS

TUESDAY, 6TH JUNE, 1916.

UNIT	TIME	PLACE
11th King's Own R. Lancs. Regt.	0.47	LILLERS.
"B" Battery, 185th Bde., R.F.A.	3.07	BERGUETTE.
13th East Surrey Regiment.	4.47	LILLERS.
"C" Battery, 185th Bde., R.F.A.	5.47	BERGUETTE.
H.Q. 120th Infy. Brigade.		
No. 3 Coy. 40th Divl. Train	9.07	LILLERS.
137th Field Ambulance		
H.Q. 185th Brigade, R.F.A.	9.47	BERGUETTE.
"A" Battery, R.F.A.		
No. 3 Section Signal Coy.		
"D" Battery, 185th Bde. R.F.A.	13.47	LILLERS.
H.Q. 40th Divl. R.E.		
231st Field Coy. R.E.	15.07	BERGUETTE.
14th Bn. Highland Light Infy.	15.47	LILLERS.

ARRIVALS

WEDNESDAY, 7TH JUNE, 1916.

UNIT	TIME	PLACE
1/1st Royal Wilts. Yeomanry)		
83rd Sanitary Section.)	0.47	LILLERS.
51st Mobile Veterinary Section)		
H.Q. 188th Brigade, R.F.A.)	3.07	BERGUETTE.
"A" Battery, 188th Bde. R.F.A.)		
H.Q. 121st Infy. Brigade.)		
No.4 Section Signal Coy.)	4.47	LILLERS.
No.4 Coy. 40th Divl. Train)		
40th Divl. Cyclist Coy)		
"B" Battery 188th Bde. R.F.A.	5.47	BERGUETTE
14th Argyll & Sutherland Highdrs.	9.07	LILLERS.
"C" Battery 188th Bde., R.F.A.	9.47	BERGUETTE
12th Suffolk Regiment	13.47	LILLERS.
"D" Battery, 188th Bde.R.F.A.	15.07	BERGUETTE.
13th Yorkshire Regt.	15.47	LILLERS.

ARRIVALS.

THURSDAY, 8TH JUNE, 1916.

	UNIT	TIME	PLACE
37	20th Middlesex Regiment	0.47	LILLERS.
38	21st Middlesex Regiment	4.47	LILLERS.
39	No. 1 Section D.A.C.	5.47	BERGUETTE.
40	No. 2 Section D.A.C.	13.47	LILLERS.
41	No. 3 Section D.A.C.	15.47	LILLERS

Remainder (viz: Headquarters, D.A.C. & No. 4 Section) will arrive
9. 6. 16.

Amended Capt AHB

ARRIVALS

FRIDAY, 9TH JUNE, 1916.

	UNIT	TIME	PLACE
42	No. 4 Section D.A.C. Part at	0.47	LILLERS.
43	" " "	4.47	LILLERS.
44	Remainder of Nos.2 & 3 Sections D.A.C.	9.07	LILLERS.
45	Headquarters and remainder of No. 1 Section D.A.C.	13.47	LILLERS.

BILLETING SCHEME.

40TH DIVISION.

DIVISIONAL HEADQUARTERS	NORRENT FONTES.
Headquarters Signal Coy. & No. 1 Section.	" "
DIVISIONAL CAVALRY	FEBVIN PALFART.
CYCLIST COMPANY	" "
MOTOR M. G. BATTERY	" "

ROYAL ARTILLERY

Headquarters	FONTAINE-LES-HERMANS.
178th Brigade, R.F.A.	~~AMES~~, BELLERY, ~~LIERETTE~~.
181st Brigade, R.F.A.	AMETTES.
185th Brigade, R.F.A.	~~AMES~~, BELLERY, LIERETTE.
188th Brigade, R.F.A.	~~AMETTES~~, NEDON, NEDONCHELLE.
Divisional Ammunition Column.	~~NEDON~~, NEDONCHELLE, FONTAINE-LES-HERMANS.

ROYAL ENGINEERS

Headquarters and 3 Field Coys.	LIGNY-LEZ-AIRE.

119th INFANTRY BRIGADE.

Headquarters.	~~ST. HILAIRE.~~ BOURECQ.
No.2 Section Signal Coy.	~~ST. HILAIRE.~~ BOURECQ.
4 Battalions.	ST. HILAIRE & BOURECQ.

120th INFANTRY BRIGADE.

Headquarters	ECQUEDECQUES.
No.3 Section Signal Coy.) 2 Battalions)	ECQUEDECQUES.
2 Battalions	LIERES, FAUCQUENHAM & LESPESSES.

121st INFANTRY BRIGADE.

Headquarters.	LILLERS.
No.4 Section Signal Coy.	LILLERS.
2 Battalions.	LILLERS.
2 Battalions.	HAM-EN-ARTOIS.

PIONEER BATTALION — RELY.

Headquarters and 2 Coys.	LILLERS.
2 Companies	LESPESSES.
DIVISIONAL TRAIN	LILLERS.

DIVISIONAL SUPPLY COLUMN	ON BUSNES ROAD.
AMMUNITION SUB PARK	AUCHEL
FIELD AMBULANCES.	
135th & 137th Field Ambulances.	~~LA COUREE.~~ NORRENT FONTES.
136th Field Ambulance.	HURIONVILLE.
51st MOBILE VETERINARY SECTION	~~AMETTES.~~ LA COUREE.
83rd SANITARY SECTION.	LILLERS.
WORKSHOP FOR MOTOR AMBULANCE CARS &C	LILLERS.
CASUALTY CLEARING STATION	AT THE BASE.

CONFIDENTIAL

BILLETS OF 40TH DIVISION IN AREA OF CONCENTRATION.

Divisional Head Quarters.	
2nd Echelon.	BRUAY.
H.Q 119th Infantry Brigade.	BRUAY.
19th Royal Welsh Fusiliers.	MARLES-LES-MINES.
12th South Wales Borderers.	-do-
17th Welsh Regiment.	-do-
18th Welsh Regiment.	DIVION.
119th Machine Gun Coy.	-do-
H.Q 120th Infantry Brigade.	J 13
11th Kings Own (R.Lanc.Regt).	BRUAY.
13th East Surrey Regiment.	-do-
14th Highland Light Infy.	-do-
14th Argyll & Sutherland Hrs.	-do-
120th Machine Gun Coy.	-do-
H.Q 121st Infantry Brigade.	-do-
12th Suffolk Regiment.	BARLIN.
13th Yorkshire Regiment.	-do-
20th Middlesex Regiment.	MAISNIL.
21st Middlesex Regiment	Q 2 - 3
121st Machine Gun Coy.	K 31
12th Yorks. Regiment (Pioneers)	Q 14 - 15
H.Q.40th Divisional Artillery.	HOUCHIN.
H.Q.& 178th Brigade. R.F.A.	FOUQUIERES.
H.Q.& 181st Brigade, R.F.A.	D 20
H.Q.& 185th Brigade, R.F.A.	D 11
H.Q & 188th Brigade, R.F.A.	LABEUVRIERE.
H.Q & Divnl. Ammunition Colmn.	D 21.
H.Q 40th Divnl. R.E.	D 21, D 15 & D 16.
224th Field Coy. R.E.	BRUAY.
229th Field Coy. R.E.	RUITZ.
231st Field Coy. R.E.	BRUAY.
H.Q 40th Divnl. Train.	DIVION.
H.Q. Coy., 40th Divnl. Train.	BRUAY.
No. 2 Coy. 40th Divnl. Train.	CHOCQUES.
No. 3 Coy. do.	I 17 01
No. 4 Coy. do.	BRUAY.
Divisional Supply Column.	RUITZ
AMMUNITION Sub Park.	CHOCQUES.
135th Field Ambulance.	AUCHEL.
136th Field Ambulance.	DIVION.
137th Field Ambulance.	BRUAY.
51st Mobile Veterinary Section.	RUITZ.
83rd Sanitary Section.	BRUAY.
Workshop for Motor Ambulance Cars &c.	BRUAY.
	CHOCQUES.

40th DIVISION.

ATTACHMENT OF UNITS TO OTHER DIVISIONS FOR INSTRUCTIONS.

UNIT	Division to which attached.	Date leaving 40th Division.	DESTINATION	Date rejoining 40th Division.
224th Fd.Coy. R.E.	15th J. Noyelles les Vermelles	12th June	Arrangements by C.R.E's of two Divisions.	28th June.
229th Fd.Coy. R.E.	16th	9th June	MAZINGARBE	30th 26th June.
231st Fd.Coy. R.E.	1st Div:	8th June	DROUVIN LES MARLES thence LES BREBIS & MAROC	30th 26th June.
178th(How)Bde. H.Q. & 1 Batty.	1st Div:	9th June	NOEUX-LES-MINES	
178th(How)Bde. 1 Battery	16th Div:	9th June	NOEUX-LES-MINES	
178th(How)Bde. 1 Battery	15th Div:	9th June	SAILLY LA BOURSE.	
178th(How)Bde. 1. 4.5 How Bty.	Attd. to H.A. Res. I Corps.	9th June	NOEUX-LES-MINES	
181st Bde. R.F.A.	16th Div:	8th June	NOEUX-LES-MINES	
185th Bde. R.F.A. less "D" Battery.	15th Div:	10th June	SAILLY LA BOURSE.	
185th Bde.R.F.A. "D" Battery	16th Div:	10th June	NOEUX-LES-MINES.	
188th Bde.R.F.A. Headquarters.	1st Div:	16th June	NOEUX-LES-MINES	
188th Bde.R.F.A. less Bde. H.Q.	1st Div:	11th June	NOEUX-LES-MINES.	
Div.Ammn.Col. No. 1 Sec:"A" Echelon	16th Div:	10th June	HOUCHIN.	
Div.Ammn.Col. No. 2 Sec:"A" Echelon	1st Div:	10th June	HOUCHIN.	
Div.Ammn.Col. No. 3 Sec:"A" Echelon	15th Div:	10th June	VERQUIGNEUL	
Div.Ammn.Col. No. 4 Sec:"B" Echelon	1st Div: & 16th.	11th June	HESDIGNEUL	

- CONTINUED -

UNIT	Division to which attached.	Date leaving 40th Division.	DESTINATION	Date rejoining 40th Division.	
119th INFY.BDE.HQ	1st Div:	9th June	HOUCHIN for BULLY, GRENAY.	21st June	at Houchin the day before
19th R.Welsh Fus:	1st Div:	9th June	BULLY MAROC	22nd June	
12th S. Wales Bordrs	1st Div:	13th June	-do-	25th June.	
17th Welsh Regt.	1st Div:	9th June	HOUCHIN	22nd June.	
18th Welsh Regt.	1st	13th June	HOUCHIN	25th June.	
120th INFY.BDE.HQ	15th Div:	11th June	BETHUNE	24th June.
11th K.O.R.L.Rgt.	15th Div:	11th June	(BETHUNE for (NOYELLES & (SAILLY LA (BOURSE.	24th June.
13th E. Surrey R.	15th Div:	15th June	(SAILLY LA BOURSE (& NOYELLES	27th June.
14th H. L. I.	15th Div:	11th June	(BETHUNE for (SAILLY LA BOURSE (AND ANNEQUIN	24th June.
14th A. & S. Hdrs	15th Div:	15th June	SAILLY LA BOURSE & NOYELLES & ANNEQUIN	27th June.
12th Yorks. Regt. (Pioneers) 1 Coy.	1st Div:	8th June	LES BREBIS AND MAROC.	30th 26th June.
12th Yorks. Regt. (Pioneers) 2 Coys	15th Div:	16th 9th June	Mazingarbe after the 14th FOUQUIERES	30th June.
12th Yorks. Regt. (Pioneers) 1 Coy.	16th Div:	10th June	MAZINGARBE	30th 26th June.

135 Fd Ambce.   A section   1st Divn   11 to 21 June
                 B   21 to 1 July
                 C   1 July 11 July

136 Fd Ambce   "   15 Divn   "   "

137   "   "   16 Divn

D

Details and dates have been arranged with the A.D.M.S. of Divisions concerned. Programme of instructions of Field Ambulances herewith:-

135th F.A.	A Section to 1st Div,	11th to 21st June.
	B "	21st to 1st July
	C "	1st to 11th July:
136th F.A.	A Section to 15th Div.	11th to 21st June.
	B "	21st to 1st July.
	C "	1st to 11th July.
137th F.A.	A Section to 16th Div.	11th to 21st June.
	B "	21st to 1st July.
	C "	1st to 11th July.

10th June 1916.

(Signed) A.J.Luther; Colonel.
A.D.M.S.
40th Division.

Original Programme passed to 1st Corps. 10/6/16

CONFIDENTIAL

WAR DIARY

OF

A. & Q. BRANCH, 40th DIVISION.

Period -- 1st to 31st, July. 1916.

VOLUME II.

WAR DIARY or INTELLIGENCE SUMMARY

Army Form C. 2118

Head Qrs } A & Q 40th DIVN.

Place	Date	Hour	Summary of Events and Information	Remarks and references to Appendices
BRUAY	JULY 1st		Two battns. nos 4/119 + nos 4/120 Inf Btns ordered to join 16 & 18th Divisions temporarily.	Copy
	2		Above countermanded. 40th Div. ordered to replace 1st Div. All moves to be completed by evening of 5 June. Orders received to hand over 13 S.A.A. Limbers G.S. Wagons in place of 13 S.A.A. carts to 1st. Divn. Exchange arranged ... place at HOCHIN at 7 p.m. today. I.G.S. Limber Wagon being taken from each battalion.	Copy
	3		Uneventful. Troops quartered in BRUAY MARLES LESMINES BARLIN area as in Appendix A.	Copy Appendix A
BRACQUEMONT	4/5		Arranging take over new area. Troops moved and quartered as in Appendix B	Copy Appendix B
NOEUX LES MINES.	5		Head Qrs of Division moved to NOEUX LESMINES on evening 5 July. Railhead at same place (NOEUX LES MINES.) Established Divl. Shop kitchen at LES BREBIS	Copy Appendix C
	6		Refilling at 9.30 A.M. Divl. Band to take over stragglers posts within Brigade + Divisional Cantines in full swing.	Copy
	7		Required. ... Casualties table from 1st to 7 July inclusive :- Killed. Officers 2, other ranks 16 — wounded other ranks 16 — wounded Offrs 4.	Copy
	8		Other ranks 47. Locations of units of 40th Divn & of troops attached quartered in 40th Divl. Area Shown in Appx D	Appx D Copy
	9		Battalions bathed at HOCHIN where the Divl. Amm. Col. are quartered. GAS School moved to HOCHIN from LA REVEILLON (near CHOCQUES).	Copy
	10		2 Regtl. transport Offrs + personnel other ranks attending a course of instruction in transport duties. This will take away officers whose services are required and who are sufficiently trained in training already by being then transferred with supervision.	Copy
	11		Candle posts, running posts, stragglers posts attached to 1st Corps - Cyclist posters (30) transferred to ... each brigade to post battalion.	Copy
	12		Orders recd. for C By 185 Bde & C & D Bdys 181st Bde to proceed with 8 & Divn. It took over 39 Divn. front. Mobilised to Bruay.	Copy
	13		... Rations drawn by HQ Divn. (Offrs nos 146 -). Nothing out routine.	
	14		Casualties from 8th - 14 July incl. Officers K.1 W.6 other ranks K.13 wounded 89.	Copy
	15		Lecture on C.T.M. duties by RSMaj 1st Army on the 13th ... has been of benefit to Staff Captains. Musketship Copy lecture are more in accordance with requirements of typed winners.	Copy

B.C.M.

Army Form C. 2118

WAR DIARY
or
INTELLIGENCE SUMMARY

(Erase heading not required.)

A & Q Head Qrs. 40th Division

Place	Date	Hour	Summary of Events and Information	Remarks and references to Appendices
BRACQUEMONT	July 16		Nil Major report	
NOEUX LES MINES	17		Arranged traffic control posts throughout, to reproduce details put under cover during summer before mobilisation. R.E. to assist to provide materials. Horse standings in bad condition. Whereabouts of men are being enquired.	copy
	18		Properties of D.Tram houses by A.D.R. 101 Army	copy
	19		Issued instructions that great care is to be taken of water at La Brebis, CALONNE & MAROC. Attention of Artillery drawn to necessity for care of horses & Hm. have been many cases of disability in trains and also of kicks.	copy
	20		Instruction received to take over additional frontage which now extends to LOOS. from night 22-23rd.	copy
	21		Casualties from 15 to 21 July inclusive. Killed officers 1, O.R.11 wounded officers 4, O.R.81	copy
	22		Arrangements made for control of night traffic to and in LOOS. Inspected Tramway which is not in use.	copy
	23			copy
	24		19 Northumberland Fusiliers Pioneers ordered up on the attached lots from on 25/26 July. to be quartered 3 Coys in LOOS. 1 Coy at PETIT SAINS. also to M. Gun Coy. quartered in LOOS.	copy
	25			copy
	26		Destruction of private property of an derelict houses consisting of woodwork chiefly, reported from front line villages. Investigation and steps taken. approved recurrence as far as possible. Difficult to make men understand that a derelict tumbledown house is still of value to the owner.	copy
	27		Morris Oxide Bomb Store. The present store to be in course trials and evenings shell fire might cause 'Trouble' owing for a different workshop.	copy
	28		Arranged Accommodation of which R.E. Cannot provide. Motor Ambces. Workshops & Pioneers workshop, from time to time and also Scheme for improving billets - 2 KOYLI at & half 206th Coy R.E. attached 6th D. Increase from 29th to 5 August quartered at La BREBIS and LOOS respectively.	copy
	29		2nd Lieut Grayston Partington 120" N. Sun Coy shot by accident by a resh of the 136 Surrey Rgt in 15 trenches in mistake for a german.	copy
	30			copy
	31		Casualties from 22 to 31 July inclusive. Killed Officers 4. other ranks 42 Wounded Officers 6 other ranks 266	copy

C.J. Huggett
Lt Col. A & Q
40 Div

CONFIDENTIAL.

BILLETS OF 40TH DIVISION ON 24TH JUNE, 1916.

A

Divisional Headquarters.	BRUAY.
2nd Echelon.	BRUAY.
H.Q. 119th Infy. Bde.	MARLES-LES-MINES.
19th Royal Welsh Fusiliers.	MARLES-LES-MINES.
12th South Wales Borderers.	Attached 1st Division.
17th Welsh Regiment.	DIVION.
18th Welsh Regiment.	Attached 1st Division.
119th Machine Gun Company.	J. 13 D.
H.Q. 120th Infantry Brigade.	BRUAY.
11th King's Own (R.Lanc.) Regt.	BRUAY.
13th East Surrey Regiment.	Attached 15th Division.
14th Highland Light Infantry.	BRUAY.
14th Argyll & Sutherland Highrs.	Attached 15th Division.
120th Machine Gun Company	BRUAY.
H.Q. 121st Infantry Brigade.	Attached 1st Division.
12th Suffolk Regiment.	Attached 1st Division.
*13th Yorkshire Regiment.	BARLIN. (Marched)
20th Middlesex Regiment.	Attached 1st Division.
*21st Middlesex Regiment.	BARLIN. (Marched)
121st Machine Gun Company.	Q. 14 - 15.
12th Yorkshire Regiment.	MAZINGARBE - MAROC.
H.Q. 40th Divisional Artillery.	FOUQUIERES.
H.Q.178th Bde.R.F.A. & 1 Battery.	Attached 1st Division.
1 Battery, 178th Brigade, R.F.A.	Attached 16th Division.
1 Battery, 178th Brigade, R.F.A.	Attached 15th Division.
1 Battery, 178th Brigade, R.F.A.	Attd. to H.A. Res. I Corps.
H.Q. & 181st Bde. R.F.A.	Attached 16th Division.
H.Q. & 185th Bde. R.F.A. (Less "D" Battery)	Attached 15th Division.
"D" Battery, 185th Bde.R.F.A.	Attached 16th Division.
H.Q. & 188th Bde. R.F.A.	Attached 1st Division.
H.Q.Divnl.Ammunition Column.	VERQUIN.
No. 1 Sec."A" Echelon, D.A.C.	Attached 16th Division.
No. 2 Sec."A" Echelon, D.A.C.	Attached 1st Division.
No. 3 Sec."A" Echelon, D.A.C.	Attached 15th Division.
No. 4 Sec."B" Echelon, D.A.C.	Attached 1st & 16th Divisions
H.Q. 40th Divisional R.E.	BRUAY.
224th Field Coy. R.E.	Attd. 15th Divn.(RUITZ from 28/6/16)
229th Field Coy. R.E.	Attd. 16th Divn.(BRUAY from 26/6/16)
231st Field Coy. R.E.	Attd. 1st Divn. (DIVION from 26/6/16)
H.Q. 40th Divnl. Train.	BRUAY.
H.Q. Coy. 40th Divnl. Train.	CHOCQUES.
No. 2 H.T.Coy. 40th Divnl. Train.	L 17 D1.
No. 3 Coy. 40th Divnl. Train.	BRUAY.
No. 4 Coy. 40th Divnl. Train.	RUITZ.
Divisional Supply Column.	CHOCQUES.
Ammunition Sub Park	AUCHEL.
135th Field Ambulance.	DIVION.
136th Field Ambulance.	BRUAY.
137th Field Ambulance.	RUITZ.
51st Mobile Veterinary Sec.	BRUAY.
83rd Sanitary Sec.	BRUAY.
Workshop for Motor Ambces.Cars &c.	CHOCQUES.

---

*These two battalions do not become attached for training till 28th. They are in Army Reserve from 10 a.m. to-day. When attached and <u>resting</u> at Barlin they are Corps Reserve.

24th June 1916.

Major-General,
Commanding 40th Division.

B

Unit				Route :- BARLIN-HERSIN-PETIT SAINS.
120th Inf. Bde complete) No 3 Coy A.S.C.	4	To arrive By 4 p.m.	BRUAY	1 Bn to PT.SAINS. remainder to LES BREBIS	3rd Inf.Bde.	
229th Field Coy R.E.	4	By day.	BRUAY	LES BREBIS	26th Field Coy.	All details of relief between Companies concerned. 229th Field Coy to arrange its march to fit in with march of 120th I.B.
231st Field Coy R.E.	4/5	Night. (relief)	DIVION	LES BREBIS	23rd Field Coy.	
135th Field Ambulance.	4	By day.	DIVION.	CALONNE	No 141 F.A.	To follow 120th Inf. Bde from BRUAY.
136th Field Ambulance.	4	By day	BRUAY	LABEUVRIERE	No 2 F.A.	To take over Corps Rest Camp.
Headquarters 119th Inf.Bde) 3 Battalions. 119th M.G.Company. 119th Trench Mortar Battery. No.2 Co. A.S.C.	4/5	Night. (relief)	BARLIN area	1st Inf. Bde area.	1st Inf.Bde.	M.G.Coy and Lewis Guns to relieve during forenoon of day of Bde relief.
Division Hd Qrs.	4th & 5th.	By day.	BRUAY.	BRAQUEMONT.	1st Division.	

N.B. To avoid possibilities of clashing, units to report proposed hours of marching and route, if not laid down, to 40th Div. H.Q.

Programme of relief of 1st Division by 40th Division.

Moves of units 40th Division.

Unit.	Date.	Hour.	Move From	Move To	To relieve.	
1 Battn 121st Inf. Bde.	2/3	Night	BARLIN area	Trenches	Battalion 2nd Inf. Bde.	To occupy billets vacated by 1 Bn 121st Infantry Brigade.
1 Battn 119th Inf. Bde.	2	Day	DIVION	BARLIN area	—	
Headquarters 119th Inf. Brigade. 3 Bns. 119th Inf.Bde. 119th M.G.Coy. 119th Trench Mortar Battery. No 2 Coy. A.S.C.	3	Forenoon	MARLES LES MINES and DIVION.	BARLIN area.	—	To occupy billets when vacated by 121st Inf. Brigade.
12th Yorkshire Pioneers.	3	By noon	HOUCHIN	S.MAROC.	16th Welsh Pioneers.	Details by arrangement between C.O's.
137th Field Ambulance.	3	By day.	RUITZ.	MAROC	No.1 F.A.	Details by arrangement between A.D's.V.S.
Mobile Vet. Section.	3	By day.	BRUAY	DROUVIN	1st Div. M.V.S.	
Headquarters 121st Inf. Brigade. 3 Bns 121st Bde. 121st M.G.Coy. 121st Trench Mortar Battery No 4 Coy A.S.C.	3/4	Night.	BARLIN area	2nd Inf. Bde. 2nd Inf. Brigade. area.		M.G.Coys and Lewis Guns to relieve during forenoon of day of Brigade relief.
1. Battn. 119th Inf.Bde.	3/4	Night	BARLIN area	Trenches.	Battn 1st Inf. Bde.	
224th Field Coy R.E.	3/4	Night	RUITZ	LES BREBIS	Lowland Fd Coy.	Officer from Coy. to meet an officer of 1st Division at 10 a.m. on 3rd at 3rd Inf.Bde H.Qrs Mine Buildings LES BREBIS to be shown over Maro3 Defences.

SECRET.

CONFIDENTIAL

A A & Q M G

C

BILLETS OF 40TH DIVISION ON 5TH JULY, 1916.

Divisional Headquarters	BRAQUEMONT.
2nd Echelon	BRAQUEMONT.
H.Q. 119th Infy. Bde.	LES BREBIS.
19th Royal Welsh Fusiliers.	TRENCHES.
12th South Wales Borderers.	TRENCHES.
17th Welsh Regiment	BULLY GRENAY.
18th Welsh Regiment	CALONNE.
119th Machine Gun Company	LES BREBIS.
119th Trench Mortar Battery	TRENCHES.
H.Q. 120th Infantry Brigade.	LES BREBIS. — Mines Offices -
11th King's Own (R.Lancs.) Regt.	PETIT SAINS.
13th East Surrey Regiment	LES BREBIS.
14th Highland Light Infantry.	LES BREBIS.
14th Argyll & Sutherland Highlanders.	LES BREBIS.
120th Machine Gun Company	GRENAY.
120th Trench Mortar Battery.	LES BREBIS.
H.Q. 121st Infantry Brigade.	LES BREBIS.
12th Suffolk Regiment	TRENCHES.
13th Yorkshire Regiment	NORTH MAROC.
20th Middlesex Regiment	TRENCHES.
21st Middlesex Regiment.	MAROC & O.G.1.
121st Machine Gun Company	LES BREBIS.
121st Trench Mortar Battery	TRENCHES.
12th Yorkshire Regiment	S. MAROC.
H.Q. 40th Divisional Artillery	BRAQUEMONT.
178th Brigade, R.F.A.)	Station
181st Brigade, R.F.A.)	to be
185th Brigade, R.F.A.)	notified
188th Brigade, R.F.A.)	later.
X 40 Trench Mortar Battery	TRENCHES.
Y 40 Trench Mortar Battery	TRENCHES.
Z 40 Trench Mortar Battery	~~TRENCHES.~~ FOUQUIERES.
A Echelon D.A.C.	HOUCHIN & DROUVIN.
B Echelon D.A.C.	HESDIGNEUL.
H.Q. 40th Divisional R.E.	BRAQUEMONT.
224th Field Coy. R.E.	LES BREBIS.
229th Field Coy. R.E.	LES BREBIS.
231st Field Coy. R.E.	LES BREBIS.
40th Divisional Train	BRAQUEMONT.
Divisional Supply Column.	HAILLICOURT.
Ammunition Sub Park	AUCHEL.
135th Field Ambulance	BRAQUEMONT.
136th Field Ambulance	LABEUVRIERE.
137th Field Ambulance	BRAQUEMONT.
51st Mobile Veterinary Section	DROUVIN.
83rd Sanitary Section	NOEUX LES MINES.
Workshop for Motor Amb. Cars &c.	HAILLICOURT.

R H Bathurst

Captain,

D.A.A. & Q.M.G.

40th Division.

3rd July, 1916.

CONFIDENTIAL

BILLETS OF 40TH DIVISION ON 8TH JULY, 1916.

Divisional Headquarters.	BRAQUEMONT.
2nd Echelon.	BRAQUEMONT.
H.Q. 119th Infantry Brigade.	LES BREBIS.
19th Royal Welsh Fusiliers.	BULLY GRENAY.
12th South Wales Borderers.	CALONNE.
17th Welsh Regiment.	TRENCHES.
18th Welsh Regiment.	TRENCHES.
119th Machine Gun Company.	TRENCHES.
119th Trench Mortar Battery.	TRENCHES.
H.Q. 120th Infantry Brigade.	LES BREBIS.
11th King's Own (R.Lancs.) Regt.	PETIT SAINS.
13th East Surrey Regiment.	LES BREBIS.
14th Highland Light Infantry.	✱ LES BREBIS.
14th Argyll & Sutherland Highlanders.	⊗ LES BREBIS.
120th Machine Gun Company.	R 6 b 2 4.
120th Trench Mortar Battery.	LES BREBIS.
H.Q. 121st Infantry Brigade.	LES BREBIS.
12th Suffolk Regiment.	TRENCHES.
13th Yorkshire Regiment.	HARROW RD. MAROC.
20th Middlesex Regiment.	NORTH MAROC.
21st Middlesex Regiment.	TRENCHES.
121st Machine Gun Company.	LES BREBIS.
121st Trench Mortar Battery.	TRENCHES.
12th Yorkshire Regiment.	S. MAROC.
H.Q. 40th Divisional Artillery.	BRAQUEMONT.
H.Q. Right Group.	L 35 d 9 0.
H.Q. Left Group.	LES BREBIS.
V 40 Trench Mortar Battery.	TRENCHES.
X 40 Trench Mortar Battery.	TRENCHES.
Y 40 Trench Mortar Battery.	TRENCHES.
Z 40 Trench Mortar Battery.	LES BREBIS.
A Echelon D.A.C.	HOUCHIN.
B Echelon D.A.C.	HESDIGNEUL.
H.Q. 40th Divisional R.E.	BRAQUEMONT.
224th Field Coy. R.E.	LES BREBIS.
229th Field Coy. R.E.	LES BREBIS.
231st Field Coy. R.E.	LES BREBIS.
40th Divisional Train.	BRAQUEMONT.
Divisional Supply Column.	HAILLICOURT.
Ammunition Sub Park.	AUCHEL.
135th Field Ambulance.	BRAQUEMONT.
136th Field Ambulance.	LABEUVRIERE.
137th Field Ambulance.	BRAQUEMONT.
51st Mobile Veterinary Section.	DROUVIN.
83rd Sanitary Section.	BRAQUEMONT.
Workshop for Motor Amb. Cars etc.	HAILLICOURT.
40th Divisional School.	PRIEUREST FRY.
40th Divisional Laundry.	BETHUNE.
173rd Tunnelling Coy. R.E.	L 13 c 5 7
255th Tunnelling Coy. R.E.	R 2A 8 4
258th Tunnelling Coy. R.E.	L 25 d 9 5
138th Army Troops, R.E.	BRAQUEMONT.
No. 2 Section 4th Reserve Park.	NOEUX LES MINES.

✱ 1 Coy. FOSSE 2.
⊗ 1 Coy. LABUISSIERE.

7th July, 1916.

[signature]
Captain,
D.A.A. & Q.M.G.,
40th Division.

ORIGINAL.

Vol 3/

WAR DIARY

OF

A & Q BRANCH

40TH DIVISION.

FROM 1st. AUGUST 1916. TO 31st. AUGUST 1916.

VOL: III

-:-:-:-:-:-:-:-:-:-

WAR DIARY

A & Q Staff
Confidential
Army Form C. 2118

INTELLIGENCE SUMMARY
40th Division

(Erase heading not required.)

Instructions regarding War Diaries and Intelligence Summaries are contained in F.S. Regs., Part II. and the Staff Manual respectively. Title Pages will be prepared in manuscript.

Place	Date August	Hour	Summary of Events and Information	Remarks and references to Appendices
BRAQUEMONT (NOEUX LES MINES)	1		Inspection of horses & mules of R.A. and Divl. Train by 1 A/Q/o Commander. of HESDRINVGE, HOUCHIN & BRACQUEMONT	Appx
	2		Instruction issued to previous front. Evacuating LOOS-f. which will be occupied by another division.	Appx
	3		Refilling at railhead delayed from 9.30 to 11 A.M. owing to reported breakdown on line.	Appx
	4		Proposed scheme for informing billets.	Appx Appx
	5		Town Major instructed. LES BREBIS occupies his appointment.	Appx
	6		Church parade at BETHUNE (Intercession 3rd year of war.)	Appx
	7		Ordinary refilling purchase of units of water and running streams forward services by troops taking over.	
	8		Scheme not being complied with. Taking steps to ensure observance of same. In order to diminish time spent at railhead by trains drawing supplies, system of refilling altered changed. Rations are to be loaded in bulk on wagons & detail issues made elsewhere away from the platform, on the	Appx
	9		same lines as a supply column works at the railhead instead of their wagons.	
	10		2 ADOS to take over Divl. Salvage dumps and arrange inspection & collection of all salvage articles by Divl. Salvage officer. The latter and 2 others to hold Salvage. Casualties to date 1 & 9 lay machine gun Divl. Supply Col. supply 30 men for work in trenches. Killed Offrs. 2 O.Rs 36. Wounded Offrs. 9 other ranks 259.	Appx Appx
	11		R.A.S.C. Supply 40 men for work in trenches.	
	12		Coop. Society NOEUX LES MINES ask for assistance of 2 soldier bakers to help in civilian local bakery. Application made for 2 ASC bakers from 2 L of C units of from tune to time, in future to be drawn by D.A.C. from railhead direct instead of from our park. (Issue me of petrol & transport)	Appx Appx
	13		Ammunition in future to be drawn by D.A.C. from railhead direct instead of from our park.	
	14		Dentist.	
	15		In Brebis shelled slightly. About 15 casualties amongst transport animals.	Appx
	16		Moved Byrd Tpt & 3 Bns to softer quarters.	Appx
	17		Mobile billets should be ready for inspection.	Appx
	18		New stabling for transport of 3 battalions found N.E. of Crown near Fosse No.2 de BETHUNE	Appx
	19		Major Gilbert of 17th Hussars of 2nd Brebis will re-arrange arrangements for scavenging etc in town.	Appx
	20		Consultation of proposed to send S.A. ammunition and Bombs to Brebis on railway instead of to LAPUGNOY	Appx
	21		amongst Divl. Concert Troupe to perform for entertainment of men just out of trenches.	Appx
	24		Orders received to take over extended area frontage including LOOS and 14 BIS sections from 16th Division. Arrangements made accordingly.	Appx

1875 W. W593/326 1,000,000 4/15 J.B.C. & A. A.D.S.S./Forms/C.2118.

the 11th and 12th being attached to the Divn.

WAR DIARY

INTELLIGENCE SUMMARY

A + Q 40th Division   Army Form C. 2118

(Erase heading not required.)

Place	Date	Hour	Summary of Events and Information	Remarks and references to Appendices
BRAQUEMONT (MOEUX LES MINES)	August 25		Orders received for 3rd Division to take over 14 Bis sector. Loos sector thus remains with 40th Division and 111th Inf Bde will be relieved on 1/9/16.	A/Q
	26		CALONNE sector to be handed over to 63rd Division on 29-30 August	A/Q A/Q
	27		Casualties from 10 August to 26th inclusive. Killed Officers 2; O.R. 60 — Wounded Officers 22, O.Ranks 30; Missing O.R.1	A/Q
	28		Arranged with 63 Divn. rehanding over of Calonne Sector	A/Q
	29		Company new bomb store dugouts at Les Brébis which will be reutilised for S.A.A & Bombs.	A/Q
	30		Inventory agreed to Loos furnished. Soup kitchen will be established in Loos.	A/Q
	31		Casualties from 27th August to 31st inclusive killed O.Ranks 12; wounded Officers 5; Other Ranks 66	A/Q

Whostock ca???
40 Divn

WAR DIARY

OF

"A" & "Q" BRANCH, 40th DIVISION.

For PERIOD 1st to 30th SEPTEMBER, 1916.

Vol. IV.

WAR DIARY or **INTELLIGENCE SUMMARY**

Army Form C. 2118

A and Q 40th Divl Staff — Confidential

Place	Date	Hour	Summary of Events and Information	Remarks and references to Appendices
BRAQUEMONT near NOEUX LES MINES	Sept 1		Units quartered as in Appendix A attached.	Appendix A
	2		Instructions received that Major Gilbert 19 Welch Regt is to put up his appointment as Town Major, Les BREBIS. This is not entirely so. Major Gilbert has arrived and has now well up to date.	
	3		Classes of instruction in shoesmaking started. Requirements of stores, lamps, braziers reported to I Corps	
	4		11 min J.I. Risk Hone attached under instruction in Baggt control duties.	
	5		Only reduction in R.F.A. establishment due to 3 Bdes of 6 gun batteries being formed instead of 4 Bdes of 4 gun batteries, the surplus vehicles & other surplus stores are being dispensed with.	Copy
	6		25% Travelling Cy transferred from I Corps to IV Corps. New 163rd Divn will take over.	Copy
	7		moving parts of footballs for footballs provided, and establishment of a Sergt kitchen in MAROC.	Copy
	8		Casualties from 1st to 8th Sept inclusive:— Killed or 16 wounded Officers 2 or 44. 200 Whitewash brushes	Copy
	9		Stony not obtainable for attachment making. Demob instruction of purchase locally.	Copy Copy
	10		issued Brooks for cleaning billets.	
			Battalion temporarily formed to form & repair uniforms when Tailors cannot be employed.	Copy
	12		Soup kitchen in MAROC will be ready this week.	Copy
	13		Performances by 40 Divl Troupe arranged. Twice a week at Les Brebis. Once at Braquemont.	Copy
	14		Arranging to take over 3 Bde. Canteens, at MAROC, LOOS + LES BREBIS, and utilize them as Divisional Canteens,	Copy
			profits to be distributed.	Copy
	15		Major Wilmus Goodsell is the Town Major, Les Brebis.	Copy
	16		Casualties 9 to 16th inclusive:— Killed Officers 1 or 15 wounded Officers 2 or 48	Copy
	17		New leave allotment of 40 Divn. changed from 5 per diem to 3 per diem – including any special leave.	Copy
	18		Approx. estimate cost of stoning for Division for straw mats to be about £400.	Copy
	19		nil–	
	20		Orders received to take over 14 BIS section.	Copy
	21		Arrangements for Canteen, French stores, including washing units loans from 3rd Divn for 14 BIS section.	Copy
	22		Took over 14 BIS SECTION from 3rd Division. 120th Inf Bde occupy Hinzestern.	Copy
	23			G.S. major with electrical apparatus for picking up nails joined Divn alts R40 Divl Train	Copy

Army Form C. 2118

September 1916 WAR DIARY A & Q 40th Division
INTELLIGENCE SUMMARY
(Erase heading not required.)

Instructions regarding War Diaries and Intelligence Summaries are contained in F. S. Regs, Part II. and the Staff Manual respectively. Title Pages will be prepared in manuscript.

Place	Date 1916	Hour	Summary of Events and Information	Remarks and references to Appendices
BRAQUEMONT near	Sept 24		Casualties 17 to 24th inclusive :- killed Offrs 1 or 16 wounded Officers 2 or 94 missing O.R. 3	OM
NOEUX LES MINES	25		Nail picking up wagon returned. It is a useful contrivance.	CM
	26		Straw forage not obtainable after 30 Sept. Straw albo L.D. with the H. Spt. animals the issues in lieu. This chaw should be chaffed but no chaff cutters are available. Central power driven machines should be established in areas.	CM
	27		All kinds in defence line are made up t authorized establishments of reserve rations turned over. also ammunition.	CM
	28		Chicory grass for use in dry weather & operations.	CM
	29		Difficulty in drying gumboots in trenches. to prevent trench foot reported satisfactory.	CM
	30		Casualties 25 to 30th inclusive :- killed Officers 3 or 5 wounded Officers 2 or 49 missing Officers 1 or 1.	CM

[signature]
O Moore ... Col ... Q gen

CONFIDENTIAL.

BILLETS OF 40TH DIVISION ON 26TH AUGUST, 1916.

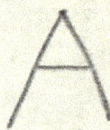

Divisional Headquarters.	BRAQUEMONT.
2nd Echelon.	BRAQUEMONT.
H.Q., 119th Infantry Brigade.	LES BREBIS.
19th Royal Welsh Fusiliers.	TRENCHES, LOOS.
12th South Wales Borderers.	TRENCHES, LOOS.
17th Welsh Regiment.	LOOS.
18th Welsh Regiment.	LOOS.
119th Machine Gun Company.	H.Q., LES BREBIS, remainder TRENCHES.
119th Trench Mortar Battery.	H.Q., LES BREBIS, remainder TRENCHES.
H.Q., 120th Infantry Brigade.	LES BREBIS.
11th King's Own (Royal Lancs.) Regt.	TRENCHES, CALONNE.
13th East Surrey Regiment.	TRENCHES, CALONNE.
14th Highland Light Infantry.	BULLY GRENAY.
14th Argyll & Sutherland Highlanders.	CALONNE.
120th Machine Gun Company.	H.Q., R 6 b 2 4, remainder TRENCHES.
120th Trench Mortar Battery.	H.Q., LES BREBIS, remainder TRENCHES.
H.Q., 121st Infantry Brigade.	LES BREBIS.
12th Suffolk Regiment.	NORTH MAROC.
13th Yorkshire Regiment.	TRENCHES, MAROC.
20th Middlesex Regiment.	TRENCHES, MAROC.
21st Middlesex Regiment.	N.E. MAROC.
121st Machine Gun Company.	H.Q., LES BREBIS, remainder TRENCHES.
121st Trench Mortar Battery.	H.Q., LES BREBIS, remainder TRENCHES.
12th Yorkshire Regiment.	SOUTH MAROC.
H.Q., 40th Divisional Artillery.	BRAQUEMONT.
H.Q., Right Group.	L 35 d 9 0.
H.Q., Left Group.	LES BREBIS.
V 40 Trench Mortar Battery.	CALONNE.
W 40 Trench Mortar Battery.	CALONNE.
X 40 Trench Mortar Battery.	CALONNE.
Y 40 Trench Mortar Battery.	MAROC.
Z 40 Trench Mortar Battery.	LES BREBIS.
A Echelon, D.A.C.	HOUCHIN.
B Echelon, D.A.C.	HESDIGNEUL.
H.Q., 40th Divisional R.E.	BRAQUEMONT.
224th Field Coy. R.E.	GRENAY.
229th Field Coy. R.E.	LES BREBIS.
231st Field Coy. R.E.	LES BREBIS (3 sections CALONNE).
40th Divisional Train.	BRAQUEMONT.
Divisional Supply Column.	HAILLICOURT.
Ammunition Sub Park.	AUCHEL.
135th Field Ambulance.	M.D.S. BRAQUEMONT; D.S. M 1 d 7 - 2; A.D.S. M 14 a 8 - 1.
136th Field Ambulance.	CORPS REST STATION, LABEUVRIERE.
137th Field Ambulance.	M.D.S. BRAQUEMONT; D.S. L 35 a 8 - 5; A.D.S. M 2 d 4 - 7; A.D.S. M 3 b 1 - 4.
51st Mobile Veterinary Section.	DROUVIN.
83rd Sanitary Section.	BRAQUEMONT.
Workshops for Motor Amb. Cars etc.	HAILLICOURT AND BRAQUEMONT.
40th Divisional School.	PRIEURE ST PRY.
40th Divisional Gas School.	HOUCHIN.
40th Divisional Laundry.	BETHUNE.
No. 2 Section 4th Reserve Park.	NOEUX LES MINES.

P.T.O.

Other Troops in 40th Divisional Area.

255th Tunnelling Company.	R 2 a PETIT SAINS.
258th Tunnelling Company.	L 25 d BRAQUEMONT.
283rd Army Troops Coy., R.E.	L 25 d BRAQUEMONT.
½ 52nd Siege Battery.	R 5 b GRENAY.
½ 2nd Siege Battery. R.G.A.	L 36 c LES BREBIS.
½ 117th Heavy Battery, R.G.A.	L 36 a FOSSE 6.
17th Northumberland Fusiliers, (less 1 Coy.)	LOOS.
11th M.M.G. Battery.	LOOS.
112th Infantry Brigade.	MAZINGARBE and 14 BIS.
152nd Field Company, R.E.	PHILOSOPHE.
1 Brigade R.F.A. (XI Corps).	NOEUX-LES-MINES.
1 Medium T.M.B. (32nd Division).	14 BIS.
2 Sections Field Amb. (32nd Divn.)	MAROC and PHILOSOPHE.
31st A.T. Company, R.E.	MINX.
173rd Tunnelling Company.	NOEUX-LES-MINES.
'B' Coy. 33rd R. Fusiliers.	MAZINGARBE.

40th Division.
26th August, 1916.

Captain,
D.A.A. & Q.M.G.,

WAR DIARY

OF

'A' and 'Q' BRANCH, 40th DIVISION.

FOR PERIOD

1st to 31st October, 1916.

Vol. V.

WAR DIARY or INTELLIGENCE SUMMARY

Army Form C. 2118

A ∙ Q   40th Division

(Erase heading not required.)

Place	Date 1916	Hour	Summary of Events and Information	Remarks and references to Appendices
BRAQUEMONT (NOEUX LES MINES)	October 1		Troops quartered as shewn in appendix A	Appendix A
	2		Question of injuries sustained by picking up nails - Further ardurousness - More nail boxes provided.	appx
	3		V.C. on Mr. immediate award will not be given for cases of wounds.	appx
	4		Question of P.B. men. Only 70 allotted to Div. area. Lieut Major Leo Portois no. in central of P.B. men.	appx
	5		All infantry battalions of Division are now equipped with full complement of Lewis Jun handcarts.	appx
	6		Sen Const Martial Leo Portois on 2 Lt. HS Bennett 20th Middx Rg., charge of drunkenness - Reprimand.	appx
	7		All returns from units. Lists of recommendations for New Years Honours due. To be forwarded to I Corps on 9/10/16	appx
	8		Orders received to evacuate southern half of MAROC Section and take over most of HULLUCH Section.	appx
	9		Maure action to be executed on 9th Hulluch section taken over on 12th	sent
			List of New Years Honours rendered. 60 allotted to the "Division". 24 went Honours + 36 mentions	appx
	10		Letter calling for names of Offrs. & other class of instruction in HATT dealts. - Do - Infantry 4 Offr + 45 OR & 45 OR & Feni Mor. Rest Camp.	AppB
			Casualties for week ending 7/10/16 Killed Offr 1, OR 10, Wounded Offr 9 OR 85.	
	11		Return rendered for officials. RA in Div. Britain wounds lasy war. - Nature was 105.	AppB
	12		Lieut col. Jordan letter from L.S. Marsden Smedale. (ng + 3 by wires in oc LES BREBIS, MAZINGARBE L PHILOSOPHE	AppB
	13		Lieut Ken appt S/Lt Captain. 120 Field Ambee ric Captain Marley, Major Appleby 1 West Ryder Shap/Bom Mermech 4+7 West Ryder	AppB
			Brevet Major L Lieut of Instruction	
	14		Medals awarded to Lgt Moore L Pte Simber 13 Yorkshire Rgt	AppB
			Casualties for week ending 14/10/16 Killed Offr 1, OR 18 Wounded Offr 10 OR 136 Missing Offr 1 OR 4	
	15		Orders received to find 2 parties of honour each of 2 Offrs & 50 on for President of Republic's visit RESERVE 18/10	AppB
	16		Rendered nth. Speaks of him m. found for 20 Middlesex	
	17		Verbal instructions received that the Division is to be relieved (The 24" Div) to about 24/1/10	AppB
			Lt. m. wounded A.E.S.M A. Gurney I Suffolks. 12 Suffolks.	
			Volunteers asked for 1 Officers in 38 Division. Verbal instructions received that Ryers was not with Division	
	18		Hathwick Ric Imft 17 West Rgt Ripeet on 18th Airship cmn awarded to Lieut Horton	AppB
	19		13 Yorks Rg TM b. Dept Captain Wolfe A Bham 13 YorkRg.	

WAR DIARY A & Q 40th Division
or
INTELLIGENCE SUMMARY

Army Form C. 2118

2 Sheet

Place	Date 1916	Hour	Summary of Events and Information	Remarks and references to Appendices
BRAQUEMONT	Oct 20		2 Lt. H.R. RUGGLES BRISE joined H.Q. Attchd up appointment A.D.C. 40th Division.	QMM
(NOEUX LES MINES)	21		Cessation bracketending 21/10/16. Killed officers 1 or 30 wounded officers 1 or 121.	—
	22		Orders for the Divn. to move from present position, to the line to Reserve Army area by end of October.	QMM
	23		Handed over to Divn. administrative book & maps to G of 20th Division which relieves 40th Division.	QMM
	24		Staff Officers shewn round the area —	QMM
	25		Canteens, Cinemas & Theatrical plant to be handed over to 24th Divn. on 27th & 28th October.	QMM
			Organization of 2 horses for storage of private property of Officers & battalion funds at Les Brebis	QMM
			also paid for out of private funds.	—
	26		Major HOPE S.W. Bombers assumed the Division, after being appointed C.O. of a battalion of the West Yorks in mistake by superior authority.	QMM
			Bomb stores prepared for handing over to 24th Division.	
	27		Refilling point for the next areas occupied during the advance of the Division to Res. Army area designated.	QMM
			Billeting areas also allotted.	
			Reformation of the Divisional Coy. M.P. personnel formed into	CMM
			groups for traffic control duties. 120th Bde group march to Bonney.	C.M Poucke B.
	28		Billets of Divisions as given in appendix B attached. 120th Bde group march to Mondy Breton area	C.M Poucke B.
	29		121 Bde group march to Bonney. 130th Bde group march to RICHEBOURG area; 121 Bd. Gde group march	QMM
			to Bonney. Two soldiers 12 Yorks charged with murdering a soldier (P.B.) working under Town Major	—
			MAZINGARBE.	
ROELLECOURT	30		121 Bde group march to Challens area. Two accused soldiers sent to custody 1 A.P.M. 1st Corps.	QMM
"	31		119 Bde group march to Bonney. Evidence against accused sent to 1st Corps. for trial.	
			Casualties from 22/10/16 to 31/10/16 Killed Officer 1 or 28 wounded Offs 2 or 93 missing or 26	

C.W.Wright
a.a + q.m.g 40 Div

CONFIDENTIAL.

BILLETS OF 40TH DIVISION ON 30TH SEPTEMBER, 1916.

Divisional Headquarters.	BRAQUEMONT.
2nd Echelon.	BRAQUEMONT.
H.Q., 119th Infantry Brigade.	LES BREBIS.
19th Royal Welsh Fusiliers.	TRENCHES, MAROC.
12th South Wales Borderers.	N.E. MAROC.
17th Welsh Regiment.	S. MAROC.
18th Welsh Regiment.	TRENCHES, MAROC.
119th Machine Gun Company.	H.Q., LES BREBIS, remainder TRENCHES.
119th Trench Mortar Battery.	H.Q., LES BREBIS, remainder TRENCHES.
H.Q., 120th Infantry Brigade.	MAZINGARBE CHATEAU.
11th King's Own (Royal Lancs. Regt.	TRENCHES, 14 BIS.
13th East Surrey Regiment.	TRENCHES, 14 BIS.
14th Highland Light Infantry.	MAZINGARBE.
14th Argyll & Sutherland Highlanders.	SUPPORT, 14 BIS.
120th Machine Gun Company.	H.Q., LES BREBIS, remainder TRENCHES.
120th Trench Mortar Battery.	H.Q., LES BREBIS, remainder TRENCHES.
H.Q., 121st Infantry Brigade.	LES BREBIS.
12th Suffolk Regiment.	TRENCHES, LOOS.
13th Yorkshire Regiment.	SUPPORT, LOOS.
20th Middlesex Regiment.	N. MAROC.
21st Middlesex Regiment.	TRENCHES, LOOS.
121st Machine Gun Company.	H.Q., LES BREBIS, remainder TRENCHES.
121st Trench Mortar Battery.	H.Q., LES BREBIS, remainder TRENCHES.
12th Yorkshire Regiment.	LOOS, (1 Coy. S. MAROC).
H.Q., 40th Divisional Artillery.	BRAQUEMONT.
178th Brigade, R.F.A.	LES BREBIS.
181st Brigade, R.F.A.	LES BREBIS.
188th Brigade, R.F.A.	LES BREBIS.
V 40 Trench Mortar Battery.	MAROC.
W 40 Trench Mortar Battery.	MAROC.
X 40 Trench Mortar Battery.	LOOS.
Y 40 Trench Mortar Battery.	MAROC.
Z 40 Trench Mortar Battery.	14 BIS.
A Echelon, D.A.C.	HOUCHIN.
B Echelon, D.A.C.	HESDIGNEUL.
H.Q., 40th Divisional R.E.	BRAQUEMONT.
224th Field Coy. R.E.	GRENAY.
229th Field Coy., R.E.	H.Q., LES BREBIS, (4 Sections LOOS)
231st Field Coy., R.E.	H.Q., LES BREBIS, (4 Sections PHILOSOPHE).
40th Divisional Train.	BRAQUEMONT.
Divisional Supply Column.	HAILLICOURT.
Ammunition Sub Park.	AUCHEL.
135th Field Ambulance.	M.D.S., BRAQUEMONT; A.D.S. LES BREBIS, SOUTH MAROC & NORTH MAROC.
136th Field Ambulance.	CORPS REST STATION, LABEUVRIERE.
137th Field Ambulance.	M.D.S., BRAQUEMONT; A.D.S. PHILOSOPHE, FORT GLATZ & ST. PATRICK.
51st Mobile Veterinary Section.	DROUVIN.
83rd Sanitary Section.	LES BREBIS.
Workshops for Motor Amb. Cars etc.	HAILLICOURT.

P.T.O.

- 2 -

40th Divisional School.	PRIEURE ST PRY.
40th Divisional Gas School.	HOUCHIN.
40th Divisional Laundry.	BETHUNE.
No. 2 Section 4th Reserve Park.	NOEUX LES MINES.

ATTACHED.

11th Motor Machine Gun Company.	LOOS.

OTHER TROOPS IN 40TH DIVISIONAL AREA, OR ATTACHED FOR CERTAIN PURPOSES.

170th Tunnelling Company.	NOEUX LES MINES.
173rd Tunnelling Company.	NOEUX LES MINES.
258th Tunnelling Company.	L 25 d BRAQUEMONT.
283rd Army Troops Coy., R.E.	L 25 d BRAQUEMONT.
½ 2nd Siege Battery.	L 36 c LES BREBIS.
124th Siege Battery.	LES BREBIS.
½ 117th Heavy Battery, R.G.A.	L 36 a FOSSE 6.
138th Heavy Battery Wagon Lines.	HOUCHIN.
Mine Rescue School.	HOUCHIN.
Det. K Cable Section, I Corps Signals.	MAROC.
8th Railway Coy., R.E. (L. of C. Unit).	FOSSE 6.
No. 7 A.A. Battery.	MAZINGARBE.
1 Section 5th Siege Battery.	FOSSE 7.

H.Q., 40th Division.

30th September, 1916.

A.F. Engelbach
Captain,
for D.A.A. & Q.M.G.,
40th Division.

CONFIDENTIAL.

BILLETS OF 40TH DIVISION ON 28TH OCTOBER, 1916.

Divisional Headquarters.	BRAQUEMONT.
2nd Echelon.	BRAQUEMONT.
H.Q., 119th Infantry Brigade.	LES BREBIS.
19th Royal Welsh Fusiliers.	SUPPORT, LOOS.
12th South Wales Borderers.	TRENCHES, LOOS.
17th Welsh Regiment.	TRENCHES, LOOS.
18th Welsh Regiment.	N. MAROC.
119th Machine Gun Company.	H.Q., LES BREBIS, remainder TRENCHES.
119th Trench Mortar Battery.	H.Q., LES BREBIS, remainder TRENCHES.
H.Q., 120th Infantry Brigade.	BRUAY.
11th King's Own (Royal Lanc.) Regt.	BRUAY.
13th East Surrey Regiment.	BRUAY.
14th Highland Light Infantry.	BRUAY.
14th Argyll & Sutherland Highlanders.	BRUAY.
120th Machine Gun Company.	BRUAY.
120th Trench Mortar Battery.	BRUAY.
H.Q., 121st Infantry Brigade.	LES BREBIS.
12th Suffolk Regiment.	LES BREBIS.
13th Yorkshire Regiment.	LES BREBIS.
20th Middlesex Regiment.	LES BREBIS.
21st Middlesex Regiment.	PETIT SAINS.
121st Machine Gun Company.	LES BREBIS.
121st Trench Mortar Battery.	LES BREBIS.
12th Yorkshire Regiment.	MAZINGARBE.
H.Q., 40th Divisional Artillery.	BRAQUEMONT.
*178th Brigade, R.F.A.	PHILOSOPHE.
188th Brigade, R.F.A.	LES BREBIS.
V 40 Trench Mortar Battery.	½ LOOS, ½ HULLUCH.
W 40 Trench Mortar Battery.	½ HULLUCH, ½ LES BREBIS.
X 40 Trench Mortar Battery.	LOOS.
Y 40 Trench Mortar Battery.	HULLUCH.
Z 40 Trench Mortar Battery.	14 BIS.
A Echelon, D.A.C.	HOUCHIN.
B Echelon, D.A.C.	HESDIGNEUL.
H.Q., 40th Divisional R.E.	BRAQUEMONT.
224th Field Coy., R.E.	GRENAY.
229th Field Coy., R.E.	LES BREBIS.
231st Field Coy., R.E.	BRUAY.
40th Divisional Train.	3 Coys., BRAQUEMONT, 1 Coy., BRUAY.
No. 40 Divisional Supply Column.	HAILLICOURT.
Ammunition Sub Park.	AUCHEL.
135th Field Ambulance.	BRUAY.
136th Field Ambulance.	BRAQUEMONT.
137th Field Ambulance.	CORPS REST STATION, LABEUVRIERE.
51st Mobile Veterinary Section.	DROUVIN.
83rd Sanitary Section.	LES BREBIS.
Workshops for Motor Amb. Cars, etc.	HAILLICOURT.
40th Divisional Gas School.	HOUCHIN.
40th Divisional Laundry.	BETHUNE.
*181st Brigade, R.F.A.	MAZINGARBE.

P.T.O.

OTHER TROOPS IN 40TH DIVISIONAL AREA, OR ATTACHED FOR CERTAIN PURPOSES.

2nd Motor Machine Gun Company.	LOOS.
No. 2 Section 4th Reserve Park.	NOEUX LES MINES.
170th Tunnelling Company.	NOEUX LES MINES.
173rd Tunnelling Company.	NOEUX LES MINES.
258th Tunnelling Company.	L 25 d BRAQUEMONT.
283rd Army Troops Coy., R.E.	L 25 d BRAQUEMONT.
½ 2nd Siege Battery.	L 36 c LES BREBIS.
138th Heavy Battery Wagon Lines.	HOUCHIN.
Mine Rescue School.	HOUCHIN.
No. 7 A.A. Battery.	MAZINGARBE.
124th Siege Battery.	LES BREBIS.
Det. K Cable Section, I Corps Signals.	MAROC.
8th Railway Coy., R.E., (L.of C. Unit).	FOSSE 6
19th Kite Balloon Section.	NOEUX LES MINES.

H.Q., 40th Division.

28th October, 1916.

Captain,
D.A.A. & Q.M.G.,
40th Division.

Original.

Vol 76

WAR DIARY

---- of ----

"A. & Q" BRANCH,

HEADQUARTERS, 40TH DIVISION

----- FOR PERIOD ------

1st to 30th NOVEMBER, 1916.

VOL: VI.

WAR DIARY
40th Division A & Q Head Quarters

INTELLIGENCE SUMMARY

November 1916

Army Form C. 2118

Place	Date	Hour	Summary of Events and Information	Remarks and references to Appendices
ROELLECOURT	1		Units quartered as shown in appendix A	appendix A
"	2		Units quartered as shown in appendix B. 40th Divn. (less RA) march to HOUVIN – REBEUVE – MAISNIL ST POL area –	appendix B
"	3		Division in rest –	appendix C
FROHEN LE GRAND	4		— Refilling points appendix B1	appendix B1
	5		Division marched to areas as shown in appendix C	appendix C
BERNAVILLE	6		Units reminded of necessity for sanitary services & cleaning of billeting areas; STABS arranging hot tin baths for battalions who report that they are required –	QAM
	7		Increased bad weather rain; local canteen opened; Transport inspected –	QM
	8		Case of stealing wine by about 20 men of 12.S.W Borderers apparently Riflemen approved into the orders of Wine + charged against the men concerned – 100 francs paid by unit –	QAM
	9		Fills & attempts to get their own back –	QAM
			Horse standings prepared in Bernaville by Divl. Coy Transport of 14 H.I. Chalk strewn locally. Orders received for 120 Inf Bde + 14 Yorks Pioneers to proceed & take over part of divn near HÉBUTERNE on 11th	QAM
	10		13th November Ile be attached to 31st Division	QAM
	11		12th Inf Bde march to DOULLENS on 12 – 14th Yorks Pioneers to Beauval on 12 – 13 – N.W. en route for front line.	QAM
	12		Moving forward Bugles to be commenced at 15 Infantry & Coy appendix D	appendix D
	13		Units quartering as shown in attached hid appendix D. Per Camphill Parvis deposited at 40 Dim on arrival also of units locally also by arrangements made to wash underclothing of men at Abbeville. Captain UPTON Jones as APM vice Major	QAM
FROHEN LE GRAND	14		Maxwell appointed APM in England – Division less 120 Inf Bde, 3 Fd Coys & 14 Yorks Pioneers, moved into Frohen le Grand area	appendix E
	15		Routine –	QAM
	16			QAM
	17		119 & 121st Inf Bdes move to LUCHEUX area on 17th & 18th. Railhead BOUQUEMAISON	QAM
	18		Br. Gen. Cunliffe Owen proceeds to England. Br. Gen. J. Campbell assumes Cd. of the division	QM
BOUQUEMAISON	19		routine. Divl. Hd. Qtrs at BOUQUEMAISON	

Army Form C. 2118

WAR DIARY
INTELLIGENCE SUMMARY
(Erase heading not required.)

1st Division
A & Q
November 1916 Enclosed

Place	Date 1916 Nov.	Hour	Summary of Events and Information	Remarks and references to Appendices
BOUQUE-MAISON	20		Orders received for Division to Entrain formation DOULLENS BERNAVAL area.	copy
"	21		120 - Bde returning from HEBURTNE to this area on 22d - Bentrie -	copy
DOULLENS	22		Marched with Doullens area.	copy
CANAPLES	23		Marched with Canaples area. Troops quartered as in appendix F	appendix F copy
AILLY LE HAUTCLOCHER	24		Marched with Ailly area - troops quartered as in appendix G	appendix G copy
	25		Preparations for improvements to billeting areas.	copy
"	26		Overhaul of all equipments etc - Damaged deficient articles to replacement.	copy
"	27		Units located as shown in appendix H. Capt Upton APM proceeds 10 days leave absence	appendix H copy
"	28		Town Majors in area appointed. Baths & Recreation rooms being established.	copy
"	29		Conference at IX Corps HQ. arrangements for move forward with Reserve Army.	copy
	30		Washing continued at Amiens. Reft. Transport units inspected during past 3 days by O.C. Suit Train & A.D.V.S. Divl Claims Officer dealing with a large number of claims by French inhabitants left by 60th Division.	copy

C.H. Marston
Lieut Colonel
A & Q Divn.

40TH DIVISION.

BILLETS :- MONCHY - BRETON AREA.

UNIT	DESTINATION
119th Infantry Brigade Group.	
Headquarters.	LA THIEULOYE.
19th Royal Welsh Fusiliers	OSTREVILLE
12th South Wales Borderers.	MONCHY BRETON.
17th Welsh Regiment.	LA THIEULOYE.
18th Welsh Regiment.	MAGNICOURT.
119th M. G. Coy.	ORLENCOURT.
119th T. M. Battery	"
231st Company, R.E.	HOUVELIN.
136th Field Ambulance.	OSTREVILLE.
No. 2 Coy. Divisional Train.	HOUVELIN.
120th Infantry Brigade Group.	
Headquarters.	FOUFFLIN RICAMETZ.
11th R. Lanc. Regiment.	MAISNIL - ST. POL -) NEUVILLE AU COMTE.)
13th East Surrey Regiment.	AVERDOINGT.
14th Highland Light Infantry.	BAILLEUL AUX CORNAILLES.
14th Argyll & Sutherland Hrs.	TERMAS.
120th M. G. Coy.	TACHINCOURT COOCHE.
120th T. M. Battery.	FOUFFLIN RICAMETZ.
No. 3 Coy. Divisional Train.	LA BELLE EPINE.
135th Field Ambulance.	To remain at ROCOURT ST. LAURENT.
121st Infantry Brigade Group.	
Headquarters.	CHELERS.
12th Suffolk Regiment.	CHELERS.
13th Yorkshire Regiment.	VILLERS-BRULIN.
20th Middlesex Regiment.	FREVILLERS.
21st Middlesex Regiment.	BETHONSART.
121st M. G. Coy.	LE TIRLET.
121st T. M. Battery.	FREVILLERS.
137th Field Ambulance, (less 4 horsed Ambulances)	Guestreville.
No. 4 Coy. Divisional Train.	FREVILLERS.
229th Field Coy. R.E.	AREA C.
12th Yorkshire Regiment.	MARQUAY.

BILLETING - HOUVIN AREA.

2nd - 4th NOVEMBER 1916.

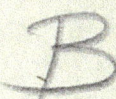

119th INFANTRY BRIGADE GROUP

Headquarters.	MAISNIL - ST. POL.
19th Royal Welsh Fusiliers.	BURNVILLE.
18th South Wales Borderers.	MONTS-EN-TERNOIS.
17th Welsh Regiment.	TROLAS.
18th Welsh Regiment.	POUFFLIN - RICAMETZ.
119th M. G. Coy.	PETIT HOUVIN.
119th T. M. Battery.	MONTS-EN-TERNOIS.
231st Field Coy. R.E.	MAISNIL - ST. POL.
No. 2 Coy. Divl. Train.	PETIT HOUVIN.
136th Field Ambulance.	HOUVILLE.
12th Yorkshire Regiment. (Pioneers).	MONCHEAUX.

120th INFANTRY BRIGADE. GROUP

Headquarters.	REBREUVE.
11th Royal Lancs. Regiment.	SERICOURT.
13th East Surrey Regiment.	REBREUVE AND LA COUTURE.
14th Highland Light Infantry.	CANETTEMONT & MONVAL.
14th Argyll & Sutherland Highrs.	PETIT BOURET & GRAND BOURET.
120th M. G. Coy.	SIBIVILLE.
120th T. M. Battery.	SIBIVILLE.
229th Field Coy. R.E.	GRAND BOURET.
No. 3 Coy. Divl. Train.	REBREUVE.
135th Field Ambulance.	SIBIVILLE.

121st INFANTRY BRIGADE. GROUP

Headquarters.	HOUVIN - HOUVIGNEUL.
12th Suffolk Regiment.	REBREUVIETTE & ROSIERE.
13th Yorkshire Regiment.	REBREUVIETTE.
20th Middlesex Regiment.	HOUVIN - HOUVIGNEUL.
21st Middlesex Regiment.	WAMIN & ETREE - WAMIN (BEUVILLERS 3rd/4th).
121st M. G. Coy.	HOUVIN - HOUVIGNEUL.
121st T. M. Battery.	HOUVIN - HOUVIGNEUL.
224th Field Coy. R.E.	½ N. of H in WAMIN.
No. 4 Coy. Divl. Train.	BROUILLY.
137th Field Ambulance.	OPPY.

REFILLING POINTS.

30th October 1916.

    119th Infantry Brigade Group..   BRAQUEMONT.
    120th Infantry Brigade Group..   ST. POL - TINQUES road near
                                              LE BELLE EPINE cross roads.
    121st Infantry Brigade Group..   FREVILLERS - BETHUNSART road.

31st October 1916.

    119th Infantry Brigade Group..   BRUAY - LABUISSERE Road.
    120th Infantry Brigade Group..   same as 30th October.
    121st Infantry Brigade Group..   same as 30th October.

1st November 1916.

    119th Infantry Brigade Group..   MONCHY BRETON.
    120th Infantry Brigade Group..   same as 31st October.
    121st Infantry Brigade Group..   same as 30th October.

2nd November 1916.

    119th Infantry Brigade Group..   Near HONVAL.
    120th Infantry Brigade Group..   MONTS en TERNOIS - GOUY en TERNOIS
                                              Road.
    121st Infantry Brigade Group..   Gnd. BOURET cross roads.

3rd. November. 1916.

    119th Infantry Brigade Group..   Road junction $\frac{1}{4}$ mile south of B
                                              in BOUQUEMAISON.
    120th Infantry Brigade Group..   Road junction $\frac{1}{4}$ mile south of H
                                              in Hte. VISEE.
    121st. Infantry BrigadeGroup..   SUS ST. LEGER - WARLUZEL road.

40TH DIVISION.

LOCATIONS OF UNITS IN FROHEN LE GRAND AREA.

Divisional Headquarters.   FROHEN-LE-GRAND.

    Divisional Train Hd. Qrs.   DRUCAS.

119th Infantry Brigade Group.

    Headquarters.   WAVANS.

      19th Royal Welsh Fusiliers.   BUIRE AU BOIS.
      12th South Wales Borderers.   FORTEL.
      17th Welsh Regiment.   NOEUX.
      18th Welsh Regiment.   ROUGEFAY & MONT HUBERT.
      119th Machine Gun Coy.   WAVANS.
      119th Trench Mortar Battery.   WAVANS.
      No. 2 Coy., Divisional Train.   HAMUR FARM.
      136th Field Ambulance.   BOFFLES.

121st Infantry Brigade Group.

    HEADQUARTERS.   REMAISNIL.

      12th Suffolk Regiment.   VILLERS L'HOPITAL.
      13th Yorkshire Regiment.   VILLERS L'HOPITAL.
      20th Middlesex Regiment.   BONNIERES.
      21st Middlesex Regiment.   BONNIERES.
      121st Machine Gun Coy.   REMAISNIL.
      121st Trench Mortar Battery.   BONNIERES.
      No. 4 Coy., Divisional Train.   BEAUVOIR.
      135th Field Ambulance.   MEZEROLLES.
      137th Field Ambulance.   MEZEROLLES.
      No. 25 Divisional Supply Col.   MEZEROLLES.

51st Mobile Veterinary Section.   FROHEN-LE-GRAND.

83rd Sanitary Section   FROHEN-LE-GRAND.

CONFIDENTIAL.   LOCATION OF UNITS.

40TH DIVISION. 19. 11. 16.

Divisional Headquarters.   BERNAVILLE.

   S.S.O.   BERNAVILLE.
   D.A.D.O.S.   BERNAVILLE.
   A.D.M.S.   BERNAVILLE.
   A.D.V.S.   BERNAVILLE.

Divisional Artillery Headquarters.   Detached under I Corps.

   178th Brigade, R.F.A.   - do -
   181st Brigade, R.F.A.   - do -
   188th Brigade, R.F.A.   - do -

Divisional Ammunition Column Hd. Qrs.   - do -

   'A' Echelon.   - do -
   'B' Echelon.   - do -

Headquarters, Royal Engineers.   BERNAVILLE.

   224th Field Coy., R.E.   COIGNEUX.
   229th Field Coy., R.E.   TOUTENCOURT.
   231st Field Coy., R.E.   DOMART-EN-PONTHIEU.

Pioneer Battalion - 12th Yorks Regt.   BEAUVAL.

119th Inf. Brigade Headquarters.   AUTHEUX.

   19th Royal Welsh Fusiliers.   HEUZECOURT and GRIMONT.
   12th South Wales Borderers.   AUTHEUX.
   17th Welsh Regiment.   BOISBERGUES.
   18th Welsh Regiment.   LE MEILLARD.
   119th Machine Gun Coy.   GRIMONT.
   119th Trench Mortar Battery.   LE QUESNEL FM.

120th Infantry Bde. Headquarters.   DOULLENS

   11th King's Own (R.Lanc.) Regt.   DOULLENS.
   13th East Surrey Regt.   DOULLENS.
   14th Highland Light Infantry.   DOULLENS.
   14th A. & S. Highlanders.   DOULLENS.
   120th Machine Gun Coy.   DOULLENS.
   120th Trench Mortar Battery.   DOULLENS.

121st Inf. Brigade Headquarters.   FIENVILLERS.

   12th Suffolk Regiment.   BERNEUIL.
   13th Yorkshire Regt.   CANDAS.
   20th Middlesex Regt.   FIENVILLERS.
   21st Middlesex Regt.   CANDAS.
   121st Machine Gun Coy.   BERNEUIL.
   121st Trench Mortar Battery.   FIENVILLERS.

Divisional Train Headquarters.   BERNAVILLE.

   No. 1 Company, Train.   Detached under 24th Division.
   No. 2 Company, Train.   LEMEILLARD.
   No. 3 Company, Train.   BEAUVAL.
   No. 4 Company, Train.   FIENVILLERS.

/Over.

No. 25 Divisional Supply Column.   BERNAVILLE.

   135th Field Ambulance.   LANCHES.
   136th Field Ambulance.   FROHEN-LE-PETIT.
   137th Field Ambulance.   GORGES.

   51st Mobile Veterinary Sect.   BERNAVILLE.

   83rd Sanitary Section.   BERNAVILLE.

Divisional Coy. (including Salvage)   BERNAVILLE.

H.Q., 40th Division.
12th November, 1916.

                              Captain,
                            D.A.A. & Q.M.G.,
                            40th Division.

40TH DIVISION.

LOCATIONS OF UNITS IN FROHEN LE GRAND AREA.

Divisional Headquarters.   FROHEN-LE-GRAND.

    Divisional Train Hd. Qrs.   DRUCAS.

119th Infantry Brigade Group.

    Headquarters.   WAVANS.

    19th Royal Welsh Fusiliers.   BUIRE AU BOIS.
    12th South Wales Borderers.   FORTEL.
    17th Welsh Regiment.   NOEUX.
    18th Welsh Regiment.   ROUGEFAY & MONT HUBERT.
    119th Machine Gun Coy.   WAVANS.
    119th Trench Mortar Battery.   WAVANS.
    No. 2 Coy., Divisional Train.   MAHUR FARM.
    136th Field Ambulance.   BOFFLES.

121st Infantry Brigade Group.

    HEADQUARTERS.   REMAISNIL.

    12th Suffolk Regiment.   VILLERS L'HOPITAL.
    13th Yorkshire Regiment.   VILLERS L'HOPITAL.
    20th Middlesex Regiment.   BONNIERES.
    21st Middlesex Regiment.   BONNIERES.
    121st Machine Gun Coy.   REMAISNIL.
    121st Trench Mortar Battery.   BONNIERES.
    No. 4 Coy., Divisional Train.   BEAUVOIR.
    135th Field Ambulance.   MEZEROLLES.
    137th Field Ambulance.   MEZEROLLES.
    No. 25 Divisional Supply Col.   MEZEROLLES.

51st Mobile Veterinary Section.   FROHEN-LE-GRAND.

83rd Sanitary Section.   FROHEN-LE-GRAND.

23/11/16 F

40TH DIVISION.
LOCATION OF UNITS IN CANAPLES AREA.

DIVISIONAL HEADQUARTERS.   CANAPLES.

119TH INFANTRY BRIGADE.

Headquarters.   ST. OUEN.
19th Royal Welsh Fusiliers.   ST. OUEN.
12th South Wales Borderers.   ST. LEGER LES DOMART.
17th Welsh Regiment.   FRANQUEVILLE.
18th Welsh Regiment.   ST. OUEN.
119th Machine Gun Company.   BARLETTE.
119th Trench Mortar Battery.   ST. LEGER LES DOMART.
No.2 Coy., Divisional Train.   BARLETTE & GENCOURT.
136th Field Ambulance.   HOUDENCOURT.

120th INFANTRY BRIGADE.

Headquarters.   FIEFFES.
11th King's Own (R.Lanc)Regt.   BONNEVILLE.
13th East Surrey Regiment.   BONNEVILLE.
14th Highland Light Infantry.   H.Q. & 1 Coy. FIEFFES,
                                            3 Coys. CANAPLES.
14th A. & S. Highlanders.   MONTRELET.
120th Machine Gun Company.   BERNEUIL.
120th Trench Mortar Battery.   FIEFFES.
229th Field Coy. R.E.   MONTRELET.
No.3 Coy., Divisional Train.   BONNEVILLE.
135th Field Ambulance.   FIEFFES.

121st INFANTRY BRIGADE.

Headquarters.   BERTEAUCOURT.
12th Suffolk Regiment.   BERTEAUCOURT.
13th Yorkshire Regiment.   BERTEAUCOURT.
20th Middlesex Regiment.   HALLOY.
21st Middlesex Regiment.   PERNOIS.
121st Machine Gun Company.   HALLOY.
121st Trench Mortar Battery.   HALLOY.
224th Field Coy. R.E.   BERTEAUCOURT.
No.4 Coy., Divisional Train.   BERTEAUCOURT.
137th Field Ambulance.   PERNOIS.

12th Yorkshire Regiment.   BERNEUIL.

No.25 Divisional Supply Column.   L'ETOILE.

51st Mobile Veterinary Section.   CANAPLES.

83rd SANITARY SECTION.   CANAPLES.

Divisional Company.   CANAPLES.

40TH DIVISION.
LOCATION OF UNITS IN AILLY AREA.

24/25 Nov 1916

G7

DIVISIONAL HEADQUARTERS.	AILLY LE HAUT CLOCHER.

119TH INFANTRY BRIGADE.

Headquarters.	BELLANCOURT.
19th Royal Welsh Fusiliers.	BELLANCOURT.
12th South Wales Borderers.	BUIGNY L'ABBE.
17th Welsh Regiment.	VAUCHELLES-LES-QUESNOY.
18th Welsh Regiment.	EAUCOURT.
119th Machine Gun Company.	EPAGNE.
119th Trench Mortar Battery.	MONFLIERS.
231st Field Coy. R.E.	VAUCHELLES-LES-QUESNOY.
No. 2 Coy. Divisional Train.	MONFLIERS.
136th Field Ambulance.	VAUCHELLES-LES-QUESNOY.

120TH INFANTRY BRIGADE.

Headquarters.	GORENFLOS.
11th King's Own (R.Lanc.) Rgt.	BUSSUS.
13th East Surrey Regt.	BUSSUS.
14th Highland Light Infantry.	GORENFLOS.
14th A. & S. Highlanders.	YAUCOURT.
120th Machine Gun Company.	GORENFLOS.
120th Trench Mortar Battery.	GORENFLOS.
229th Field Coy., R.E.	YAUCOURT.
No. 3 Coy., Divisional Train.	GORENFLOS.
135th Field Ambulance.	GORENFLOS.

121ST INFANTRY BRIGADE.

Headquarters.	PONTREMY.
12th Suffolk Regiment.	PONTREMY.
13th Yorkshire Regiment.	FRANCIERES.
20th Middlesex Regiment.	FAMECHON.
21st Middlesex Regiment.	ERGNIES.
121st Machine Gun Company.	PONTREMY.
121st Trench Mortar Battery.	FAMECHON.
224th Field Coy. R.E.	PONTREMY.
No. 4 Coy., Divisional Train.	PONTREMY.
137th Field Ambulance.	PONTREMY.

PIONEER BATTALION.

12th Yorkshire Regiment.	AILLY LE HAUT CLOCHER.
No. 25 Divisional Supply Column.	L'ETOILE.
51st Mobile Veterinary Section.	AILLY LE HAUT CLOCHER.
83rd Sanitary Section.	AILLY LE HAUT CLOCHER.
Divisional Company.	L'ETOILE. (AILLY on 25th).

40TH DIVISION.

LOCATION OF UNITS IN AILLY AREA, 26th NOVEMBER, 1916.

DIVISIONAL HEADQUARTERS.   AILLY LE HAUT CLOCHER.

119TH INFANTRY BRIGADE.

    Headquarters.   BELLANCOURT.
    19th Royal Welsh Fusiliers.   BELLANCOURT.
    12th South Wales Borderers.   PONTREMY.
    17th Welsh Regiment.   VAUCHELLES-LES-QUESNOY.
    18th Welsh Regiment.   EAUCOURT.
    119th Machine Gun Company.   EPAGNE.
    119th Trench Mortar Battery.   MONFLIERS.
    231st Field Coy. R.E.   BUIGNY L'ABBE
    No. 2 Coy. Divisional Train.   MONFLIERS.
    136th Field Ambulance.   VAUCHELLES-LES-QUESNOY.

120TH INFANTRY BRIGADE.

    Headquarters.   GORENFLOS.
    11th King's Own (R.Lanc.) Rgt.   BUSSUS.
    13th East Surrey Regiment.   BUSSUS.
    14th Highland Light Infantry.   GORENFLOS.
    14th A. & S. Highlanders.   YAUCOURT.
    120th Machine Gun Company.   ALLIEL.
    120th Trench Mortar Battery.   ALLIEL.
    229th Field Coy. R.E.   YAUCOURT.
    No. 3 Coy., Divisional Train.   GORENFLOS.
    135th Field Ambulance.   FAMECHON.

121ST INFANTRY BRIGADE.

    Headquarters.   VAUCHELLES-LES-DOMART.
    12th Suffolk Regiment.   MOUFLERS - 1 Coy. VAUCHELLES-
                                                            LES-DOMART.
    13th Yorkshire Regiment.   VILLERS SOUS AILLY.
    20th Middlesex Regiment.   BRUCAMPS.
    21st Middlesex Regiment.   ERGNIES.
    121st Machine Gun Company.   BRUCAMPS.
    121st Trench Mortar Battery.   BRUCAMPS.
    224th Field Coy. R.E.   L'ETOILE.
    No. 4 Coy., Divnl. Train.   VAUCHELLES-LES-DOMART.
    137th Field Ambulance.   L'ETOILE.

PIONEER BATTALION.

    12th Yorkshire Regiment.   AILLY LE HAUT CLOCHER.

No. 26 Divisional Supply Column.   L'ETOILE.

51st Mobile Veterinary Section.   FAMECHON.

83rd Sanitary Section.   AILLY LE HAUT CLOCHER.

Divisional Company.   AILLY LE HAUT CLOCHER.

Vol 7

WAR DIARY

OF

"A" AND "Q" BRANCH

40TH DIVISION.

FROM 1/12/1916 TO 31/12/1916.

VOLUME VII.

WAR DIARY or INTELLIGENCE SUMMARY

Army Form C. 2118

A. & Q. Staff
Hd. Qrs. Confidential
40th Divn.

Dec. 1916

Place	Date 1916	Hour	Summary of Events and Information	Remarks and references to Appendices
AILLY LE HAUT CLOCHER	Dec 1		The division will shortly move forward and of the present area the question of billets & RE Stores Dumps for improving billets and area require decision as regards Materiel. Left the base in limited way force will.	Appx
	2		Battalions & practice marching over periods for the march forward. Parks & Parks & carries interior duty. Blankets & ammunition.	Appx
	3		2nd Baths company at PONT REMY & BUSSUS. Washing contract for linen at A.M. I.E.M.S.	Appx
	4		Visited 14th Yorks Pioneers area now occupied by 33 Division with view to finding sites for Divl. School	Appx
	5		ALLERY approved suitable in arch allotted.	Appx
			Instructions received to move 3 Fd. Corps RE & the 12 Yorks Pioneers to MAUREPAS on the 7th Dec. Proceeded by transport on 8th Dec.	Appx
	6		Area commandants appointed to take over areas from French, areas BRESSAIRES, CELESTINS and SAILLY LAURETTE	Appx
	7		Allery chosen as Divl. School out. Lt. Col GUNN 14 A.I.S. Hohs appointed commandant.	Appx
	8		Transport 17 Yorks & 3 Fd Corps proceeded to ARGOEUVES & LONGPRÉ enroute to MAUREPAS on the 9th	Appx
	9		Personnel of RE & 12 Yorks move by rail 2 & 3 Fd Corps RE to SAILLY LE SEC. Transport of 119 Bde to ST. SAUVEUR	Appx
	10		Personnel of 119 Bde group by rail & camps 111 & 112. Transport of 121 Bde group to ST. SAUVEUR. Transport of 119 Bde to camps 111 & 112.	Appx
	11		Personnel of 121 Bde group to camps 12 & 13.	Appx
	12		General Court Martial. Final Verdicts. Barber & Hollinsfield Do Miller P/g charges of cowardice.	Appx
	13		Find proceeded & completed. Lt. M. Barber found not guilty. 2nd Lt Hollinsfield convicted. Sentence dismissed awaits confirmation.	Appendix A
CHIPILLY	14		Divl. Head Qrs. moved to CHIPILLY. Divison concentrated as 15th	Appendix A
	15		Location of units, offenders. A Company very dirty state so left by French troops.	Appx
	16		Division busily engaged chiefly in cleaning up camps & carrying building accommodation	Appx
	17		Area re-allotted by XIV Corps. 4th Division & units commandants for CHIPILLY and SAILLY LE SEC areas.	Appx
	18		Supply billhead at BELAIR	Appx
	19		Railways, accoutrements changed from EDGEHILL (DERNANCOURT) to LE PLATEAU	Appx
	20		Outline for move of division out of our lines – Division shifted on 21st 22nd 23rd Dec. Takes over from 33rd Division	Appx

Army Form C. 2118

WAR DIARY or INTELLIGENCE SUMMARY

December 1916 A+Q Staff HQ 9th Div. September

(Erase heading not required.)

Instructions regarding War Diaries and Intelligence Summaries are contained in F.S. Regs., Part II. and the Staff Manual respectively. Title Pages will be prepared in manuscript.

Place	Date 1916 DEC.	Hour	Summary of Events and Information	Remarks and references to Appendices
CHIPILLY	21		Instructions received that all Lorry are to be provided with a white disc to precede traffic control.	Appx
	22		Officers to be appointed to working parties trained in Horsemanship & Care of Horses	Appx
	23		A Works battalion formed by the Divn in reinforcement. II Corps when under command of Major TURTON	Appx
	24		A.K. Army arranged a contract for washing Shirts etc. at BEAUVAIS. 60 miles away. 12 yards left.	Appx
	25		130 men detailed to form a washing company.	Appx
	26		119 Bde send 120 Bde men forward attack over front line from 3rd Division 121 Bde moves in 27th	Appx
	27		Works battalion move to MAVREPAS' winter canvas.	Appx
MAVREPAS	28		do. bid. Head Qtrs established in dug outs in front line. relieved in middle area by 4th Division.	Appx
	29		Casualties: wounded officers killed B others men wounded 21 other ranks —	
	30		Units treated as above in attached Appendix B	Appendix B.
	31		68 cases of "trench feet." Front trenches deteriorating all water water & deep in mud, as taken over—	Appx

CHMontefiore
A+Q, 9th Divn.

SECRET

40TH DIVISION.

DISTRIBUTION OF UNITS. - From 15th Decr. 1916.

Divisional Headquarters.	CHIPILLY.
40th Divnl. Signal Coy.	CHIPILLY.

ROYAL ARTILLERY.
Headquarters. — SAILLY LE SEC.
178th Brigade, R.F.A. — Attached 33rd Division.
181st Brigade, R.F.A. — Attached 33rd Division.
188th Brigade, R.F.A. — Attached 8th Division.
40th D.A.C. (less No. 4 Sect.). — Attached 33rd Division.
No. 4 Section, D.A.C. — Attached 8th Division.

ROYAL ENGINEERS.
Headquarters. — CHIPILLY.
224th Field Coy., R.E. — Attached 4th Division.
229th Field Coy., R.E. — Attached 4th Division.
231st Field Coy., R.E. — SAILLY LE SEC.

119th INFANTRY BRIGADE.
Headquarters. — SAILLY LAURETTE.
19th Royal Welsh Fusiliers. — Camp No. 12.
12th South Wales Borderers. — Camp No. 12.
17th Welsh Regiment. — Camp No. 12.
18th Welsh Regiment. — Camp No. 12.

120th INFANTRY BRIGADE.
Headquarters. — Camp No. 111.
11th King's Own (R.Lanc.) Rgt. — Camps No. 111 & 112.
13th East Surrey Regiment. — Camps No. 111 & 112.
14th Highland Light Infantry. — Camps No. 111 & 112.
14th Argyll & Sutherland Hrs. — Camps No. 111 & 112.

121st INFANTRY BRIGADE.
Headquarters. — SAILLY LAURETTE.
12th Suffolk Regiment. — Camp No. 124.
13th Yorkshire Regiment. — Camp No. 124.
20th Middlesex Regiment. — Camp No. 125.
21st Middlesex Regiment. — Camp No. 12.

12th Yorkshire Regt. (Pioneers). — Attached 4th Division.

DIVISIONAL TRAIN.
Headquarters. — SAILLY LAURETTE.
Headquarter Company. — SAILLY LAURETTE.
No. 2 Company. — Camp No. 12.
No. 3 Company. — Camps No. 111 & 112.
No. 4 Company. — Camp No. 124.

No. 25 Divisional Supply Column. — SAILLY LAURETTE.

R.A.M.C.
135th Field Ambulance. — Camps No. 111 & 112.
136th Field Ambulance. — Camp No. 12.
137th Field Ambulance. — SAILLY LAURETTE.

51st Mobile Veterinary Section. — CHIPILLY.

83rd Sanitary Section. — No. 12 Camp.

SECRET.

40TH DIVISION.

LOCATION OF UNITS.

Divisional Headquarters.	B.21.c.
Echelon B.	L.16.d.1.9.
40th Divnl. Signal Coy.	B.21.c.

ROYAL ARTILLERY.

H.Q., 33rd Divnl. Artillery.	B.21.c.
H.Q., 156 Bde. R.F.A.	B.16.d.1.4.
H.Q., 162 Bde. R.F.A.	B.16.d.1.6.
H.Q., 178 Bde. R.F.A.	B.11.b.3.8.
H.Q., 181 Bde. R.F.A.	B.24.d.7.6.
H.Q., 33rd D.A.C.	L.10.b.5.5.
No. 1 Sect. 33rd D.A.C.	L.10.c.5.2.
No. 2 Sect. do.	L.10.d.1.4.
Section, 40th D.A.C.	L.10.d.1.9.
do. do.	L.12.c.5.7.
B Echelon, 33rd D.A.C.	L.16.c.5.8.

ROYAL ENGINEERS.

Headquarters.	B.21.c.
224th Field Coy. R.E.	B.16.b.3.4.
229th Field Coy. R.E.	B.16.d.
231st Field Coy. R.E.	L.15.c.

119TH INFANTRY BRIGADE.

Headquarters.	B.16.b.3.6.
19th Royal Welsh Fusiliers.	Reserve.
12th South Wales Borderers.	Trenches.
17th Welsh Regiment.	Trenches.
18th Welsh Regiment.	Support.
119th Machine Gun Coy.	Camp 17.
119th Trench Mortar Batty.	Camp 21.
Rear Party.	Camp 21.
Transport.	B.14.c.

120TH INFANTRY BRIGADE.

Headquarters.	B.16.d.4.7.
11th King's Own (R.Lanc). Rgt.	Reserve.
13th East Surrey Regt.	Support.
14th Highland Light Infantry.	Trenches.
14th A. & S. Highlanders.	Trenches.
120th Machine Gun Coy.	B.17.c.0.5.
120th Trench Mortar Batty.	A.23.d.
Rear Party.	Camp 20. A.27.c.8.1.
Transport.	A.23.d.

121ST INFANTRY BRIGADE.

Headquarters.	BRAY.
20th Middlesex Regiment.	Camp 21.
21st Middlesex Regiment.	Camp 21.
12th Suffolk Regiment.	Camp 17.
13th Yorkshire Regiment.	Camp 17.
121st Machine Gun Coy.	Camp 17.
121st Trench Mortar Batty.	Camp 17.
Rear Party.	Camp 17.
Transport.	With Units.
12th Yorkshire Regt. (Pioneers).	B.20.a.1.8.
Transport.	B.20.a.1.2.

/Over.

- 2 -

DIVISIONAL TRAIN.
   Headquarters.   BRAY.
   Headquarters Coy.   BRAY.
   No. 2 Company.   L.15.b.
   No. 3 Company.   BRAY.
   No. 4 Company.   BRAY.

No. 25 Divisional Supply Column.   K.31.c.

   135th Field Ambulance.   Camp 17.
   136th Field Ambulance.   Camp 17.
   137th Field Ambulance.   Camp 17.

51st Mobile Veterinary Section.   BRAY.

83rd Sanitary Section.   Camp 17.

Divisional Gas School.   Camp 21.

A.P.M.   Camp 17.

D.A.D.O.S.   BRAY.

French Mission.   Place L'Eglise, BRAY.

H.Q., 40th Division.
29th December, 1916.

(RSJ).

A.H. Engelbach
Captain,
for D.A.A. & Q.M.G.,
40th Division.

CONFIDENTIAL.

WAR DIARY

"A" and "Q" BRANCH

40TH DIVISION.

From 1st January TO 31st January, 1917.

VOL. VIII.

Confidential

WAR DIARY
or
INTELLIGENCE SUMMARY

(Erase heading not required.)

A & Q Head Qtrs Staff   Army Form C. 2118
40th Division

Place	Date 1917	Hour	Summary of Events and Information	Remarks and references to Appendices
near MAUREPAS	Jany 1		Wardes Battalion Rfts increased from 600 men to about 1000 men.	Cdhh
	2		At army learning centred at BEAUVAIS. not satisfactory at present.	Cdhh
	3		Difficulties of arranging returns to be carried up properly to front line owing to divisions and back slate of communication.	Cdhh
	4		Offrs refns particularly for night sector. Pack animals are used as much as possible. Cases of Trench feet all preventive measures possible taken - weather conditions & localities of trenches render it difficult. Glycerine Solution paraffin issued in excess of authorized scale. In what immediate condition of men in trenches shall be personally inspected.	Cdhh
	5		Sist of Artillery wagon lines. Corps Car. not satisfied that they have been looked after by artillery units. Dispatches fromentry.	Cdhh
	6		Casualties 1st & 7th inclusive:- Killed offrs nil. ORs 19. Wounded offrs nil 3 ORs. Tanks 59	Cdhh
	7		Reserve Bns of 152d - 2nd line are to form foot baths. Arrangements to prepare dug outs func'n frameworks.	Cdhh
	8		Arrangements made for provision of huts &c. where men can be treated with preparation for acute trench feet.	Cdhh
	9		Lack of Dr. Mors. in Battalion nof 119 Bde represented.	Cdhh
	10		Area Commandants as arranged by XV Corps not proving a success. Smaller areas required for their supervision.	Cdhh
	11		Amended instructions concerning attachment of offrs as learners on staff duties. 10 days with Div. HQ. One more Tank Bde.	Cdhh
	12		Lt. Col. A'Kins 2/5 Leicester Rgt detached to Battalion for one month.	Cdhh
	13		CRE as "Divn" acting as CE. XV Corps from today for about a fortnight.	Cdhh
	14		Capt Crawford RAMC awarded M.C.	Cdhh
	15		21 Blyt proceeds to XV Corps HQ. on 18th as Camp Commandant XV Corps.	Cdhh
	16		Capt UPTON APM ordered for 2nd Division as APM - Snowy front. Cases of trench feet 82.	Cdhh
	17		Arrangements made to attach Capt GOUGH 3 Lthan Sco. as a learner in staff duties.	Cdhh
	18		18 treated.	Cdhh
	19		Casualties 8 to 17th inclusive:- Killed officers nil. OR Tanks 14. Wounded officers 1 OR Tanks 74.	Cdhh
	20		Lt Hunter Rodwell joined as ADC Major A Bryant Gloucester Rgt to command 17 Welsh Rfts.	Cdhh
	21		Preparations for move of Division out of line with reserve area on 25-26-27th Jany.	Cdhh
	22		Use of steam Bantams for elongation of certain of units to be discontinued. No further sanction drafts.	Cdhh
	23		Ambulance drawn away to utilized by men proceeding on leave.	Cdhh
	24		The treatment of front feet preventive of "french feet" by means of camphor lotn. etc. as recommended by the French has not given conclusive results.	Cdhh
	25		121 Inf Bde jump march to camps 12 & 13. Three battalions move for railhead duties on 27 at BRAY, PLATEAU & BELAIR	Cdhh

Confidential

WAR DIARY
INTELLIGENCE SUMMARY
(Erase heading not required.)

Army Form C. 2118

A & Q Head Quarters 40th Division

Instructions regarding War Diaries and Intelligence Summaries are contained in F.S. Regs., Part II and the Staff Manual respectively. Title Pages will be prepared in manuscript.

Place	Date 1917 December	Hour	Summary of Events and Information	Remarks and references to Appendices
Near MAUREPAS	26		Owing to congestion on railway all leave cancelled – except for officers entitled to proceed by our letter – 121/2/ Inf Bde marched to rest area – 120th F. Camps 12 en route for Gobles CORBIE.	
	27			
	28		119th Inf Bde proceeded to camps 12 & 124, rest area. Divl Head Qrts moved to CORBIE.	
CORBIE	29		Deficiencies in Infantry officers in battalions brought to notice. D. Nos particularly required.	
"	30		Recommendations for rewards Italian decorations to be submitted.	
"	31		Schemes for improvement of camps to be later up. Areas divided into Bdd-groups – Casualties from 18 to 31 Dec. inclusive :- killed Officers nil or. 29 wounded Officers 5 or. 71	

C. Moore Mol
A & Q LN
40 Div

ORIGINAL

Vol 9

WAR DIARY

of

Q BRANCH

40th DIVISION

for

FEBRUARY 1917.

Confidential

WAR DIARY
or
INTELLIGENCE SUMMARY
(Erase heading not required.)

Army Form C. 2118

A & Q Staff
Head Quarters 40th Division

Place	Date 1917 FEB.	Hour	Summary of Events and Information	Remarks and references to Appendices
CORBIE	1		Units 40th Division located as shown in Appendix A.	Appendix A.
	2		Divl. Baths at SAILLY LAURETTE, Camp 12 and CORBIE. The latter have been arranged by XIV Corps, & are under Town Major Corbie.	App A
	3		No. 200 Machine Gun Coy. to form Divisional Strops —	Appx A
	4		Divisional MG Coy. divisional troops. "Thaw" which commenced about January 15th still continues. Traffic and supply arrangements in event of thaw.	App A
	5		836 Sanitary Section of 115 40th Division not to be located permanently in Reserve area. Whilst the division is in the	App A App A Appx A
	6		XV Corps — instructions received that HQ Division is Reserve with Div RANCOURT SECTOR on a one Bde front S.A.A. portion of 140 SAA Column is located at Cartel VAUX whilst the Division is in G HQ reserve.	App A App A App A
	7		Division will take over RANCOURT SECTOR on the evening 12 January.	App A
	8			
	9		Units move on 10th & 11th	
	10		119th Bde & Camps 17 & 21	Appx A
	11		120th Bde to Camp 111 with 3 battalions at Railhead for loading trucks, 121 Inf Bde & Camps 20 & 21+11+ 1112	Appx A Appendix B.
	12		H.Q. Division at P.C. BONNET. MAUREPAS	App A
MAUREPAS	13		Units located as in Appendix B.	App A App A
	14		Applications for commissions in Highland Regts. will not be considered till end of March.	
	15		Leave allotment to division — 3 daily. Battalions will be reshauffered to contrary —	App A App A
	16		Contingency transferred to infantry. Battalions supply 3 Bde Major, 119 Inf Bde do —	
	17		Capt. GOODLIFFE Royal Fusiliers Thaw precautions ordered — to save break up of roads —	
	18		No lorries allowed on the roads. all divisional arrangements for thaw working satisfactorily	
	19		Lens ashowl convert party coming to BRAY. Shortly for a week	
	20		Major MacDonald 2nd R. Berkshire Regt protem command N.R. O.R. Lanc. Regt. vice Lt Col Ritchie Sick.	
	21		Casualties to date from 12 February - Killed Officers 1 O.R. 1 Wounded Officers 1 O.R. 26	
	22		Lumber wagons to be issued to battalions in other than 12 Lancs Regt —	
	23		Proposed to form an Officers club at Bray — considered unnecessary under present circumstances	
	24			
	25		D.C.M. Awarded to Pte. JONES (R) 136 Field Ambulance	
	26		P.B. men at last Scenery available. Aeroplane men doing duties behind the line who are fit for the trenches —	
	27		P.B. Officers required & Specialists and medically unfit	
	28		Casualties from 22 to 28 February inclusive — Killed Officers — OR 9 Wounded Officers 1 O.R. 30	

C/Moore Lt Col AA and QMG 40th Division

SECRET.

40TH DIVISION.

DISTRIBUTION OF UNITS. - 2nd FEBRUARY, 1917

DIVISIONAL HEADQUARTERS.   CORBIE.

  40th Divnl. Signal Coy.   CORBIE.

ROYAL ARTILLERY.
  Headquarters.   CORBIE.
  178th Brigade, R.F.A.   Attached 8th Divn. Camps 20 & 21.
  181st Brigade, R.F.A.   Attached 8th Divn. Camp 21.
  V/40 T.M. Battery.   CHIPILLY.
  X/40 T.M. Battery.   CHIPILLY.
  Y/40 T.M. Battery.   VAUX EN AMIENOIS.
  Z/40 T.M. Battery.   CHIPILLY.
  40th Divnl. Ammn. Column.   Attached 8th Divn. H.Q. & B Echelon,
                                                    L.16.c. A Echelon, L.18.a.
                                                    S.A.A. portion, VAUX SUR SOMME.

ROYAL ENGINEERS.
  Headquarters.   CORBIE.
  224th Field Coy. R.E.   Camp 14. K.23.a. (Under XV Corps)..
  229th Field Coy. R.E.   H.Q. & 2 Sects. SAILLY LE SEC.
                                                    1 Sect. CHIPILLY. 1 Sect. CORBIE.
  231st Field Coy. R.E.   Nissen Huts. A.30.b. (Under XV Corps).

119TH INFANTRY BRIGADE.
  Headquarters.   SAILLY LAURETTE.
  19th Royal Welsh Fusiliers.   Camp No. 12. (a). K.33.b.
  12th South Wales Borderers.   Camp No. 124.   J.35.b.
  17th Welsh Regiment.   Camp No. 124.   J.35.b.
  18th Welsh Regiment.   Camp No. 12. (a). K.33.b.
  119th Machine Gun Coy.   Camp No. 12. (e). K.33.d.
  119th Trench Mortar Batty.   Camp No. 12. (e). K.33.d.

120TH INFANTRY BRIGADE.
  Headquarters.   CORBIE.
  11th King's Own (R.Lanc) Rgt.   CORBIE.
  13th East Surrey Regiment.   CORBIE.
  14th Highland Light Infantry.   CORBIE.
  14th A. & S. Highlanders.   CORBIE.
  120th Machine Gun Coy.   CORBIE.
  120th Trench Mortar Batty.   CORBIE.

121ST INFANTRY BRIGADE.
  Headquarters.   SAILLY LAURETTE.
  12th Suffolk Regiment.   BELAIR STATION.
  13th Yorkshire Regiment.   BRAY.
  20th Middlesex Regiment.   Camp No. 12. K.33.b.
  21st Middlesex Regiment.   H.Q. & 1 Coy. Camp 111. L.2.b.
                                                   2 Cos. PLATEAU STN, 1 Co. ETINEHEM.
  121st Machine Gun Coy.   Camp 12. K.33.b.
  121st Trench Mortar Batty.   Camp 12. K.33.b.

12th Yorkshire Regt. (Pioneers).   H.Q. & 1 Coy. Camp 14. K.23.a.
                                                   3 Coys. Nissen Huts, A.30.b.

40th Divnl. Works Battn.   L.17.b.

DIVISIONAL TRAIN.
  Headquarters.   CORBIE.
  No. 1 Company.   BRAY.
  No. 2 Company.   SAILLY LAURETTE.
  No. 3 Company.   CORBIE.
  No. 4 Company.   CHIPILLY.

No. 25 Divnl. Supply Column.   SAILLY LAURETTE.

/Over.

135th Field Ambulance.   CORBIE.
136th Field Ambulance.   SAILLY LAURETTE.
137th Field Ambulance.   Camp No. 12. K.33.b

51st Mobile Veterinary Sect.   CHIPILLY.

83rd Sanitary Section.   SAILLY LAURETTE.

Divisional Gas School.   Camp No. 12. K.33.b

A. P. M.   CORBIE.

D.A.D.O.S.   CHIPILLY.

French Mission.   CORBIE.

SECRET.

40TH DIVISION.

DISTRIBUTION OF UNITS. - 12th FEBRUARY, 1917.

40TH DIVISION.
- Advanced Headquarters.   P.C. BONNET. - B.21.c.2.6.
- Rear Headquarters.   L.16.d.1.9.
- Signal Company.   P.C. BONNET. - B.21.c.2.6.

ROYAL ARTILLERY.
- Headquarters.   P.C. BONNET. - B.21.c.2.6.
- 178th Brigade, R.F.A.   Camp 21.
- 181st Brigade, R.F.A.   P.C. CRANIERES. - B.16.d.0.7.
- 45th Brigade, R.F.A.   APPLE. - B.11.b.3.8.
- V/40 Trench Mortar Batty.   CHIPILLY.
- X/40 " " "   CHIPILLY.
- Y/40 " " "   CHIPILLY.
- Z/40 " " "   CHIPILLY.
- 40th Divnl. Ammn. Column.   BRAY.
- Wagon lines.   Camps 20 and 21.

ROYAL ENGINEERS.
- Headquarters.   P.C. BONNET. - B.21.c.2.6.
- 224th Field Coy. R.E.   H.Q. and 3 Secs. Camp 14. - K.23.a. - Under XV Corps. 1 Sec. SAILLY LE SEC.
- 229th Field Coy. R.E.   B.16.b.3.4.
- 231st Field Coy. R.E.   Nissen Huts. A.30.b. (Under XV Corps).

119TH INFANTRY BRIGADE.
- Headquarters.   LE FOREST. - B.16.b.3.6.
- 19th Royal Welsh Fusiliers.   ARTHUR'S SEAT. - C.8.a.0.6.
- 12th South Wales Borderers.   B.14.c.central.
- 17th Welsh Regiment.   ALBANY. - B.6.d.4.2.
- 18th Welsh Regiment.   APOLLO. - C.1.d.1.9.
- 119th Machine Gun Coy.   C.1.c.1.4.
- 119th Trench Mortar Bty.   B.14.c.

120TH INFANTRY BRIGADE.
- Headquarters.   Camp 111.
- 11th King's Own (R.Lanc) Rgt.   BELAIR.
- 13th East Surrey Regt.   BRAY TOURBIERES.
- 14th Highland Light Infantry.   Camp 112.
- 14th A. & S. Highrs.   BRAY.
- 120th Machine Gun Coy.   Camp 112.
- 120th Trench Mortar Bty.   VAUX-EN-AMIENOIS. (T.M. Course).

121ST INFANTRY BRIGADE.
- Headquarters.   BRAY.
- 12th Suffolk Regt.   Camp 111.
- 13th Yorkshire Regiment.   Camp 21.
- 20th Middlesex Regt.   Camp 111.
- 21st Middlesex Regt.   Camp 21.
- 121st Machine Gun Coy.   Camp 111.
- 121st Trench Mortar Bty.   Camp 111.

Transport of Brigade in line.   B.14.c.
Details of " " "   Nissen Huts, B.14.c.

12TH YORKSHIRE REGIMENT.(PIONEERS)
- Hd.Qrs. and 2 Coys.   MAUREPAS RAVINE. - B.20.a.3.5.
- 2 Companies.   Nissen Huts. - A.30.b. (Under XV Corps)

40th Divnl. Works Battn.   L.17.b.

/Over.

200th Machine Gun Company.	Camp 111.

DIVISIONAL TRAIN.

Headquarters.	BRAY.
No. 1 Company.	BRAY.
No. 2 Company.	L.15.b.
No. 3 Company.	BRAY.
No. 4 Company.	BRAY.
No. 25 Divnl. Supply Column.	SAILLY LAURETTE.
135th Field Ambulance.	Camp 112.
136th Field Ambulance.	Camp 21.
137th Field Ambulance.	BRAY.
51st Mobile Veterinary Sect.	BRAY.
83rd Sanitary Section.	SAILLY LAURETTE.
Divnl. Gas School.	Camp 20.
D.A.D.O.S.	BRAY.
French Mission.	BRAY.

CONFIDENTIAL.

WAR DIARY

OF

"A" AND "Q" BRANCH,

40TH DIVISION.

VOL. X.

FROM 1st to 31st MARCH, 1917.

Confidential

WAR DIARY *or* **INTELLIGENCE SUMMARY**

Army Form C. 2118

A & Q Staff
40th DIVISION HDQRTRS.

Place	Date 1917 March	Hour	Summary of Events and Information	Remarks and references to Appendices
MAVREPAS (P.C. BONNET)	1		Instructions received for the Divn. to take over a new front at a date to be notified later.	Appy
	2		Half yearly list of officers & OR for honours & rewards submitted shortly.	Appy
	3		40 Divn. will relieve 31st Division on 6th & 7th over an extended front.	Appy
	4		arrangements for camps etc. as shown in appendix A.	A Appy
	5		Preparations in event of a forward movement.	Appy
	6		Lt Col Dunlop rejoins Divn. & took over 20 Midd Regt.	Appy
	7		II Corps prepare Bristol & Chaff cutting machine in Hearne.	Appy
P.C. CHAPEAU (near CURLU)	8		All French troops in the area to be collected & sent in to France.	Appy
	9		Casualties 1 of. 6 O.R. inclusive killed officers O.R. wounded officers O.R.	Appy
	10		Capt. DOCWRA 37th Rl Fusiliers attached to the division under instruction for staff duties.	Appy
	11		Men sent to Railway Construction Corps. May be taken off other fatigue work.	Appy
	12		ADOS with inspect ammunition dumps.	Appy
	13		Units quartered as shown in appendix B.	appendix B
	14		Casualties 9 to 11 inclusive Officers O.R. killed - Officers O.R. wounded.	
	15		Germans reported to retire opposite 40th Divn front - Preparations made to carry ammunition out supplies forward by pack mules and forward dumps for artillery to be established.	(Vince)
	16		19 RWF & 12 SWB placed under II Corps for work on the roads across the German Nimmers.	P
	17		Germans commenced to retire - Drawn from front covered by his Division. Policy of Supply. Important discussed with Que 6 pgn - proposals for Appendix I. That they can not be brought into force till the	R APPENDIX I
	18		St QUENTIN & firing in our hand. Informed by II Corps that the wells at BARLEUX poisoned with arsenic - board allowed by wire. Mr St QUENTIN - HAUT-ALLAINES evacuated as out first line. Orders issued for transfer of 120th & 121st Bde to move at 9 am 19/3/17 from TRISE BEND to CLÉRY.	g

WAR DIARY / INTELLIGENCE SUMMARY

Army Form C. 2118

A + Q staff
40th Division Head Qrs.

Place	Date 1917 March	Hour	Summary of Events and Information	Remarks and references to Appendices
P.C. Chapeau (nr CURLU)	18.		Supply echelons of Div Train to deliver rations to ITEM, to be collected by 1st line transport units. Many dry near the limit of delivery at Outskirts of Hvre Transport from the Bergers at TROISSY. TROISSY is out, put the 1st-St QUENTIN – HAUT-ALLAINES is 14 miles, issued half rations for CLERY. 120" x 12. 11 only Bdy M'Zani transport moved to CLERY. Appointed a D.A.A. as commandant CLERY. Corps explored the cavalry reconnaissance CLERY. 20 other men as Cyclo Brevet. Asked Corps to return transport agents transferred into fund for horses (30 GS wagons & 15 pairs from now under truck for Div) Convinced the advisability of moving the Div Train to FRISE BEND.	(appendix)
	19.		Inspected the roads from CLERY to HAUT-ALLAINES & CLERY – PERONNE. Orders issued that no wheeled vehicles other than G.S. lorries to go beyond CLERY also opened	Appendix II
	20th		Traffic enquiry CURLU – HEM – CLERY. BOIS DE HEM. Div Train instructions 15 FRISE BEND water supplied by 6th 21st. Refilling point fixed at CURLU, Div trains to draw is CLERY. Unit to send in furcos up to pick. Item up there.	

Confidential

WAR DIARY or INTELLIGENCE SUMMARY

Army Form C. 2118

A.T.Q
Staff
30th Div A.Q.M.G

Place	Date	Hour	Summary of Events and Information	Remarks and references to Appendices
P.C. CHAPEAU	1918 Nov			III
	21st		M.V.S. ordered to move to CURBU 22nd March. Rear HQr (ADMS DADMS ADVS Camp Cmdt) to move to P.C. CHAPEAU 22nd March. Dismounted Grooms & Mobile Officers will be born by orders being issued for A.Q Corps - Extra Lorries details of regiment of ordnance beyond I.W. forcent out from time. Pt Line transport & advanced H.Qrs. Bths ordered to HAUT ALLAINES on FEUILLAUCOURT & 2 Field Coys ordered to move to HAUT ALLAINES on FEUILLAUCOURT confirmed in Q'stores order No 63. of 21/3/19	
	22nd		Argo Line 178 Bde R.F.A moves to PARICWOOD, CLERY — PERONNE road — A.P.M reports the traffic enroute to CLERY on new working road — but the traffic is much less congested. Some 30 cars of 704-Indians ? — the German line ? PERONNE are hunted back. D.A.D.Q.M.G II Corps called hear to discussed road policy which is being taken up by 1st Transportation Dept. Complained the 3 Batts on road trading work cannot fulfil enough 30 unit. it. Engr officers sent to chief ? things. Others deemed that Div is being withdrawn for read training work. No detailed instructions for Corps asked to sent entire move the moves beyond CLERY are not to be met till next morning.	
		8 pm		Q

Confidential

Army Form C. 2118

WAR DIARY
or
INTELLIGENCE SUMMARY

(Erase heading not required.)

A + Q Staff
40th Division HQrs

Place	Date 1917 March	Hour	Summary of Events and Information	Remarks and references to Appendices IV.
P.C. CHAPEAU	23rd		Location of units at 12 noon attached. Informing XV Corps HQrs A. Bde wanted for work in the CLERY - HAUT ALLOINES road. Camp near Canal du Nord FEUILLAUCOURT. B Bde in along rds BOUCHAVESNES, ANDOVER, & LITTLEDALE for work on RANCOURT - BOUCHAVESNES - MOISLAINS road.	Appendix III.
	24.		B Bde 1 Bn for Road work, 1 Bn for Light Trie 2 Bns for railway. 1st wk Zingu Camp Moislains road. Msn C.R.E. Lt Col A.C. BAYLAY DSO reported for duty. Arrangements for location of duty Bde Groups for works on the roads to accompany concentration in Brigade Groups.	
	25th	2/0/17	Division concentrated in Brigade Groups. Commenced 26th March. DA & QMG Capt Conlan from Staff Capt Douro HQ Rds arrangements. Location Tpt allotted.	Appendix IV
26			Difficulty in obtaining remounts. 144 L.D. Horses have been sent to R.A. As Divisional remounts.	
P.C. JEAN near CURLU	27 28 29 30 31		Units moved elsewhere as shown in appendix C. Units engaged in repair of roads. Rfl Tpt used for conveying road material, as well as all other transport available. Captain Murphy 11 Hampshire Regt. appointed District Cdt. at BILLON. Heavy roads & work in the more forward of division in area vacated by Germans has felt on the Rfl Tpt animals. Arrangements for accommodation of division in a more forward area. Villages practically no cover.	CMG CMG Appendix D CMG CMG CMG CMG CMG

O. Wheeler Capt
A.D. See

1875 Wt. W593/826 1,000,000 4/15 J.B.C.&A. A.D.S.S./Forms/C. 2118.

40th Division No. 505 (Q)

A.

Reference XV Corps Administrative Instruction No 18 dated 2-3-1917, on reverse.

1. The Right Divisional Area will be divided for the purpose of administration of accommodation as follows:-

DISTRICT.	HEADQUARTERS.	COMMANDANT.
SUZANNE - Camps 18, 19.) VAUX)	SUZANNE.	Major PUGH, 18th Welsh Regt.
MOULIN DE FARGNY, CURLU,) Camps 162 & 164 (Linger) Camp))	CURLU.	Major McCullough, 21st Middlesex Regiment.
FRISE BEND (District) North of Frise bounded by) the River SOMME on the N.) and the Canal on the S.)	FRISE. (G.18.b.7.8.)	Major Gilbert, 17th Welsh Regt.

2. Major Pugh 18th Welsh Regiment, and Major Gilbert, 17th Welsh Regiment will proceed to take over their districts as soon as they are relieved in their present districts.
Major McCullough, 21st Middlesex Regiment will proceed to CURLU on the 5th March.
These Officers will become acquainted with their districts before the departure of the present Commandants, (3 days after 40th Division move in).

3. (a) Reference para B. 1. of instructions on reverse.
Major Pugh will take over SUZANNE from 33rd Division Commandant of Area 4; Camps 18 and 19 from 33rd Division Commandant of Area 3; VAUX from 33rd Division Commandant of Area 1.

(b) There are at present two Commandants of CURLU one found by 8th Division and one found by 33rd Division, both administrating different areas, which will be taken over by Major McCullough as follows:-
MOULIN DE FARGNY from 8th Division Commandant.
Camps 162 and 164 (Linger Camps) from 8th Division Commandant.
CURLU from 33rd Division Commandant.

(c) The northern portion of FRISE BEND Area is under 33rd Division Commandant of CURLU, and Southern portion under the Commandant, FRISE (office at G.18.b.7.8.)
The above two portions will be taken over by Major Gilbert accordingly.

March 3rd 1917.
(FH)

(Sd) C.F.Moores Lt.Col:
A.A.&Q.M.G.,
40th Division.

SECRET.

XV CORPS ADMINISTRATIVE INSTRUCTION NO 18.

Subject- REDISTRIBUTION OF CORPS AREA.

Reliefs of Town Majors and Camp Commandants will take place as follows:-

A. 1. Town Majors SAILLY-LE-SEC and VAUX will take over the SAILLY LAURETTE and CHIPILLY Areas, and will relieve the Town Majors of those places now found by 40th Division.

He will establish his Headquarters at SAILLY LAURETTE.

2. Town Major CORBIE will take over the Corps Area west of VAUX.

3. These reliefs will take place at once.

B. 1. Pending the appointment of "P.B" Officers, 40th Division will relieve Camp Commandants of Areas 1, 2, 3, and 4, now found by 33rd Division, and Camp Commandants of Areas "C" and "B" now found by 8th Division.

2. These reliefs will take place three days after the completion of the relief of 33rd Division by 40th Division, to facilitate taking over.

3. Names of Officers appointed will be reported to Corps Headquarters in due course.

(Sd) C.W. Jebb Brigadier General,
1-3-1917.   D.A. & Q.M.G., XV Corps.

P.T.O.

S E C R E T.   4 0 T H   D I V I S I O N.

DISTRIBUTION OF UNITS - 9TH MARCH, 1917.

	Headquarters.	Wagon & Transport Lines.
40TH DIVISION.		
Advanced Headquarters.	P.C. CHAPEAU (A.29.d)	
Rear Headquarters.	SUZANNE CHATEAU.	
Signal Company.	P.C. CHATEAU (A.29.d)	
ROYAL ARTILLERY.		
Headquarters.	P.C. CHAPEAU (A.29.d.)	
181st Brigade, R.F.A.	P.C. EARTHWORKS (H.3.b. central)	G.16.a.90.80.
178th Brigade, R.F.A.	H.16.a.05.50.	(G.16.b.40.40. A Bty. (G.21.a.50.50. B, C, (& D Btys.
14th Brigade, R.F.A.	B.23.b.0.3.	G.10.c.
V/40 T.M. Battery.	G.18.b.1.4.	
X/40 do. do.	- do -	
Y/40 do. do.	- do -	
Z/40 do. do.	- do -	
40TH DIVNL. AMMN. COLUMN.		
No. 1 Section.	L.17.b.7.8.	L.17.b.7.8.
No. 2 "	L.18.a.2.9.	L.18.a.2.9.
"B" Echelon.	L.16.c.6.0.	L.16.c.6.0.
ROYAL ENGINEERS.		
Headquarters.	P.C. JEAN (H.1.c.1.9.)	
224th Fld. Coy. R.E.	H.11.a.5.9.	G.18.b.4.5.
229th Fld. Coy. R.E.	G.18.b.8.4.	G.18.b.4.5.
231st Fld. Coy. R.E.	B.30.c.5.5.	H.13.a.3.5.
119TH INFANTRY BRIGADE.		
Headquarters.	P.C. WURZEL.(H.11.a.5.7)	
19th R.W. Fusiliers.	Brigade Support.	FRISE BEND (G.18.a)
12th S.W. Borderers.	Left Sub-Sector.	do.
17th Welsh Regt.	Right Sub-Sector.	do.
18th Welsh Regt.	Brigade Reserve.	do.
119th M.G. Company.	Trenches.	do.
119th T.M. Battery.	Trenches.	
120TH INFANTRY BRIGADE.		
Headquarters.	P.C. EARTHWORKS (H.3.b.central)	
11th King's Own (R.L) R.	Right Sub-Sector.	FRISE BEND (G.6.c.)
13th E. Surrey Regt.	Left Sub-Sector.	do. do.
14th High. Lt. Inf.	Brigade Reserve.	do. do.
14th A. & S. Highrs.	Brigade Support.	do. do.
120th M.G. Company.	Trenches.	do. do.
120th T.M. Battery.	Trenches.	
121ST INFANTRY BRIGADE.		
Headquarters.	P.C. JEAN. (H.1.c.1.9.)	
12th Suffolk Regt.	CAMP 19.	CAMP 19.
13th Yorks. Regt.	LINGER CAMP. (A.30.d)	LINGER CAMP (A.30.d)
20th Middlesex Regt.	CAMP 19.	CAMP 19.
21st Middlesex Regt.	LINGER CAMP. (A.30.d.)	LINGER CAMP (A.30.d)
121st M.G. Company.	CAMP 18.	CAMP 18.
121st T.M. Battery.	CAMP 18.	
12TH YORKS. RGT. (PIONEERS)		
Hd.Qrs. & 2 Coys.	H.1.c.	H.1.c.
1 Company.	C.25.a.	C.25.a.
1 Company.	H.3.b.	H.3.b.

P.T.O.

	Headquarters.	Wagon & Transport Lines.
40TH DIVNL. WORKS BATTN.	L.17.b.	
DIVISIONAL TRAIN.		
Headquarters.	BRAY.	BRAY.
No. 1 Company.	BRAY.	BRAY.
No. 2 Company.	BRAY.	BRAY.
No. 3 Company.	BRAY.	BRAY.
No. 4 Company.	BRAY.	Bray.
No. 25 DIVNL. SUPPLY COLUMN.	BAILLY LAURETTE.	
135th Field Ambulance.	SAILLY LAURETTE.	SAILLY LAURETTE.
136th " "	SUZANNE.	SUZANNE.
137th " "	HEM.	HEM.
51st Mobile Vet. Section.	SUZANNE.	
83rd Sanitary Section.	SAILLY LAURETTE.	
Divisional Gas School.	CAMP 18.	
D.A.D.O.S.	BRAY.	
A.P.M.	SUZANNE.	
French Mission.	BRAY.	

(RSJ)

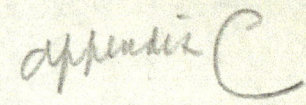
Appendix C

SECRET.

40TH DIVISION.

DISTRIBUTION OF UNITS - 28TH MARCH, 1917.

UNIT.	LOCATION.	LOCATION OF TRANSPORT LINES.
40TH DIVN. HEADQUARTERS.		
'G' Branch,		
'A & Q' Branch.		
Camp Commandant.	P.C. JEAN. H.1.c.1.9.	
D.A.D.O.S.		
Signal Company.		
A.D.M.S.		
A.D.V.S.	P.C. CHANIERE.	
Senior Chaplain.	B.16.d.3.8.	
A.P.M.	G.18.b.8.2.	
Divnl. Traffic Officer.		
ROYAL ARTILLERY.		
Headquarters.	H.1.c.2.7.	
178th Brigade, R.F.A.	Attached 20th Divn.	With Brigade.
181st Brigade R.F.A.	Attached 8th Divn.	With Brigade.
V/40, X/40, Y/40 & Z/40 T.M. Btys.	P.C. EARTHWORKS. (H.3.b.central)	
40TH DIVNL. AMMN. COLUMN.		
Headquarters.	L.18.a.0.7.	
No. 1 Section.	Attached 20th Divn.	With Section.
No. 2 Section.	Attached 8th Divn.	With Section.
'B' Echelon.	VAUX.	VAUX.
ROYAL ENGINEERS.		
Headquarters.	P.C. JEAN.	
224th Fld.Coy. R.E.	Dug-outs by P.C.WURZEL (H.11.a.5.9)	H.5.c.8.3.
229th Fld.Coy. R.E.	H.Q.& 2 Secs. Dug-outs at G.6.b.8.6. 2 Secs. at P.C. WURZEL.	With Headquarters of Company.
231st Fld.Coy. R.E.	LITTLEDALE DUMP, (B.3.0.b)	MIMOSA DUMP. (H.6.b.5.9)
119TH INFANTRY BRIGADE.		
Headquarters.	LE FOREST, B.16.b.3.5.	
19th R.W. Fusiliers.	H.Q. P.C MADAME C.25.b. 3 Coys. ROAD WOOD, C... (C.25.a.) 1 Coy. MARRIERS WOOD.	CLERY.
12th S.W. Bordrs.	H.Q. P.C.VIOLETTE B.30.c. 2 Coys. LITTLEDALE B.30.b.	CLERY.
17th Welsh Regt.	H.Q.& 3 Coys. LANGTON BARRACKS (C.14.a) 1 Coy. BOUCHAVESNES.	CLERY.
18th Welsh Regt.	H.Q.& 2 Coys. LOOK BARRACKS (C.11.c) 2 Coys. BOUCH-AVESNES.	CLERY.
119th M.G. Company.	LIVERPOOL (C.15.b)	CLERY.
119th T.M. Batty.	On Course of Instruction.	

/over.

120TH INFANTRY BRIGADE.

Headquarters.	P.C.EARTHWORKS, H.3.b.cent.	
11th King's Own Rgt.	H.Q.& 2 Coys.LINGER CAMP. 2 Coys.Huts nr.P.C. JEAN.	LINGER CAMP.
13th East Surrey Rgt.	LINGER CAMP.	LINGER CAMP.
14th H. L. I.	HOWITZER WOOD.	FRISE BEND.
14th A.& S. Highrs.	LINGER CAMP.	FRISE BEND.
120th M.G. Company.	HOWITZER WOOD.	FRISE BEND.
120th T.M. Battery.	HEM WOOD.	

121ST INFANTRY BRIGADE.

Headquarters.	OMNIECOURT-LES-CLERY.	
12th Suffolk Regt.	}	
13th Yorks. Regt.	}	
20th Middlesex Rgt.	} Camp about I.8.central.	FEUILLAUCOURT.
21st Middlesex Rgt.	}	
121st M.G. Company.	}	
121st T.M. Battery.	}	

12TH YORKS.RGT.(PIONEERS).	ANDOVER (C.13.a)	CLERY.
40TH DIVN. WORKS BATTN.	CURLU.	

DIVISIONAL TRAIN.

Headquarters.	FRISE BEND.	With Companies.
No. 1 Company.	FRISE BEND.	do.
No. 2 Company.	do.	do.
No. 3 Company.	do.	do.
No. 4 Company.	do.	do.

No. 25 Divnl. Supply Col.	L.4.d. BRAY-MARICOURT Rd.	
135th Fld. Ambulance.	SAILLY LAURETTE.	With Ambulance.
136th Fld. Ambulance.	HEM (A.D.S.at CLERY)	do.
137th Fld. Ambulance.	Camp 163 (B.14.c.central)	do.
51st Mobile Vet. Sect.	CURLU.	
Divnl.Sanitary Off.	Dug-out at H.7.a.3.7.	
83rd Sanitary Section.	Hut close to P.C.JEAN.	
Divnl. Gas School.	P.C. 6. (L.18.a)	
French Mission.	BRAY. (23 Rue d'Albert).	

(RSJ)

APPENDIX 1.

Water points to be established at H.5.c.9.3. (B.213 Decauville Station) and at H.12.d.9.8. CLERY.

A reserve of 2000 - 2 gall. petrol tins to be established at A.R.P. B.207.

1st Line Transport of the 2 Advanced Brigades and Field Coys. R.E. to CLERY, H.6.a. and H.6.c. or in CLERY South of the CLERY - PERONNE Road.

Water troughs required on river bank. H.12.a.0.8. suitable ?

D.A.C. Echelon "B" to move to Camp 19.

Nos. 1 and 2 Sections to CURLU.

Wagon lines to FRISE BEND and HEM.

Train Coys. to FRISE BEND, CURLU, or neighbourhood.

APPENDIX II

Hd Qrs. 40th Divn. No. 12 (A).

TRAFFIC INSTRUCTIONS -- CURLU - CLERY Roads.

1. The Map overleaf shows the traffic circuits to and from CLERY.

2. The A.P.M. will establish controls at points marked ⊕

3. No motor cars, motor ambulances, lorries, G.S. wagons or Ambulance wagons to proceed beyond point marked ✲ , road junction CLERY & HAUT ALLAINES and CLERY & PERONNE roads.

   Only G.S. Limbers with supplies or R.E. material, gun limbers with ammunition, and pack animals, may pass this point.

   The A.P.M. will arrange for the Traffic Officer to be at this point and he is authorised to stop all ranks who are not on duty, and turn them back. Names to be reported to Divisional Head Quarters.

4. The M.M.P. to constantly patrol CLERY - HAUT ALLAINES - PERONNE roads to stop double banking and regulate traffic.

20th March, 1917.

Major,
D. A. Q. M. G.,
40th Division.

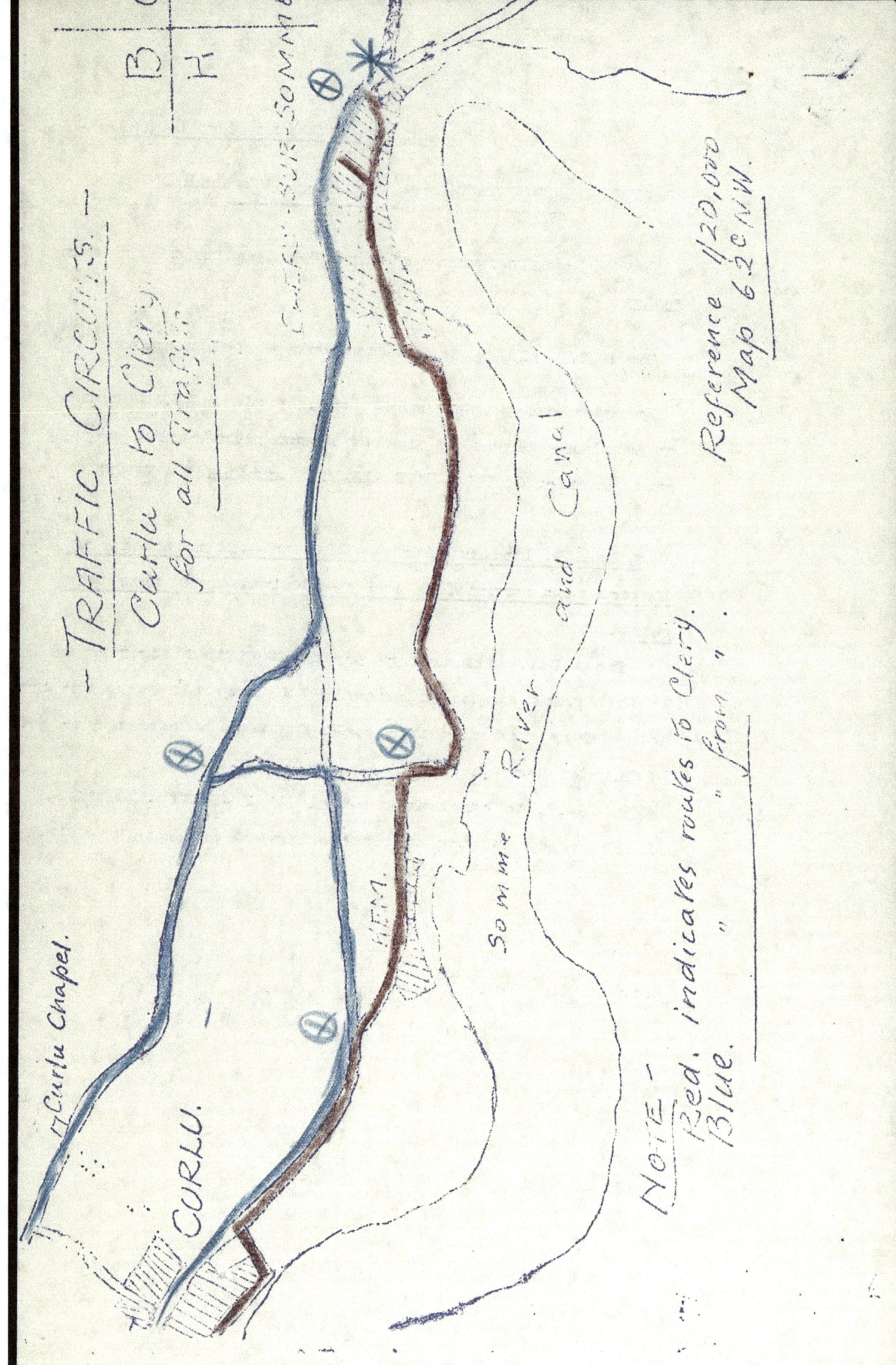

MOISLAINS.

AIZECOURT LE-HAUT.

HAUT ALLAINS

BUSSU.

ALLAINS

FEUILLAU-COURT.

MT ST QUENTIN.

CLERY.

Main Route

HALLE

PERONNE

REFERENCE 1/40,000
MAP — 62C.

SECRET.   40TH DIVISION.   Appdx III

DISTRIBUTION OF UNITS - 23RD MARCH, 1917.

40TH DIVISION.
  Advanced Headquarters.   P.C. CHAPEAU. (A.29.d)
  Rear Headquarters.   P.C. JEAN. (H.1.c.1.9)
  Signal Company.   P.C. CHAPEAU. (A.29.d)

ROYAL ARTILLERY.
  Headquarters.   P.C. CHAPEAU. (A.29.d)
  181st Brigade, R.F.A.   I.4.b.5.8.
  178th Brigade, R.F.A.   I.22.b.4.4.
  V/40, X/40 and Y/40
    T.M. Batteries.   EARTHWORKS.
  Z/40 T.M. Battery.   Fourth Army Sch. of Mortars.

40TH DIVNL. AMMN. COLUMN.
  Headquarters.   L.18.a.0.7.
  No. 1 Section.   L.17.b.7.8.
  No. 2 Section.   L.18.a.2.9.
  "B" Echelon.   L.16.c.6.0.

ROYAL ENGINEERS.
  Headquarters.   P.C. JEAN. (H.1.c.1.9)
  224th Fld. Coy. R.E.   I.21.c.9.8.
  229th Fld. Coy. R.E.   P.C. WURZEL. (H.11.a.5.7)
  231st Fld. Coy. R.E.   HAUT ALLAINES.

119TH INFANTRY BRIGADE.
  Headquarters.   HAUT ALLAINES.
  19th R.W. Fusiliers.   H.Q. & 2 Coys. Camp 18 or 19. 2 SUZANNE.
  12th S.W. Borderers.   Camp 20 or 21.
  17th Welsh, 18th Welsh,)
  119th M.G.Co. 119th T.M.Bty.)   Left Advanced Brigade.

120TH INFANTRY BRIGADE.
  Headquarters.   P.C. EARTHWORKS. (H.3.b.central)
  11th King's Own Regt.   H.Q.& 2 Cos. HOWITZER WOOD.
       2 Cos. MERTON (H.6.a.7.6)
  13th East Surrey Regt.   LINGER CAMP.
  14th Highland Lt. Inf.)
  14th A. & S. Highlanders.)   Left Advanced Brigade.
  120th M.G. Company.   HOWITZER WOOD.
  120th T.M. Battery.   do. do.

121ST INFANTRY BRIGADE.
  Headquarters.   P.C. WURZEL (H.11.a.5.7)
  12th Suffolks, 13th Yorks.)
  20th Middx., 21st Middx,Rgts.)   Right Advanced Brigade.
  121st M.G.Co. 121st T.M.Bty.)

12TH YORKS. RGT.(PIONEERS).   BERLIN VALLEY.
40TH DIVNL. WORKS BATTN.   CURLU.
DIVISIONAL TRAIN.   FRISE BEND (Portion H.Q.Coy. BRAY).
No. 25 Divnl. Supply Column.   L.4.d. (BRAY - MARICOURT Road).

  135th Field Ambulance.   SAILLY LAURETTE.
  136th Field Ambulance.   HEM.
  137th Field Ambulance.   HAUT ALLAINES.

51st Mobile Vet. Section.   CURLU.

83rd Sanitary Section.   P.C. JEAN (H.1.c.1.9)
Divisional Gas School.   P.C. 6. (L.18.a.)
  D. A. D. O. S.   P.C. JEAN (H.1.c.1.9)
  A. P. M.   P.C. JEAN (H.1.c.1.9.
  French Mission.   BRAY (23 Rue d'ALBERT).

Appendix IV

S E C R E T.   40TH DIVISION.

DISTRIBUTION OF UNITS - 25TH MARCH, 1917.

40TH DIVISION.
  Advanced Headquarters. P.C. CHAPEAU (A.29.d)
  Rear Headquarters. P.C. JEAN (H.1.c.1.9)
  Signal Company. P.C. CHAPEAU (A.29.d)

ROYAL ARTILLERY
  Headquarters. P.C. CHAPEAU (A.29.d)
  178th Brigade, R.F.A. Attached 20th Division.
  181st Brigade, R.F.A. " 8th "
  V/40; X/40, Y/40 &)
    Z/40 T.M. Btys.) P.C. EARTHWORKS (H.3.b.central)

40TH DIVN. AMMN. COLUMN.
  Headquarters. L.18.a.0.7.
  No. 1 Section. Attached 8th Division.
  No. 2 Section. " 20th 8th "
  'B' Echelon. L.16.c.6.0.

ROYAL ENGINEERS.
  Headquarters. P.C. JEAN (H.1.c.1.9)
  224th Fld. Coy. R.E. Dug-outs at P.C. WURZEL.
  229th Fld. Coy. R.E. H.Q.& 2 Secs. LINGER CAMP,
    2 Secs. LITTLEDALE BARRACKS.
  231st Fld. Coy. R.E. LITTLEDALE DUMP. (B.30.b)

119TH INFANTRY BRIGADE.
  Headquarters. LE FOREST (B.16.b.3.5)
  19th R.W. Fusiliers. H.Q. P.C. MADAME (C.25.b) 3 Coys. ROAD
    WOOD (C.25.a) 1 Coy. MARRIER.
  12th S.W. Borderers. H.Q. P.C. VIOLETTE (B.30.c) 4 Coys.
    LITTLEDALE (B.30.b)
  17th Welsh Regiment. H.Q.& 3 Coys. LANGTON BARRACKS (C.14.a)
    1 Coy. BOUCHAVESNES.
  18th Welsh Regiment. H.Q.& 2 Coys. LOCK BARRACKS (C.14.c),
    2 Coys. BOUCHAVESNES.
  119th M.G. Company. LIVERPOOL (C.15.b)
  119th T.M. Battery. MARJORIE. (C.20.a)

120TH INFANTRY BRIGADE.
  Headquarters. P.C. EARTHWORKS (H.3.b.central)
  11th King's Own Regt. H.Q.& 2 Coys. LINGER CAMP, 2 Coys.
    Dug-outs nr. P.C. JEAN.
  13th East Surrey Regt. LINGER CAMP.
  14th Highland Lt. Inf. HOWITZER WOOD and HEM WOOD.
  14th A. & S. Highlanders. LINGER CAMP.
  120th M.G. Company. HOWITZER WOOD.
  120th T.M. Battery. HOWITZER WOOD.

121ST INFANTRY BRIGADE.
  Headquarters. OMNIECOURT-les-CLERY.
  12th Suffolk Regt. CAMP about I.8.central.
  13th Yorks. Regt. do. do.
  20th Middlesex Regt. do. do.
  21st Middlesex Regt. do. do.
  121st M.G. Company. do. do.
  121st Trench Mortar Batt. do. do.

12TH YORKS. REGT.(PIONEERS) ANDOVER (C.13.a)

40TH DIVNL. WORKS BATTN. CURLU.

/Over.

DIVISIONAL TRAIN.
   Headquarters.   FRISE BEND.
   No. 1 Company.   FRISE BEND (Portion at BRAY).
   No. 2 Company.   do.
   No. 3 Company.   do.
   No. 4 Company.   do.

No. 25 Divnl. Supply Col.   L.d.d. (BRAY - MARICOURT Road).

135th Field Ambulance.   SAILLY LAURETTE.
136th Field Ambulance.   HEM (A.D.S. at CLERY).
137th Field Ambulance.   CAMP 163 (B.14.c.central)

51st Mobile Vet. Section.   CURLU.

83rd Sanitary Section.   P.C. JEAN (H.1.c.1.9)

Divisional Gas School.   P.C.6. (L.18.a)

   D.A.D.O.S.   P.C. JEAN (H.1.c.1.9)

   A. P. M.   P.C. JEAN (H.1.c.1.9)

   French Mission.   BRAY (23 Rue d'ALBERT)

(RSJ)

WAR DIARY

OF

"A. & Q". BRANCH, 40th DIVISION.

-o-o-o-o-o-o-o-o-o-o-

Period -- 1st to 30th April, 1917.

WAR DIARY or INTELLIGENCE SUMMARY

Army Form C. 2118

April 1917. Confidential
A & Q Staff 40th Division

Place	Date April 1917	Hour	Summary of Events and Information	Remarks and references to Appendices
Pt JEAN	1		Strength 93 men for 17th Welch Regt. 119 Bde. This Bde is much reduced in numbers, averaging about 500 men per battalion.	Copy
	2		Military medal awarded to A/Bdr Walker and Gr. McEachern R.F.A.	Copy
near CURLU	3		Recommended that 2 vets per man be issued instead of 1 pair - winter scale clothing.	Copy
	4		Forage ration only 9 lbs per animal increased to 12 lbs for 20% of animals.	Copy
	5		Captain Lawless, General List appointed Staff Captain 121 Inf. Bde.	Copy
MANANCOURT	6		10 hours vacation a day allotted to Division. Bu.H.Q. 2A.t. moved to MANANCOURT.	Copy
	7		Division all employed in improving road communication. One Bde in front line. One Bde in back area or training.	Copy
	8		Divisional School to be moved from JALLERY to DAOURS. Units located as shown in Appendix A.	Appendix A
	9		Formation of "Employment Coys" proposed - embodying unit known as Divisional Coy.	Copy
	10		A.D.M.S. proceeded to IV Corps H.Q. to act as D.D.M.S.	Copy
	11		3 days. Reserve rations to be stored permanent.	Copy
	12		Majors Gilbert, Pugh and McCullough appointed District Commandants in IV Corps area.	Copy
	13		Major W. G. CHARLES appointed G.S.O.1, 20th Division vice Lt. Col. Walker who proceeds to Poland.	Copy
	14		Bde Notes Battalion. Bde HQ moved to MOISLAINS. NURLU & AIZECOURT LE HAUT.	Copy
	15		System of attaching officers & N.C.O.s under instruction to be discontinued for the present.	Copy
	16		Bde Works Battalion to be broken up. One Coy is to be attached to each Inf Bde north unit appointed Fd Coy RE	Copy
	17		Casualties from 1/4/17 to 16/4/17	Appendix B
	18		Units located as in appendix B	Copy
	19		Major RIGG Royal Artillery assumed command 18 Welsh Regt. not to join until completion of a Constantine period he is a member.	Copy appendix B.
	20		Redistribution of transport for conveyance of S.A.A., T.M. ammunition & grenades, no next a Bde Reserve may be formed for T.M. ammunition.	Copy
	21		Reinforcements were sent at LA CHAPPELLETTE near Peronne, which is railhead.	Copy
	22		Enemy prisoners attacked Casualties - see appendix D. - german prisoners Captured 4 4	Copy appendix C.
	23		Units located as in appendix C	Copy appendix D.
	24		Enemy positions attacked. Casualties - see appendix D.	Copy appendix D.
	25			Copy
	26		Reserve supplies (3 days) held forward are now the Commandant. Corps prisoners cage now at U3od 75° near MOISLAINS.	Wd Copy
	27		Divisional test station for animals formed at MOISLAINS. An issue of frozen rabbit to be made occasionally as a ration	Copy
	28		8 candidates sent for Commissions are required to be sent each month from 40th Division.	appendix E
	29		Lt Col Paget DSO 12 S.W. Borderers evacuated sick.	
	30		Location of units - appendix E. 285 Sent to m/ Division to reduce deficiencies. Animals the the number of 285 Sent to m/ Div. to reduce deficiencies. Division is still 198 animals under establishment	C.J.H. Moore Lt Col AA QMG 40 Div

SECRET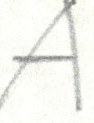

40TH DIVISION.

DISTRIBUTION OF UNITS - 8TH APRIL, 1917.

UNIT.	LOCATION.	LOCATION OF HORSE LINES.

40TH DIVN. HEADQUARTERS.
'G' Branch.
'A & Q' Branch.
Camp Commandant.
A.P.M.
H.Q. No.1 Sec. 40th Divn. Signal Coy. R.E.
Divnl. Sanitary Officer.
83rd Sanitary Section.
} MANANCOURT. V.13.c.5.2.

A.D.M.S.
A.D.V.S.
S.C.F.
French Mission.
} P.C. CRANIERE. B.16.d.3.8.

D.A.D.O.S.
O.C., Divnl. Coy.
Divnl. Salvage Officer.
Divnl. Gas School.
} LOCK BARRACKS, BOUCH-AVESNES. (C.14.c)

ROYAL ARTILLERY.
Headquarters. — With Divnl. Hd. Qrs.
178th Bde. R.F.A. — In the line.
 H.Q. V.4.c.9.4.
 A Bty. V.10.d.2.3.
 B Bty. V.10.b.2.7.
 C Bty. V.8.a.3.7.
 D Bty. V.10.c.5.9.
181st Bde. R.F.A. — In the line.
 H.Q. V.19.b.6.7.
 A Bty. V.19.b.9.8.
 B Bty. V.19.b.3.8.
 C Bty. V.13.d.6.3.
 D Bty. V.13.d.9.4.

V/40, X/40, Y/40 & Z/40 T.M. Battys. } P.C. EARTHWORKS. (H.3.b.central)

40TH DIVNL. AMMN. COLUMN.
Headquarters. — MOISLAINS (C.12.c.7.6)
No. 1 Section.
No. 2 Section.
} C.6.a.5.5. — With Sections.
Echelon B. — CLERY (H.5.c.9.8) — With unit.

ROYAL ENGINEERS.
Headquarters. — With Divnl. Hd. Qrs.
224th Fld. Coy. R.E. — FINS. (V.12.a.4.1) — With Company.
229th Fld. Coy. R.E. — { H.Q. & 2 Secs. Dugouts at G.6.b.3.6. 2 Secs. P.C. WURZEL. } — With Headquarters of Company.
231st Fld. Coy. R.E. — ETRICOURT. — With Company.

119TH INFANTRY BRIGADE.
Headquarters.
19th R.W. Fusiliers.
12th S.W. Borderers.
17th Welsh Regt.
18th Welsh Regt.
119th M.G. Company.
} ETRICOURT. } With units.
119th T.M. Battery. — On Course of Inst'n.

/Over.

UNIT.	LOCATION.	LOCATION OF HORSE LINES.
120TH INFANTRY BRIGADE.		
Headquarters.	P.C. EARTHWORKS. (H.3.b.central)	
11th K.O.R.L. Regt.	H.Q. & 2 Coys. LINGER CAMP, CURLU. 2 Coys. Huts, P.C. JEAN.	LINGER CAMP.
13th East Surrey Regt.	LINGER CAMP.	LINGER CAMP.
14th Highland Lt.Inf.	HOWITZER WOOD.	FRISE BEND.
14th A.& S. Highrs.	LINGER CAMP.	FRISE BEND.
120th M.G. Company.	HOWITZER WOOD.	FRISE BEND.
120th T.M. Battery.	HEM WOOD.	
121ST INFANTRY BRIGADE.		
Headquarters.	The Quarry, FINS.	
12th Suffolk Regt.		
13th Yorkshire Regt.		
20th Middlesex Regt.	In the line.	N.E. End of MANANCOURT.
21st Middlesex Regt.		
121st M.G. Company.		
121st T.M. Battery.		
12TH YORKS.RGT. (PIONEERS)	RIVERSIDE WOOD. V.19.c.	With Unit.
40TH DIVNL.WORKS BATTN.	CURLU.	
DIVISIONAL TRAIN.		
Headquarters.	MOISLAINS. C.12.c.8.4.	
No. 1 Company.	C.12.b.0.0.	
No. 2 Company.		
No. 3 Company.	FRISE BEND.	With Companies.
No. 4 Company.	C.12.b.0.0.	
No. 25 Divnl. Supply Col.	L.4.d. BRAY-MARICOURT Road.	
135th Fld. Ambulance.	SAILLY LAURETTE.	With Ambulance.
136th Fld. Ambulance.	H.Q. MANANCOURT. Adv. Dress.Stn. FINS.	With H.Q. of Amb.
137th Fld. Ambulance.	Vickers Lane, MOISLAINS.	With Ambulance.
51st Mobile Vet.Section.	MOISLAINS.	

SECRET.   40TH DIVISION.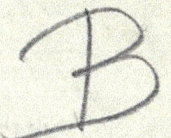

DISTRIBUTION OF UNITS - 16TH APRIL, 1917.

UNIT.	LOCATION.	LOCATION OF HORSE LINES.
40TH DIVISIONAL HEAD-QUARTERS, complete.	MANANCOURT. (V.13.c.5.2)	
D.A.D.O.S. O.C. Divnl. Coy. Divnl. Salvage Officer. Divnl. Gas School.	BOUCHAVESNES. (C.14.c)	
Divnl. Sanitary Offr. 83rd Sanitary Section.	MANANCOURT.	
ROYAL ARTILLERY.		
Headquarters	With Divnl. Hd.Qrs.	
178th Bde. R.F.A.	In the line.	H.Q. V.4.c.9.4. A Bty. V.10.d.2.3. B Bty. V.10.b.2.7. C Bty. V.8.a.8.7. D Bty. V.10.c.5.9.
181st Bde. R.F.A.	In the line.	H.Qrs. V.19.b.6.7. A Bty. V.19.b.9.8. B Bty. V.19.b.3.8. C Bty. V.13.d.6.3. D Bty. V.13.d.9.4.
V/40, X/40, Y/40 & Z/40 T.M. Battys.	P.C. EARTHWORKS. (H.3.b.central)	
40TH DIVNL. AMMN. COLUMN.		
Headquarters.	MOISLAINS (C.12.c.7.6)	
No. 1 Section. No. 2 Section.	C.6.a.5.5.	With Sections.
Echelon B.	CLERY. (H.5.c.9.8)	With unit.
ROYAL ENGINEERS.		
Headquarters.	With Divnl. Hd.Qrs.	
224th Fld.Coy. R.E.	FINS. (V.12.a.4.1)	With Company.
229th Fld.Coy. R.E.	H.Q. & 2 Secs. EQUANCOURT. 2 Secs. at I.21.b.	EQUANCOURT.
231st Fld.Coy. R.E.	ETRICOURT.	With Company.
119TH INFANTRY BRIGADE.		
Headquarters. 19th R.W. Fusiliers. 12th S.W. Borderers. 17th Welsh Regt. 18th Welsh Regt. 119th M.G. Company. 119th T.M. Battery.	ETRICOURT	With units.
120TH INFANTRY BRIGADE.		
Headquarters. 11th K.O.R.L. Regt. 13th East Surrey Regt.	EQUANCOURT.	V.2.d.
14th High. Light Inf.	I.21.b. (N. of PERONNE)	With Battalion.
14th A.& S. Highrs.	ETRICOURT.	V.2.d.
120th M.G. Company.	EQUANCOURT.	V.2.d.
120th T.M. Battery.	Equancourt.	-

/Over.

UNIT.	LOCATION.	LOCATION OF HORSE LINES.
121ST INFANTRY BRIGADE.		
Headquarters.	The Quarry, FINS.	
12th Suffolk Regt.		
13th Yorkshire Regt.		
20th Middlesex Regt.	In the line.	N.E. END of MANANCOURT.
21st Middlesex Regt.		
121st M.G. Company.		
121st T.M. Battery.		
12TH YORKS. REGT. (PNRS).	RIVERSIDE WOOD. V.19.c.	With unit.
DIVISIONAL TRAIN.		
Headquarters.	MOISLAINS (C.12.c.8.4)	
Nos. 1, 2, 3 and 4 Companies.	C.12.b.0.0.	With Companies.
No. 25 Divnl. Supply Col.	I.15.b.	
135th Fld. Ambulance.	SAILLY LAURETTE.	With Ambulance.
136th Fld. Ambulance.	H.Q. MANANCOURT - Advd. Dress.Stn. FINS.	With H.Qrs. of Ambulance.
137th Fld. Ambulance.	Vickers lane, MOISLAINS.	With Ambulance.
51st Mobile Vet.Sec.	MOISLAINS.	

SECRET.

40TH DIVISION.

DISTRIBUTION OF UNITS - 23RD APRIL, 1917.

UNIT.	LOCATION.	LOCATION OF HORSE LINES.
40TH DIVNL. HD.QRS., complete.	MANANCOURT, (V.13.c.5.2)	
D.A.D.O.S.	MOISLAINS.	
Divnl. Gas School.	FINS.	
O.C., Divnl. Coy.)	BOUCHAVESNES (C.14.c)	
Divnl. Salvage Offr.)		
Divnl. Sanitary Offr.)	Out of Divnl. Area.	
83rd Sanitary Section.)		
ROYAL ARTILLERY.		
Headquarters.	With Divnl. Hd.Qrs.	
178th Bde. R.F.A.	In the line.	Hd.Qrs. V.4.c.9.4. A Bty. V.10.d.2.3. B Bty. V.10.b.2.7. C Bty. V.8.a.8.7. D Bty. V.10.c.5.9.
181st Bde. R.F.A.	In the line.	Hd.Qrs. V.10.d.6.3. A Bty. V.16.b.5.8. B Bty. V.11.c.1.3. C Bty. V.16.b.9.8. D Bty. V.10.d.7.2.
V/40, X/40, Y/40 and Z/40 T.M. Battys.	FINS.	
40TH DIVNL. AMMN. COLUMN.		
Headquarters.	MOISLAINS. (C.12.c.7.6.)	
No. 1 Section.)	C.6.a.5.5.	With Sections.
No. 2 Section.)		
Echelon B½	CLERY. (H.5.c.9.8)	With Unit.
ROYAL ENGINEERS.		
Headquarters.	With Divnl. Hd.Qrs.	
224th Fld.Coy. R.E.	FINS. (V.12.a.4.1)	With Company.
229th Fld.Coy. R.E.	H.Q.& 2 Secs. EQUANCOURT. 2 Secs. I.21.b.	EQUANCOURT.
231st Fld.Coy. R.E.	ETRICOURT.	With Company.
119TH INFANTRY BRIGADE.		
Headquarters.	FINS.	
19th R.W. Fusiliers.		
12th S.W. Borderers.		
17th Welsh Regiment.	In the line.	FINS.
18th Welsh Regiment.		
119th M.G. Company.		
119th T.M. Battery.		-
120TH INFANTRY BRIGADE.		
Headquarters.	EQUANCOURT.	EQUANCOURT.
11th K.O.R.L. Regt.		EQUANCOURT.
13th East Surrey Regt.		V.2.d.
14th High. Light Inf.	In the line.	V.2.d.
14th A. & S. Highrs.		ETRICOURT.
120th M.G. Company.		EQUANCOURT.
120th T.M. Battery.	EQUANCOURT.	-

/Over.

121ST INFANTRY BRIGADE.
```
    Headquarters.
    12th Suffolk Regt.      ⎫
    13th Yorkshire Regt.    ⎬  ETRICOURT.           ⎫
    20th Middlesex Regt.    ⎭                       ⎬ ETRICOURT.
    21st Middlesex Regt.       EQUANCOURT.          ⎪
    121st M.G. Company.     ⎫  ETRICOURT.           ⎭
    121st T.M. Battery.     ⎭

12th YORKS. REGT. (PNRS).      RIVERSIDE WOOD, V.19.c.   With Unit.
```

DIVISIONAL TRAIN.
```
    Headquarters.              MOISLAINS.
                               (C.12.c.8.4.)
    Nos. 1, 2, 3 and  )
        4 Companies.  )        C.12.b.0.0.              With Companies.

No. 25 Divnl. Supply Col.      I.15.b.

    135th Fld. Ambulance.      SAILLY LAURETTE.         With Ambulance.
                              ⎧H.Q. MANANCOURT - Adv. With Hd.Qrs. of
    136th Fld. Ambulance.     ⎨Dress.Stn. FINS.         Ambulance.
    137th Fld. Ambulance.      Vickers Lane, MOISLAINS. With Ambulance.

    51st Mobile Vet. Sec.      MOISLAINS.
```

SUMMARY OF CASUALTIES

FROM

21st to 27th APRIL 1917.

Unit.	Killed. Off.	Killed. o.r.	Wounded. Off.	Wounded. o.r.	Missing. Off.	Missing. o.r.	Total. Off.	Total. o.r.
119th Bde.	3	51	17	190	-	12	20	253
120th Bde.	8	101	24	455	1	52	33	608
121st Bde.	-	2	-	15	-	-	-	17
12th York.	-	-	-	1	-	-	-	1
R.A.	-	-	-	1	-	-	-	1
R.E.	-	-	-	5	-	-	-	5
R.A.M.C.	-	-	-	1	-	-	-	1
TOTAL	11	154	41	668	1	64	53	886

SECRET.

40TH DIVISION.

DISTRIBUTION OF UNITS - 29TH APRIL, 1917.

UNIT.	LOCATION.	LOCATION OF HORSE LINES.
40TH DIVNL. HD.QRS. complete.	MANANCOURT (V.13.c.5.2)	
D.A.D.O.S.	MOISLAINS.	
Divnl. Gas School.	FINS.	
O.C., Divnl. Coy.)	BOUCHAVESNES (C.14.c)	
Divnl. Salvage Offr.)		
Divnl. Sanitary Offr.)		
83rd Sanitary Secrion.)	Out of Divnl. Area.	
ROYAL ARTILLERY.		
Headquarters.	With Divnl. Hd.Qrs.	
178th Bde. R.F.A.	In the line.	Hd.Qrs. V.4.c.9.4. / A Bty. V.10.d.2.3. / B Bty. V.10.b.2.7. / C Bty. V.8.a.8.7. / D Bty. V.10.c.5.9.
181st Bde. R.F.A.	In the line.	Hd.Qrs. V.10.d.6.3. / A Bty. V.16.b.5.8. / B Bty. V.11.c.1.3. / C Bty. V.16.b.9.8. / D Bty. V.10.d.7.2.
V/40, X/40, Y/40 and) Z/40 T.M. Battys.)	FINS .	
40TH DIVNL. AMMN. COLUMN.		
Headquarters.	V.13.d.3.6.	
No. 1 Section.	V.13.d.7.3.)	
No. 2 Section.	V.19.b.5.3.)	With sections.
Echelon B.	CLERY (H.5.c.9.8)	With unit.
ROYAL ENGINEERS.		
Headquarters.	With Divnl. Hd.Qrs.	
224th Fld.Coy. R.E.	Hd.Qrs. FINS (V.12.a.4.1)	
229th Fld.Coy. R.E.	Hd.Qrs. EQUANCOURT.	With Company
231st Fld.Coy. R.E.	Hd.Qrs. ETRICOURT.	Hd.Qrs.
119TH INFANTRY BRIGADE.		
Headquarters.	W.4.a.0.4.	
19th R.W. Fusiliers.)		
12th S.W. Borderers.)		
17th Welsh Regiment. }	In the line. }	FINS.
18th Welsh Regiment.)		
119th M.G. Company.)		
119th T.M. Battery.)		
120TH INFANTRY BRIGADE.		
Headquarters.	ETRICOURT.	ETRICOURT.
11th K.O.R.L. Regt.	DESSART WOOD.	EQUANCOURT.
13th East Surrey Regt.	EQUANCOURT.	V.2.d.
14th H.L.I.	ETRICOURT.	V.2.d.
14th A. & S. Highrs.	ETRICOURT.	ETRICOURT.
120th M.G. Comapny.	EQUANCOURT.	EQUANCOURT.
120th T.M. Battery.	EQUANCOURT.	EQUANCOURT.

/Over.

- 2 -

UNIT.	LOCATION.	LOCATION OF HORSE LINES.
121ST INFANTRY BRIGADE.		
Headquarters.	DESSART WOOD (W.1.a)	
12th Suffolk Regt.	⎫	⎫
13th Yorkshire Regt.	⎬ In the line.	⎬ MANANCOURT (V.13.a)
20th Middlesex Regt.	⎪	ETRICOURT (V.8.c)
21st Middlesex Regt.	⎭	
121st M.G. Company.		MANANCOURT (V.13.a)
121st T.M. Battery.	DESSART WOOD.	
12TH YORKS. REGT. (PNRS).	H.Q. & 3 Cos. V.11.b. 1 Coy. DESSART WOOD.	With Hd.Qrs.
DIVISIONAL TRAIN.		
Headquarters.	MOISLAINS. (C.12.c.8.4)	
Nos. 1, 2, 3, and 4 Companies.	C.12.b.0.0.	With Companies.
No. 25 Divnl. Supply Col.	I.15.b.	
135th Fld. Ambulance.	SAILLY LAURETTE.	
136th Fld. Ambulance.	H.Q. FINS; A.D.S. at GOUZEAUCOURT.	With Ambulance. FINS.
137th Fld. Ambulance.	H.Q. MANANCOURT; detachment MOISLAINS.	MANANCOURT.
51st Mobile Vet. Sec.	MOISLAINS.	

ORIGINAL.   SECRET

WAR   DIARY

"A" and "Q" BRANCH,

HEADQUARTERS, 40TH DIVISION

MAY 1917.

Confidential

A & Q Staff
40th Div. Head Qrts.

WAR DIARY
INTELLIGENCE SUMMARY
(Erase heading not required.)

Army Form C. 2118

Instructions regarding War Diaries and Intelligence Summaries are contained in F.S. Regs, Part II. and the Staff Manual respectively. Title Pages will be prepared in manuscript.

Place	Date 1916	Hour	Summary of Events and Information	Remarks and references to Appendices
MAIMANCOURT	May 1		Number of horses on establishment of M.Vet. Section to be reduced by 5.	Appx
	2		Lt Col Pope C.dg. 11 S.W. Borderers to England sick.	Appx
	3		Divisional Employment Coy. consisting of P.B. men to be started.	Appx
	4		Divisional "Schedule A" Untalented aim Schedule A trades across country to be marked to save main roads.	Schedule A
	5		Captain LOCKETT to 2/Lt RYAN, 2/Midds Rgt wounded M.C. Major Collins Bde.Major, 121 Inf Bde. appointed C.R.E. 8th Division. Two candidates for commission to be dispatched to England from the Division each Tuesday & Friday.	Appx
	6		Lt. Col Sherard R.F.A. posted to B.A. Col. vice Lt. Col Dunlop gone sick.	Appx
	7		Church Army marquee asked for, to be sited near F.I.N.S.	Appx
	8		Units to state amount of clothing saved from recent pediculi.	Appx
	9		Following casualties occurred during raid in enemy lines at LAVACQUERIE. K. Offrs 2, OR 31. W. Offrs 11 or 174, M. Offrs mr.	Appx
	10		Major McCullough 21/Middx Rgt appointed to command a Chinese Labour Company of 50.	Appx
	11		Captain R.C. Matthews R. Lancs Rgt appointed Bde. Major 121 Inf Bde.	Appx
	12		Names of officers recommended for appointment of Corps Agricultural Officer to be submitted.	Appx
	13		Sick horses likely to recur within a month are not to be evacuated from the division.	Appx
	14		Major White KOYLI apptd Lieutenant 19 R West Yorks.	Appx
	15		Divl. Employment Coys. to be established in due course with personnel chiefly from Infantry of Class B(I) category.	Appx
	16		Arrangements to safeguard fields which may produce crops of hay, clover etc.	Appx
	17		20 N.C.Os & men awarded military medal.	Appx
	18		Leave allotment to division is the 29 instead of 10.	Appx
	19		Proposed to sell certain articles of ordnance stores in Divl. Canteens. There is a question & there is some hint to no difficulty in issuing articles aliced from ordnance trains will have difficulty in keeping up a/cs etc.	Appx
	20		Casualties since 1st May: Offrs killed, Officers 20 OR 391 missing OR 41	Appx
	21		Chain rivers to be taken into use with steel helmets although adversely reported upon	Appx
	22		with a view to ascertain preferably sunny crops of lucerne, clover etc. Horses & mules must not present indiscriminate over the country.	Appx

Confidential

2d page Army Form C. 2118

WAR DIARY
or
INTELLIGENCE SUMMARY
(Erase heading not required.)

A/q Staff 40th Divl Head Qrs

Place	Date 1917 MAY	Hour	Summary of Events and Information	Remarks and references to Appendices
NANCOURT	23		10 N.C.O.s were awarded the military medal.	Copy
	24		IIId Corps klothe over XII Corps area - on 2 June when the IIId Corps.	Copy
	25		A new form of unit to the tried to replace the petrol tin usually used.	Copy
	26		3 men 17 Welch Rgt awarded the military medal	Copy
	27		Employment Coys. arrived. 105 men with 1 Officer - medical examination of all personnel returned medically employed within the Division to be held.	Copy
	28		D.S.O. awarded to Major Radleigh RFA, Mily Cross to 5 Officers, D.C.M. to 2 N.C.O.s and military medal to 3 N.C.O.s	Copy
	29		Captain Hope M.C. S.S.O.3. posted to 1/5 Lancs Fusiliers as Major in Head Qrs. Lieut. R.M.L. Chapman 14 A.T.S. appt G.S.O.3 40th Division.	Copy
	30		Inspector of Infantry to Army reports favourably on the musing arrangements generally of the 40th Division	Copy
	31		Casualties from 21st May to 31st May inclusive Killed Officers 1 O.R 11 Wounded Officers 4 O.R 67 Missing Officers 1 O.R 2	

C J Wynne Mac
A/Sup.Lm 40 Div.

SECRET.

40TH DIVISION.

DISTRIBUTION OF UNITS - 4TH MAY, 1917.

UNIT.	LOCATION.	LOCATION OF HORSE LINES.
40TH DIVNL. HD.QRS. complete.	MANANCOURT (V.13.c.5.2)	
D.A.D.O.S.) Divnl. Gas School.) O.C., Divnl. Coy.) Divnl. Salvage Offr.)	FINS.	
Divnl. Sanitary Offr.) 83rd Sanitary Section.)	Out of Divnl. Area.	
ROYAL ARTILLERY.		
Headquarters.	With Divnl. Hd.Qrs.	
178th Bde. R.F.A.	In the line.	Hd.Qrs. V.4.c.9.4. A Bty. V.10.d.2.3. B Bty. V.10.b.2.7. C Bty. V.8.a.8.7. D Bty. V.10.c.5.9.
181st Bde. R.F.A.	In the line.	Hd.Qrs. V.10.d.6.3. A Bty. V.16.b.5.8. B Bty. V.11.c.1.3. C Bty. V.16.b.9.8. D Bty. V.10.d.7.2.
V/40, X/40, Y/40 and) Z/40 T.M. Battys.)	FINS.	
40TH DIVNL. AMMN. COLUMN.		
Headquarters.	V.13.d.3.6.	
No. 1 Section.	V.13.d.7.3.)	With Sections.
No. 2 Section.	V.19.b.5.3.)	
Echelon B.	VAUX WOOD (U.30.c)	With unit.
ROYAL ENGINEERS.		
Headquarters.	With Divnl. Hd.Qrs.	
224th Fld.Coy. R.E.	H.Q. FINS (V.12.a.4.1)	FINS.
229th Fld.Coy. R.E.	H.Q. W.2.a.0.1.	EQUANCOURT.
231st Fld.Coy. R.E.	H.Q. W.2.a.6.0.	ETRICOURT.
119TH INFANTRY BRIGADE.		
Headquarters.	W.4.a.0.4.	
19th R.W. Fusiliers. 12th S.W. Borderers. 17th Welsh Regiment. 18th Welsh Regiment. 119th M.G. Company. 119th T.M. Battery.	In the line.	FINS.
120TH INFANTRY BRIGADE.		
Headquarters.	DESSART WOOD.	ETRICOURT.
11th K.O.R.L. Regt.		EQUANCOURT.
13th East Surrey Regt.		V.2.d.
14th H.L.I.		V.2.d.
14th A. & S. Highrs.	In the line.	ETRICOURT.
120th M.G. Company.		EQUANCOURT.
120th T.M. Battery.		

/Over.

- 2 -

UNIT.	LOCATION.	LOCATION OF HORSE LINES.
121ST INFANTRY BRIGADE.		
Headquarters.	DESSART WOOD (W.1.a)	
12th Suffolk Regt.		
13th Yorkshire Regt.		MANANCOURT (V.13.a)
20th Middlesex Regt.		
21st Middlesex Regt.	In the line.	ETRICOURT (V.8.c)
121st M.G. Company.		MANANCOURT (V.13.a)
121st T.M. Battery.	DESSART WOOD.	
12TH YORKS. REGT. (PNRS).	H.Q: & 3 Coys. V.11.b.	With Hd.Qrs.
	1 Coy. DESSART WOOD.	
DIVISIONAL TRAIN.		
Headquarters, Nos.1, 2, 3 and 4 Coys.)	MANANCOURT. (U.24.b)	With Companies.
No. 25 Divnl. Supply Col.	I.15.b.	
135th Fld. Ambulance.	SAILLY LAURETTE.	With Ambulance.
136th Fld. Ambulance.	H.Q. FINS; A.D.S. at GOUZEAUCOURT.	FINS.
137th Fld. Ambulance.	H.Q. MANANCOURT; detachment MOISLAINS.	MANANCOURT.
51st Mobile Vet. Sec.	MOISLAINS.	

ATTACHED UNITS.

25th Brigade, R.F.A.	In the line.	RIVERSIDE WOOD.
4th Guards' Machine Gun Coy.	H.Q. DESSART WOOD.	EQUANCOURT.

SECRET

WAR DIARY.

"A. & Q" BRANCH

HEADQUARTERS
40TH. DIVISION.

JUNE 1917.

WAR DIARY — Contents
INTELLIGENCE SUMMARY — A.Q. Head Quarters 40 Divn

Army Form C. 2118

June 1917

Place	Date	Hour	Summary of Events and Information	Remarks and references to Appendices
MANAN-COURT	JUNE 1917 1		Lt. Col. Dunlop resumes command 20th Middx Rgt returning from England recovered from wounds –	Copy
	2		Church Army Marquees required for SOREL & DESSART WOOD.	Copy
	3		Leave allotment of Divisn next "5".	Copy
	4		Capt. Evans A.P.M 40 Divn to be A.P.M TARANTO. T/Captain C.L.B. Proule Cyclist Corps apptd A.P.M 40 Divn.	Copy
	5		Lt. Col. Dick Cag 14 HLI reported too medically unfit to command a battalion in England.	
	6		Lt. & Qr. Mr. Hampton for duty as Qr. Mr. Mr W.A.A. Stkd H.Qrs.	
	7		Stay residing party detailed from the Division about 80 all ranks –	
	8		Major Evans 238 A.T.Coy R.E to exchange duties with Major Ormston 229 A. Coy R.E for one month.	Copy
	9		Capt. Naunton 13 E. Surrey Rgt & 2/Lt Walla 17 Welsh Rgt awarded the D.S.O.	Copy
	10		Capt. J. Murphy 11 K.O.R Lanc Rgt appointed Lt. Commandt No 11 P.O.W Cag.	Copy
	11		Lt. Col. Hart-Synnot DSO selected for next vacancy in command of an Inf. Bn. Lt. Col. Hartsynnot to now G.S.O 2	Copy
	12		Bonus granted to be trained for employment in case of heavy fighting.	Copy
	13		A.C. Instructions received ref. formation of Divl Employment Companies	Copy
	14		a/ Major Kennedy M.G. 12 Bn H.L.I apptd 2nd Cd of 12 S. Wales Borderers. Major + Chutte D.S.O & njon.	Copy
	15		7 L. KOYLI from Leave from command of 19 R.l. Welsh Fus.	Copy
	16		Capt. Varga apptd 2 in Cd 13 Yorks Rgt and Major JUPE D.S.O 2 in Cd of 11 K.O.R. Lancs Rgt.	Copy
	17		Capt. Newman 17 Welsh Rgt awarded D.C.M.	Copy
	18		All Bns to be collected & salvage – appointment of boot. apptd to each Inf. Bn internal extra pay, approved. Preparation of accommodation for extra Divisions in the Corps area. would as arrangement for reconstruction of winter quarters.	Copy
	19		83 L.D horses drawn for Divl. Artillery.	Copy
	20		2 P.B. Officers posted R.Divisn. Hon.Col. LYON + Capt FRANKLIN attached to Town Major Instn. incht.	Copy
	21		2 Lt. Williams 17 S.W. Borders awarded M.C.	Copy
	22		Major S. Pugh 18 Welsh Rgt. appointed C.W. of Dessart Wood and area East of thro' of COUVERIUCOURT and VILLERS PLOUICH.	Copy
	23		Troops of Hd. Divn. located as shown in Appendix A	Appendix A

Army Form C. 2118

Page 2.

WAR DIARY

Confidential

INTELLIGENCE SUMMARY

A & Q Head Qrs
4th Division

(Erase heading not required.)

Place	Date	Hour	Summary of Events and Information	Remarks and references to Appendices
MANAN-COURT	24		Haymaking party formed near Morlancourt.	AH/CO1
	25		Lt.Col. A. Hart Prymat O/or to Command the 1/5th E Lancs Rgt (42nd Division) Major (temp) Capt Bunbury to be G.S.O.2 40th Division	Com
	26		65 Remounts to be drawn. Maj Jas Willoughby CMG proceeds on 3 days' leave of absence. 12th Bde to be Commanded temporarily by Lt Col A. Bergard DSO (Cdg. 17 Welsh Rgt)	Com
	27		Major Newbury joins 4th Divn as G.S.O.2.	Army
	28		Military medal awarded to Sgt Jones, Corpl Isaac and Pte Phees 17 Welsh Rgt.	AHH
	29		Major E.H.S.L.G. Gilbert 17 Welsh Rgt posted to Chinese Labour Coy.	AHH
	30		Casualties for month June Offrs killed 2 O.R. killed 12 24 Officers wounded 12 O.R. wounded 229	
			Offrs missing — O.R. missing 2.	

C. Moore
Lt Col
ant & QMG
4th Div

30/6/17

SECRET.

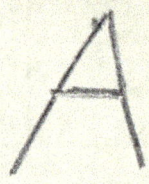

40TH DIVISION.

DISTRIBUTION OF UNITS - 20TH JUNE, 1917.

UNIT.	LOCATION	LOCATION OF HORSE LINES.
40TH DIVNL. HD.QRS.		
Complete.	MANANCOURT (V.13.c.5.2)	
D.A.D.O.S.)		
Divnl. Gas School.)	FINS (V.11.b.3.0.)	
Divnl. Salvage Offr.)		
ROYAL ARTILLERY.		
Headquarters.	With Divnl. Hd.Qrs.	
178th Bde. R.F.A.	In the Line.	Hd.Qrs. W.7.d.2.9. / A Bty. W.8.c.5.6. / B Bty. W.7.b.2.2. / C Bty. W.8.d.3.6. / D Bty. W.8.c.8.7.
181st Bde. R.F.A.	In the Line.	Hd.Qrs. V.10.d.5.0. / A Bty. V.16.b.5.7. / B Bty. V.11.c.5.5. / C Bty. V.16.b.9.8. / D Bty. V.11.c.1.3.
V/40, X/40, Y/40 and) Z/40 T.M. Battys.)	FINS.	
40TH DIVNL. AMMN. COL.		
Headquarters.	V.13.d.3.6.	
No. 1 Section.	V.13.d.7.4.)	
No. 2 Section.	V.19.b.5.3.)	With Sections.
Echelon B.	VAUX WOOD (U.30.c & d)	With unit.
ROYAL ENGINEERS.		
Headquarters.	With Divnl. Hd.Qrs.	—
224th Fld.Coy.R.E.	H.Q. FINS (V.12.a.4.1).	FINS.
229th Fld.Coy.R.E.	H.Q., DESSART WOOD.	SOREL.
231st Fld.Coy.R.E.	H.Q., DESSART WOOD.	FINS.
119TH INFANTRY BRIGADE.		
Headquarters.	DESSART WOOD.	
19th R.W. Fusiliers.	SOREL.	
12th S.W. Borderers.	DESSART WOOD.	
17th Welsh Regiment.	DESSART WOOD.	FINS.
18th Welsh Regiment.	SOREL.	
119th M.G. Company.	DESSART WOOD.	
119th T.M. Battery.	DESSART WOOD.	
120TH INFANTRY BRIGADE.		
Headquarters.	DESSART WOOD.	
11th K.O.R.L. Regt.)		
13th E. Surrey Regt.)		
14th H.L.I.)	In the Line.	SOREL. (East).
14th A.& S. Highrs.)		
120th M.G. Company.)		
120th T.M. Battery.	W.4.a.1.3.	—

/Over.

121ST INFANTRY BRIGADE.
  Headquarters.
  12th Suffolk Regt.
  13th Yorks. Regt.
  20th Middlesex Regt.
  21st Middlesex Regt.
  121st M.G. Company.
  121st T.M. Battery.

W.9.d.8.7.

In the Line.

SOREL. (West).

12TH YORKS. RGT. (PNRS.) H.Q., V.11.b; 1 Coy. DESSART WOOD.   With Hd.Qrs.
3 Coys. in cutting from W.3.c.5.7. to W.9.a.5.5.

DIVISIONAL TRAIN.
  H.Q., Nos. 1, 2, 3 & 4 Coys.   MANANCOURT (U.24.b).   With Companies.

No. 25 Divnl. Supply Col.   I.15.b.   ---

135th Fld. Ambulance.   Corps Rest Stn. MARICOURT. Offs. Rest Stn. BOIS L'ABBE.

136th Fld. Ambulance.   H.Q., FINS; Aid Posts and Bearer posts E. of FINS.   With Hd.Qrs.

137th Fld. Ambulance.   H.Q., MANANCOURT; Detachment at NURLU.   With Hd.Qrs.

51st Mobile Vet. Sec.   MOISLAINS.   ----

SECRET.
ORIGINAL.

WAR DIARY

A & Q BRANCH.

HEADQUARTERS

40TH. DIVISION.

@@@@@@@

JULY 1917.

@@@@@@@

CONFIDENTIAL　　Army Form C. 2118

WAR DIARY
or
INTELLIGENCE SUMMARY

(Erase heading not required.)

A.T.Q.
40th DIVISION

Place	Date 1917	Hour	Summary of Events and Information	Remarks and references to Appendices
MANAN-COURT	July 1st	11 a.y.	A & Q arrangements for relief of 36th Div. on 1/2 July, 2/3 July completed. Copies attached.	See Appendix I
"	2nd	—	Arranged for new D.A.D.O.S. at SOREL to take part in hand. To be completed by 6th July.	copy
"	3rd	—	Capt. CRUISE sent to Division by GHQ 1st Eqn way he still says attachment for Instructor is not approved yet tells all C.O.'s of 119th Inf Bde. in GOMMIECOURT sector and discussed it question of Eng. instruction with him.	copy
"	4th	—	The General obtained Instrns from FIFTH to new Lt Col in the SOUZEAUCOURT-FINS road. Transferred British Army for ammunition on 4/5 July 1917. Issued S.B. 1st No. heavy for armed letter held as a warm approved	copy
"	5th	—	by A.D.S.I.T. 4th Army (Eavesworth, A.D.S.I.T. 3rd Army on 4th July.	copy
"	6th	—	HQs. G.O.C. Genl Staff R.A. C.R.E. + Signals opened at SOREL LE GRAND 10 a.m. ATQ office remained at MANAMCOURT.	copy
SOREL LE GRAND	7th	—	Closed at MANAMCOURT 10 a.m. opened SOREL LE GRAND same time. A.D.M.S. + A.P.M. remain at MANAMCOURT.	copy

1875 Wt. W593/826 1,000,000 4/15 J.B.C. & A. A.D.S.S./Forms/C. 2118.

CONFIDENTIAL   WAR DIARY   A Q
                of   40th Div.
            INTELLIGENCE SUMMARY
            (Erase heading not required.)

Army Form C. 2118

Place	Date 1917 July	Hour	Summary of Events and Information	Remarks and references to Appendices
SOREL LE GRAND	8th	—	9 A.T.S. horses for Div Train to work on roads at NURLU. 1st S. with this horses from this unit detached for hay making drawn only sufficient for supply duties and 11 officers.	Appx I
"	9th	—	Commandant of Div Horse Transport shows report arrangements completed. Programme attached.	Appx II
"	10th	—	Horse Transport shows 2 Bn. Localising of next relief. III Corps asked to move 48th Sanitary Section to MARICOURT. 135th Field Ambulance moved Division from NURLU Corps Reserve at MARICOURT. A.P.M., D.A.D.S., & D.A.D.V.S. clear MAYNON COURT Offices of arms. Open at SOREL LE GRAND 10 am. Horse transport shows 2 Bn.	Appx III, Appx IV
"	11th	—	4 Infantry Brigade Baths completed in this Div. area & ready for use 12/July 1917.	

CONFIDENTIAL

Army Form C. 2118

A.D.S.D
30th DIV

WAR DIARY
or
INTELLIGENCE SUMMARY

(Erase heading not required.)

Instructions regarding War Diaries and Intelligence Summaries are contained in F. S. Regs., Part II. and the Staff Manual respectively. Title Pages will be prepared in manuscript.

Place	Date	Hour	Summary of Events and Information	Remarks and references to Appendices
SOREL LE GRAND	12th		No 48 Sanitary Section into Hd.Qts at St.Pierre Farm, near Nurlu, is allotted to the Divl. area. "Pourvoi" train - Decauville to Peronne, thence by broad gauge terminé - near daily - Military Metal awarded to Flight Sergeant to Pte. Cresshall 12th S.W. Buntingus. 5 sets of spring seised harness for him to pt. Weigh 130lb - no machinery when worn. General Petain draws apparent grounds (?) from to 2 Lt WALTON, 17 Puddleton. The officer is in England wounded.	AGM
	13			AGM
	14			AGM
	15			AGM
	16		Decided to institute large laundries, in certain areas, to be working for all formations. When this is done present certain personnel of Division now employed in laundries will be released for duty - Remounts for division - not practically complete in arrivals -	AGM
	17		2 Many making barden still employed -	AGM
	18		Division made arrangements for W.D. Army Inspector of Catering to deliver lectures -	AGM
	19		L. Capt. Ross 21 Miller Regt. awarded bar to Military medal. No 244 MG Coy. joins the Division.	AGM
	20		Town Major appointed as follows:- Major Turton, 12 Yorks at FINIS; Capt. Hill 12 Suffolks at NURLU	AGM
	21		Capt. Franklin, P.B. Officer, at SOREL; 2U.Walker H.A.O.R Junes at HEUDICOURT.	AGM
	22		Major A.T. LACEY appointed to Dvd. Machine Gun Officer	AGM
	23		Leave allotment to Division 10 daily from 28th to 3rd July -	AGM
	24		Scheme for accommodating 3 Divisions in a 2 Division area, abandoned - Winter hutting to be pushed on - Horse Standings being erected as material becomes available.	AGM
	25		Conference of Dn. Divs. 1st Sorel. AA.QMGs. & DADOS to explain certain arrangements necessary as to accommodation which should benefit all concerned.	AGM
	26		M/4105 Pad.mo. Schuse-stone recommended the military medal.	AGM
	27		Sgt.-Brenton DCM Gunnell 1st take prents. Care of bicycles in his charge. Units instructed to take prents. care of bicycles in his charge, also that winter quarters in reserve support lines	AGM
	28		Accommodation in forward area proceeding pleasantly.	AGM
	29		Acts Kany comminicated 13 E. Surrey Pgt. awarded military medal.	AGM
	30		Corpl. Richards 13 E. Surrey Pgt. awarded military medal.	AGM
	31		Inspection of Catering III D Army Delivered a lecture.	AGM

Casualties month July killed Offrs 6 O.R. 64 Wounded Offrs 29 O.R. 505 missing O.R. 33

SECRET.   H.Q., 40th Division No. 6/Q1/Q.

_____

_____

40 Div War Diary
A & Q Appendix I

Reference 40th Division Order No. 87 dated 29/6/17.

1. TRANSPORT LINES.
    The transport lines and r.Mr. Stores of 121st Inf. Brigade will remain in their present locations. The transport lines of the 224th Field Coy. and 137th Field Ambulance will be located at HEUDICOURT and NURLU respectively. Application for standings to be made to the Town Majors concerned.

2. ACCOMMODATION.
    The 35th Division have arranged to hand over all trench shelters and accommodation in the forward area "in situ". The Camps at DESSART WOOD and SOREL will be struck by 10 a.m. on the day they are being vacated by Units. A total of 150 tents are to be collected at the roadsides at W.1.d.9.0. and at V.18.b.8.2. They will be handed over to a representative of the 35th Division and receipts obtained.

3. MEDICAL ARRANGEMENTS.
    The A.D.M.S. will arrange to move the 137th Field Ambulance to NURLU and will notify all concerned of the arrangements for the evacuation of the sick and wounded from the area being taken over.

4. DIVISIONAL BATHS.
    The A.D.M.S. will arrange to take over the baths at HEUDICOURT.

5. DIVISIONAL BOMB STORE.
    The Officer i/c 40th Divnl. Bomb Store will take over the 35th Divisional Bomb Store at W.14.c. on the 1st July, 1917.

6. TRENCH STORES.
    All trench stores, grenades, rockets, trench mortar ammunition, Strombos Horns, will be taken over. Returns to be sent to this office by the 4th July, 1917.

7. CONTROL POSTS.
    The A.P.M. will arrange direct with the A.P.M., 35th Division, to take over Control Posts and Stragglers' Posts. A list to be sent to this office by 1st July.

8. DIVISIONAL CANTEENS.
    A Divisional Canteen will be opened near VAUCETTE FARM on the 2nd July, 1917. If found feasible a Canteen will be established in VILLERS GUISLAIN. The Canteen at DESSART WOOD will be closed on the 1st July, 1917.

9. CEMETERIES.
    The authorised cemeteries to be used have been published in D.R.O. No. 1211 of 3rd June, 1917. They are

    HEUDICOURT - Extension of German Cemetery which is behind the Church. Sheet 57c. W.21.a.4.5.
    VILLERS GUISLAIN. - Sheet 57c. X.2.d.9.9. The piece of land on N.W. side of the French Communal Cemetery should be used,

- 2 -

where there are already 6 or 7 British soldiers buried in one grave. (Existing German Cemetery should not be used as it is under observation.

H.., 40th Division.
29th June, 1917.
J.

Major,
D.A.Q.M.G.,
40th Division.

APPENDIX II

40TH DIVISION HORSE TRANSPORT SHOW.

P R O G R A M M E.

1st Day, TUESDAY, 10th July, 1917.

Commencing at 2 p.m.

TRANSPORT CLASSES.

Class I.
Best pair of "Heavy Draught" horses in G.S. Wagon.
Open to Units having H.D. and G.S. Wagons on their War Establishment, or Field Ambulance.
Confined to 2 pairs per Unit.

    1st Prize. ... 20 Francs.
    2nd Prize. ... 15 Francs.
    3rd Prize. ... 10 Francs.

Class III.
(a). Best pair of "Light Draught" horses in limber G.S. or S.A.A. Cart, or Maltese Cart.
Confined to 2 pairs per unit, except as in (b).
(b). As above, but confined to Inf. Battns. and M.G. Coys.

(a). 1st Prize. 20 Francs.   (b). 1st Prize. 20 francs.
    2nd Prize. 15 Francs.   2nd Prize. 15 francs.
    3rd Prize. 10 Francs.   3rd Prize. 10 francs.

Class V.
Best 6 Mule team in G.S. Wagon. Open to R.A., R.E., and D.A.C. 2 Teams per unit only.

    1st Prize. ... 60 Francs.
    2nd Prize. ... 40 Francs.
    3rd Prize. ... 20 Franes.

Class VII.
Best "Pack" animal, complete set of pack saddlery without load.
Open to Battns. of Infantry and M.G. Coys. only.
Confined to 2 animals per Unit.

    1st Prize. ... 20 Francs.
    2nd Prize. ... 15 Francs.
    3rd Prize. ... 10 Francs.

RIDING CLASSES.

Best Turn-out Mounted. - Drill Order.

Class II.
Junior N.C.O's, from Corporal downwards.
Must be the one allotted to the N.C.O. showing it.

    1st Prize. ... 15 Francs.
    2nd Prize. ... 10 Francs.
    3rd Prize. ... 5 Francs.

/Over.

2nd Day, WEDNESDAY, 11th July, 1917.

Commencing at 2 p.m.

TRANSPORT CLASSES.

Class II.
Best pair of "Heavy Draught" horses in Field Kitchen.
Open to Battalions of Infantry only.
Confined to 2 pairs per battalion.

    1st Prize. ... 20 Francs.
    2nd Prize. ... 15 Francs.
    3rd Prize. ... 10 Francs.

Class IV.
(a). Best pair of "Mules" in limber G.S. or S.A.A. Cart or Maltese Cart.
Confined to 2 pairs per Unit, except as in (b).
(b). As above, but confined to Inf. Battns. and M.G. Coys.

    (a). 1st Prize. 20 Francs.   (b). 1st Prize. 20 Francs.
         2nd Prize. 15 Francs.   2nd Prize. 15 Francs.
         3rd Prize. 10 Francs.   3rd Prize. 10 Francs.

Class VI.
Best 6 horse Gun team in Q.F. Wagon, drill order. No ammunition to be carried.
Open to Royal Artillery only.
Confined to 2 teams from any one Battery, or Section D.A.C.

    1st Prize. ... 60 Francs.
    2nd Prize. ... 40 Francs.
    3rd Prize. ... 20 Francs.

RIDING CLASSES.

Best Turn-out Mounted. - Drill Order.

Class I.
W.O., Staff Sergt. or Sergeant.
Must be the one allotted to the W.O. or N.C.O. showing it.

    1st Prize. ... 15 Francs.
    2nd Prize. ... 10 Francs.
    3rd Prize. ... 5 Francs.

Special consideration and extra marks will be given to a "Turn out" that has been in possession of the unit since 1st September, 1916.

SECRET.   APPENDIX
                                                                    III

40TH DIVISION.

DISTRIBUTION OF UNITS - 10TH JULY, 1917.

UNIT.	LOCATION.	LOCATION OF HORSE LINES.
40TH DIVNL. HD.QRS.		
"G" and "A & Q" Branches)	SOREL-LE-GRAND.	
Camp Commandant.)	(V.18.d.5.7)	
A.D.M.S.		
D.A.D.V.S.		
A.P.M. }	MANANCOURT.	
Sen. Chaplain (C.of E.)	(V.13.c.5.2)	
O.C., French Mission.		
Sen. Chaplain (Non C.of E)	With 136th Fld.Amb.	
D.A.D.O.S.		
Divnl. Gas School. }	FINS (V.11.b.3.0)	
Div. Salvage Offr.		
O.C. Divnl. Employ't Coy.		
ROYAL ARTILLERY.		
Headquarters.	With Divnl.Hd.Qrs. (SOREL).	
178th Bde. R.F.A.	IN the Line.	Hd.Qrs. W.7.d.2.9. A Bty. W.8.c.5.6. B Bty. W.7.b.2.2. C Bty. W.8.d.3.6. D Bty. W.8.c.8.7.
181st Bde. R.F.A.	In the Line.	Hd.Qrs. V.10.d.5.0. A Bty. V.16.b.5.7. B Bty. V.11.c.5.5. C Bty. V.16.b.9.8. D Bty. V.11.c.1.3.
V/40, X/40, Y/40 and Z/40 T.M. Battys.	FINS.	
40TH DIVNL. AMMN. COL.		
Headquarters.	V.13.d.3.6.	
No. 1 Section.	V.13.d.7.4.)	
No. 2 Section.	V.19.b.5.3.)	With Sections.
Echelon B.	VAUX WOOD (U.30.c & d)	With Unit.
ROYAL ENGINEERS.		
Headquarters.	With D.H.Q. SOREL.	—
224th Fld.Coy.R.E.	HEUDICOURT.	HEUDICOURT.
229th Fld.Coy.R.E.	H.Q. W.9.d.8.7.	SOREL.
231st Fld.Coy.R.E.	H.Q. DESSART WOOD.	FINS.
119TH INFANTRY BRIGADE.		
Headquarters.	R.31.c.8.7.	
19th R.W. Fusiliers.		
12th S.W. Borderers.		
17th Welsh Regt. }	In the Line. }	FINS.
18th Welsh Regt.		
119th M.G. Coy.		
119th T.M. Batty.		—
120TH INFANTRY BRIGADE.		
Headquarters.	Q.29.b.1.3.	
11th K.O.R.L. Regt.		
13th E. Surrey Regt.		
14th H.L.I. }	In the Line. }	SOREL (East).
14th A.& S. Highrs.		
120th M.G. Company.		
120th T.M. Battery.	W.4.a.1.3.	—

/Over.

- 2 -

121ST INFANTRY BRIGADE.
Headquarters.   W.23.b.3.1.
12th Suffolk Regt.   ⎫
13th Yorkshire Regt.   ⎪
20th Middlesex Regt.   ⎬ In the line.   SOREL (West).
21st Middlesex Regt.   ⎪
121st M.G. Company.   ⎪
121st T.M. Battery.   ⎭

12TH YORKS. REGT. (PNRS) H.Q. & 3 Coys. in cutting
                           from W.3.c.5.7. to   With Hd.Qrs.
                           to W.9.a.5.5. 1 Coy.
                           DESSART WOOD.

DIVISIONAL TRAIN.
H.Q. Nos.1,2, 3   MANANCOURT (U.24.b).   With Companies.
& 4 Coys.

No. 25 Divnl. Supply Col. I.15.b.   ----

135th Fld. Amb.   ⎰ H.Q. FINS; Aid Posts &   With Hd.Qrs.
                           ⎱ Bearer Posts E. of FINS.

136th Fld. Amb.   ⎰ H.Q. V.18.c. (Divnl.   With Hd.Qrs.
                           ⎱ Main Dressing Station)

137th Fld. Amb.   ⎧ H.Q. HEUDICOURT. Aid Posts
                           ⎪ & Bearer Posts E. of   With Hd.Qrs.
                           ⎨ HEUDICOURT).
                           ⎩ Det'mt. at NURLU.

51st Mobile Vet. Sec.   MOISLAINS.   ----

A T T A C H E D.

296th Bde. R.F.A.   In the line.   W.21.d.8.4. and
                                                           W.27.b.3.3.

No. 2 Section, 35th   D.10.a.
      D.A.C.   (Sheet 62.c)

CONFIDENTIAL.

WAR DIARY

of

"A" and "Q" BRANCH, 40TH DIVISION.

-o-o-o-o-o-o-o-o-o-o-o-o-o-

VOLUME XV.

From 1st to 31st AUGUST, 1917.

35807. W16879/M1879 500,000 3/17 R.T. (1074) Forms/W3091/3   Army Form W.3091.

Cover for Documents.

Nature of Enclosures.

Notes, or Letters written.

Confidential

WAR DIARY

AUGUST 1917

INTELLIGENCE SUMMARY

A + Q Head Quarters 40th DIVISION

Army Form C. 2118

(Erase heading not required.)

Instructions regarding War Diaries and Intelligence Summaries are contained in F. S. Regs., Part II. and the Staff Manual respectively. Title Pages will be prepared in manuscript.

Place	Date AUG.	Hour	Summary of Events and Information	Remarks and references to Appendices
AUGUST / SOREL	1		Military medal awarded to Gunner CALDECOURT. 181 Bde R.F.A. Locating of units schedule A	A Coy
	2		Reduction in establishment of horses of Div. H.Q. Military police + RE Artillery	Copy
	3		Military Cross awarded to Lieut Wallace 17 Welsh Regt and 2/Lt Robins 12 Suffolk Regt	Copy Copy
	4		Lt.Col. Henricker P.B. Officer appointed Town Major HEUDICOURT.	Copy Copy
	5		Lt.Col. G. Gunn to be struck off establishment of 14 A.V.S.Ste. Hches.	Copy
	6		Haymaking parties to be closed down on 15 August	
	7		Holding arrangements for winter accommodation of troops	Copy Copy
	8		Indian meded awarded to L/Cpl Rogers 17 Welsh Regt. M. Cross awarded to 221 Wilson 13 E.Surrey Regt.	Copy
	9		Estimates of Stores required for winter accommodation, stores, lamps etc -	Copy
	10		Military medal awarded to 2 N.C.Os. 21st Middx Regt and 2 men 17 Welsh Regt. H.Cpl Jones Cpl. 19.	Copy
	11		R.Welsh Fus to fire at War Office	Copy
	12		Corps Salvage Depot for ammunition, grenades etc formed at F.W.S.	Copy
	13		Arrangements for leave parties proceeding to Rest Camp at Valery Sur Somme.	Copy
	14		Water to be pumped to Buisson on a scale of 3000 per division	Copy
	15		Corps Commanders written appreciation of good work done by Haymaking party -	Copy
	16		Lt.Col Brick DSO 14.H.L.I. awarded ordre de Leopold (Belgian Decoration)	Copy
	17		Major Wilkinson, 2 in Cd 12 Yorks Regt - England sick.	Copy
	18		Military medal awarded Sgt. Hollis + Pte O'Sullivan 14 H.L.I. s/Major Andrews to be 2 i/c 17 Welsh.	Copy
	19		Hosp! Thorpe awarded a Belgian decoration.	Copy
	20		Relinquishment of acting rank of 2/Lt. by Majr Hedlis 18 Welsh Regt - Majr Kennedy appointed Commant Military Medals awarded to 8 NCOs + men 17 Welsh Regt. Majr MacDonald to be acting Lt. Colonel 11th o. RL Lancs Regt.	Copy
	21		Military Cross awarded to S. Lt. Evans 21 Br. Middx Regt. - Majr Ormondy R.B. officer posted as Town Major FINS	Copy
	22		Capt. Higgins 6/Queens. RW Surrey Regt. appted Corps O. Martial Officer. F.G.C.M. will be convened at Divl Head Qrtrs. for the present -	Copy

Army Form C. 2118

WAR DIARY
INTELLIGENCE SUMMARY

Second Page. A + Q Head Quarters 40th Division

Place	Date August	Hour	Summary of Events and Information	Remarks and references to Appendices
SOREL	23		Preparations for prevention of Trench feet. Gumboot stores - Soup Kitchens - medical treatment shelters.	Copy
	24		Military Cross awarded to 2/Lt Parker 14 H.L.I. Brigadier Ruggles Brise proceeded home & assumed a dummy.	Copy
	25		Major Genl. J. PONSONBY CMG, DSO, assumed command of the 40 Division arrangements for selecting & marking grounds to be placed on axes.	Copy
	26		Reorganization of Bgde. Ammunition Column - S.A.A. section formed -	Copy
	27		W.Os. & N.C.Os not wanted [?] to listen in the field selected home	Copy
	28		Small eight tube form formed in connection with Corps Rest Station. Medical examination of all Divl. Employment Coy. 41 Class A men retained Ktoese -	Copy
			Lt Col. Warden transferred 13 E. Surrey Rgt. Three hospital Nissen huts for recreation	Copy
	29		purposes in Divl. area.	
			Further applications for transfer of officers to Tank Corps [?] submitted. Reduction of Divl. Trains -	Copy
	30		Class A men being exchanged by men of low Physical category.	
	31		Casualties 40 Division month of August.	Copy
			Killed Officers 2 wounded Officers 15 killed O.R. 17 wounded O.R. 200	
			Missing Officers 1 O.R. 5	

C.J. Moore
Lt Col
AA & QMG
40 Div.

S E C R E T.   "A"

40TH DIVISION.
DISTRIBUTION OF UNITS - 1st AUGUST 1917.

UNIT.	LOCATION.	LOCATION OF HORSE LINES.
40TH DIVNL. HD.QRS. complete.	SOREL-LE-GRAND. (V.18.d.5.7).	
Sen. Chaplain (Non.C.of.E.) with 136 Fld Amb.		
D.A.D.O.S. DIV. Salvage Officer. O.C. Divl. EMPLY'T Coy.	FINS (V.12.b.7.3.)	
Divl. Gas School.	FINS (V.12.c.3.9.)	
ROYAL ARTILLERY. Headquarters.	With Divnl. Hd.Qrs.	
178th Bde R.F.A.	In the Line.	Hd.Qrs. W.7.d.2.9. A Bty. W.8.c.5.6. B Bty. W.7.b.2.2. C Bty. W.8.d.3.6. D.Bty. W.8.c.8.7.
181st Bde R.F.A.	In the Line.	Hd.Qrs. V.10.d.5.0. A Bty. V.16.b.5.7. B Bty. V.11.c.5.5. C Bty. V.16.b.9.8. D.Bty. V.11.c.1.3.
V/40, X/40, Y/40 and Z/40 T.M. Battys.	FINS.	
40th DIVNL. AMMN. COL. Headquarters. No.1 Section. No.2 Section. B Echelon.	V.29.d.3.5. V.28.c.8.0. V.27.d.9.3. V.28.d.&.b.	With Sections. With unit.
Royal Engineers. Headquarters. 224th Field Coy.R.E. 229th Field Coy.R.E. 231st Field Coy.R.E.	With Divnl. Hd.Qrs. HEUDICOURT H.Q. W.9.d.8.7. H.Q. Q.34.c.4.8.	--- HEUDICOURT. SOREL. FINS.
119TH INFANTRY BRIGADE. Headquarters. 19th R.W.Fusiliers. 12th S.W.Borderers. 17th Welsh Regt. 18th Welsh Regt. 119th M.G.Coy 119th T.M.Batty.	R.31.c.8.7. In the Line.	FINS.
120th Infantry Brigade. Headquarters. 11th K.O.R.L.Regt. 13th E.Surrey Regt. 14th H.L.I. 14th A.&S.Hldrs. 120th M.G.Coy. 120th T.M.B.	Q.29.b.1.3. In the Line	SOREL (East)

/OVER.

121ST INFANTRY BRIGADE.		
Headquarters.	W.23.b.3.1.	
12th Suffolk Regt.	⎫	⎫
15th Yorkshire Regt.		
20th Middlesex Regt.	In the Line.	SOREL (West).
21st Middlesex Regt.		
121st M.G.Coy.		
121st T.M.Battery.	⎭	⎭
12TH YORKS. RGT. (PNRS).	H.Q.& 2 Coys in cutting from W.3.c.5.7. to W.9.a.5.5. 2 Coys, W.18.b.	With H.Q.
204TH MACHINE GUN COY.	HEUDICOURT.	HEUDICOURT.
DIVISIONAL TRAIN. H.C., Nos.1,2,3, and 4 Coys.	V.29.a.3.4.	With Coys.
No.25 Divl.Supply.Clm.	I.15.b.	----
135th FD.Ambulance.	H.Q. FINS;Aid Posts & Bearer Posts E. of FINS	With H.Q.
136th FD.Ambulance.	H.Q.V.10.c.(Divl.Main Dressing Station).	With.H.Q.
137th FD.Ambulance.	H.Q. HEUDICOURT.Aid Posts & Bearer Posts East of HEUDICOURT. Det'mt. at NURLU.	With H.Q.
51st Mobile Veterinary Section.	H.Q. MOISLAINS. Det'mt NURLU.	-------

---

ATTACHED.

296th Bde. R.F.A.	In the Line.	W.21.d.8.4.& and W.27.b.3.3.
No 2 Section, 59th D.A.C.	D.10.a. (Sheet 62.c.)	-------
III Corps Cyclist Battn.	HEUDICOURT.	-------

CONFIDENTIAL.

WAR DIARY

OF

"A" AND "Q" BRANCH

40TH DIVISION

From 1ST TO 30TH SEPTEMBER, 1917.

VOLUME XVI.

28031 W3125/M2250 1000m 6/17 M.R.Co.,Ltd. (1367) Forms W3091.   Army Form W. 3091.

Cover for Documents.

Nature of Enclosures.

Notes, or Letters written.

Army Form C. 2118

WAR DIARY
or
INTELLIGENCE SUMMARY   A & Q Hd Qrs 40th Division

(Erase heading not required.)

Confidential September 1917

Instructions regarding War Diaries and Intelligence Summaries are contained in F. S. Regs., Part II and the Staff Manual respectively. Title Pages will be prepared in manuscript.

Place	Date	Hour	Summary of Events and Information	Remarks and references to Appendices
SOREL	Sept. 1		13 E. Surrey Rgt.	Copy
	2		2/Lt. Newton 20 Middx Rgt. Approved England. List of Officers recommended for advancement on the Staff to be forwarded. Mil. medal awarded to 2/Corpl Cadney 13 E. Surrey Rgt. — Military Cross awarded to 2/Lt Mullins 19 R. Welch Fus.	Copy
	3		Military advancements. Units located as shewn in appendix A	Appendix A
	4		Military Cross awarded to Lt. V. Scott. 13 E. Surrey Rgt.	Copy
	5		Period of stay in Army rest camps at Valley sur Somme reduced from 14 to 7 days.	Copy
	6		2/Lt. Collins t/s Leicester Rgt. to be struck off establishment of 13 E. Surrey Rgt. Capt. Renwick R.A. A.C. officer	Copy
	7		a member of IV Corps Board on brood mares. Military medal awarded to 1 man 229 Fd by R.E. and to	Copy
	8		3 men 19th Rl. Welsh Fusrs. —	Copy
	9		Vacancies at Schools of Cookery Courses & Catering Course — Military police establishment of horses not	Copy
			to be reduced as originally ordered.	
	10		Agreed that Rest Camps at Valery sur Somme might well be continued during winter months, provided that men were properly housed and entertainment catered for.	Copy
	11		Ordered to notify what quantities of cut apples existed in the area for the making of French cider.	Copy
	12		Names of officers for Course at Staff School Cambridge to be submitted.	Copy
	13		2/Lt. Dunlop 20 Middx Rgt. transferred to 121. M. Gun Coy.	Copy
	14		Coal for Division now arriving by rail at FINS.	Copy
	15		Military Cross awarded to Lieut. Bain 121. M. Gun Coy.	Copy
	16		3 Medical Officers of U.S. Army joined the division. To be sent home daily from 1st October 1917.	Copy
	17		One candidate for Infantry Cadet Units approved to India.	Copy
	18		Major Kidner O.C. Brig. Signal Coy. approved to India.	Copy
	19		No names to submit of Brigadier recommended command brigades at home for 6 months.	Copy
	20		Names of candidates not recommended for commission should not be submitted.	Copy
	21		Medal ribbons to be presented by Corps Commander on parade ground near Dessart Wood on 25th September	Copy

Army Form C. 2118

second page
A & Q
Hd. Qrs. 40 Division

WAR DIARY
or
INTELLIGENCE SUMMARY
(Erase heading not required.)

September 1917

Place	Date 1917 SEPT	Hour	Summary of Events and Information	Remarks and references to Appendices
SOREL	22		Hay cut in area & now stacked to the rear. Necessitates issue of 1/3 Feed hay 2/3 ration hay each day. Arrangements made accordingly.	
	23		Military medal awarded to 2 N.C.O.s & Pte. 19th Bn. Welsh Fusrs.	
	24		Issue approved of underclothing at extra scale being issued for use of Divl. Baths.	
	25		Officers & 60 O.R. proceed to rest camp at Valery Sur Somme.	
	26		Lt Col. A Bryant DSO Glourcesters Regt. Commanding 17th Welsh Regt. to assume cd. of a Battalion 3rd Division.	
	27		Major Ormsden R.E. to proceed home.	
			New Year Honours Gazette allotment - 116 - Ratio of 2 Honours to 3 mentions.	
	28		Corps Training Camp formed at Hand All ranks for training of drafts incl. Divl. arrangements	
	29		a/Capt. Carpenter appt. O.C. Divl. Signal Coy. Military medals awarded to 4 N.C.O.s	
	30		Military Cross awarded to Capt. Williams 19 R.W. Fusrs.	
			Casualties month Sept. Killed Officers 3 O.R. 39 wounded Officers 18 O.R. 274 missing Officers - 23 other ranks - 3018 (other 1 or 20).	
			Reinforcements month Sept. Officers 23 other ranks - 3018	

3/10/17

ORIGINAL.

Vol 17

WAR DIARY

A. & Q. BRANCH,   HEADQUARTERS, 40TH. DIVISION.

for

OCTOBER, 1917.

VOL. XVII

28031 W3125/M2250 1000m 6/17 M.R.Co.,Ltd. (1367) Forms W3091.   Army Form W. 3091.

Cover for Documents.

Nature of Enclosures.

Notes, or Letters written.

WAR DIARY or INTELLIGENCE SUMMARY

Army Form C. 2118

Month and year: October 1917
Unit: A & Q Head Qrs 40th Divn.

Place	Date	Hour	Summary of Events and Information	Remarks and references to Appendices
SOREL	Oct 1917 1		Instructions received that 40th Division to be relieved by 20th Division. Relief will take place between 5th and 11th October.	Appx
	2		Military medal awarded to 11 N.C.Os + men. 9/12 Suffolk Regt. 10 of 13 Yorks + 1 of R.A. T.M. By.	Appx
	3		Proposal to reorganize M.T. by formation of Army, Corps + Divl. M.T.Coys. embracing A. Supply Parks.	Appx
	4		Arrangements made for evacuation of area thanking over to 20th Division.	Appx
	5		Rail Road to area West of ARRAS commencing on 6th October.	Appx
	6		Of a draft of 60 men sent to 14 H.L.I. from 18th H.L.I. (35th Division) 24 men are found medically unfit.	Appx
	7		120 Inf. Bde. proceeded by lorry + decauville from SOREL staging area to PERONNE, relieved by 60 Inf. Bde. in the line. 59th Inf. Bde. in SOREL staging area. 2 officers 4 NCOs + horsed to trace the Staires in administration of Indians to the divisions of D. Ammn. Col.	Appx
	8		61st Inf. Bde. arrived in SOREL staging area relieving 119 Inf. Bde. jump proceeded from Decauville to Peronne area	Appx
	9		120 Inf. Bde. entrain at Peronne for BOISEUL. Transport by road via BAPAUME	Appx
FOSSEUX	10		119 Inf. Bde. entrain at Peronne for BEAUMETZ. 121 Bde. jumps move to Peronne. 119 Bde. Tpt. by road	Appx
	11		121 Inf. Bde. entrain at Peronne for BEAUMETZ. 121 Bde. Tpt. by road.	Appx
	12		Units of Division quartered as shewn in attached schedule appendix A	Appendix A
	13		Arrangements made for Divl. Ammunition to support all rifles, Lewis guns, machine guns and prey etc another Division by 22 W.O.Cm., SAADOS to report trucks of the respective.	Appx
	14		All supplies drawn by Hqrs. transport from Railhead BEAUMETZ: Lewis & No 2 S.A.S.C. laid up except for ordnance or fuel work.	Appx
	15		Arranged for OC Divl. Train, SAADS 16 inspect transport, inall Units during the week to report on the condition of animals, vehicles + standing.	Appx
	16		Visited HENU - COIRSEUX - SOUASTRE area with Gen Staff with a view of move to front.	Appx

SECRET Army Form C. 2118

WAR DIARY
or
INTELLIGENCE SUMMARY
(Erase heading not required.)

October 1917 A.T.Q. Major 20 Div

Place	Date 1917	Hour	Summary of Events and Information	Remarks and references to Appendices
FOSSEUX	17 Oct		Telephone instruction received that 2 Field Coys Divnl Batt'n will report on 19th Oct. Arrangements to be made to accommodate them in present area.	
	18.		Instructions from III Corps to III Corps at 12 noon. In charge is location of units. 2nd Divnl Depot Batt'n at PERONNE will report with the Pioneers & R.E. Coys on 19th Oct.	
	19.		On receipt of warning order that the Div will be transferred by Rail on 27th 28th & 29th Oct to DUBLIN & 2nd or 3rd Pioneers and GHQ reserve arranged with DADOS to hold in readiness, arrange to ship stores from the base on 24th Oct.	
	20.		Reinforcement rail-head for Div (two allg) from PERONNE to BEAUMETZ	
	21.		Lequ Lucis. G.O.C. inspected 121st Bde Sptrs Poty near BARLY at 10.30am, presented medals to others & inspected the ranks. Brigade then marched past in column.	
	22.		Obtained Traffics AVESNES regarding entraining arrangements for SAULTY and BEAUMETZ.	
	23.		27th Oct. Div will entrain at SAULTY and BEAUMETZ. Wire from 3rd Army re: dates of entraining at BEAUMETZ & SAULTY not confirmed	
	24		Divl. Commander inspected 119 Bde. near SIMENCOURT. Bde marched past.	

WAR DIARY
—or—
INTELLIGENCE SUMMARY
(Erase heading not required.)

Third Sheet. Army Form C. 2118

Secret.
October 1917.
A. D. Vet. Services H.Q. 46th Division

Place	Date 1917 Octr	Hour	Summary of Events and Information	Remarks and references to Appendices
FOSSEUX	25		Divl. Artillery trekking at PERONNE on 27th & 28th October to occupy NORDPEENE area	Copy
	26		detraining at GODEWAERSVELDE. Arrangements made to obtain Sulla from Bully tins in lieu —	Copy
	27		Divl. Artillery returns to PERONNE area.	Copy
	28		Instructions received (Control name of an officer recommended for Order of the Merite Agricole. (No names forward)	Copy
LUCHEUX	29		46 Divn (Less artillery & services + Pionier Bn.) marched to LUCHEUX area	Copy
"	30		quartered as shewn in appendix B. Reinforcement rathead at BEAUMETZ. Supply Refilling pt. at POMMERA. COULLEMONT and WARLUZEL.	Copy appendix B —
"	31		Casualties killed officers nil others nil 17 wounded officers 4 others ranks 72 month October	Copy

C. J. Moorehouse
A.D.V.S.
46th Divn.

SECRET.

40TH DIVISION.

DISTRIBUTION OF UNITS ON AND FROM 13TH OCTOBER, 1917.

A.

Unit.	Location.	Remarks.
40TH DIVNL. HD.QRS. Complete.	FOSSEUX.	
Senior Chaplain, (Non-C.of E.)	BERNEVILLE.	With 135th Fld.Amb.
D.A.D.O.S.	BEAUMETZ.	Close to Station.
O.C., Divnl. Employment Co) Divnl. Salvage Officer.)	MONCHIET.	
ROYAL ARTILLERY. Complete.	Detached to III Corps.	Personnel Railhead, PERONNE.
ROYAL ENGINEERS. Headquarters. 224th Fld.Coy. R.E. 231st Fld.Coy. R.E. 229th Fld.Coy. R.E.	Detached to III Corps. GOUY-EN-ARTOIS.	Personnel Railhead, PERONNE.
119TH INF. BRIGADE. Headquarters. 19th R.W. Fuslrs. 12th S.W. Bordrs. 17th Welsh Regt. 18th Welsh Regt. 119th M. G. Coy.) 119th T. M. Batty.)	GOUY-EN-ARTOIS. SIMENCOURT. GOUY-EN-ARTOIS. SIMENCOURT. GOUY-EN-ARTOIS. MONCHIET.	
120TH INF. BRIGADE. Headquarters. 11th K.O.R.L. Regt. 13th E. Surrey Regt.) 14th H. L. I.) 14th A.& S. Highrs. 120th M. G. Coy.) 120th T. M. Batty.)	BERNEVILLE. SIMENCOURT. BERNEVILLE. SIMENCOURT. BERNEVILLE.	
121ST INF. BRIGADE. Headquarters. 12th Suffolk Regt. 13th Yorkshire Regt. 20th Middlesex Regt. 21st Middlesex Regt. 121st M. G. Coy. 121st T. M. Batty.	BARLY. BAVINCOURT. BARLY. BAVINCOURT. FOSSEUX. LA HERLIERE. BARLY.	
12th YORKS. REGT.(Pnrs).	Detached to III Corps.	Personnel Railhead, PERONNE.
244th MACHINE GUN COY.	LA HERLIERE.	

S E C R E T.

40TH DIVISION.

DISTRIBUTION OF UNITS, ON NIGHT 29/30TH OCTOBER, 1917.

Unit.	Location.	Remarks.
40TH DIVNL. HD.QRS.		
Complete.	LUCHEUX.	
S.C. (Non C. of E.)	With 135th Fld.Amb.	
D.A.D.O.S.	MONDICOURT.	
O.C., Divnl. Emplyt. Coy.)	LUCHEUX.	
Divnl. Salvage Officer)		
ROYAL ARTILLERY.		
Complete.	PERONNE.	Detached.
ROYAL ENGINEERS.		
Headquarters.)		
½/224 Fld.Coy.R.E.)	PERONNE.	Detached to III Cps.
231 Field Coy.R.E.)		
229 Field Coy.R.E.	MOISLAINS.	Detached to III Cps.
½/224 Fld.Coy. R.E.	SUS-ST-LEGER.	With 121 Inf.Bde.
119TH INF. BRIGADE.		
Headquarters.	COUTURELLE.	
19th R.W. Fusiliers.	COUTURELLE.	
12th S.W. Borderers.	HUMBERCOURT.	
17th Welsh Regiment.	COULLEMONT.	
18th Welsh Regiment.	LUCHEUX.	
119th M.G. Company.)	HUMBERCOURT.	
119th T.M. Battery.)		
120TH INF. BRIGADE.		
Headquarters.	POMMERA.	
11th K.O.R.L. Regt.	HALLOY.	
13th E. Surrey Regt.	GRENAS.	
14th H.L.I.	POMMERA.	
14th A.& S. Highrs.	HALLOY.	
120th M.G. Company.)	POMMERA.	
120th T.M. Battery.)		
121ST INF. BRIGADE.		
Headquarters.)		
12th Suffolk Regt.)	SUS-ST-LEGER.	
13th Yorkshire Regt.)		
20th Middlesex Regt.)	WARLUZEL.	
21st Middlesex Regt.)		
121st M.G. Company.)	SOMBRIN.	
121st T.M. Battery.)		
12th YORKS. REGT. (Pnrs.)	MOISLAINS.	Detached to III Corps.
244TH MACHINE GUN COY.	WARLINCOURT.	
40TH DIVNL. TRAIN, A.S.C.		
Headquarters.	POMMERA.	
No. 1 Company.	PERONNE.	With 40th Divnl. Arty.
No. 2 Company.	COULLEMONT.	
No. 3 Company.	POMMERA.	
No. 4 Company.	WARLUZEL.	

/Over.

Unit.	Location.	Remarks.
No. 25 DIVNL. SUPPLY COL.	POMMERA.	
No. 55 A.S.P.		
S.A.A. SECTION.	POMMERA.	
H.Q. & Remainder.	PERONNE.	With 40th Divnl. Arty.
135th Fld. Ambulance.	GRENAS.	
136th Fld. Ambulance.	LUCHEUX.	
137th Fld. Ambulance.	WARLUZEL.	
51st Mobile Vet. Sec.	WARLINCOURT.	
40th Divnl. Depot Bn.	SAULTY.	

(RSJ)

SECRET.   ORIGINAL.
-------------------   -------------------

WAR   DIARY

O F

"A"   AND   "Q"

B R A N C H.

40TH   DIVISION.

For period -   1st to 30th November, 1917.

———————————

VOL   XVIII.

WAR DIARY

November 1917
A & Q
Hd Qrts 40th Division

Army Form C. 2118

INTELLIGENCE SUMMARY
(Erase heading not required.)

Instructions regarding War Diaries and Intelligence Summaries are contained in F.S. Regs., Part II. and the Staff Manual respectively. Title Pages will be prepared in manuscript.

Secret

Place	Date Nov 1917	Hour	Summary of Events and Information	Remarks and references to Appendices
LUCHEUX	1		Division to be transferred from III Army to Third Corps for administrative purposes	A&Q
	2		Leave extended from 10 to 14 days - (15 days via Havre).	A&Q
			Nothing definite known of length of stay of Division in this area, causing difficulties as regards formation of Canteens and arrangements for divisional troops, as well as training programmes.	A&Q
	3		Canteens at each Bde. Head Qtrs. arranged for.	A&Q
	4		Winds of Division quartered as shewn in Appendix A.	A&Q / Appendix A
	5		Canteens established at LUCHEUX, WARLUZEL and POMMERA. The divisional band plays daily at different localities. Divisional troops perform 4 times weekly at various Centres.	A&Q / A
	6		ADOS required to move from MONDICOURT (wanted by III Corps as a reinforcement depot) to near SAULTY.	A&Q
	7		50 additional leave vacancies allotted to the Division.	A&Q
	8		Gymnasium starts a week ago to obtain expertise staff from tent, doing good work.	A&Q
	9		R & H Corps of the Div. Artillery quartered at STRICOURT & MOISLAINS, away from Division under III Corps	A&Q
	10		Boxing competitions arranged. Finals to take place at BELLEVUE on the 12th + 13th.	A&Q
	11		Through mischances of transport - inspection - of pack animals & of farry, XI Corps laundry at ARRAS unable to return clean clothing. Arrangements made by DADOS to obtain clothing elsewhere.	A&Q
	12		Div. Arty. attached to Division not received clean clothes for some time. Clean clothes obtd. from this Division.	A&Q
	13		Lt.Col. J. Leckie CMG to Div.Train evacuated to base sick.	A&Q
	14		Lt.Col. Carmichael to proceed to England vacancy quartermaster of 14 A & S Hrs.	A&Q
	15		Depot Bn to move to LEALVILLERS. Reinforcement railhead at BELLEEGLISE at a date to be fixed - as shewn in appendix B.	Appendix B
FOSSEUX	16		Divn. moved to FOSSEUX area, quartered as shewn in appendix C.	Appendix B / Appendix C
ACHIET LE PETIT	17		Divn moved to Achiet-le-Petit area quartered as shewn in appendix C.	A&Q
	18		DADOS moved to South of BAPAUME.	

1875 Wt. W593/826 1,000,000 4/15 J.B.C. & A. A.D.S.S./Forms/C. 2118.

Secret

WAR DIARY
or
INTELLIGENCE SUMMARY
(Erase heading not required.)

November 1917 Army Form C. 2118

A.& Q.
H.Q. 2th "Division"

Place	Date Nov 1917	Hour	Summary of Events and Information	Remarks and references to Appendices
ACHIET LE PETIT	19		Division marches to areas as shown in appendix D. Divisional HQ. established at N.of Haplincourt.	appendix A.
N. HAPLINCOURT	20		Arrangements made to bivouac & encamp. Staff pushes to DOIGNIES, BEAUMETZ and LE BUCQUIERE respectively. 2 Sqdns. N. Irish Horse & 2 Cyclist Coys. attached to Division.	appx D. appx E.
"	21			appx
BEAUMETZ	22		No 2nd Division bivouacked. Beaumetz 21.20d. moved to HAVRINCOURT in lorries 22nd. 2 R.F. Bttns. moved to GRAINCOURT one (18th) staying at LE BUCQUIERE. Div.Train went to HERMIES.	appx
HAVRINCOURT	23		Attack of 4th Divn. on BOURLON. No further advance. moved up to ATTR ESCAULT. Route in very indifferent condition. Congestion of transport. Roads not sufficient for amount of traffic in wet weather. Bivouac station established at GRAINCOURT. S.A. Rear H.Qrs. at NEUVILLE - BOURJONVAL.	appx
"	24		BOURLON Village & Wood captured. Repeated counter attacks repulsed. Ammunition supply:- amounts brought fwd. to GRAINCOURT. 1,315,000 rounds S.A. also grenades, flares etc.	appx
"	25		Prisoners captured number 409. excluding wounded. Casualties estimated at Offrs 172 O.R. 4017. Division Relieved by 42nd Division.	appx appendix E.
"	26			appx
NEUVILLE BOURJONVAL	27		Sudden orders Divn. moved by rail to Basseux area. Location of units shown in appendix	appendix F.
BASSEUX	28		Units quartered as shown in appendix F.	
"	29		Ordered to relieve 16th Divn. in front line, near Croisilles & BULLECOURT.	appx
"	30		Standing by for a move at 2 hours notice. Orders to relieve 16th Divn. cancelled.	

C.S. Moggit aaQmg
Lt.Col.

SECRET.

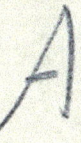

40TH DIVISION.
DISTRIBUTION OF UNITS, 4TH NOVEMBER, 1917.

Unit.	Location	Remarks.
40TH DIVNL. HD.QRS. Complete.	LUCHEUX.	
S.C.(Non C of E).	With 135th Fld Amb.	
D.A.D.O.S.	MONDICOURT.	
O.C., Divnl.Emplyt.Coy.	LUCHEUX.	
Divnl.Salvage Officer.	MONDICOURT.	
ROYAL ARTILLERY.		
Headquarters.	PERONNE.	
178th Brigade.R.F.A.)		
40th Div.Ammn.Col.)		Detached to III Corps.
40th D.T.M's.)	NURLU.	
181st Brigade.R.F.A.	EQUANCOURT WOOD.	
ROYAL ENGINEERS.		
Headquarters.)		
½/224 Field Coy.)	EQUANCOURT	Detached to III Corps.
231 Field Coy.)		
229 Field Coy.	MOISLAINS.	Det. to III Corps.
½/224 Field Coy.	SUS-ST-LEGER.	With 121 Inf.Bde.
119TH INF. BRIGADE.		
Headquarters.	COUTURELLE.	
19th R.W.Fusiliers.	COUTURELLE.	
12th S.W.Borderers.	HUMBERCOURT.	
17th Welsh Regiment.	COULLEMONT.	
18th Welsh Regiment.	LUCHEUX.	
119th M.G.Company.)		
119th T.M.Battery.)	HUMBERCOURT.	
120TH INF.BRIGADE.		
Headquarters.	POMMERA.	
11th K.O.R.L.Regt.	HALLOY.	
13th E.Surrey Regt.	GRENAS.	
14th H.L.I.	POMMERA.	
14th A & S Hdrs.	HALLOY.	
120th M.G.Company.)		
120th T.M.Battery.)	WARLINCOURT.	
121ST INF. BRIGADE.		
Headquarters.)		
12th Suffolk Regt.)		
13th Yorkshire Regt.)	SUS-ST-LEGER.	
20th Middlesex Regt.		
21st Middlesex Regt.)	WARLUZEL.	
121st M.G.Company.)		
121st T.M.Battery.)	SOMBRIN.	
12TH YORKS? REGT.(P).	MOISLAINS.	Detached to III Corps.
244TH MACHINE GUN COY.	WARLINCOURT.	

/Over.

- 2 -

Unit.	Location.	Remarks.
40TH DIVNL. TRAIN, A.S.C.		
Headquarters.	POMMERA.	
No. 1 Company.	PERONNE.	With 40th Divnl.Arty.
No. 2 Company.	COULLEMONT.	
No. 3 Company.	POMMERA.	
No. 4 Company.	WARLUZEL.	
NO. 25 DIVNL. SUPY. COL.	POMMERA.	
NO. 55 A.S.P.		
S.A.A. SECTION.	POMMERA.	
H.Q. & remainder.	PERONNE.	With 40th Divnl.Arty.
135th Field Ambulance.	GRENAS.	
136th Field Ambulance.	LUCHEUX.	
137th Field Ambulance.	WARLUZEL.	
51st Mobile Vet. Sec.	WARLINCOURT.	
40th Divnl. Depot Bn.	SAULTY.	

(WB).

SECRET.

40TH DIVISION.

DISTRIBUTION OF UNITS IN FOSSEUX AREA, 16th November, 1917.

Unit.	Location.	Remarks.
40th DIVNL. HD.QRS.	FOSSEUX.	
S.C.F. (Non C.of E.)	With 135th Field Ambulance.	
D.A.D.O.S.)		
Divnl.Salvage Offr.)	LA HERLIERE.	
Divnl.Claims Offr.)		
Divnl. Employment Company.	FOSSEUX.	
ROYAL ARTILLERY.		
Headquarters.	PERONNE.	)
178th Brigade R.F.A.)		)
40th Divnl.Ammn.Col.)	NURLU.	) Detached
40th Div. Trench Mtrs)		) to III Corps.
181st Brigade R.F.A.	EQUANCOURT WOOD.	)
ROYAL ENGINEERS.		
Headquarters.)		)
½/224 Field Coy.)	EQUANCOURT.	) Detached to
231st Field Coy.)		) III Corps.
229th Field Coy.	MOISLAINS.	)
½/224th Field Coy.	LA HERLIERE.	With 121st Infy. Bde.
119th INFANTRY BRIGADE.		
Headquarters.	GOUY-EN-ARTOIS.	
19th R.Welsh Fusrs.	SIMENCOURT.	
12th South Wales Bdrs.	GOUY-EN-ARTOIS.	
17th Welsh Regt.	SIMENCOURT.	
18th Welsh Regt.	GOUY-EN-ARTOIS.	
119th Machine Gun Coy.)	MONCHIET.	
119th Trench Mortar Bty)		
120th INFANTRY BRIGADE.		
Headquarters.	BERNEVILLE.	
11th Kings Own (R.Lanc.Rgt).	SIMENCOURT.	
13th East Surrey Regt.)	BERNEVILLE.	
14th High.Light Infy.)		
14th A.& Suth. Highrs.	SIMENCOURT.	
120th Machine Gun Coy.)	BERNEVILLE.	
120th Trench Mortar Bty)		
121st INFANTRY BRIGADE.		
Headquarters.	BARLY.	
12th Suffolk Regt.	BAVINCOURT.	
13th Yorkshire Regt.	BARLY.	
20th Middlesex Regt.	BAVINCOURT.	
21st Middlesex Regt.	FOSSEUX.	
121st Machine Gun Coy.	LA HERLIERE.	
121st Trench Mortar By	BARLY.	
12th YORKS. REGT. (P).	MOISLAINS.	Det.to III Corps

/Over.

Unit.	Location.	Remarks.
244th MACHINE GUN Coy.	LA HERLIERE.	
40th DIVISIONAL TRAIN, ASC.		
Headquarters.	FOSSEUX.	
No.1 Company.	ETRICOURT.	With 40/Div.Arty.
No.2 Company.	GOUY-EN-ARTOIS.	
No.3 Company.	BERNEVILLE.	
No.4 Company.	BARLY.	
No.25 DIVNL.SUPPLY Col.	GOUY-EN-ARTOIS.	
Detachment.	ETRICOURT.	With Det.Troops.
No.55 AMMN.SUB PARK.		
S.A.A. Section.	GOUY-EN-ARTOIS.	With 25 D.S.C.
Hd.Qrs. & remainder.	GURLU WOOD.	Detached.
135th Field Ambulance.	BERNEVILLE.	
136th Field Ambulance.	GOUY-EN-ARTOIS.	
137th Field Ambulance.	BARLY.	
51st Mobile Vet.Sec.	MONCHIET.	
40th Divnl.Depot Battn.	SAULTY.	

S E C R E T.   40TH DIVISION --- LOCATION OF UNITS.

Unit.	Night 18/19th Novr.	Night 19/20th Novr.
40th Divnl.Hd.Qrs.	ACHIET-LE-PETIT.	Camp 1 mile N. of HAPLINCOURT.
119th Brigade Group.	GOMIECOURT.	BARASTRE.
120th Brigade Group.	COURCELLES-LE-COMTE.	BEAULENCOURT.
121st Brigade Group.	ACHIET-LE-PETIT.	ROCQUIGNY.
Royal Artillery.	PERONNE.	PERONNE.
Field Coys. R.E.	)Detached III Corps Area.	(With groups as follows :-
	)Railhead PERONNE.	(C.R.E. 40/Div.H.Q.; 224/Fd.Co. - 121/Bde Group.
	)	(229/Fd.Co. - 119/Bde Group;
	)	(231/Fd.Co. - 120/Bde Group.
12th Yorks.Regt. (P).	COURCELLES-LE-COMTE.	BEAULENCOURT.
244th M.G. Company.	ABLAINZEVELLE.	ABLAINZEVELLE.
No.25 Div.Sup.Colmn.	SAULTY.	SAULTY.
Divnl. Depot Battn.		
RAILHEAD.	ACHIET-LE-GRAND.	BAPAUME.

UNITS OF BRIGADE GROUPS.

119th Brigade Group.
Headquarters.
19th Royal Welsh Fus.
12th South Wales Borderers.
17th Welsh Regt.
18th Welsh Regt.
119th Machine Gun Company.
119th Trench Mortar Batty.
No.2 Cy. A.S.C.
136th Field Ambulance.

229th Field Coy. R.E.

120th Brigade Group.
Headquarters.
11th Kings Own (R.Lanc.Regt.)
13th East Surrey Regt.
14th Highland Light Infy.
14th A. & Suth. Hrs.
120th Machine Gun Coy.
120th Trench Mortar Batty.
No. 3 Coy. A.S.C.
135th Field Ambulance.
and R.E. Companies as follows :-
231st Field Coy. R.E.

121st Brigade Group.
Headquarters.
12th Suffolk Regt.
13th Yorkshire Regt.
20th Middlesex Regt.
21st Middlesex Regt.
121st Machine Gun Coy.
121st Trench Mortar Batty.
No. 4 Coy. A.S.C.
157th Field Ambulance.

224th Field Coy. R.E.

S E C R E T.   40TH DIVISION.

TABLE SHEWING ALLOTMENT OF ACCOMMODATION ON NIGHT OF 19/20TH NOVEMBER, 1917.

Map Ref. Sheet 57 c. 1/40,000.

Unit.	Area.	Detail and map reference of Camps.	Huts in terms of Nissen Huts.	Billeting parties to report to	Remarks.
40th Divnl.Hd.Qrs. complete incl. C.R.E.	-	I.34.a.3.5.	-	Direct to Camp.	
119th Brigade Group incl. 229th Field Coy. R.E.	BARASTRE.	Bde.H.Q. 0.15.b.9.7. 1 Bn. 0.9.d.9.4. 1 Bn. 0.10.c.9.2. 1 Bn. 0.16.d.0.9. 1 Bn. 0.16.d.1.6. M.G.Coy. 0.16.d.1.7. T.M.Bty. 0.16.cent. Fld.Amb. 0.15.b.9.9. Fld.Coy. 0.10.c.2.5.	8 40 40 40 26 plus tents 1 plus tents 5 16 15	Area Commandant, 'P' Area, BARASTRE.	Should the Fld.Coy. Camp be occupied by troops of 1st King Edwards' Horse they are to be left in and Fld.Coy. accommodated in Bn. Camps. A.S.C. Coy. to be allotted accommodation in area by Bde. Hd.Qrs.
Hd.Qrs., 40th Divnl Train, A.S.C.	BARASTRE.	To be allotted by 119th Inf. Bde. from their Area.	-	H.Q., 119th Inf. Brigade.	
120th Brigade Group incl. 231 Fld.Coy. R.E. and 12th Yorks. (P).	BEAULENCOURT	Bde.H.Q. N.24.b.1.3. 1 Bn. N.18.c.3.8. 1 Bn. N.18.c.5.5. 1 Bn. N.18.c.4.3. 1 Bn. N.24.b.3.0. 1 Fld.Coy. N.18.c.6.3. M.G.Coy. N.18.a.9.3. T.M.Bty. N.18.a.5.2. Fld.Amb. N.24.d.5.5.	9 35) 44 9) 44 43 44 13 13 5 17	Area Commandant, 'M' Area BEAULENCOURT.	35 Huts in Camp at N.18. c.3.8. allotted to 12th Yorks. (P). Remainder of all Camp in BEAULENCOURT Area allotted to 120th Bde. Group incl. 231 Fld.Coy. R.E. A.S.C. Coy. to be allotted accommodation in Area by Bde. Hd.Qrs.

Unit.	Area.	Detail and Map reference of Camps.	Huts in terms of Nissen Huts.	Billeting Parties to report to.	Remarks.
244th Machine Gun Coy.	BEAULENCOURT.	N.18.b.0.3.	13	Area Commandant, 'M' Area, BEAULENCOURT.	
51st Mobile Vet. Sec.	BEAULENCOURT.	In same camp as 244th Machine Gun Coy., by arrangement direct between 2 Units concerned.			
121st Brigade Group. including 224th Field Coy.R.E.	IV Corps Musketry and Reinfct. Camps, South of ROCQUIGNY.	C.33.b. and O.34.a.	Total accomdn. for 4,500 men.	Commandant at Camp.	Troops of King Edward's Horse and of 1 Motor M.G.Batty. will also be in this area.

No 25 D S C E remains at ablainzeville

S E C R E T.

LOCATION OF UNITS OF 40TH DIVISION on 26TH November, 1917.

Map Reference Sheet 57c. 1/40,000.

Unit.	Location.	Wagon Lines	Remarks.
40TH DIVNL. HD.QRS. (Complete).	NEUVILLE-BOUR-JONVAL.	-	-
S.C.F. (Non C.of E.)	With 135th Fld.Amb.		
D.A.D.O.S.) O.C., Divnl.Emplyt.Co.)	Sugar Factory, BEAULENCOURT.	-	-
Divnl. Claims Offr.	SAULTY.		
ROYAL ARTILLERY.			
Headquarters.	With Divnl. Hd.Qrs.		
178th Bde. R.F.A.	In the Line.	HAVRINCOURT.	
181st Bde. R.F.A.	In the Line.	FLESQUIERES.	
40th Div.Ammn.Col. H.Q. & Nos.1 & 2 Sons.	TRESCAULT.	With Unit.	
S.A.A. Section.	NEUVILLE-BOURJONVAL.	do.	
40th Div.Trench Mtrs.	TRESCAULT.		
ROYAL ENGINEERS.			
Headquarters.	HAVRINCOURT Chateau Grounds.		
224 Fld.Coy.R.E.	HAVRINCOURT.	With Unit.	
229 Fld.Coy.R.E.) 231 Fld.Coy.R.E.)	HAVRINCOURT.	do.	
119TH INF. BRIGADE.			
19th Royal Welsh Fus. 12th South Wales Bdrs. 17th Welsh Regt. 18th Welsh Regt. Headquarters. 119th M.G. Coy. 119th T.M. Batty.	LECHELLE Area.	With Units.	
120TH INF. BRIGADE.			
Headquarters. 11th K.O.R.L. Regt. 13th E.Surrey Regt. 14th High.Lt.Inf. 14th A.& S. Hrs. 120th M.G. Coy. 120th T.M. Batty.	Q.15.b.	With Units.	
121ST INF. BRIGADE.			
Headquarters. 12th Suffolk Regt. 13th Yorkshire Regt. 20th Middx. Regt. 21st Middx. Regt. 121st M.G. Coy. 121st T.M. Batty.	BERTINCOURT.	With Units.	
12th YORKS. RGT.(PNRS).	HAVRINCOURT.	With Unit.	
244TH MACHINE GUN COY.	In the Line.	S.W.of GRAIN-COURT.	

/Over.

- 2 -

Unit.	Location.	Wagon Lines.	Remarks.
40TH DIVNL.TRAIN, ASC.			
Headquarters.	With Div.H.Q.		
No. 1 Company.	Q.20.b.		
No. 2 Company.	With 119th Bde.	With Units.	
No. 3 Company.	NEUVILLE-BOUR-JONVAL.		
No. 4 Company.	With 121st Bde.		
No. 25 DIVNL. SUPPLY Col.	BERTINCOURT.		
No. 55 Ammn.Sub-Park.	ERVILLERS-BAPAUME Rd. (H.8.d. & H.15.a.)		
135th Field Amb.	With 120th Bde.		
136th Field Amb.	With 119th Bde.		
137th Field Amb.	With 121st Bde.		
51st Mobile Vet.Sec.	RUYAULCOURT.		
40th Divnl.Depot Bn.	SAULTY.		

(RSJ)

S E C R E T.

LOCATION OF UNITS OF 40TH DIVISION ON 28TH NOVEMBER, 1917.

Unit.	Location.	Wagon Lines	Remarks.
40TH DIVNL. HD.QRS. (Complete).	BASSEUX.		
S.C.F. (Non C.of E.)	With 135th Fld.Amb.		
D.A.D.O.S.) O.C.,Divnl.Emplyt.Co.)	BEAUMETZ.		
Divnl. Claims Officer.	SAULTY.		
ROYAL ARTILLERY.			
Headquarters.	With Divnl. Hd.Qrs.		
178th Bde. R.F.A.	In the Line.	HAVRINCOURT.	Detached to IV Corps.
181st Bde. R.F.A.	In the Line.	FLESQUIERES.	
40th Div.Ammn.Col.			
H.Q.& Nos.1 & 2 Secs.	TRESCAULT.	With Unit.	
S.A.A. Section.	NEUVILLE-BOURJONVAL.	do.	
40th Div.T.M.Battys.	TRESCAULT.		
ROYAL ENGINEERS.			
Headquarters.	HAVRINCOURT Chateau. (Grounds).		Detached to IV Corps.
224 Fld.Coy. R.E.	HAVRINCOURT.	With Unit.	
229 Fld.Coy. R.E.	HAVRINCOURT.	do.	
231 Fld.Coy. R.E.	HAVRINCOURT.	do.	
119TH INF. BRIGADE.			
Headquarters.	POMMIER.		
19th R.W. Fuslrs.	BIENVILLERS.		
12th S.W. Bordrs.	BERLES-AU-BOIS.	With Units.	
17th Welsh Regt.	POMMIER.		
18th Welsh Regt.	BERLES-AU-BOIS.		
119th M.G. Coy.	POMMIER.		
119th T.M. Batty.	POMMIER.		
120TH INF. BRIGADE.			
Headquarters.	Quarry at BLAIREVILLE.		
11th K.O.R.L. Regt.			
13th E.Surrey Regt.	Hutments between BLAIREVILLE and HENDECOURT.	With Units.	
14th High.Lt.Inf.			
14th A.& S. Hrs.			
120th M.G. Coy.			
120th T.M. Batty.			
121ST INF. BRIGADE.			
Headquarters.	BAILLEULMONT.		
12th Suffolk Regt.	BAILLEULMONT.		
13th Yorks. Regt.	BELLACOURT.	With Units.	
20th Middx. Regt.	BAILLEUVAL.		
21st Middx. Regt.	BAILLEUVAL.		
121st M.G. Coy.	BELLACOURT.		
121st T.M. Batty.	BELLACOURT.		
12TH YORKS. RGT.(PNRS).	HAVRINCOURT.	With Unit.	Detached to IV Corps.
244TH MACHINE GUN COY.	With 120 Bde. Grp.	With Unit.	

/Over.

Unit.	Location.	Wagon Lines.	Remarks.

40TH DIVNL.TRAIN, ASC.
Headquarters.	With Divnl.H.Q.		
No. 1 Company.	Q.20.b.		Detached to IV Corps.
No. 2 Company.	With 119th Brigade.	With Units.	
No. 3 Company.	With 120th Brigade.		
No. 4 Company.	With 121 Bde. at BAILLEULMONT.		

No. 25 DIVNL.SUPPLY COL.   BEAUMETZ.

No. 55 AMMN. SUB PARK.
    ERVILLERS - BAPAUME Rd.(H.3.d. & H.15.a.)

135th Field Amb.	With 120th Brigade.
136th Field Amb.	With 119th Bde. at BIENVILLERS.
137th Field Amb.	With 121st Bde. at BAILLEULMONT.
61st Mob.Vet. Sec.	BASSEUX.
40th Divnl. Depot Bn.	SAULTY.

(RSJ)

SECRET.

ORIGINAL.

WAR DIARY OF

'A AND Q'

BRANCH

40TH DIVISION.

VOLUME XIX.

From 1st December, 1917 to 31st December, 1917.

28031 W3125/M2250 1000m 6/17 M.R.Co.,Ltd. (1367) Forms W3091. Army Form W. 3091.

Cover for Documents.

Nature of Enclosures.

Notes, or Letters written.

WAR DIARY
INTELLIGENCE SUMMARY
(Erase heading not required.)

Army Form C. 2118

40th Division A.F.A. December 1917

Place	Date 1917	Hour	Summary of Events and Information	Remarks and references to Appendices
BASSEUX	1		Orders received to relieve 16th Division in the line. Relief to be completed by the 8th. Casualties in recent fighting near BOURLON shown in appendix A.	Appendix A
	2		121st Bde Group proceed to HAMELINCOURT by motor lorry. Arrangements for move of Bdes.	Copy App A
BAHAG-NIES	3		119 Bde Group proceed by lorries to take over right sector. 121st Bde Inf. now Left sector.	
	4		120th Bde Group & Divl Head Quarters proceed to HAMELINCOURT. Div. Hd. Qtrs. & BAHAGNIES. Units located as shown in appendix B. 37th Coy RE & Pioneer Bn. rejoin the division.	App Appendix B
	5		Meeting of VI Corps Officers Club & discusses opening of torch club.	Copy
	6		Arrangements for opening canteens – Baths – gumboot stores & amp; kitchens in new area – only canteens existing. Baths require repair; gumboot stores & kitchens not existing.	Copy
	7		Items forming Trench Foot treatment Centres. No lists of trench stores handed over – then officers to be a very large amount of grenades in front line trenches; necessary to reorganize & arrange for better storage. No 250 D.S.F. in Division.	Copy
	8		Guise Head Qtrs. move to GOMMIECOURT. where bombing mission units to be carried out.	Copy
	9		Leave vacancies of division available average 120 a day. Proposed Xmas cards designed within the division. He played a role at 2 each.	Copy
	10		Lt. Col. E.J. Evans joined Command Historic Train vice Lt. Col. J.R. Leakie. Stores allotted to units out of Divl. Gnds. Grants for Xmas.	Copy
	11		Divl. Depot Battalion officered from SAULTY & ACHIET LE PETIT on 13th December.	Copy
	12		50 men to be transferred from 10 Yorks Regt to R.E. base depot as reinforcements.	Copy
	13		Names of NCOs & men recommended for M. Serva Medal additions to New Years Honours List – for Commander.	Copy
COMME-COURT	14		Divl. Hd. Qtrs. moved to GOMIECOURT, being new hutted camp built. Units located as shewn in appendix C.	Appendix C

WAR DIARY or **INTELLIGENCE SUMMARY**
(Erase heading not required.)

Army Form C. 2118

40th Divn
A + Q
December 1917. 2 pages

Place	Date 1917	Hour	Summary of Events and Information	Remarks and references to Appendices
GOMIECOURT	DEC 15		Reinforcements received since 1st Dec. Officers 53 Other ranks 1034	
			Casualties since 1st Dec'r. Killed - Officers - Other ranks 13 wounded Offs 8 O.r. 132 missing O.r. 2	
	16		3d Division require Khati over tents absolutely - Necessary to build shelter to obtain up African hut -	
	17		Category "B" men - Banbonin of not 3d Band to be transferred from R.A. to Divl. Supply Cy. -	CRA
	18	(wounded)	placed under open arrest in charge made by officer 38 Divn. that he was drunk	CRA
			at Doignies when acting as Town Major. One candidate for duty for a commission. the sub-joining the Army	
	19		Report signally allied that from a Frenchman at Warlugat. Probable trace authors of theft	CRA
	20		awards gained by the Divn in Bourlon Wood operations - V.D.S.O., 3 MoC's, 27 DCM's, 48 MC's, 27 DCM's, 15 Photo -	CRA
	21		Military medals. Major Lake S.S.O. returned for duty in England. Lieutcom Major Craig -	
	22		Lt Gen Sir C.Woollcombe Cd II Corps presented military medals to some of 170th Bde and Congratulated the Division on its gallant conduct when by Bourlon Wood and Village they were Captured - specially mentioning to 14 H.L.I. 3 Dni. in reserve.	CRA
	23		Orders for the "Divn" stoke over Corps front. 3 Bdes in line. 3d Divn. on the left 3 Divn in reserve. Brigade of reserve - Capt NWLC. Asst adjy S.S.O. Sanitation upon infantry. 100 men in each Pioneer Bn to be taken	CRA
	24		Major Bradshaw 550 protem to command 17 Welsh Pgt	CRA
	25		by 100 B1 men. Major Metcalfe offtg to command. H.Q.R.C.F. Lt. Col. Samuel 21 Middx Regt. Approved by England. Approved by Gen. Vice Br Gen. McLaren for England (CRA North Army) Palmer BG offtg T/Brfgd. CRA to been Vice Br Gen McLaren for England (CRA North Army)	CRA
	26		Capt of the Post lt and necessary Khaki returns in sufficient points.	CRA
	27		Major Scarlett offtg to command 181 Bde RFA vice Col Palmer	CRA
	28	(wounded)	Lott Prevost Bde Major no post offtg G.S.O 2 62d Division killed by G.C.A. "Babes in the Wood" Pantomime 40 Divn Theatre Endless 3 times	Appendix D
	29		Units merry stoke over 3d Divl front -	CRA
	30		a week. Units located as shown in Appendix D wounded 130	
	31		Casualties 16 Dec to 31 Dec. Officers killed - wounded 14 - wounded 130	
			Other ranks killed 13	

C.Y.Moore Alc Lt Col
a+q 40 Divn.

40TH. DIVISION.

CASUALTIES TO DATE.

1st December.

UNIT.	ACTUAL CASUALTIES.						ESTIMATED CASUALTIES.	
	Killed.		Wounded.		Missing.			
	Off.	o. r.	Off.	o. r.	Off.	o. r.	Offrs.	o. r.
119th INF. BRIGADE.								
19th R. W. Fusrs.	6	31	11	288	1	85	16	443
12th S.W. Bords.	8	46	13	245	1	77	18	390
17th Welsh Regt.	3	44	8	105	6	145	13	240
18th Welsh Regt.	7	59	9	110	1	152	13	400
119th M.G. Coy.	1	8	3	34	-	6	4	44
120th INF. BRIGADE.								
11th R. Lancs. Regt.	-	7	4	65	-	15	8	250
13th E. Surrey Regt.	3	40	1	111	2	79	20	500
14th H. Lt Infy. o.r.466.	1	x	2	x	14	x	20	550
14th A & S. Hrs.	2	34	5	124	-	24	11	300
120th M.G. Coy.	-	-	-	-	-	-	1	10
121st INF. BRIGADE.								
12th Suffolk Regt.	-	23	6	100	1	25	7	150
13th Yorks. Rgt.	6	20	9	122	3	72	17	300
20th Middx. Regt.	2	22	10	149	-	18	11	250
21st Middx. Regt.	2	18	7	95	-	6	10	150
121st M. G. Coy.	2	4	3	21	-	-	3	40
12th Yorks. Rgt.(P).	-	2	1	14	1	-		
178th Brigade RFA.	-	4	2	14	-	-		
181st Brigade RFA.	-	3	-	12	-	-		
40th D. A. C. RFA.	-	-	-	1	-	-		
224th Field Coy. RE.	-	-	1	-	-	-		
229th do	-	3	-	12	-	-		
231st do	1	-	-	-	-	-		
Signal Coy.	-	-	-	2	-	-		
135 Field Ambce.	-	-	-	3	-	-		
136 do	-	-	-	4	-	-		
137 do	1	-	-	-	-	-		
244th M. G. Coy.	-	-	1	22	-	-		
RAMC att. 21 Middx.	-	-	1	-	-	-		
TOTAL.	45	368	97	1653	30	704	172	4017.

Total actual casualties,
Offrs. 172   o.r. 2725
Add:-   o.r. 466 H.L.I. not classified
Total   Offrs. 172   o.r. 3191

S E C R E T.

LOCATION OF UNITS OF 40TH DIVISION ON 3RD DECEMBER, 1917.

Map Refs. Sheets 57c. and 51b. 1/40,000.

Unit.	Location.	Wagon Lines.	Remarks.
40TH DIVNL. HD.QRS. (Complete). S.C.F.(Non C.of E.)	BEHAGNIES CAMP. (H.2.a.4.7). With 135th Fld.Amb.		
D.A.D.O.S. O.C., Div.Emplyt.Coy.	ERVILLERS. (B.19.b.5.6.)		
Divnl. Claims Offr.	SAULTY.		
ROYAL ARTILLERY.			
Headquarters.	With Divnl.Hd.Qrs.		
178th Bde. R.F.A.	In the Line.	HAVRINCOURT.	
181st Bde. R.F.A.	In the Line.	FLESQUIERES.	Detached
40th Div.Ammn.Col.			to
H.Q. & Nos.1 & 2 Secs.	TRESCAULT.	With Unit.	V Corps.
S.A.A. Section.	NEUVILLE-BOURJONVAL.	do.	
40th Div.T.M. Battys.	TRESCAULT.		
ROYAL ENGINEERS.			
Headquarters.	With Divnl. Hd.Qrs.		
224 Fld.Coy. R.E.	BOIRY BECQUERELLE. (T.8.c.45.10.)	With Units.	Arrive on 4/12/17.
229 Fld. Coy.R.E.	ST.LEGER (B.4.a.8.7.)		
231 Fld.Coy. R.E.	HAMELINCOURT (S.29.d.3.4)		
Div.Signal Coy.H.Q.	With Divnl. Hd.Qrs.		
119TH INFANTRY BRIGADE.			
Headquarters.	L'HOMME MORT (B.17.a.9.8.)		
19th R.W. Fuslrs.			
12th S.W. Bordrs.			
17th Welsh Regt.	In the Line.	ERVILLERS.	
18th Welsh Regt.	Right Sector.		
119th M.G. Coy.			
119th T.M. Batty.			
120TH INF. BRIGADE.			
Headquarters.	HAMELINCOURT (A.5.b.2.1)		
11th K.O.R.L. Regt.	CLONMEL CAMP (A.5.a.8.8)		
13th E. Surrey Regt.	ARMAGH CAMP (S.23.c.5.0)		
14th High.Lt.Inf.	BELFAST CAMP (B.13.a.9.4)	With Units.	
14th A.& S. Hrs.	INNISKILLING CAMP (B.13.b.6.4)		
120th M.G. Coy.	MOYNE CAMP (S.28.d.4.4)		
120th T.M. Batty.			
121ST INF. BRIGADE.			
Headquarters.	T.21.d.6.8.	CLONMEL Cp.(A.5.a.8.8)	
12th Suffolk Regt.		BELFAST Cp.(B.13.a.9.4)	
13th Yorkshire Regt.		INNISKILLING Cp.(B13b64)	
20th Middx. Regt.	In the Line.	ARMAGH Cp.(S.23.c.5.0)	
21st Middx. Regt.	Left Sector.	ERVILLERS.	
121st M.G. Coy.			
121st T.M. Batty.			

/Over.

Unit.	Location.	Wagon Lines.	Remarks.
12TH YORKS.RGT.(PNRS).	BOYELLES CAMP. (T.13.a.1.6)	With Unit.	Arrives 4/12/17.
244th M.G. Coy.	With 120th Bde.Grp. (At BELFAST Camp).	With Unit.	
40TH DIVNL.TRAIN, A.S.C. Headquarters.	BOIRY ST.MARTIN. (S.14.b.1.5.)	} With Units.	No.1 Coy. detached With V Cps.
No. 1 Company.	Q.20.b.		
No. 2 Company.	S.10.d.3.1.		
No. 3 Company.	S.14.b.3.5.		
No. 4 Company.	S.14.b.1.1.		
No.25 DIVNL.SUPPLY COL.	RANSART.		
No.55 AMMN.SUB PARK.	ERVILLERS-BAPAUME RD. (H.8.d. & H.15.a)		
135th Fld. Ambulance.	SAPIGNIES.	} With Unit.	
136th Fld. Ambulance.	HAMELINCOURT.		
137th Fld. Ambulance.	ERVILLERS.		
51st Mobile Vet. Sec.	S.14.c.6.4.		
40th Divnl. Depot Bn.	SAULTY.		

(RSJ)

SECRET.   40TH DIVISION.

LOCATION OF UNITS on EVENING OF 14TH DECEMBER, 1917.

UNIT.	LOCATION.	WAGON LINES.
40TH DIVNL.HD.QRS. (Complete).	GOMIECOURT.	
S.C.F.(non C.of E.)	With 136th Fld.Amb.	
D.A.D.O.S.) O.C.,Div.Emplyt.Coy.)	ERVILLERS. (B.19.b.5.6.)	
Divnl. Claims Offr.	SAULTY.	

ROYAL ARTILLERY.
Headquarters.	With Divnl.Hd.Qrs.	
178th Bde., R.F.A.	In the Line.	ARGYLE Cmp.(S.17.a.6.2)
181st Bde., R.F.A.	In the Line.	Southern portion, HAMELINCOURT.

40th Divnl.Ammn.Col.
H.Q. & 1 Section.	S.28.d.9.1.
1 Section.	S.29.a.4.9.
S.A.A. Section.	S.30.c.1.7.

40th Divnl.T.M. Battys.   ST. LEGER.

ROYAL ENGINEERS.
Headquarters.	With Divnl.Hd.Qrs.	
224th Fld.Coy. R.E.	BOIRY BECQUERELLE. (T.8.c.45.10.)	
229th Fld.Coy. R.E.	ST. LEGER (B.4.a.8.7)	With Units.
231st Fld.Coy. R.E.	HAMELINCOURT (S.29.d.3.4)	
Div.Signal Coy.H.Q.	With Divnl.Hd.Qrs.	

119TH INF. BRIGADE.
Headquarters.	L'HOMME MORT (B.17.a.9.8)	Camp along ERVILLERS-ST.LEGER Road.
19th R.W. Fuslrs.		
12th S.W. Bordrs.	—	— INNISKILLING CAMP.
17th Welsh Regt.	In the Line.	
18th Welsh Regt.	Right Sector.	Camp along ERVILLERS-ST.LEGER Road.
119th M.G. Coy.		
119th T.M. Batty.		

120TH INF. BRIGADE.
Headquarters.	T.31.d.6.8.	
11th K.O.R.L. Regt.		CLONMEL Cmp.(A.5.a.8.8)
13th E.Surrey Regt.		ARMAGH Cmp.(S.23.c.5.0)
14th High.Lt.Inf.	In the Line.	BELFAST Cp.(B.13.a.9.4)
14th A.& S. Highrs.	Left Sector.	INNIS'G Cp.(B.13.b.6.4)
120th M.G. Coy.		MOYNE Cmp. (S.28.d.4.4)
120th T.M. Batty.		do. do.

121ST INF. BRIGADE.
Headquarters.	HAMELINCOURT(A.5.b.2.1)	CLONMEL CAMP.
12th Suffolk Regt.	CLONMEL CAMP.	do.
13th Yorks. Regt.	BELFAST CAMP.	BELFAST CAMP.
20th Middx. Regt.	BOYELLES Cmp.(T.13.a.1.6)	With Unit.
21st Middx. Regt.	ARMAGH CAMP.	ARMAGH CAMP.
121st M.G. Coy.	In the line with Left Bde.	MOYENVILLE.
121st T.M. Batty.	Detached to 119 Bde.	do.

/Over.

UNIT.	LOCATION.	TRANSPORT LINES.
<u>12th YORKS.RGT.(PNRS).</u>	H.Q.& 3 Coys.ST.LEGER. 1 Coy. CROISILLES.	BOYELLES CAMP. (T.13.a.1.6.)
244th Machine Gun Coy.	In the Line, Right Sec.	BELFAST CAMP.

<u>40TH DIV.TRAIN, A.S.C.</u>
  Headquarters.
  No. 1 Company.
  No. 2 Company.
  No. 3 Company.
  No. 4 Company.
	
	BOIRY ST MARTIN(S.14.b.1.5)
	do. do.
	S.10.d.3.1.
	S.14.b.3.5.
	S.14.b.1.1.
		}With Units.

<u>No.40 Div.Supply Col.</u>	ABLAINZEVELLE.	
<u>No. 55 Ammn.Sub Park.</u>	ERVILLERS-BAPAUME Road. (H.8.d. & H.15.a.)	
135th Fld. Ambulance. 136th Fld. Ambulance. 137th Fld. Ambulance.	BOIRY-BECQUERELLE. HAMELINCOURT. CLONMEL & ARMAGH Camps.	}With Units.
51st Mob.Vet. Section.	BOIRY ST MARTIN(S.14.c.6.4)	
40th Divn.Depot Battn.	ACHIET-LE-PETIT.	

ATTACHED UNITS.

No.14 Squadron, M.G.C. (Cavalry).	Camp at B.7.d.4.4.	
14th Army Fld.Artillery Brigade.	In the line.	BOISLEUX-ST-MARC, (S.12.c.3.8)
<u>16th Divnl. Artillery.</u> 177th Bde. R.F.A.	In the line.	Southern portion, HAMELINCOURT.
180th Bde. R.F.A. 16th Divnl.Ammn.Col.	In the Line. Same positions as 40th D.A.C.	Camp at B.7.c.

H.Q., 40th Division.

14th December, 1917.

(RSJ).

R. L. Cowtan.
Captain,
D.A.A.G.,
40th Division.

SECRET.

40TH DIVISION.

LOCATION OF UNITS ON 30TH DECEMBER, 1917.

UNIT.	LOCATION.	TRANSPORT LINES.
40th Div.Hd.Qrs. S.C.F. (Non C.of E). D.A.D.O.S. Divnl. Gas Officer. O.C. Div.Emp.Coy.	GOMIECOURT. With 136th Field Amb. ERVILLERS.	
ROYAL ARTILLERY. Head Qrs. 178th Bde. R.F.A. 181st Bde. R.F.A. 40th Div.Ammn.Column. H.Q. & 1 Section. 1 Section. S.A.A. Section.	 With Div. Hd. Qrs. In the Line. --do-- S.28.d.9.1. S.29.a.4.9. S.30.c.1.7.	 ARGYLE CAMP (S.17.a.6.2) HAMELINCOURT (South).
40th Div.T.M.Battys.	ST. LEGER.	
ROYAL ENGINEERS. Headquarter. 224 Fld. Coy. 229 Fld. Coy. 231 Fld. Coy. H.Q.Signal Coy.	 With Div.Hd.Qrs. ERVILLERS. ST. LEGER. Tunnl'g Cmp. MORY. (B.22.b.7.7) With Div.Hd.Qrs.	 With Unit. With Unit. With Unit.
119TH INF. BRIGADE. Headquarters. 19th R.W. Fuslrs. 12th S.W. Bordrs. 17th Welsh Regt. 18th Welsh Regt. 119th M.G. Coy. 119th T.M.Bty.	L'HOMME MORT B.17.a.9.8. In the Line, with Reserve Battn.in MORY North Camp, MORY. DYSART Camp.(B.14.c.6.2) and ERVILLERS. In the Line.	B.16.a.2.3. CLONMEL Cmp.(A.5.A.8.8.) INNISKILLING Cp(B13b64) BELFAST Cp.(B.13.a.9.4.) ARMAGH Cp. (S.23.c.5.0.) MOYENNEVILLE.
120TH INF. BRIGADE. Headquarters. 11th K.O.R.L.Regt. 13th E.Surrey Regt. 14th High.Lt.Inf. 14th A.& S.Highrs. 120th M.G. Coy. 120th T.M. Bty.	NOREUIL.(C.9.d.8.5). In the Line with Reserve Battn. in MORY South Camps A & B, MORY. In the Line. In the Line.	 DYSART CAMP.
121st INF. Brigade. Headquarters. 12th Suffolk Regt. 13th Yorks. Regt. 20th Middx.Regt. 21st Middx.Regt. 121st M.G. Coy. 121st T.M. Bty.	B.17.a.9.8. In the Line with Reserve Battn. in MORY ABBAYE CAMP, MORY. In the Line. In the line.	 South ERVILLERS.
12th Yorks. Regt. (P). H.Q. & 2 Coys. 2 Companies	 ST. LEGER. Tunnlg. Cmp. MORY.	BOYELLES (Temporarily). Move to nr. MORY by 31/12/17.

/Over.

- 2 -

Unit.	Location.	Transport Lines.
244th Machine Gun Coy.	In the line.	South ERVILLERS, with 121 and 233 M.G. Coys.
40th DIVNL. TRAIN, ASC. H.Q. and all Coys.	GOMIECOURT.	With Units.
40th DIV. SUPPLY COL.	RANSART.	
40TH AMMN. SUB PARK.	M.26.central. (Sheet 51.B)	
R.A.M.C.		
135th Fld. Amb.	BEHAGNIES.	With Unit.
136th Fld. Amb.	HAMELINCOURT.	do.
137th Fld. Amb.	ERVILLERS.	do.
51st Mobile Vet. Sec.	BOIRY St.MARTIN. (S.14.c.6.4)	
40th Divnl. Depot Battn.	ACHIET-LE-PETIT.	

ATTACHED UNITS.

Unit	Location	Transport Lines
14th Army Fld.Arty. Bde.	In the Line.	BOISLEUX-ST-MARC. (S.12.c.3.8)
18th Army Fld.Arty. Bde.	In the Line.	MOYENNEVILLE.
3rd Divnl. Artillery. 40th Bde. R.F.A.	In the line.	2 Battys. B.26.c.2.2. 1 Batty. H.1.d.0.5. 1 Batty. H.1.b.central.
42nd Bde. R.F.A.	In the Line.	A.5.d.central.
3rd Divn. T.M. Battys.	MORY.	
3rd Divn. D.A.C. Headquarters. Nos. 1 & 2 Secs. S.A.A. Section.	GOMIECOURT. A.16.d.5.0. A.24.a.0.2.	
233rd Machine Gun Coy.	S.ERVILLERS.	South ERVILLERS.

H.Q., 40th Division.

29th December, 1917.

(RSJ)

Captain,
D.A.A.G.,
40th Division.

ORIGINAL. CONFIDENTIAL.

WAR DIARY

OF

'A' AND 'Q' BRANCH

40TH DIVISION.

VOLUME XX.

FROM 1st to 31st JANUARY, 1918.

WAR DIARY or INTELLIGENCE SUMMARY

(Erase heading not required.)

Army Form C. 2118

Secret
A & Q
Headquarters 40th Division
Jan 1918

Place	Date 1918	Hour	Summary of Events and Information	Remarks and references to Appendices
GOMIECOURT	Jan 1		Military Medals awarded to 9 NCOs & men of 121 Inf/Bde & 15 NCOs & men of 40th Divl. Artillery - Improvements to mens' billets & places & baths in hand. Supply rooms to be established.	A & Q
	2		Lt Col. R.S. Grant Thorold D.S.O. struck off establishment of 18 Welsh Rgt.	A & Q
	3		85 francs forwarded to VII Corps for Xmas dinner.	A & Q
	4		Capt Will M.C. Worcestershire Rgt to be posted to 18 Welsh Rgt as 2 in Cd.	A & Q
	5		Divl. Head Qrtrs. to be moved to BAHAGNIES on 7th - exchanging with 3rd Division	A & Q
BAHAGNIES	7		13 limber wagons, ammunition, salved from HAVRINCOURT & BOURLON returned to ordnance	A & Q
	8		18 German prisoners, including 1 wounded, captured and sent to Corps A.P.M.	A & Q
	9		Salvage of huts sec. & sadly continued by the 'Brin'. Erection of huts, stabling progressing. Reserve Battalion Camps at MORY are in	A & Q
	10		a bad state & require much improvement to be effected. This would seem superfluous if such divisions & Corps propose to form a Corps Concert troupe.	A & Q
	11		Use of decauville or light tramways for supplies as well as ammunition & R.E. stores employing ho Hal horse transport so much as well as the roads.	A & Q
	12		Thaw precautions referred. Hebernian Katacki. Lt. McTavish S. Staff Rgt. appointed Staff Captain (vice Captain HOWE) 119 Inf. Bde. Capt Howe K.R. SAMG. 62 Division	A & Q
	13		Wire received no action to be taken pending further orders through Lt. McTavish has reported.	A & Q
	14		Maps for Poranby, Cog Bingen awarded Belgian Croix de Guerre.	A & Q
	15		Officers & wired. Kinsland for 8 months army relieved by corresponding ranks (the Kaplain John Hyland 5 B6.) now posted Kantileries as wire indigence.	A & Q
	16		All printers and chaffeuters now taken over by public.	A & Q
	17		Capt Howe Somerset Staff Capt. 119 Bde. Corps Rest Camp for officers & O.Rs. & opened at BOISLEUXAUMONT.	A & Q
	18		Instructions regarding recommendations for advancement of staff other officers received - the 8 only in -	A & Q
	19		Notifications received that Drums will be in 10 Bn. Bands instead of 13 - (3 Bands per Bde.)	A & Q

Army Form C. 2118

Scan
2 page Jany 1918
ADS Hebuterne 46 Divn

WAR DIARY
INTELLIGENCE SUMMARY
(Erase heading not required.)

Instructions regarding War Diaries and Intelligence Summaries are contained in F.S. Regs., Part II. and the Staff Manual respectively. Title Pages will be prepared in manuscript.

Place	Date 1918 JAN	Hour	Summary of Events and Information	Remarks and references to Appendices
BEHAGNIES	20		Improvements to Res. Bn. Instnl. Camps Continuing, and building of transport lines proceeding in spite of difficulties — lack of material & labour.	CMS
	21		Heavy snow — trenches full in places. Result 10 cases Trench feet between 13th & 19th Jany. — average 10 a day.	CMS
	22		The anti-trench foot treatment still to me fully used by Bde. A medical centre established at Mory Smith to control incipient trench foot cases. All stations shortly to be summarily inspected to prohibit unsound boots.	CMS
	23		Stuffs who made & repair number of "A" Frames men are all technically skilled i.e. bootmakers, tailors, clerks, bargemen etc. & unless B men who are equally skilled are sent to Divn. they cannot well be replaced. Major Barbury GSO₂ apptd GSO I Corps. Change in Divl. Sign approved. The white diamond to be superimposed on a red pine cock with an acorn in the diamond.	CMS
	24		attached to Divnl. Sup./Coys. This is difficult as these men are	CMS
	25			CMS
	26		Two field hyp RE from 59 Divn. taking tribute etc. etc.	CMS
	27		Units located & drawn in attached Appendix "A"	Appendix A CMS
	28		Reinforcement Battalion Rg moved to MONDECOURT by 30th Jany —	CMS
	29		Two field hyp RE from 59 Divn. join on 30th. 20 casualties trenches of 119 M.G. Coy by enemy trench mortars. 21	CMS
	30		Cases of Trenchfeet 115 during month.	CMS
	31		Casualties during month: Officers killed, Other ranks killed — Officers wounded & shell-shocked wounded & missing OR 22 O.R. 48 321 nice	CMS

C.M. Westhodaven
Lt Col

SECRET.

40TH DIVISION.

LOCATION OF UNITS ON 27TH JANUARY, 1918.

UNIT.	LOCATION.	TRANSPORT LINES.
40th Div.H.Qrs.	BEHAGNIES.	
S.C.F. (Non C.of E).	With 136th Field Amb.	
D.A.D.O.S.)		
Divnl.Gas Officer.)	ERVILLERS.	
O.C. Div.Emp.Coy.)		
ROYAL ARTILLERY.		
Headquarters.	With Div. Hd.Qrs.	
178th Bde. R.F.A.	In the Line.	ARGYLE CAMP.(S.17.a.6.2.)
181st Bde. R.F.A.	-do-	HANELINCOURT.(South).
40th Div.Ammn.Column.		
H.Q. & 1 Section.	S.28.d.9.1.	
1 Section.	S.29.a.4.9.	
S.A.A.Section.	S.30.c.1.7.	
40th Div. T.M.Battys.	ST. LEGER.	
ROYAL ENGINEERS.		
Headquarters.	With Div.Hd.Qrs.	
224 Fld. Coy.	ERVILLERS.	With Unit.
229 Fld. Coy.	ST. LEGER.	With Unit.
231 Fld. Coy.	Tunnl'g Cmp.MORY.	With Unit.
	(B.22.b.7.7.)	
H.Q.Signal Coy.	With Div.H.Qrs.	
119th INF.BRIGADE.		
Headquarters.	L/HOMME MORT B.17.a.9.8.	B.16.a.2.3.
19th R.W.Fuslrs.)		CLONMEL Cmp.(A.5.d.8.8.)
12th S.W.Bordrs.)	In the Line, with	INNISKILLING.C.(B13b64).
17th Welsh Regt.)	Reserve Battn. in MORY.	BELFAST Cp.(B.13.a.9.4.)
18th Welsh Regt.)	North Camp.MORY	ARMAGH Cp.(S.23.c.5.0.)
119th M.G.Coy.	In the Line.)	
119th T.M.Batty.	In the Line.)	MOYENNEVILLE.
120th INFANTRY BDE.		
Headquarters.	C.19.c.2.3.	
11th K.O.R.L.Regt.)	In the Line with	
13th E.Surrey Regt.)	Reserve Battn. in MORY	Dysart
14th High.Lt.Inf.)	South Camps A. & B.	
14th A.& S.Highrs.)	MORY.	Camp.
120th M.G.Coy.	In the Line.	
120th T.M.Batty.	In the Line.	
121st INF. BRIGADE.		
Headquarters.	B.17.a.9.9.	
12th Suffolk Regt.)	In the Line with	
13th Yorks. Regt.)	Reserve Battn. in MORY	South.
20th Middx.Regt.)	ABBAYE CAMP.MORY.	ERVILLERS.
21st Middx.Regt.)		
121st M.G.Coy.	In the Line.	
121st T.M.Batty.	In the Line.	
12th Yorks.Regt. (P).		
H.Q. & 3 Coys.	ST LEGER.)	
1 Company.	Tunnlg.Cp.MORY.)	Tunneling C.MORY.

/Over.

- 2 -

Unit.	Location.	Transport Lines.
244th Machine Gun Coy.	DURROW CAMP.	South ERVILLERS, with 121 and 102 M.G.Coys.
40TH DIVNL.TRAIN.A.S.C. H.Q. & all Coys.	GOMIECOURT.	With Units.
40TH DIV. SUPPLY COL.	BIHUCOURT.	
40TH AMMN. SUB PARK.	M.26.Central. (sheet 51.B.).	
R. A. M. C.		
135th Fld Amb.	BEHAGNIES.	With Unit.
136th Fld Amb.	HAMELINCOURT.	do.
137th Fld. Amb.	ERVILLERS.	do.
51st Mobile Vet.Sec.	BOIRY St.MARTIN. (S.14.c.6.4).	
40th Divl.Depot Battn.	MONDICOURT.	

ATTACHED UNITS.

3rd Divnl. Artillery. 40th Bde. R.F.A.	In the Line.	2 Battys.B.26.c.2.2. 1 Batty. H.1.d.0.5. 1 Batty. H.1.b.Central.
42nd Bde. R.F.A.	In the Line.	A.5.d.Central.
3rd Divn. T.M.Battys.	MORY.	
3rd Divn. D.A.C. Headquarters. Nos. 1 & 2 Sections. S.A.A. Section.	GOMIECOURT. A.16.d.5.0. A.24.a.0.2.	
102nd Machine Gun Coy.	DURROW CAMP.	South ERVILLERS.
181st (T) Company R.E.	DURROW CAMP.	

H.Q., 40th Division.
27th January, 1918.

Captain,
A/D.A.A.G.
40th Division.

SECRET.   ORIGINAL.

WAR DIARY

"A & Q"

BRANCH

40TH DIVISION.

From 1st to 28th FEBRUARY, 1918.

VOLUME XXI.

SECRET

Feby 1918

Army Form C. 2118

WAR DIARY
or
INTELLIGENCE SUMMARY
(Erase heading not required.)

A & Q   HQ 40 Div

Place	Date 1918	Hour	Summary of Events and Information	Remarks and references to Appendices
BEHAGNIES	Feby 1st		10/11 A21 arrival ERVILLERS on bcg 16. 15th Inf Bde fm 15th Div for reorganisation. Orders for relief of Div by 59th Div discussed with G.A. 59th Div. Must wait for some 59 Div officials who have been appointed fm 18 Corps D. Rly officer. Reports re drafting situation fm units received. Not one is short. T. to him after note fm Lichts air crafts is being passed on Mats. Could not shorn is appendix I.	Appendix I.
"	2nd		Went through reorganisation scheme with Major General & proceeded when released from line 1/2/18. Orders received to dispatch men from units as undermentioned. appendix II. Orders received that "C" in C will visit DAQE 3.40 pm 4th Feby 18.	Appendix II
"	3rd		Visit of C in C cancelled - orders received to dispatch. officers + men of units being broken up in ungr to camp, part of route march. See appendix I.	Appendix I.
	4th		11" Kings Own R. Lancs 15 Officers 300 OR by lorry on 7th Feby to 12th K.O.R. Regt 11 do do do 15 - 300 OR by mand route 5th Feby 1-8th do do 11 do do do 7 - 1570 OR by rail on 6th Feby to 2/5 do do 11 do do do 7 - 150 OR by rail on 6th Feby to 2nd R.W.F. Regt 19 RI Wels Fus 8 - 150 OR AA TQMG n relief 10-13 Feby. Went fully into the administration of the area. 3 officers D/who handed over.	Appendix III

SECRET.

WAR DIARY or INTELLIGENCE SUMMARY

Army Form C. 2118

Feby. 1918

A. & Q.   HQ 40 Division

Place	Date	Hour	Summary of Events and Information	Remarks and references to Appendices
BEHAGNIES	5/2		Reinforcements under Reorganization scheme — Into & under ritiques	
			13th East Surrey Regt — 260 other ranks	
			21 Middlesex Regt — 300 " "	
			12 Yorks Regt (P) — 250 " "	
			13 Yorks Regt — 200 " "	
			Draft 9 Officers 197 OR for 12 Suffolk Regt arrived	
			Draft of 11th K.Own.R.Lanc 6 Officers 224 other ranks left for 3rd Div by march route.	
	6/2		Draft 19th R.W.F. & 11 Kings Own R Lancs (see 3rd) left by rail. Administration instruction issued a 40 Div order No 117 of 5/2/1918. Relief in the 2nd on 10-13 Feby by 1st. 59th Div — Div withdraws to Corps Reserve to be locality as shown in — Appendix IV. Surplus 19th R.W.F. proceeded by motor lorry to BAILLEULMONT. 16 E. Corps Surplus personnel camp. Return of draftery sent in the Division shows an informer doing 4500 Ubo instead of 1300 Ubo — The Salvage of units has improved and the highly satisfactory. A large monover	

SECRET

WAR DIARY
or
INTELLIGENCE SUMMARY
(Erase heading not required.)

Army Form C. 2118

A & Q   Feby 1918   HQrs 40th Divn

Place	Date	Hour	Summary of Events and Information	Remarks and references to Appendices
BEHAGNIES	7th		Notification Received that O i/c with most Dn HQ at 10.15 am 9th Feby. Train and 1st Line Transport 11th KRRC left to join the 15th Divn. 11 am Surplus Personnel 11th KRRC sent to Corps Surplus Camp à PUISIEUX al Mont from Dn HQ's units rail.	Appendix I
	8th		2 Officers 50 ORs 12 & 6/13 2 Officers 50 ORs 17th Welch by Lorry to 19th Divn. Gen. C. noticed Dn HQ 3.30 p.m. When in Q Office he was informed of the B1 men received for the places of 12 Yorks Pioniers who were only B2. CinC took a typed statement of this office any note Re: demis for relief of 120th Bde in this demn or the 16 Febr. demandery.	Appx II
	9th		Surplus 17th Welch & Rgts proceeded to Corps Surplus Personnel Camp by Lorry & Railway H.T. 20 wagons from Rev Dn Train being used.	Appx II
	10th		2 Officers 50 OR 17th Welch Rgt for 2nd Welch Rgt) proceeded by 5 Others 100 ORs 12th SWB for 1st SWB) rail from 6 Officers 100 ORs 12 SWB for 2nd SWB) ACHIET by rail. 10.17 am. Surplus 12 SWB left for Corps Camp by Lorry. Re arrangements as Regards disposal of units personnel Elmo enclosed	See Appendix II

Army Form C. 2118

WAR DIARY
INTELLIGENCE SUMMARY
(Erase heading not required)

SECRET   Feby 1918

A. & Q.   H.Q. 40th Div.

Place	Date	Hour	Summary of Events and Information	Remarks and references to Appendices
BEHAGNIES	10th		120th Infy Bde relieved in the Right Sector by the 176th Infy Bde 59th Div & concentrated in HAMELINCOURT area by 12 noon.	
"	11th		119th Infy Bde relieved in the Left Sector by the 178th Infy Bde 59th Div by Day. 119 Infy Bde concentrated in MERCATEL area by Eveng. 120th Infy Bde moved to BLAIRVILLE area fm HAMELINCOURT.	
"	12th		121st Infy Bde relieved in the Right Sector & concentrated in HAMELINCOURT area. G.O.C. inspected 51st M.V. Section. Drafts held appendix VI joined the Division, and details shown thereon. Handed in all A.T.Q. documents to 59th Div and took in those in this area.	APPENDIX VI
GOMIECOURT	13th		DHQ closed BEHAGNIES at 10 a.m. & opened GOMIECOURT same hour. Units of the Division located as shown in appendix VII	APPENDIX VII
"	14th		Arrangements made for 136th Field Ambulance entertainment to give performance to 715th Infy Bde at BOISLEUX.	
"	15th		10/11 H21 handed over to 120 Infy Bde fm 119th Infy Bde since Murra to take place on 16th Feby by march route.	

SECRET

WAR DIARY
or
INTELLIGENCE SUMMARY

Army Form C. 2118

Feb 1918

Place	Date	Hour	Summary of Events and Information	Remarks and references to Appendices
GOMIECOURT	Feb 1918 16th		In accordance with G.R.O 3269 Brigade for Committees appointed for each area – nil appendix VIII	Appendix VIII
	17		Instructing Battalion Busy formed for Sappers presence under Corps H.Q. This to being done by Corps Group to the Division has set to deal with this.	
			French authorities awarded "Medaille de Sauvetage en Bronze" to No 24782 L/Cpl C. Read Yorkshire Rgt. This NCO received a drowning Frenchman from the R. Somme in April 1917 –	Roster
	18		L.G.S. Bruner 2.Lt. Officer R.A. ac Div. the G.S.O.3 Intelligence at G.H.Q.	CRW
	19		Major Craig 5.50 Hi Bn – Reported Employee	CRW
	20		I/Col. P.E. Ralston Cay. 17 Webb Rgt & perceived England. Reports on sanitation of Bnd. area formed to II Corps during the 4 Camps when division entrink occupation as they remain to Freely	CRW
	21		2.Lt. Col. R. Benzie 7.10 Commands 14 Apple Battalion Her –	CRW
	22		Instructions received for compilation of recommendation for kings Birthday Honors. Dispatch Class.	CRW
	23		Division move to BASSEUX area to be in G.H.Q. reserve whilst relieved Latin –	CRW
	24		Reconstructions normal in Div. area fitted with Tables Forms & Lamps –	CRW
	25		Proposal K allots the imposing patches to Brid. Troops.	CRW
	26		C in C. visits Divd. area on 27/2/18.	CRW
	27		L in L. and 18th Webb Rgt in attack scheme – Units to be located in Buresens area as shown	Appendix IX
			in Appendix IX. Div Kheredy Sentries at 24 hours notice.	CRW
BASSEUX.	28th		DHQ in Buresens. Casualties month Feby Killed officers 1 O.R. 4 Wounded officers 1 O.R. 91	CRW

O. Moore-Weil Ky/m
act ADM
L.Don

APPENDIX 1.

ALLOTMENT OF ACCOMODATION TO UNITS OF 40TH DIVISION SHOWING NOT REFERRED TO IN 40TH DIVISION O.O. NO. 117

DATE OF MOVE IN CASE OF UNITS DATED 5TH. FEBRUARY 1918.

Unit.	9th Feby: Right Bn:	10th Feby: Left Bn:	11th Feby:	12th Feby.	13th Feb:	REMARKS.
X 120th Bde.		Mory South.	No.2 Cp. Blairville.	---	---	
Y 120th Bde.	Left Bn:	Armagh Cp.	No.4 Cp. Hendecourt.	---	---	Taken over from 177th Brigade, 59th Division. Under the Area Commandant BLAIREVILLE & HENDECOURT.
Z 120th Bde.	Suppt.Bn:	Enniskillen Camp.	No.3 Cp. Hendecourt.	---	---	
Surplus, 12th S.W.B. Surplus, 17 Welsh 120 M.G.C.	N. Mory. Mory L' Abbaye. R.Sector.	Durham Cp. Mercatel. Durham Cp. Mercatel. R. Sector.	Durham Cp. Mo.1. Mercatel. Durrow Cp.	M.G.Cp. Blaireville.	---	To occupy one battalions accommodation only until disposed of to Corps Reinforcement Camp.
120 T.M.B. X 119th Bde.	R. Sector. R.Bn:	Under Brigade Arrangements. R.Bn:	Enniskillen. R.Bn:	York.Cp. Mercatel.	---	Vacated by 178th Brigade.
Y 119th Bde.	L. Bn:	L. Bn:	Mory L' Abbaye	Northumberland Cp.Mercatel.	---	Vacant.
Z 119th Bde.	Suppt.Bn:	Suppt Bn:	Durham Cp.2 Mercatel.		---	Vacated by 178th Brigade on 10th.
119 M.G.C.	Durrow Cp.	Durrow Cp.	Neuville Vitasse.	---	---	At disposal of 3rd Division from 6 p.m. 11th Feb.
119 T.M.B. X 121st Bde.	L.Sector R. Bn:	L. Sector. R. Bn:	Under Brigade Arrangements. R. Bn: Mory L' Abbaye.		Clonmel Cp. Armagh Cp. Belfast Cp.	
Y 121st Bde. Z 121st Bde. 121st MGC.	L. Bn: Suppt.Bn: Cen.Sect.	L. Bn: Suppt.Bn: Cen.Sect.	L. Bn: Suppt.Bn: Cen.Sect.	Armagh Cp. Belfast Cp. Moyne Cp. Moyenneville.	--- --- ---	
121 T.M.B. 135 Fld.Amb. 136 Fld.Amb. 137 Fld.Amb. D.A.D.O.S.	Cen.Sect. Behagnies. Hamelinct. Ervillers. Ervillers.	Cen. Sect. Ervillers. Hamelinct. Ervillers. Ervillers.	Cen.Sect. Gouy en Artois Hamelinct. Ervillers. Ervillers.	Under Bde. Arrangements. Blairville. Blenvillers. Boiry St. Rictrude S.14.b.	--- --- --- ---	Under arrangements to be made by A.D.M.S. —do— —do—
224 F.Coy. 229 F.Coy.	Rt.Sector. L. Sector.	Ervillers. L. Sector.	Hamelinct. L.Sector.	Henin HQ & Tpt.Mory B20.a.4.6.	--- ---	Under arrangements to be made by C.R.E. —do—
231 F.Coy.	B.Sector.	Cen.Sect.	Mory B.22. b.7.7.		---	—do—
244 M.G.Coy. 237 EmpCoy.	L.Sector. Ervillers.	L.Sector. Ervillers.	L.Sector. Ervillers.		--- ---	
HC.Train.	Gomiecourt. Boiry St. Rictrude.	Boiry St. Rictrude. S.14.b.	---	Durrow Cp. Enniskilling Cp.	Durrow Gp. ---	Come under orders of 59th Division on 13th Feb:
Coys.Train. 51st M.V.S.	Gomiecourt. Do not move.	S.9.c.	---	---	---	

NOTES ON AREAS.

BLAIREVILLE & HENDECOURT. Accommodation is under the Area Commandant BLAIREVILLE.
BLAIREVILLE. Camps are on BLAIREVILLE - HENDECOURT Road.

MERCATEL. Map. Sheet 51 B.
Location. DURHAM CAMP. (Nos. 1 and 2) S/11/a/3/6,
YORK CAMP. (M/22/d/9/8.)
NORTHUMBERLAND CAMP. (M/23/c/3/4).

BDE. H.QRS. as follows:-
119th Bde. M/36/c/8/0. (Mercatel Area)
120th Bde. QUARRY, BLAIREVILLE.
121st Bde. HAMELINCOURT. (A/5/B/2/2).

S E C R E T.

40TH DIVISION.

LOCATION OF UNITS ON 27TH JANUARY, 1918. 1st Feby

UNIT.	LOCATION.	TRANSPORT LINES.
40th Div. H.Qrs.	BEHAGNIES.	
S.C.F. (Non C. of E).	With 136th Field Amb.	
D.A.D.O.S.)		
Divnl. Gas Officer.)	ERVILLERS.	
O.C. Div. Emp. Coy.)		
ROYAL ARTILLERY.		
Headquarters.	With Div. Hd. Qrs.	
178th Bde. R.F.A.	In the Line.	ARGYLE CAMP. (S.17.a.6.2.)
181st Bde. R.F.A.	-do-	HANELINCOURT. (South).
40th Div. Ammn. Column.		
H.Q. & 1 Section.	S.28.d.9.1.	
1 Section.	S.29.a.4.9.	
S.A.A. Section.	S.30.c.1.7.	
40th Div. T.M. Battys.	ST. LEGER.	
ROYAL ENGINEERS.		
Headquarters.	With Div. Hd. Qrs.	
224 Fld. Coy.	ERVILLERS.	With Unit.
229 Fld. Coy.	ST. LEGER.	With Unit.
231 Fld. Coy.	Tunnl'g Cmp. MORY.	With Unit.
	(B.22.b.7.7.)	
H.Q. Signal Coy.	With Div. H.Qrs.	
119th INF. BRIGADE.		
Headquarters.	L/HOMME MORT B.17.a.9.8.	B.16.a.2.3.
19th R.W. Fuslrs.)		CLONMEL Cmp. (A.5.d.8.8.)
12th S.W. Bordrs.)	In the Line, with	INNISKILLING.C. (B13b64).
17th Welsh Regt.)	Reserve Battn. in MORY.	BELFAST Cp. (B.13.a.9.4.)
18th Welsh Regt.)	North Camp, MORY	ARMAGH Cp. (S.23.c.5.0.)
119th M.G. Coy.	In the Line.)	
119th T.M. Batty.	In the Line.)	MOYENNEVILLE.
120th INFANTRY BDE.		
Headquarters.	C.19.c.2.3.	
11th K.O.R.L. Regt.)	In the Line with	
13th E. Surrey Regt.)	Reserve Battn. in MORY	Dysart
14th High. Lt. Inf.)	South Camps A. & B.	
14th A. & S. Highrs.)	MORY.	Camp.
120th M.G. Coy.	In the Line.	
120th T.M. Batty.	In the Line.	
121st INF. BRIGADE.		
Headquarters.	B.17.a.9.9.	
12th Suffolk Regt.)	In the Line with	
13th Yorks. Regt.)	Reserve Battn. in MORY	South.
20th Middx. Regt.)	ABBAYE CAMP. MORY.	ERVILLERS.
21st Middx. Regt.)		
121st M.G. Coy.	In the Line.	
121st T.M. Batty.	In the Line.	
12th Yorks. Regt. (P).		
H.Q. & 3 Coys.	ST LEGER.)	
1 Company.	Tunnlg. Cp. MORY.)	Tunneling C. MORY.

/Over.

- 2 -

Unit.	Location.	Transport Lines.
244th Machine Gun Coy.	DURROW CAMP.	South ERVILLERS, with 121 and 102 M.G.Coys.
40TH DIVNL.TRAIN A.S.C. H.Q. & all Coys.	GOMIECOURT.	With Units.
40TH DIV. SUPPLY COL.	REBART.	
40TH AMMN.SUB PARK.	M.26.Central. (sheet 51.B.).	
R.A.M.C.		
138th Fld.Amb.	BEHAGNIES.	With Unit.
136th Fld Amb.	HAMELINCOURT.	do.
137th Fld.Amb.	ERVILLERS.	do.
51st Mobile Vet.Sec.	BOIRY St.MARTIN. (S.14.c.6.4).	
40th Divl.Depot Battn.	MONDICOURT.	

ATTACHED UNITS.

Unit	Location	Transport Lines
3rd Divnl. Artillery. 40th Bde. R.F.A.	In the Line.	2 Battys.B.26.c.2.2. 1 Batty. H.1.d.0.5. 1 Batty. H.1.b.Central.
42nd Bde. R.F.A.	In the Line.	A.5.d.Central.
3rd Divn. T.M.Battys.	MORY.	
3rd Divn. D.A.C. Headquarters. Nos. 1 & 2 Sections. S.A.A. Section.	GOMIECOURT. A.16.d.5.0. A.24.a.0.2.	
102nd Machine Gun Coy.	DURROW CAMP.	South ERVILLERS.
181st (T) Company R.E.	DURROW CAMP.	

H.Q., 40th Division.
27th January, 1918.

Captain,
A/D.A.A.G.
40th Division.

Appendix II

FROM			TO			
Unit.	Officers	Other Ranks.	Unit.	Division	Corps	Army.
11th King's Own (R.L.) Regt.	15	300	1st K.O.R.L. Regiment.	4th	XVII	Third
- do -	15	300	8th K.O.R.L. Regiment.	3rd	VI	Third
- do -	7	150	2/5th K.O.R.L. Regt.	57th	XV	First
19th Royal Welsh Fuslrs.	8	150	2nd Royal Welsh Fuslrs.	33rd	VIII	Fourth
17th Welsh Regiment.	2	50	2nd Welsh Regiment.	1st	II	Fourth
- do -	2	50	9th Welsh Regiment.	19th	V	Third
- do -	10	200	18th Welsh Regiment.	40th	VI	Third
12th South Wales Borderers.	5	100	1st South Wales Borderers.	1st	II	Fourth
- do -	5	100	2nd South Wales Borderers.	29th	VIII	Fourth
- do -	2	50	5th South Wales Borderers.	19th	V	Third.

Appendix III

Headquarters, 40th Division.
4th February, 1918.

11th King's Own R. Lancs
19th RWF
12th SWB

To all ranks of the 18 Welsh Regt
who are now leaving the 40th Division I wish to express my deep regret at the loss occasioned by myself personally and to the Division as a whole by your departure. Although the Battalion in which you have served so long in this Country is to be broken up, the memory of its splendid achievements will never fade. The record of your past services, the fine fighting spirit you have invariably displayed, and your constant determination to maintain the lofty traditions of your Battalion, not only redound to your own credit and to that of the 40th Division, but will add still further to the glorious reputation of your Regiment.

I am assured that wherever you may go you will justify the character you have already gained for courage in the field and devotion to duty, and continue to deserve the confidence that has been reposed in you in the past.

As your Divisional Commander I wish to thank all ranks for the active and unfailing support you have so readily afforded me during the last six months of arduous fighting under the most trying conditions. Once again let me express to you my sincere regret at losing your services, my warm appreciation of your past work, and my very best wishes for your future welfare and success.

4/2/18

Sd
J. Ponsonby Maj Genl
Cmd 40 Div

Appendix IV

H.Q., 40th Division No. S/122/Q.

ADMINISTRATIVE INSTRUCTIONS - REFERENCE 40TH DIVISION ORDER No. 117 dated 5/2/1918.

1. **ACCOMMODATION.**

   Accommodation and moves of Units not referred to in above Order, are as shewn in the attached Appendix I.

2. **SUPPLIES.**

   Railhead will be BOISLEUX-AU-MONT from 11th February, 1918, inclusive.
   Supplies will be delivered as follows :-

Group I.	By Horse Transport.
Group II.	By Decauville.
Group III.	By Horse Transport.
Group IV.	By Horse Transport.

   Refilling Point - Railhead.
   Fuel Dump - BOISLEUX (S.9.d.2.8.)

   All units of the Division, whether detached or not, will continue to be rationed by the Division.
   The following units will be transferred to 59th Division. Details to be arranged between S.S.Os. concerned direct :-

Unit.	Men.	L.D.Horses.	H.D.Horses
Y.M.C.A., ERVILLERS.	2	-	-
27 Labour Company.	425	3	2
Town Major, MORY.	102	6	2
467th Field Coy. R.E.	150	-	-
469th Field Coy. R.E.	186	-	-

   The following Haystacks in the Divnl. Area will be handed over by the S.S.O. :-

Location.	Tons.	Condition.
ST. LEGER (B.4.d.3.8.)	20 tons.	Inferior quality.
HOMME MORT (B.11.c.4.4.)	12 tons.	Fair quality.
SUGAR FACTORY (B.24.d.2.6.)	12 tons.	Poor quality.

3. **ORDNANCE STORES.**

   D.A.D.O.S. will transfer to D.A.D.O.S., 59th Division, the following units for Ordnance Services :-

347th Road Construction Coy.	338th Road Construction Coy.
27th Labour Company.	5th Group, Lovats Scouts.
14th Rly.Engineers, U.S.Army.	6 Ord. Mob.Workshops, A.O.D.
701 Labour Company.	Area Officer, No. 6 Area.
Area Officer, No. 9 Area.	Town Major, COURCELLES.
Town Major, ERVILLERS.	Area Officer, MOYENNEVILLE.
Area Officer, ERVILLERS.	Area Officer, MORY.

4. **TRENCH AND AREA STORES.**

   Trench Stores and Area Stores as defined in A.R.O. 1438 dated 31st January, 1918, will be handed over.
   They will be classified in separate lists as under :-

   List I. S.A.A., Grenades, 3" Stokes Ammn., Rockets, S.O.S. Grenades, etc.

   /List II.

- 2 -

List II. Trench Stores. (At least 280 water or petrol tins to be handed over in each Brigade Sector).

List III. Area Stores.

Receipts to be taken and preserved, and consolidated lists for formations to be forwarded to this office by the 14th February.

The A.D.M.S. will arrange to hand over the equipment in the Anti-Trench Foot Treatment Centres.

5. DIVISIONAL STORES.

Yukon Packs and white patrol suits will not be handed over but brought out of the line under Brigade arrangements.

6. RESERVE RATIONS.

Reserve Rations will be handed over and receipts forwarded to this office by the 13th February.

7. CLOTHING EXCHANGE AND BATHS.

The Clothing Exchange at ERVILLERS will be closed on 10th February and opened at BOIRY ST.MARTIN on 11th February.
The Divnl. Baths will be closed on 11th February.
The Divnl. Baths Officer will arrange to open Baths as under on 13th February in conjunction with the Field Ambulances concerned:-

MERCATEL.
BLAIREVILLE.

Personnel to be moved in conjunction with the A.D.M.S.

8. CANTEENS.

Canteens will be opened at MERCATEL, BLAIREVILLE and HAMEL-INCOURT on 11th February.

9. LEAVE TRAIN.

The Leave train departs from BOISLEUX-AU-MONT at 10.18 p.m. There is an E.F.C. Canteen and Y.M.C.A. Hut at Railhead.

10. AMMUNITION &c., FOR TRAINING PURPOSES.

Demands for ammunition and grenades for training purposes for week ending 23rd February to be submitted at once to this office.

11. HANDING OVER CERTIFICATES.

All units will obtain a certificate from Area Commandants that their camps and transport lines were left clean on being vacated.

12. EXTRA REGIMENTALLY EMPLOYED PERSONNEL WITHIN PRESENT DIVNL.AREA.

Divnl. arrangements will be made for the relief of the personnel shown by units as extra-regimentally employed in the return called for in this Office letter No. 153(A) dated 4/2/1918. All other extra-regimentally employed personnel in the area is to be relieved by incoming Division under Unit arrangements.

13. REINFORCEMENTS AND ARRIVALS.

Reinforcement Railhead remains at MONDICOURT. 40th Divnl. Depot Battalion does not move. 40th Divnl. Railhead Officer will

/move

- 3 -

move from ACHIET-LE-GRAND to BOISLEUX-AU-MONT on 11th February.
40th Divnl. Depot Battalion will send reinforcements to BOISLEUX from and including 11th February.

14. MOVES.

40th Divnl. Employment Coy: Gas Officer: Salvage Officer: Claims Officer: Baths Officer: Entertainments Officer: will move to ENNISKILLEN CAMP on 12th February.

15. THE GAMECOCKS.

The Gamecocks will give performances in each Brigade area weekly, commencing at BLAIREVILLE on 11th February. Inf. Brigade Hd.Qrs. are requested to assist Lieut. DAVIES as regards accommodation for the Troupe and Band.

16. LORRIES.

Demands for lorries on the attached pro forma to reach this office by 9 a.m. 8th February.

17. ACKNOWLEDGE.

H.Q., 40th Division.
6th February, 1918.
(RSJ)

Major,
for A.A. & Q.M.G.,
40th Division.

UNITS TO MOVE BY LORRY (a) vide RELIEF TABLE.

Unit.	Strength.	No. of Lorries or H.T.	Starting Point.	Debussing Point.	Time.	Date.

LORRIES OR H.T. REQUIRED FOR BLANKETS (b).

Appendix V

H.Q., 40th Division No. 327(A).

A grant as under from the 40th Divisional Fund will be made. Cheques will be forwarded at an early date.

The Divisional Commander wishes this money to be spent on the welfare and comfort of the troops.

    C.R.A.   £70. 0. 0.

    C.R.E.   £20. 0. 0.

    Infantry Brigades.   each   £100. 0. 0.

    12th Yorks. Regt.   £30. 0. 0.

    Divisional Train, A.S.C.   £10. 0. 0.

    A.D.M.S.   £15. 0. 0.

    Machine Gun Battn.   £20. 0. 0.

    Mobile Vet. Section.   £2. 0. 0.

    Divnl. Supply Column.   £4. 0. 0.

    Divnl. Headquarters.   £2. 0. 0.

    Divnl. Employment Coy.   £1. 0. 0.

It is hoped to make a similar grant in about 3 months time.

H.Q., 40th Division.
7th February, 1918.
(RSJ)

Major,
D.A.Q.M.G.,
40th Division.

Appendix VI

S E C R E T.

POSTINGS TO 40TH DIVISION UNDER REORGANIZATION SCHEME.

From.		Posting Strength.		To.	Actual strength on arrival.		Date of arrival.	REMARKS.
Unit.	Division.	Offrs.	O.R.		Offrs.	O.R.		
9th Suffolks.	6th	12	250	12th Suffolks.	10	197	5th Feby.	
17th Welsh.	40th	10	200	18th Welsh	7	179	5th Feby.	
7th E.Surrey.	12th	12	250	13th E.Surrey.	4	180	6th Feby.	
17th Midd'x.	2nd	15	300	21st Midd'x,	13	270		
7th Yorks.	17th	12	250	12th Yorks.(P).	7	154		
7th Yorks.	17th	10	200	13th Yorks.	7	180		
16th Midd'x.	29th	15	300	20th Midd'x	10	235	12th Feby.	
17th H.L.I.	32nd	?	?	14th H.L.I.	3	79		
17th H.L.I.	32nd	?	?	10/11 H.L.I.	2	92		
Total.				Total.	63.	1566.		

S E C R E T.

Appendix VII

40TH DIVISION.

LOCATION OF UNITS ON 13th FEBRUARY, 1918.

UNIT.	LOCATION.	TRANSPORT LINES.
40th Div. Hd.Qrs.	GOMIECOURT.	
S.C.F. (Non C. of E).	With 136th Field Ambce.	
D.A.D.O.S.	BOIRY St. RICTRUDE.	
O.C. Div.Emp. Coy.	Enniskillen Camp, ERVILLERS. (B.13.b.4.4)	
Divnl. Gas Officer.	--do--	
ROYAL ARTILLERY.		
Headquarters.	With Divnl.Hd.Qrs.	
178th Brigade R.F.A.	In the Line.	Argyle Camp.(S.V.a.6.2)
181st Brigade R.F.A.	--do--	HAMELINCOURT (South).
40th Divnl.Ammn.Colmn.		
Hd.Qrs.& 1 Section.	S.28.d.9.1.	
1 Sec.(Det.to 59/Div).	S.29.a.4.9.	
S.A.A.Section (Det. to 3rd Divn).	S.30.c.1.7.	
40th Div.T.M.Battys. (Det.to 59/Div).	ST. LEGER.	
ROYAL ENGINEERS.		
Headquarters.	With Divnl.Hd.Qrs.	
224th Field Coy.	HAMELINCOURT.	With Unit.
229th Field Coy.	HENIN.	MORY.
231st Field Coy.	MORY. (B.22.b.7.7).	With Unit.
H.Q. Signal Coy.	With Div.Hd.Qrs.	
119th INF. BRIGADE.		
Headquarters.	M.36.c.8.0. MERCATEL Area.	York Camp.
18th Welsh Regt.	Durham Camp (S.11.a.3.6) MERCATEL Area.	York Camp.
21st Middlesex Rgt.	Northumberland Camp. (M.23.c.3.4.)MERCATEL Area.	--do--
10/11th High.Lt.Inf.	York Camp. (M.22.d.9.2) MERCATEL Area.	--do--
19th R.W.Fus. (Transpt only).		--do--
119th M.G.Coy.	NEUVILLE VITASSE.	With Unit.
119th T.M.Batty.	Durham Camp (S.11.a.3.6) MERCATEL AREA.	
120TH INF. BRIGADE.		
Headquarters.	The Quarry, BLAIREVILLE.	With Unit.
13th E.Surrey Regt.	No.4 Camp, HENDECOURT.	--do--
14th High.Lt.Inf.	No.2 Camp, HENDECOURT.	--do--
14th A.& S. Highrs.	No.5 Camp, HENDECOURT.	--do--
17th Welsh Regt. (Transport only).		No.3 Camp, BLAIREVILLE.
120th M.G. Coy.	No.3 Camp, HENDECOURT.	With Unit.
120th T.M.Batty.	No.5 Camp, HENDECOURT.	

121st INF. BRIGADE.

UNIT.	LOCATION.	TRANSPORT LINES.
121st INF. BRIGADE.		
Headquarters.	HAMELINCOURT.(A.5.b.2.2.).	With Unit.
12th Suffolk Regt.	CLONMEL CAMP (A.5.b.2.8) HAMELINCOURT.	--do--
13th Yorks. Regt.	Belfast Camp (B.13.a.9.2) ERVILLERS.	--do--
20th Middlesex Regt.	Armagh Camp (S.22.c.4.5)	--do--
12th S.Wales Bdrs. (Transport Only).		Enniskillen Camp (B.13.b.4.4.) ERVILLERS.
121st M.G. Coy.	No.3 Camp, HENDECOURT. (Moving on 14th Feb).	With Unit.
121st T.M. Batty.	Moyne Camp (A.4.a.6.7) MOYENNEVILLE.	
12th YORKS.REGT. (P).		
H.Q. & 2 Coys.	MORY. (B.22.b.7.7)	)
1 Company.	ST. LEGER.	) B.21.b.2.5.
1 Company.	ECOUST.St.MEIN.	)
244th Machine Gun Coy.	Durrow Camp, MORY. (B.21.a.7.6)	S.ERVILLERS (With 177 M.G.Coy).
40TH DIVNL.TRAIN,A.S.C.		
H.Q. & all Coys.	BOIRY ST. RICTRUDE. S.14.b. & S.2.c.	With Unit.
40TH DIV.SUPPLY COL.	RANSART.	
R. A. M. C.		
135th Field Ambulance.	GOUY EN ARTOIS.	With Unit.
136th Field Ambulance.	BLAIREVILLE.	With Unit.
137th Field Ambulance.	Durham Camp.(S.11.a.3.6). MERCATEL Area.	York Camp.
51st MOB.VET.SECTION.	BOIRY ST. MARTIN. (S.14.c.6.4).	
40TH DIVL.DEPOT BATTN.	MONDICOURT.	
SURPLUS PERSONNEL.		
11th K.O.R.Lanc.Regt.)		
19th R.Welsh Fus.)	At VI Corps surplus personnel camp, BAILLEULVAL.	
12th S. Wales Bdrs.)		
17th Welsh Regt.)		

--------oooOOOOooo--------

&APPENDIX 9.

H.Q., 40th Division No. 139(Q).

H.Q., 40th Divnl. Artillery.
H.Q., 119th Inf. Brigade.
H.Q., 120th Inf. Brigade.
H.Q., 121st Inf. Brigade.
O.C., 40th Divnl. Train, A.S.C.
Area Commdt., MERCATEL.
    do.   BLAIREVILLE.
    do.   ERVILLERS.
    do.   BOIRY ST RICTRUDE.
    do.   GOMIECOURT.

Reference G.R.O. 3269 and C.R.O. 3071 of 13/2/1918.

The Divisional Area is divided into the following grouping for Fire Committees :-

40th Divnl. Artillery.	MOYENNEVILLE	--- ARGYLE CAMP.
119th Inf. Brigade.	MERCATEL	--- DURHAM LINES.
120th Inf. Brigade.	BLAIREVILLE	--- HENDECOURT.
121st Inf. Brigade.	HAMELINCOURT	--- ERVILLERS (To include D.H.Q.Camp, GOMIECOURT).
Divisional Train.	BOIRY ST RICTRUDE	- BOIRY ST MARTIN.

Units as shown on the Divisional Location List (copy attached for Area Commandants) to be included in the Brigade Fire Committee Schemes if they are in their area as given above.

R.A. and Brigade Headquarters will appoint a President and Committee of which the Area Commandant is to be a member.

Area Commandants should see that there is no overlapping as regards the schemes of other Divisions.

These Committees will be formed at once and draw up a scheme for dealing with an outbreak of fire in its area, and review the Fire Orders and Fire fighting appliances of all Units in their area.

Report to reach this office by 25th February, 1918.

16th February, 1918

(Sgd). A. Gordon, Major,
D.A.Q.M.G., 40th Division.

Copy to :-
    Corps.
    C.R.E., 40th Division.
    A.D.M.S., 40th Division.

Appdx IX

SECRET.

40TH DIVISION.

LOCATION OF UNITS IN "BASSEUX" AREA.

UNIT.	LOCATION.	REMARKS.
40th Divnl.Hd.Qrs. (Complete).	BASSEUX.	
D.A.D.O.S.) O.C. Div.Emp.Coy) Div. Claims Offr)	BEAUMETZ.	
ROYAL ARTILLERY. Head Quarters.	HUMBERCAMP.	
178th Bde. R.F.A.) 181st Bde. R.F.A.) 40th Div.Amn.Col.)	SOUASTRE.	Move on 5th March.
ROYAL ENGINEERS. Head Quarters.	With Div. Hd. Qrs.	
H.Q.& ½ 224 Fd.Co.	BAILLEULMONT.	
½ 224 Field Coy.	Detached.	
229th Field Coy.) 231st Field Coy.)	BELLACOURT.	
119th INFANTRY BRIGADE. Head Quarters.) 2 Battalions.)	GOUY-EN-ARTOIS.)	
1 Battalion.	MONCHIET.	Move back to previous Camps in BLAIREVILLE Area on 3rd March.
1 T.M.Battery.	GOUY-EN-ARTOIS.	
120TH INFY. BRIGADE. Hd.Qrs. and 1) Battalion.)	POMMIER.	
1 Battalion.) 1 Battalion.)	BERLES-AU-BOIS.	
1 T.M.Battery.	POMMIER.	
121st INFY.BRIGADE. Head Qrs.) 1 Battalion.)	BAILLEULMONT.	
2 Battalions.) 1 T.M.Battery.)	BAILLEULVAL.	
12th YORKS.REGT.(P).	BIENVILLERS.	
40th Div.M.Gun Bn.	No.4 Camp, BLAIREVILLE.	Moves in on 3rd March.
40TH DIVNL. TRAIN. Head Quarters.	With Divnl. Head Qrs.	
No.1 Company.	With Divnl.Artillery.	
No.2 Company.	GOUY-EN-ARTOIS.	Joins 119/Bde. and will move with them to BLAIREVILLE on 3rd March.
No.3 Company.	POMMIER.	With 120th Infy.Bde.
No.4 Company.	BAILLEULVAL.	With 121st Infy.Bde.
		R.A.M.C.

UNIT.	LOCATION.	REMARKS.
R.A.M.C.		
135th Fd. Amb.	GOUY-EN-ARTOIS.	No move. Corps Rest Station.
136th Fd. Amb.	BLAIREVILLE.	No move.
137th Fd. Amb.	BAILLEULMONT.	
51st Mob.Vet.Sec.	BELLACOURT.	

NAME OF PLACE.	Area Officer to whom application should be made for billets.
BASSEUX.	Town Major, BASSEUX.
BAILLEULVAL.) BAILLEULMONT.) BELLACOURT.)	Sub Area Officer BAILLEULVAL (Capt. Tucker).
POMMIER.) BIENVILLERS.) BERLES-AU-BOIS.)	Sub Area Officer, BERLES-AU-BOIS (Major STEWART).
GOUY-EN-ARTOIS.) MONCHIET.)	Sub Area Officer, BARLY (Col.Wright).

WAR DIARY

A & Q BRANCH,

HEADQUARTERS, 40TH. DIVISION.

MARCH 1918.

WAR DIARY
INTELLIGENCE SUMMARY

Army Form C. 2118

Secret.

A "D" Head Quarters 40th Division

March 1918

(Erase heading not required.)

Place	Date 1918	Hour	Summary of Events and Information	Remarks and references to Appendices
BASSEUX	March 1		Entraining Stations for 40th Division will be GOUY; BEAUMETZ; & SAULTY.	Appendix A
	2		Units warned to adhere to attached appendix A	Appx A
	3		Entraining stations changed - Preliminary places - Division displaying in Division being quartered in area thermaville for a night when Division will be AUBIGNY, SAVY and TINQUES - or in area Le Carnoy, when H.Q's are at Ste POL, PETIT HOUVIN, and FREVENT.	Appx A
	4		No 148 - "Div" Arty when in GOVIN area will entrain at DOULLENS and FREVENT.	Appx A
			MONDICOURT.	
	5		Lt. Col. Charles GSO₁ appointed 65D1. There army représen 16/3/18. Provisional boundaries fixed.	Appx A
	6		Major Hutt appointed Divl Gas Officer - Certain number of Trafficontrol Personnel to be B/category.	Appx
	7		Allotment of recommendations for Kings Birthday Gazette. 150 Hororo mentions.	Appx
	8		Prision Pen. on a 3 day basis - Major Lacey D.H.G.O appta 6 Corps. M.G. Officer. Every unit to have its equipment checked when out of Picline.	Appx
	9		14 remounts arrived. Lecture on Supplies by Major Jewman Army Service Corps - Every unit to be printed with several acoustic meeting's. Report and that the meeting of partially visibile audio from dis'rty imprivers the dust chields not satisfactory.	Appx
	10		Major Jupp appta 2nd in Col 10/11 HLI Major Brown 2nd in Col of 18th Weish Rgt.	Appx
	11		Major Gordon D.A.Q.M.G. to "Div" appta A.Q.M.G. 7th Corps. Captain Dawson appta D.A.Q.M.G. 40 Div.	Appx
	12		Establishment of Employment transport (3 Bns) due to restriction of Battalions, Reschedulest strength - Cos + 2½ inch of these Battalions (Re-planted 2 months leave.	Appx
	13		100 Cotton acts of Packsaddling drawn for use in event of roads being impossible by evening fire.	Appx
	14		All war dogs of replies the and to staples - Arrangements made for Bde pack dumps + District to be left in cond of Division going into action on account of Enemy offensive.	Appx
	15		Capt. Oakley M.C. appta Staff Captain R.A. 40 Div. - Return of Officers who have distinguished themselves in civil life to be send in.	Appx

WAR DIARY

INTELLIGENCE SUMMARY

Army Form C. 2118

A. & B. Head Qrs.
H.Qrs. Div.
2 pages

Secret — March 1918

Place	Date March 1918	Hour	Summary of Events and Information	Remarks and references to Appendices
BASSEUX	16		Major Gilman appts O.C. No. 2 Div. M.T. Coy. - 6th formation of D.S.Col. & A. Supply Park Divisional with Units formed as shewn in Appendix B.	Appendix B. Copy
	17		Submits instructions which is HQ 7/see Appendix C.	Appendix C. Copy
	18		Return of Italian speaking NCOs & men called for and sent in. Only 3 names -	Copy
	19		Lt.Col. Culver 17 Welch Regt. & Bryland sick. Br.Gen. Willoughby Coy. 120th Inf. Bde applies to create Appt. on grounds of ill health - Leave vacancies of division reduced to 29 per diem.	Copy
	20		Bde M.Gun Bn. establishment of 2 line Tpt. transport horsed requirements considering large number of animals and the Coys being liable to be split up. Bread, Letter Services now ironed is	Copy
	21		Appointed the Course of scrap loans enemy bombardment, enemy lines - 55 Regiments sent to Armistead intense bombardment Croisilles. 120th Bde ordered to hold line of defence W. of Mory. 121 Bde moves from Blairville & Hamelincourt, Nos Divn. June sent out admin. Supply Railhead changed from BOISLEURCMONT to SAULTY at 22.	Appendix Copy
HAMELIN-COURT	22		All leave stopped. Details of Bde tps left at Berles au Bois, Bailleulval and Blairville - with the dumps. adv. Div. HQ. at HAMELINCOURT near Div. HQ. to BUCQUOY. All transport withdrawn to BIENVILLERS	Appendix D.
BUCQUOY	23		from Hamelincourt. Appendix D. Transport moved on 24"& to locations shewn appendix E.	Appendix E.
BUCQUOY MONCHY = AU BOIS	24		Lt.Col. Dudley Wilmot killed. O.C. 17 Suffk.Regt. - Lt.Col. Becker O.C. 11/Yorks Regiment wounded. Br.Gen. HOBKIRK Coy. E. joined & assumed command of 120th Inf. Bde. Rum issued nightly during operations - Head Rtrs. & Bdes established at GOMMICOURT.	Copy
HABARCQ	25		RANSART ADINFER Noot line. Railheads changed for SAULTY to FREVENT. 42 Divn. coming to relieve Nos Divn. Divn. withdrawn to	Copy
LUCHEUX WARLUZEL	26		HABARCQ area - Troops in march concentration during night - Oders received to concentrate in the LUCHEUX area. Troops diverted with difficulty. quarters as shewn in Appendix F. Artillery to	Appendix F. Copy
LUCHEUX	27 28		remain in VI Corps - Endeavours made to re-equip division - difficulties any to combat moves and Units being unable to send in requirements to D.A.D.S. Clean socks issued throughout Division	Copy

WAR DIARY

Army Form C. 2118

40 Div HQ 96
A & Q
March 1918 Title Page

INTELLIGENCE SUMMARY

Place	Date 1918 March	Hour	Summary of Events and Information	Remarks and references to Appendices
CHELERS	29		Divn. entered wire trench route to Chelers area. Capt. GAFFIKIN RAMC appt'd DADMS HQ Divn. Captain DAWSON DADVS to be temporary major.	am
	30		H.M. The King visited the Divn.; Comd. 15 Divl. Head Stn. where HqStff was presented. Attached Coy of circular letter issued. Brigade Appendix G1. Railhead changed 6TNQUES Appendix G.	am Appendix G
MERVILLE	31		Divn. moved by bus on 31st & 1st April from XIII Corps to IV Corps area, to relieve 57th Divn. in the line. Instructions received late on night of 30th. 119 Bde moved on 1st. April. Casualties during operations 23 March to date. Officers killed 25 wounded 74 missing 34. O.R. killed 236 wounded or 1188 missing 1442.	Appx

[signature]
asstun
LtCom

31/3/18.

SECRET.

40TH DIVISION.

LOCATION OF UNITS IN BASSEUX AREA, 1st March, 1918.

Unit.	Location.	Remarks.
40th Divnl. Hd.Qrs. (Complete).	BASSEUX.	
D.A.D.O.S.)		
O.C., Divnl. Emplyt. Coy.)		
Divnl. Claims Officer.)	BEAUMETZ.	
Divnl. Gas Officer.)		
Divnl. Salvage Officer.)		
ROYAL ARTILLERY.		
Headquarters.	HUMBERCAMP.	Move on 5th March.
178th Bde. R.F.A.)		Until then are in for-
181st Bde. R.F.A.)	SOUASTRE. →	ward area in previous
40th Divnl. Ammn. Col.)		locations.
ROYAL ENGINEERS.		
Headquarters.	With Divnl. Hd.Qrs.	
H.Q. & ½ 224 Fld. Coy.	BAILLEUIMONT.	
½ 224 Field Coy.	Detached.	
229th Field Coy.	BARLY.	
231st Field Coy.	BIENVILLERS.	
119TH INF. BRIGADE.		
Headquarters.	GOUY-EN-ARTOIS.	Move to previous Camps
13th E. Surrey Regt.	MONCHIET.	in BLAIREVILLE Area
18th Welsh Regiment.)		on 3rd March.
21st Middlesex Regt.)	GOUY-EN-ARTOIS.	
119th T.M. Battery.)		
120TH INF. BRIGADE.		
Headquarters.	POMMIER.	
10/11th High. Lt. Inf.	BERLES-AU-BOIS.	
14th High. Lt. Inf.	POMMIER.	
14th A.& S. Highrs.	BERLES-AU-BOIS.	
120th T.M. Battery.	POMMIER.	
121ST INF. BRIGADE.		
Headquarters.)		
12th Suffolk Regt.)	BAILLEUIMONT.	
13th Yorks. Regt.)	BAILLEULVAL.	
20th Middlesex Regt.)		
121st T.M. Battery.	BELLACOURT.	
12TH YORKS. REGT (Pnrs).	BELLACOURT.	
40TH BATTN. M.G. CORPS.		
Headquarters.)	ARMAGH CAMP	Move to No.4 Camp
A Coy.(late 119th Coy.))	(HAMELINCOURT).	HENDECOURT
B Coy.(late 120th Coy.)	Attached 3rd Divn.	on 3rd March.
C Coy.(late 121st Coy.)	Attached 59th Divn.	
D Coy.(late 224th Coy.)	DURHAM Camp, BOISLEUX.	
40TH DIVNL. TRAIN, A.S.C.		
Headquarters.	With Divnl. Hd.Qrs.	
No.1 Company.	With Divnl. Artillery.	
No.2 Company.	GOUY-EN-ARTOIS.	With 119th Bde.
No.3 Company.	POMMIER.	With 120th Bde.
No.4 Company.	BAILLEULVAL.	With 121st Bde.
40TH DIVNL. SUPPLY COLUMN.	RANSART.	

/Over.

S E C R E T.

40TH DIVISION.

LOCATION OF UNITS - 12TH MARCH, 1918.

B

Unit.	Location.	Remarks.
40th Divnl. Hd.Qrs. (Complete).	BASSEUX.	
D.A.D.O.S.	BOIRY ST.RICTRUDE (S.14.a).	Moves on 13th M'ch.
O.C. Div.Emplyt.Coy.)		
Div.Claims Offr.)		
Div.Gas Officer.)	With D.A.D.O.S.	
Div.Salvage Offr.)		
S.C.F., C.of E.)		
S.C.F. Non C.of E.)	With Divnl. Hd.Qrs.	

ROYAL ARTILLERY.
  Headquarters.   HUMBERCAMP.
  178th Bde. R.F.A.   S.15.c.
  181st Bde. R.F.A.   MOYENNEVILLE.
  40th Div.Ammn.Col.   S.15.c.
  O.C. Details R.A.   SOUASTRE.

ROYAL ENGINEERS.
  Headquarters.   With Divnl. Hd.Qrs.
  224th Fld.Coy. RE.   No.6 Camp, BLAIREVILLE.
  229th Fld.Coy. RE.   DURHAM 'A' Camp.
  231st Fld.Coy. RE.   ARMAGH CAMP, HAMELINCOURT.

119TH INF. BRIGADE.
  Headquarters.   M.36.c.8.0.
  13th E.Surrey Regt.   CARLISLE YORK CAMP.
  18th Welsh Regt.   NORTHUMBERLAND CAMP.
  21st Middlesex Rgt.   DURHAM 'B' Camp.
  119th T.M. Batty.   - do -
  O.C. Details, 119 Bde.   The Quarry, BLAIREVILLE.

120TH INF. BRIGADE.
  Headquarters.   HAMELINCOURT, A.5.b.2.2.
  10/11th H.L.I.   BELFAST CAMP, ERVILLERS.
  14th H.L.I.   ENNISKILLEN CAMP, do.
  14th A.& S. Hrs.   CLONMEL CAMP, HAMELINCOURT.
  120th T.M. Batty.   BELFAST CAMP, ERVILLERS.
  O.C.Details, 120 Bde.   FERLES-AU-BOIS.

121ST INF. BRIGADE.
  Headquarters.   The Quarry, BLAIREVILLE.
  12th Suffolk Regt.   No.3 Camp,   do.
  13th Yorks. Regt.   No.5 Camp,   do.
  20th Middx. Regt.   No.2 Camp,   do.
  121st T.M. Batty.   No.5 Camp,   do.
  O.C.Details, 121 Bde.   BAILLEULVAL.

12TH YORKS.RGT.(PNRS.)   No.4 Camp, BLAIREVILLE.

40TH BATTN. M.G.C.
  Headquarters.   CARLISLE YORK CAMP.
  'A' Coy (late 119 Coy)   do.
  B Coy. (late 120 Coy)   ENNISKILLEN CAMP.
  C Coy. (late 121 Coy)   NORTHUMBERLAND CAMP.
  D Coy. (late 244 Coy)   CLONMEL CMP. HAMELINCOURT.

40TH DIVNL. TRAIN? ASC.
  Headquarters.)
  No.1 Company.)
  No.2 Company.)   HENDECOURT.
  No.3 Company.)
  No.4 Company.)

/Over.

- 2 -

Unit.	Location.	Remarks.
40TH DIV. SUPPLY COL.	RANSART.	
R.A.M.C.		
135th Field Amb.	ARMAGH CAMP, HAMELINCOURT.	With 120th Brigade.
136th Field Amb.	BLAIREVILLE.	With 121st Brigade.
137th Field Amb.	DURHAM 'A' Camp.	With 119th Brigade.
51ST MOBILE VET. SEC.	HENDECOURT.	
40TH DIVN. DEPOT BATTN.	MONDICOURT.	

H.Q., 40th Division.
12th March, 1918.
(RSJ)

for Captain,
D.A.A.G.,
40th Division.

SECRET.

COPY NO ....

40th Divn. No. S/22/Q.4.

ENTRAINING INSTRUCTIONS FOR 40TH DIVISION WHILE IN G. H. Q. RESERVE.

40th Division No. S/22/Q.3. dated 3rd March 1918 and No. S/22/Q dated 11th March, 1918, are cancelled.

1. Reference 40th Division Order No. 131 dated 13th March, 1918, the Division will be prepared to entrain according to the STANDARD ORDER OF ENTRAINMENT OF UNITS OF A DIVISION IN G.H.Q. RESERVE, APPENDIX "D", Third Army SQ/108 issued under this office No. C/22/Q of 26.2.18.

2. The entraining stations for the Division are :-

    A.   BOISLEUX-AU-MONT.
    B.   BAPAUME WEST.
    C.   BAPAUME MAIN.

The standard programme (9 Battalion Division) is modified as under :-
Train 18 is less cable section, train 21 is less 1 Coy. & Cooker of Pioneer Battalion. H.Q. 40th Bn. M.G.C. in Train 18 vice Cable Section with balance in Train 21 vice 1 Coy. Pioneer Battalion.
Train 20 takes Pioneer Battalion complete. Trains Nos. 33 & 34 each takes half B.A.A. Section D.A.C., and one Trench Mortar Battery. Train No.35 is not required.

3. Infantry Brigade Groups will en-train as under :-

    Station A.   119th Infantry Brigade Group.
    Station B.   121st Infantry Brigade Group.
    Station C.   120th Infantry Brigade Group.

4. The instructions for units entraining contained in Third Army No. SQ/108 will be complied with.

5. Rations will be taken on the train for consumption the day following detrainment. The number of days to be taken will be notified when known. Units entrain with their baggage and supply wagons.

6. Arrangements for advance parties (if any) will be notified when known.

7. Infantry Bde. Hd.Qrs. and Divnl. Artillery will detail a Staff Officer to superintend the entraining of units of their groups.

8. Infantry Brigades will detail two Officers, not under the rank of Captain, to report to the R.T.O's of Stations and remain there to assist units entraining until the last unit of the Division leaves.

9. Trains leave each station at 3 hours intervals. The time the first train leaves each station will be notified by wire.

10. Separate instructions will be given for the move of No. 40 Divnl. Supply Column, No. 40 Ammunition Sub Park and the surplus first line and train transport by road.

11. Lorries to move blankets and heavy baggage to the entraining stations will be provided. Requirements to be notified to this office at once, stating unit, number of lorries, and rendezvous.

/ 12

- 2 -

12. Divnl. Headquarters, H.Q. No. 1 Sec. 40th Divnl. Signal Coy., H.Q., 40th Divnl. Engineers, will entrain in the fifth train to leave BOISLEUX-AU-MONT (train No.13).

13. The departure of each train, giving the train number, with a statement of the units travelling in it, is to be wired to these Headquarters immediately on departure by the Staff Officer i/c entrainment of the formation concerned.

14. ACKNOWLEDGE.

H.Q., 40th Division.

13th March, 1918.

Captain,
D.A.Q.M.G.,
40th Division.

DISTRIBUTION :-

Copy No.			
1.	G.O.C.	17	Camp Commandant.
2.	119th Bde.	18	G.
3.	120th Bde.	19	VI Corps.
4.	121st Bde.	20)	War Diary.
5.	C.R.A.	21)	
6.	C.R.E.	22	File.
7.	12th Yorks.	23	DADRT, AVESNES.
8.	40th Bn. M.G.C.	24	DADRT, ALBERT.
9.	Signals.	25	R.T.O., BAPAUME WEST.
10.	A.D.M.S.	26	R.T.O., BAPAUME MAIN.
11.	D.A.D.V.S.	27	R.T.O., BOISLEUX.
12.	A.P.M.	28	Employt. Coy.
13.	D.A.D.O.S.		
14.	D. Gas Offr.		
15.	Divnl. Train.		
16.	Div. Supp. Col.		

(RSJ)

SECRET.   40th Division Adv: No. S/17/Q.

Rear Hd. Q
....

1.   Railhead until further orders will remain at SAULTY.
      Refilling point from 23rd. March inclusive will be on road
      MONCHY-AU-BOIS - ADINFER.

2.   In the event of Unit Transport withdrawing from present
      position, it will proceed to AYETTE Area, (West of DOUCHY-LES-
      AYETTE about F.3.c & d.). Sites to be selected by Units concerned.

3.   The following moves will take place forthwith
      (a) S.A.A. Section, D.A.C. from present position to
          Camping ground about F.10.d., F.16.b & d.
          South of AYETTE.
      (b) 40th Divisional Train to ADINFER Area (at ADINFER-
          MONCHY-AU-BOIS Road X.20.c & d.)
      (c) 137th Field Ambulance from DURHAM CAMP to ARMAGH
          Camp.

4.   Location of transport lines and Artillery Wagon Lines.
R.A. 178th & 181st Brigades R.F.A.   ERVILLERS.
119th Brigade Transport.   HAMELINCOURT.
120th Brigade Transport.   -do-
121st Brigade Transport.   -do-
224th Field Coy. R.E.   ARMAGH Camp.
229th Field Coy. R.E.   ARMAGH Camp.
231st Field Coy. R.E.   ARMAGH Camp.
12th Yorks Regt. (P).   CLONMEL Camp.
40th Bn: M.G.C. H.Q.   -do-
"A" Coy.   CARLISLE Camp to move to CLONMEL or
                                                                        ARMAGH.
"B" Coy.   INNISKILLEN Cp. to move to ARMAGH
                                                                        or CLONMEL
"C" Coy.   NORTHUMBERLAND Cp. to move to
                                            CLONMEL or ARMAGH.
"D" Coy.   CLONMEL Camp.
135th Field Ambce.   ARMAGH Camp.   Ayette
136th   -do-   BLAIREVILLE.
137th   -do-   ARMAGH Camp.
51st M.V.S.   BEHENCOURT.

5.   In the event of it being necessary to withdraw transport
from the HAMELINCOURT Area it will proceed via MOYENNEVILLE -
AYETTE - DOUCHY-LES-AYETTE.

                                                          Captain,
22nd March 1918.   D.A.Q.M.G., 40th Division.
FH.

SECRET.   H.Q., 40th Division No. C/131/A.

1. The following moves of Transport lines will take place at 6 a.m. on morning of 24th March, 1918 :-

Unit.	To.
40th Divnl. Train, A.S.C. and attd. Companies 59th Divnl. Train.	HANNESCAMPS.
51st Mobile Vet. Section.	To join 40th Divnl. Train at HANNESCAMPS.
224th Field Coy. R.E.) 229th Field Coy. R.E.) 231st Field Coy. R.E.)	West of BUCQUOY on BUCQUOY - HANNESCAMPS Road.
119th Inf. Brigade.) 120th Inf. Brigade.) 121st Inf. Brigade.) 12th Yorks. Regt. (P).)	Camping grounds in vicinity of BUCQUOY-ABLAINZEVILLE Road.

Sites for these units will be selected by a Divnl. Staff Officer in direct consultation with Staff concerned or Officer in charge of transport of above units.

2. The Transport lines of the undermentioned Units will remain in present positions :-

Unit.	Present site.
40th Divnl. Amn. Column.) 40th Battn. M.G. Corps.)	BUCQUOY-AYETTE Road.
135th Field Ambulance.) 136th Field Ambulance.) 137th Field Ambulance.)	AYETTE.

3. Orders are being issued direct by Divnl. Hd.Qrs. for the move to the Officers i/c of the Transport of units referred to in para. 1 of this instruction.

4. D.A.D.O.S., 40th Division, will move on morning of 24th March to BUCQUOY.

5. SOUASTRE is "earmarked" for 40th Division Rear Hd.Qrs.

6. In the event of transport having to move farther Westward the direction of the move would be towards HANNESCAMPS and FONQUE-VILLERS. Normally the orders for such a move would be issued from Divnl. Hd.Qrs.

Major,
D.A.A.G., 40th Division.

H.Q., 40th Division.
23rd March, 1918.

Distribution :-
40th Divnl. Artillery.   12th Yorks. Regt. (P).
C.R.E., 40th Division.   40th Battn. M.G.Corps.
O.C., Signals.   O.C., 40th Div.Train.
119th Inf. Brigade.   A.D.M.S., 40th Division.
120th Inf. Brigade.   D.A.D.V.S. 40th Division.
121st Inf. Brigade.   A.P.M., 40th Division.
VI Corps (G)   'G'.
    (For information.)   'Q'.
                                D.A.D.O.S.

LOCATION OF UNITS.

26th March, 1918.

40th Divl.Hd.Qrs.	LUCHEUX.
Divl.Artillery.	With Divl.H.Q.
1 Brigade R.F.A.) 1 Section D.A.C.)	With 3rd Division.
1 Brigade R.F.A.) 1 Section D.A.C.)	With Guards Division.
A.A.Section D.A.C.	OPPY.
224th Field Coy.R.E.) 229th Field Coy.R.E.) 231st Field Coy.R.E.)	SOMBRIN.
119th Infantry Brigade.	SOMBRIN.
120th Infantry Brigade.	WARLUZEL.
121st Infantry Brigade.	SUS-ST-LEGER.
177th Infantry Brigade.	SUS-ST-LEGER.
12th Yorkshire Regt.(P).	BEAUDRICOURT.
40th Bn. M.G.Corps.	BEAUDRICOURT.
40th Divl Train.	HERBERCOURT & COULLEMONT.
40th Divl. M.T.Coy.	AVESNES-LE-COMTE.
135th Field Ambulance.	WARLUZEL.
136th Field Ambulance.	SOMBRIN.
137th Field Ambulance.	SUS-ST-LEGER.

His Majesty the King visited the Division to-day and was pleased to express to the Divisional Commander his great appreciation of the gallant behaviour and bearing of the 40th Division during the recent operations. He was fully conversant with the work accomplished by the Division and while offering his sincere congratulations thereon he deplored the losses which have been incurred.

The Major General directs that the above be communicated to all ranks.

H.Q., 40th Division. (Signed) A.L.Cowtan, Major,
30th March, 1918. D.A.A.G.,
  40th Division.

Distribution :-
    To all Units of the Division on scale of Routine Orders.

(WB).

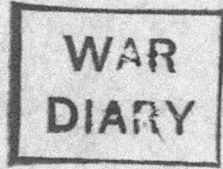

A. & Q.

40th DIVISION.

APRIL. 1918

Appendices attached:-
　　Location Returns.
　　Battle Casualties　31st March-6th April
　　Battle Casualties　9th-23rd April.

CONFIDENTIAL.   ORIGINAL.

WAR DIARY

'A' AND 'Q' BRANCH.

40TH DIVISION.

VOLUME XXIII.

FROM :- 1st to 30th April,
              1918.

WAR DIARY or INTELLIGENCE SUMMARY

Army Form C. 2118

A.D. APRIL 1918
Head Quarters 40 Divn

(Erase heading not required.)

Place	Date 1918	Hour	Summary of Events and Information	Remarks and references to Appendices
CROIX DU BAC	April 1		Reported that the Divl. Artillery will rejoin the Divn. At present 57 D. Arty. will be in line with the Divn.	(A/M)
	2		Reinforcements from base:- 12 Suff.k Rgt 1 Offr, 169 O.R., 13 E Surrey Rgt 82 O.R., 4th M.G. Bn. 157 Offrs and 150 O.R. Further Reinforcements :-	(A/M)
	3		Major W E Brown M.C. to command 18 Welsh Rgt. All transport with Divn: 2 Mid x Rgt 1 Off 574 or, 12 Suff k Rgt 62 or., 10/11 H.L.I 1 Offr 20 or. Divl. Reinforcement Wing joined at	(A/M)
	4		posted & placed at disposal of S.M.T.O. 15 "Cops" - Capt. G.V. GOODLIFFE M.O. Bde Major 119 Bde. appointed G.S.O 2 XVIII "Cops" -	(A/M)
	5		Reinforcements: 12 Yorks 82 o, 13 Yorks 233 or, 20 Middx. 1 off., 120 or, 13 E Surrey 1 off. or. 18 Welsh Rgt 100 n ; 4 Offrs R.M.G. Bn. -	(A/M)
	6		Major Smyth 18 Welsh Rgt. reported to Divn. proposed issue of dungaree clothing for Cooks recommended. Reinforcements: 2 R. Scots Fus.	(A/M)
	7		199 or. 2 R.I. Scots Fus. joined the Divn. In discharge for 11 c.A + 3 hr Bn. transferred to 38 "Divn" -	(A/M)
	8		Reported that Lancer units were not required with RE units of the Divn -	(A/M)
	9		Enemy attacked Portuguese on right in force and took in Divn. Frts. in rear. Divl. Head Qrs. moved to DOULIEU + thence to VIEUX BERQUIN. All transport withdrawn. Neighbouring	(A/M)
VIEUX BERQUIN	10		of Brit. Head Qtrs. Major Carlisle DSO MC RE appt'd command 12 Yorks (Pioneers)	(A/M)
	11		Divl. Head Qrs moved temporarily to LAMOTTE thereafter by XV Corps. Ambulances also lent there - Divl. M Q removed to LA SOUVERAIN south of HAZEBRUCK. All transport	(A/M)
	12		moved to north of HAZEBROUCK and East West of Hazebrouck. Bdes. being concentrated in neighbourhood of STRAZEELE. Divl. Troops Head Qrs and 4 Divl shop pretories and	(A/M)
	13		instruments by enemy action.	(A/M)
RENESCURE	14		Troops concentrated on transport lines near Hazebrouck. Units moved by march route to RENESCURE - STAPLE	(A/M)

Secret

A & Q
Head Qrtrs 40th Divn.

WAR DIARY
INTELLIGENCE SUMMARY
(Erase heading not required.)

Army Form C. 2118

Instructions regarding War Diaries and Intelligence Summaries are contained in F.S. Regs., Part II. and the Staff Manual respectively. Title Pages will be prepared in manuscript.

Place	Date	Hour	Summary of Events and Information	Remarks and references to Appendices
LONGUE- NESSE	15		Orders from GHQ reorganising the Divn. for use as a Divn. Blankets allowed at Scale of 1 per man. The second Army withdrawn. Reinforcements; 2/Middx Rgt 24 Or. 18 Welsh Rgt 365 O.R. H.Q.R.F. Forbes OJJ 10/11 H.L.I appointed Commandant First Army School.	Appx I Appx II
	16			Appx II
WIZERNES	17.		Units located as shown in attached list Appendix A. 14 Officers & join 1/Suffolk Rgt - Remainder to rejoin in attached.	Appendix A Appx
	18		Reinforcement 15 OR LUMBRES. Army interchange from ARQUES.	Appx
	19		Units to find drafts for other divisions - perhaps tomy to return in attd. Appendix B	Appx III appendix B
	20.		Composite Bde. to be formed and sent to East of CASSEL. to help to stop a Gap. Bde Composition & H.Q. Pl. & 121 Bde. and details of Other Bdes. (119 & 120) together with 229 Fd. by RE, one	Appx IIII
	21		M.G. Coy + No 4 Coy ASC with 137th Ambce & Section of S.A.A. Section DAC shown	C Appx
	22		Battle all settled as shown in attached appendix C.	appendix C
	23		attached list. Appendix D. Divn Casualties incurred since "April by 40 Divn	Appx D IIII
	24		Appendix E. Divn Casualties incurred by this Divn. from 21/3/18 to 6/4/18	Appx E IIII
	25		Captain A.J. MUIRHEAD appt'd. Bde. Major 119 Bde vice Capt. GOODLIFFE - Wounds. Clothing to be withdrawn.	C Appx IIII
	26		82 Divn. Pioneers & Pn General J. Campbell Coy 121 Inf Bde. appointed to command	C Appx IIII
	27		a second composite Bde. to be formed ready to move to East of Cassel. 119 Bde. Hd Qrs + 2 Composite Bdes.	Appendix F Appx IIII
			Details of no Coys. Appendix F. above constitution of 2 Composite Bdes. 121 Composite moves to PROVEN. 119 Comp Bde to Esquard.	
	28		2 Composite Bdes. move to neighbourhood of POPERINGHE.	C Appx
	29		Reconnaissance officers receive advance notice of units of the Divn. either forward or back	Appx
			Croise de Guerre awarded to 1/4 Cpl R.J. Arnowd. DSO Me. & 17 Welsh by Capt. I.H.G. EADY M.C. Bde Major 120 Inf Bde No 99442 Cpl Webster 229 Fd Coy R.E. Medaille Militaire to No 99942 Cpl Webster 229 Fd Coy R.E.	
ST. OMER	30		Divn Head Quarters moved into St. Omer.	

C.P. Moore Lt. Col.
AA & QMG
40th Divn.

S E C R E T.

40TH DIVISION.

LOCATION OF UNITS - 17TH APRIL, 1918.

A

40th Divnl. Hd.Qrs.
    (Complete).   WIZERNES.

ROYAL ARTILLERY.
   Headquarters)
   178th Bde. R.F.A.)
   181st Bde. R.F.A.)   Detached to VI Corps.
   40th D.A.C.(less SAA. Sec.))

ROYAL ENGINEERS.
   C.R.E.   With Divnl. Hd.Qrs.
   224th Fld.Coy. R.E.)
   229th Fld.Coy. R.E.)   CORMETTE.
   231st Fld.Coy. R.E.)

119TH INF. BRIGADE.
   Headquarters.   TILQUES.
   13th E.Surrey Regt.   MOULLE.
   18th Welsh Regt.   MOULLE.
   21st Middx. Regt.   TILQUES.
   119th T.M. Batty.   TILQUES.

120TH INF. BRIGADE.
   Headquarters.   TATINGHEM.
   2nd Royal Scots Fus.   TATINGHEM.
   10/11th H.L.I.   TATINGHEM.
   14th Bn. H.L.I.   TATINGHEM.
   120th T.M. Batty.   LONGUENESSE.

121st INF. BRIGADE.
   Headquarters.   ST.MARTIN-AU-LAERT.
   12th Suffolk Regt.   ST.MARTIN-AU-LAERT.
   13th Yorks. Regt.   ST.MARTIN-AU-LAERT.
   20th Middx. Regt.   ST.MARTIN-AU-LAERT.
   121st T.M. Battery.   ST.MARTIN-AU-LAERT.

12th Yorks. Regt.(Pnrs).   SALDERWICK.

40th Battn. M.G. Corps.   MOULLE.

R.A.M.C.
   135th Fld. Amb.   LONGUENESSE.
   136th Fld. Amb.   TILQUES.
   137th Fld. Amb.   SCADERBOURG.

/Over.

- 2 -

S.A.A. SECTION, 40th D.A.C.	LONGUENESSE.
D.A.D.O.S.	ST.MARTIN-AU-LAERT.
51st Mobile Vet. Section.	With S.A.A. Sec. 40th DAC.

<u>40TH DIVNL. TRAIN? ASC.</u>
   Headquarters. — LONGUENESSE.
   No. 1 Company. — With Divnl. Artillery.
   No. 2 Company. — With 119th Inf. Brigade.
   No. 3 Company. — With 120th Inf. Brigade.
   No. 4 Company. — With 121st Inf. Brigade.

237th Divnl. Employment Coy. — WIZERNES.

<u>40th DIVN. M. T. COY.</u>
   H.Q. & Workshops. — MOULLE.
   Park. — ST.MARTIN-AU-LAERT.

<u>40TH DIVNL. WING,</u>
   Corps Reinfct. Camp. — MOULLE.

Divnl. Clothing Exchange. — No. 3 Billet, WIZERNES.

H.Q., 40th Division.
17th April, 1918.

                           Captain,
                        for D.A.A.G.,
                        40th Division.

CONFIDENTIAL.

URGENT.

H.Q., 40th Division No. A16(A).

H.Q., 119th Inf. Brigade.
H.Q., 120th Inf. Brigade.
H.Q., 121st Inf. Brigade.
O.C., 12th Yorks. Regt. (Pnrs.)

---

1. Under instructions received from G.H.Q. the following repostings are to take place. The parties will be prepared to-day and despatched to-morrow, 20th April, 1918.
Transport arrangements are being notified later by 'Q'.

Total Number of Other Ranks.	From.	To.
250	13th Yorks. Regt.	4th Yorks. Regt. 50th Division.
250	13th Yorks. Regt.	5th Yorks. Regt. 50th Division.
150	12th Yorks. Regt.	5th Yorks. Regt. 50th Division.
200	21st Middx. Regt.	1st Middx. Regt. 33rd Division.
100	14th H.L.I.	9th H.L.I. 33rd Division.
100	14th H.L.I.	15th H.L.I. 32nd Division.
200	10/11th H.L.I.	15th H.L.I. 32nd Division.

2. Officers up to 5 % are to be sent with these parties if available.

3. As far as possible 1 Sergeant and 2 Corpls. per 50 men are to be included and 1 C.S.M. is to be included in all parties of and over 200 strong.

- 2 -

4. Nominal rolls of the parties are to be made out and disposed of as follows :-

    (a). One copy to be sent by the Unit to 3rd Echelon (reference D.A.G., G.H.Q. 3rd Echelon wire No. C.F.523 dated 18th April, 1918).

    (b). One copy to accompany each party.

    (c). One copy to be retained by the unit for reference.

    (d). One copy to be sent to Divnl. Hd.Qrs. by 12 noon, 19th April, 1918.

A. L. Corotan.
Major,
D.A.A.G.,
40th Division.

H.Q., 40th Division.

19th April, 1918.

Copies to :-
    C.R.E., 40th Division.
    O.C., 40th Divnl. Train.
    'G'.
    'Q'.

(RSJ)

H.Q., 40th Division No. 271(Q).

[handwritten annotation: 119.120 Composite Bde 12th Yorks, 2 M.G. Bn, S.A. Sec. 40 DAC / Reinf Wing. M.G. Coy, Employ. Coy, Signals, 12th Yorks (P) ...]

The following is the allotment of Baths to Units of the Division for period 22nd - 27th April, 1918 :-

ST. OMER.

	Times.	Units.
Monday, 22nd April.	9.30 to 1 & 2 to 5.	120th Inf. Brigade.
Tues. 23rd April.	do. do.	Composite Brigade.
Wednes. 24th April.	do. do.	120th Inf. Brigade.
Thurs. 25th April.	do. do.	Composite Brigade.
Friday, 26th April.	9.30 a.m. to 1.0 p.m.	Composite Brigade.
do. do.	2 p.m. to 3 p.m.	135th Fld. Amb.
do. do.	3 p.m. to 5 p.m.	137th Fld. Amb.
Saty. 27th April.	9.30 a.m. to 1 p.m.	12th Yorks. (P).
do. do.	2 p.m. to 5 p.m.	S.A.A. Sec. 40th DAC.

MOULLE.

Monday, 22nd April.	9.0 to 1 & 2 to 5 p.m.	119th Inf. Brigade.
Tues. 23rd April.	do. do.	do.
Wednes. 24th April.	do. do.	do.
Thurs. 25th April.	do. do.	M.G.C. Battn.
Friday, 26th April.	9 a.m. to 1 p.m.	Reinfct. Wing.
do. do.	2 p.m. to 4.30 p.m.	136th Fld. Amb.
Saty. 27th April.	9 a.m. to 1 p.m.	119th Inf. Brigade.
do. do.	2 p.m. to 4.30 p.m.	40th Div. M.T. Coy.

WIZERNES.

Monday, 22nd April.	9.0 to 1 & 2 to 4.30.	237th Div. Employt. Coy.
Wednes. 24th April.	do. do.	Headquarters Troops.
Friday, 26th April.	do. do.	do. do.

H.Q., 40th Division.

19th April, 1918.

(RSJ)

Major,
D.A.Q.M.G.,
40th Division.

LIST OF TOTAL CASUALTIES INCURRED DURING BATTLE
FROM 9-4-1918, AMENDED TO DATE.

40TH. DIVISION.

UNIT.	Killed		Wounded.		Missing.	
	Off.	o.r.	Off.	o.r.	Off.	o.r.
Divisional Headquarters.	-	-	-	1	-	-
119th Infantry Brigade.						
13th Bn: E. Surrey Regt.	1	7	-	56	18	428
18th Bn: Welsh Regt.	1	18	12	187	15	306
21st Bn: Middlesex Regt.	6	25	12	107	10	233
120th Infantry Brigade.						
2nd Bn: Rl. Scots Fusrs.	1	10	3	72	-	81
10/11th Bn: H.L.I.	1	4	5	58	8	341
14th Bn: H. Lt. Infy.	-	23	3	128	11	317
120th T.M. Battery.	-	-	-	1	-	2
121st Infantry Brigade.						
12th Bn: Suffolk Regt.	-	21	5	114	1	293
13th Bn: Yorkshire Regt.	3	26	5	90	2	200
20th Bn: Middlesex Regt.	1	6	3	42	15	379
121st T.M. Battery.	1	-	1	9	2	8
12th Bn: Yorkshire Regt.(P)	3	28	3	155	3	133
178th Brigade R.F.A.	-	2	-	6	-	-
181st Brigade R.F.A.	-	2	-	2	-	-
40th D.A.C. (British)	-	-	1	3	-	-
40th D.A.C. (Native)	-	1	-	2	-	-
224th Field Coy. R.E.	1	2	-	31	-	10
229th Field Coy. R.E.	-	3	1	23	-	6
231st Field Coy. R.E.	1	3	-	24	-	12
40th Div: Signal Coy RE.	-	-	1	2	-	8
137th Field Ambulance RAMC.	-	2	-	-	1	25
40th Bn: Machine Gun Corps.	5	12	5	67	6	141
40th Divnl: Train A.S.C.	-	-	1	4	-	-
Army Chaplains Department.	1	-	1	-	1	-
M.M.P. attd. D.H.Q.	-	-	-	3	-	-
Traffic Control att. D.H.Q.	-	-	-	2	-	-
MORC., USA. att. 13 E.Surr.	-	-	-	-	1	-
RAMC½ attd. 18th Welsh.	-	-	-	-	1	-
-do- 21st Middx.	-	-	-	-	1	-
-do- 20th Middx.	-	-	-	-	1	-
TOTAL.	26	195	62	1189	97	2923

Divnl: H. Qrs.,
23rd April 1918.

DETAILS OF CASUALTIES TO OFFICERS.

UNIT.	RANK	INITIALS & NAME.	Casualty. Nature.	Date.	In Army List
119th Inf. Bde.				April	
13th Bn: E. Surrey R.	Major	W.G. WEST	'M'	9th.	Notts & Derby.
	T/Capt.	G. BEAUMONT, MC.	'K'	9th.	
	T/Capt.	F.S. AINGER	'M'	9th.	
	Capt.(TF)	W.G. PRICE	'M'	9th.	6th TF.Bn:
	T/Capt.	C.E. LINGE	'M'	9th.	
	a/Capt.	A.B. BURTON, MC	'M'	9th.	
	T/Lieut.	R.R. WEBB	'M'	9th.	7th Bn:
	Lt.(TF)	L.W. PINNICK	'M'	9th.	6th (TF) Bn:
	Lt.(TF)	J.E.M. MICHELMORE	'M'	9th.	-do-
	T/Lt.	R.H.T. PEACOCK	'M'	9th.	
	Lieut.	H.W. ALLASON	'M'	9th.	3rd Bn: (1192b)
	T/Lieut.	W.A. MORRIS	'M'	9th.	
	T/2/Lt.	A.C. COWLIN	'M'	9th.	
	T/2/Lt.	H. BUCK.	'M'	9th.	
	T/2/Lt.	E. JORDON	'M'	9th.	
	2Lt.(TF)	W.B. PARKER, MC.	'M'	9th.	5th TF Bn:
	T/2/Lt.	J.A.V. CAMI	'M'	9th.	
	do	H.J. SMITH	'M'	9th.	7th Bn:
	do	H.E. BLATCH	'M'	9th.	7th Bn:
18th Bn: Welsh Regt.	Capt.(TF)	R.H. BASKERVILLE	'K'	9th.	Glam.Yeo.
	T/Capt.	F.M. MATHIAS, DSO.	'W'	9th.	a/Major.
	T.2/Lt.	G.I. TURNBULL	'W'	9th.	Reg. Bn:
	T.2/Lt.	J.J. BOWEN	'W'	9th.	
	T/Maj.	W.P. STRATTON	'W'	9th.	17th Bn:
	T/Lieut.	O. SALISBURY	'W'	9th.	
	2Lt.(TF)	W.B. RODERICK	'W'	9th.	4th TF Bn:
	2/Lt.(TF)	A. BARTLETT	'W'	9th.	do.

/Over.

-2-

UNIT.	RANK.	INITIALS & NAME.	Casualty. Nature.	Date.	In Army List.
18th Bn: Welsh Regt. (Contd).				April.	
	T/2Lt.	A.F. ANTHONY	'W'	10th.	
	a/Major.	H.P.B. GOUGH, MC.	'W'	13th.	17th Bn:
	2Lt. a/Cpt.	T.G. WHITE	'W' & 'M'	9th.	
	T/Lt.	J.G.S. HACKNEY	'M'	9th	
	T/Lt.	E.V. EVANS.	'M'	9th.	Col: 1579 p.
	T.2Lt.	S.H. DUFF.	'M'	9th.	
	2Lt.	W.P. GARNER	'M'	9th.	
	2Lt.(TF)	G.S. THOMAS		9th.	
	T.2Lt.	D.M. DAVIES, MC.	'M'	9th.	4thTF Bn:
	T.2Lt.	J.O. HILL	'M'	9th.	17th Bn:
	T.2Lt.	W.M. WILLIAMS.	'M'	9th.	17th Bn:
	T.2Lt.	E.A. SPINKS.	'M'	9th.	
	T.2Lt.	A.J. FRANKLIN	'M'	9th.	Reg. Bn:
	T/Lt.	J.I. RICHARDS	'M'	9th.	17th Bn:
	2/Lt.	R.O. OWENS	'M'	9th.	9th Bn:
	T.2Lt.	J.C. TUCKER	'M'	9th.	
	2Lt.(TF)	G. OWENS.	'M'	9th.	
	T/Capt.	C.R. EVANS, MC.	'W'	10th.	4th R.W.F.
18th Welsh R. att.)	T.2Lt.	R.P. JONES.	'W'	9th.	17th Bn:
119th T.M.Batty.)	T.2Lt.	R.C. COOPER	'W'	10th.	Reg. Bn:
21st Bn: Middx. Rgt.	T/2Lt.	A.E. HONESS	'K'	9th.	
	2Lt.TF.	C.H. SULLENS	'K'	9th.	8th Bn:
	T.2Lt.	S.H. LEAVER	'K'	5th Bn:	17th Bn:
	do	J. BEGGS	'K'	9th.	17th Bn:
	do	J. FREEMAN	'K'	9th.	
	T/Capt.	G.A. COLEMAN	'W'	9th.	
	do	C.A. SLIGHT.	'W'	9th.	
	T/Lt.	C.W. TABBUSH	'W'	9th.	

/Contd.

(3).

UNIT. RANK	RANK.	INITIALS & NAME.	Casualty. Nature.	Casualty. Date.	In Army List.
21st Bn: Middx. Regt. (Contd).				April.	
	T.2Lt.	E.G. HUNT	'W'	9th.	
	T/Lt.	A.P. COOPER	'W'	8th.	Reg. Bn:
	T/Lt.	E.G. BEAUMONT	'W'	9th.	1650 h.
	2/Lt.(TF)	A.T. JAGGARD	'W'	9th.	8th Bn:
	T/Lieut.	H.R. WALDEN	'W'	10th.	
	T/Lieut.	L.A. LUCAS	'W'	10th.	
	T/Capt.	R.C. SHEEN	'M'	9th.	
	T/Capt.	J.H. DALGARNO	'M'	9th.	Reg. Bn:
	T/Capt.	A.P. HEARD	'M'	9th.	1570 x.
	T/Capt.	R.A. HORNBY	'W'&'M'	9th.	Reg.Bn:
	2/Lt.	E.D. HUSSEY.	'M'	9th.	
	T.2Lt.	A.S. DUNCAN	'M'	9th.	17th Bn:
	T.2Lt.	E.J. CONYNGHAM	'M'	9th.	
	T/2Lt.	R.L. SEARS	'M'	9th.	
	T/2Lt.	R. BOULTON	'M'	9th.	
	T.2Lt.	P.M. HESTER	'M'	9th.	
	T/Capt.	A.G. SYMONS.	'W'	9th.	
	a/Lt.Col:	H.C. METCALFE.	'W'	11th.	Northants R.
	Major.	W.J. BROOKE	'K'	9th.	K.S.L.I.
	2/2Lt.	H. ALFORD.	'W'	9th.	
120th Inf. Brigade. 2nd. Rl. Scots. Fus.	2/Lieut.	J. BOYD.	'K'	12th.	
	Lieut.	F.W. FRANCIS	'W'	9th.	
	Lieut.	J. FRAME	'W'	10th.	
	2Lt.aCapt.	J.L. RIDDEL.	'W'	9th.	
10/11th H.L.I.	T/Major.	P.W. JUPE, DSO.	'W'	9th.	R.Lancs. R.
	Capt.	W.G.D.G. RORISON	'K'	9th.	
	T/Lieut.	A.A. BOWMAN	'W'	10th.	
	2/Lt.	R. AITKEN	'W'	10th.	

/Over.

(4).

UNIT.	RANK.	INITIALS & NAME.	CASUALTY.		In Army List.
			Nature.	Date.	
10/11th H.L.I. (Contd).	T/2Lt.	A.L. KING.	'W'&'M'	April. 9th.	
	T.2/Lt.	S. DUNCAN	'W'	9th.	Reg. Bn:
	T.2/Lt.	A.C. RUSSELL	'W'	9th.	3rd. Bn:
	T/Lt.a/Cpt.	T. CHRISTIE.	'M'	9th.	T/Lt.
	Lt(TF)	G.W. WOTHERSPOON.	'M'	9th.	6th Bn:
	2/Lt.(TF)	R.A. CUTHBERTSON.	'M'	9th.	7th Bn:
	Lt.	J.D. COUSIN	'M'	9th.	4th Bn:
	T/Lt.	D. STALKER.	'M'	9th.	Reg. Bn:
	2/Lt(TF)	J. ELLIS.	'M'	9th.	Lovat's Scts.
	T.2Lt.	P. HUGHES.	'M'	9th.	Reg. Bn:
14th H. L. I.	T/2Lt.	E.D. JOHNSTON	'W'	9th.	
	T/Lt.	J.R. BARCLAY	'W'	11th.	
	2Lt.(TF)	R.L.N.FREW	'W'	9th.	9th Bn:
	T/Capt.	R.D. BLACKLEDGE MC.	'M'	9th.	
	T/Capt.	H.N.S. MUMMERY	'M'	9th.	Reg. Bn:
	T/Lt.a/Cpt.	H.Y.G. HENDERSON.	'M'	9th.	
	2/Lt.	J.C. PICKEN, M2.	'M'	9th.	3rd Bn:
	Lt(TF)	G.L.DICKSON.	'M'	9th.	8th Bn:
	T/Lt.	G.C. JENNINGS.	'M'	9th.	9th Bn:
	2/Lt(TF)	J.S. ROBERTSON	'M'	9th.	4th Bn:
	2/Lt.	K. REED.	'M'	9th.	
	T.2Lt.	W. HENDERSON	'M'	9th.	6th Bn:
	2Lt.(TF)	J.D. EDWARD	'M'	9th.	18th Bn:
	T/Lt.	A.C. CURLE	'M'	9th.	
121st Inf. Brigade.					
12th Bn: Suff: Regt.	T/Capt.	H.A. REDDING, MC.	'W'	10th.	a/Capt.
	2/Lt.	L.C. WILLIAMS, MC.	'W'	10th.	3rd. Bn:
	T.2Lt.	A. JOHNSON	'W'	10th.	Reg. Bn:
	T.2Lt.	H.A. PANTON	'W'	9th.	1st Garr. Bn:
	T.2Lt.	S.H. HABERSHON.	'M'	10th.	9th Bn:
12th Suff.attd. from 20th Middx.	a/Capt.	R.H. FORSTER, MC.	'W'		

/Contd.

(5).

UNIT.	RANK.	INITIALS & NAME.	Casualty. Nature.	Date.	In Army List
13th Bn: Yorks. R.	T/Major	T.I. MITCHELL	'K'	9th April	Midx. Regt
	2.Lt.	F.T. McBAIN	'K'	9th.	
	2.Lt.	L. WARD	'K'	10th.	4th Bn:
	T.2Lt.	W.J. LUCAS	'K'	10th.	7th Bn:
	T/Lt.a/Capt.	G.H. PERKINS, M.C.	'W'	10th.	
	T.2Lt.	F.C. WALKER	'W'	10th.	
	T/Lt.	L.G. COLLINS	'W' & 'M'	10th.	7th Bn:
	T/Capt.	R.G. de QUETTEVILLE, MC	'M'	10th.	7th Bn:
	T/Lieut.	E. PEPPER	'W'	10th.	10th Bn:
	T.2Lt.	C.F. JAMESON	'W'	10th.	10th Bn:
20th Middlesex Reg.	Major	F.R. HILL	'M'	9th.	16th Bn:
	T/2Lt.	W.H. BOWDEN	'K'	12th.	
	T/Capt.	D.O. LIGHT	'W'	10th.	16th Bn:
	T/Lieut.	A.S. ALEXANDER	'W'	13th.	A.S.C.
	T/2Lt.	W.C. MASON	'W'	12th.	
	T/Lieut.	L.W. FREEMAN	'M'	9th.	Reg. Bn:
	T/2Lt.	H.P. CRITTALL, M.C.	'M'	5th.	16th Bn:
	T/2Lt.	J.A. ROLLS.	'M'	5th.	Reg. Bn:
	T/2Lt.	G.F. WHITBREAD	'M'	9th.	16th Bn:
	T/2Lt.	R.D. STEINBURG	'M'	9th.	
	T/2Lt.	H.G. BAYLIS	'M'	9th.	16th Bn:
	T/Lt. aCapt.	E.D. SAMUEL, M.C.	'M'	9th.	16th Bn:
	T.2Lt.	A.R. HULLS.	'M'	9th.	A.K.
	2Lt. (TF)	F. IZOD.	'M'	9th.	E.Denton.
	2Lt. (TF)	T.S. MOORE	'M'	9th.	8th Bn:
	T.2Lt.	A. ROBERTSON	'M'	9th.	8th Bn:
	T.2Lt.	T.W.R. FAIRALL	'M'	5th.	
	T.2Lt.	R.E. GROVES	'M'	9th.	
	T/Capt.	L. PRICE.	'W'bel'd:'	9th.	
121st T.M. Battery.	T/Capt.	H.C. KILLINGBACK	'W'	9th.	Reg.Bn: Mx.Rgt
	T/Lt.	L.C.R. MILLER	'K'	9th.	do att. from 13 Yk
	T.2Lt.	G. HENDERSON, MC.	'M'	10th.	do 21st Mx.
	T.2Lt.	C.F. SMITH.	'M'	9th.	do 12 Suff.

(6)

UNIT.	RANK.	INITIALS & NAME	Casualty Nature.	Date.	In Army List
12th Bn: Yorks. R.(P)	T/Lt.	B.C. PEACH	'K'	April 10th	
	T.2Lt.	S.F. HUTTON	'K'	11th	
	T.2Lt.	H.D. A. CHAMPNEY.	'K'	6th	
	T.2Lt.	A.E. LORD	'W'	9th.	
	T.2Lt.	S. POTT	'W'	10th.	
	T.2Lt.	G.F.W. JENNINGS.	'W'	10th.	
	T.2Lt.	A.V. DEANS.	'W'&'M'	9th.	
	T/Capt.	A.M. SHAW.	'M'	11th	
	2Lt.	J. BINNS	'M'	11th	3rd Bn:
40th DAC. RFA.	Lieut.	T. THORPE	'W' at duty 9th.		
224 Field Coy. RE.	T/Lt.	C. CARR, MC.	'K'	11th	
229th Field Coy.RE.	T/Lieut.	E.F. FORRIE, MC.	'W'	11th.	
231st Field Coy.RE.	Lieut.	M.C. BALL	'K'	6th.	
Signal Coy. RE	T.2Lt.	H. CAMPBELL, MC.DCM	'W'	9th.	
137th Field Amb.	T/Capt.	A.H. LITTLE	'M'	6th.	
40th Bn: M.G.Corps.	Hon.Lt.& QM.	G.W. MILNES	'W'	9th.	RWF.
	Lt. a Maj.	D.J.AMERY-PARKES, MC	'W'	9th.	Mx. Rgt
	T/Lt.	E. HEMSOLL	'W'	6th.	
	Lieut.	J.G. DUNCAN	'W'	6th.	9th Bn: R.S.
	T.2Lt.	V.M. DALEY	'W'	13th.	
	T/Lt.aCapt.	E.G. HERBERT	'K'	9th.	
	T.2Lt.	R.A. BOTHAMLEY	'K'	6th.	
	T.2Lt.	T.E. ELLIS	'K'	10th.	
	T.2Lt.	J.B. NORMAN	'K'	10th.	
	T.2Lt.	E.L. WILLIAMS.	'M'	9th.	
	T.2Lt.	W.G. FINCH	'M'	9th.	
	T.2Lt.	C.P. DUNN	'M'	9th.	
	T.2Lt.	W.C. WICKHAM	'M'	9th.	
	T.2Lt.	T. BOWKER	'M'bel 'K'	9th.	
	Lt.	V.C. LOWRY	'K'	9th.	
	T/Lt.	J.G. EMITT	'M'	9th.	1564 t.

/Contd.

LIST OF TOTAL CASUALTIES INCURRED DURING BATTLE FROM 21-3-18 AMENDED TO DATE.

40TH. DIVISION.

UNIT.	Killed. O.	Killed. O.R.	Wounded. O.	Wounded. O.R.	Missing. O.	Missing. O.R.	REMARKS.
Divisional H. Qrs.	-	-	1	1	-	-	
119th Inf. Brigade.							
13th E.Surrey Rgt.	1	18	8	138	-	51	
18th Welsh Regt.	-	22	7	113	1	86	
21st Middx. Regt.	-	21	7	186	2	64	
120th Inf. Brigade.							
10/11th H.L.I.	3	23	5	88	7	234	
14th H.L.I.	2	22	3	103	1	122	
14th A & S Hrs.	3	23	5	152	3	112	
121st Inf. Brigade.							
12th Suffolk Regt.	5	14	6	45	11	297	
13th Yorks. Regt.	2	45	7	109	-	104	
20th Middx. Rgt.	-	11	4	69	3	93	
121st T.M.B.	-	-	-	3	-	-	
12th Yorks. Rgt.(P)	-	3	3	23	-	0	
40th Div: Artillery.							
178th Bde. RFA.	1	11	5	39	-	2	
181st Bde. RFA.	1	7	4	34	-	-	
V/40 T.M.B.	-	1	-	1	-	-	
40th D.A.C. R.F.A.	-	-	-	-	-	2	
Royal Engineers.							
224th Fld. Coy. RE.	-	-	-	6	-	-	
231st Fld. Coy. RE.	-	1	-	2	-	-	
Signal Coy.	-	-	-	2	-	-	
Ambulances.							
135th Fld. Amb:	-	2	-	8	-	-	
137th Fld. Amb,	-	4	-	8	-	-	
40th Bn: M.G.Corps.	5	8	8	58	5	87	
RAMC.att.18 Welsh.	1	-	-	-	-	-	
RAMC.att 13 Yks.	1	-	-	-	-	-	
RAMC att 178 Bde RFA.	-	-	-	-	1	-	
USMC att 13 E.Surr.R.	-	-	1	-	-	-	
TOTAL.	25	236	74	1186	34	1242	

UNIT.	RANK.	INITIALS.	NAME	Diff.in Army List.	Nature of Casualty.	DATE.
NAMES OF OFFICERS.						March
119th INF. BRIGADE.						
13th Bn: E. Surrey Regt.	Lt.(TF)	W.V.L.	MATLEY	5th Bn:	Killed.	23rd.
	T/Capt.	O.G.	NORMAN	-	Wounded.	23rd.
	T/Lieut.	J.E.M.	CROWTHER	-	Wounded.	25th.
	T/Lieut.	A.J.G.	ALTMAN	T/2/Lt.	Wounded.	25th.
	2nd.Lt.	H.M.S.	BATTEY	4th Bn:	Wounded.	23rd.
	T/2.Lt.	F.A.	SIMMONDS.	Reg. Bn:	Wounded.	23rd.
	T/2.Lt.	G.R.	TARKY.	7th Bn:	Wounded.	25rd.
	T/2.Lt.	E.	SKIDMORE.	Reg. Bn:	Wounded.	25rd.
	T/Capt.	R.W.H.	KING.	T/Lieut.	Wounded.	26th.
18th Bn: Welsh Regt.	T/Lt.a/Cpt.	B.A.K.	ROBINSON	-	Wounded.	23rd.
	2/Lt.(TF)	S.	PRITCHARD.	4th RWF.	Wounded.	23rd.
	T/2.Lt.	J.H.	EVANS.	-	Wounded.	25rd.
	T/2.Lt.	J.	McCRISON.	Reg. n:	Wounded.	22nd.
	T/2.Lt.	F.P.	LAYLAND.	Reg. Bn:	Wounded.	24th.
	T/2.Lt.	H.	BARKER.	Reg. Bn:	Wounded.	24th.
	T/Lieut.	G.I.	TURNBULL.	T/2.Lt.	Wounded (at duty)	25th.
	T/Capt.	J.P.	JONES.	Col:1645f.	'W' & 'M'	24th.
21st Bn: Middlesex Regt.	T/Lt.	H.T.	MACAN	-	Missing bel: 'K'	23rd.
	T/Capt.	F.	GREGORY.	17th Bn:	Wounded.	25rd.
	T/2.Lt.	V.	ELLIOTT.	Reg. Bn:	Wounded.	25th.
	T/2.Lt.	FFW.	WARTNABY.	Not shewn.	Wounded.	25rd.
	T/2.Lt.	W.G.	GALLEY.	Not shewn.	Wounded.	25rd.
	T/Capt.	H.J.	SKIVG.	Reg. Bn:	Missing.	24th.
	Lieut.	P.H.	WOOLERY.	Reg. Bn:	Wounded.	24th.
	2/Lieut.	H.	PARKER.	Reg. Bn:	Wounded.	24th.
	2/Lieut.	B.J.	WARNE	Reg. Bn:	Wounded.	24th.

/Contd.

- 2 -

UNIT.	Rank.	Initials.	Name.	Differences in Army List.	Nature of Casualty.	DATE.
120th INF. BRIGADE.						March
10/11th Bn: H.L.I.	T/2.Lieut.	E.A.	GORDON.	Reg. Bn:	Killed.	21st.
	T/2.Lieut.	J.	McINTOSH.	Reg. Bn:	Wounded.	21st.
	T/2.Lieut.	J.B.	HOWIE.	Reg. Bn:	Wounded.	21st.
	Capt.	A.O.	FORBES.	2.Lt. A.Forbes. (Reg.Bn:)	Wounded.	21st.
	T/2.Lieut.	H.B.	ORR.		Killed.	22nd.
	T/Lieut.	R.G.	HUGO.	—	Wounded.	22nd.
	T/2.Lieut.	I.D.	McNEILL.	Reg.Bn:	Killed.	22nd.
	T/2.Lieut.	M.	ROSS.	Reg. Bn:	Wounded.	22nd.
	Captain.	H.T.B.	BOSHELL.	4th Bn:	'W' and 'M'	22nd.
	2nd. Lieut.	M.G.	CAMPBELL	M Campbell (Reg,Bn)	'W' and 'M'	22nd.
	2nd. Lieut.	L.A.	SHUTTE	SHUTTER 3rd.BN:	Missing.	22nd.
	T/2.Lieut.	M.G.	HOOD.	17th Bn:	Missing.	22nd.
	Capt.(TF)	H.T.	KINLOCH	6th Bn:	Missing.	22rd.
	T/Lieut.	J.B.	BLACK.	Col: 1579 1	Missing.	22nd.
	T/2.Lt.	W.D.	WHITE.	W.A.Col: 1452.	Missing.	22nd.
14th Bn: H.L.I.	Lieut.(TF)	J.C.	PRATT	J	Killed.	22nd.
	Lieut.(TF)	W.F.	ROXBURGH.	7th Bn:	Killed	23rd.
	Maj.T/Lt.Col:	J.F.N.	BAXENDALE.	Hants Yeo.	Wounded.	25th.
	2nd.Lt.(TF)	R.	WILSON.	6th Bn:	Wounded.	22nd.
	T/2nd.Lt.	R.	STEVEN.	—	Wounded.	23rd.
	Lt.(a/Cpt)(TF)	JGB.	WALKER,MC.	9th Bn,MC not shewn.	Missing.	25th.

/Contd.

- 3 -

UNIT.	Rank.	Initials.	Name.	Differences in Army List.	Nature of Casualty.	Date.
						March
14th Bn: A & S. Hrs.						
	T/2.Lieut.	J.	ALLISON.	-	Killed.	21st.
	T/2.Lieut.	D.W.	MELVILLE	Reg. Bn:	Killed.	21st.
	T/2.Lieut.	I.D.	MACKAY	Reg. Bn:	Killed.	21st.
	T/Lt.Col:	R.	BENZIE, DSO.	12th S. W. Bords.	Wounded.	25th.
	Lieut.	W.A.	WHITELAW.	3rd Bn:	Wounded.	21st.
	T/Lieut.	J.H.	SHARP	Reg. Bn:	Wounded.	25th.
	T/2.Lieut.	A.	KINNEAR.	Reg. Bn:	Wounded.	25th.
	T/2.Lieut.	A.	BROWN.	-	Wounded at duty.	21st.
	Capt. (TF).	H.B.	SANDEMAN.	9th Bn:	'W' and 'M'	21st.
	T/Lt.a/Capt.	A.	MACMILLAN	T/2.Lt.	'W' and 'M'	25th.
	T/2.Lieut.	G.	McADIE	Reg. Bn:	'W' and 'M'	21st.
121st INF. BRIGADE.						
12th Bn: Suffolk Regt.	Maj.(T/Lt.Col)	T.	EARDLEY-WILMOT,DSO.	-	Killed.	22nd.
	T/Lieut.	J.E.	HAMBLIN	T/2.Lt.	Killed.	24th.
	T/2.Lieut.	L.	SCOTT	Col:102ld.	Killed.	24th.
	T/2.Lieut.	G.R.	PEDRICK	-	Killed.	22nd.
	T/Lt.a/Capt.	A.M.	CROSS, MC.	-	Wounded.	25th.
	T/2.Lieut.	R.	TRICKER	7th Bn:	Wounded.	21st.
	T/2.Lieut.	R.E.	GOOCH	-	Wounded.	24th.
	2nd.Lieut.(TF)	L.H.	KNOWLES MC.	4th Bn:	Wounded.	24th.
	T/2.Lieut.	G.H.	COCKERTON	-	Wounded.	24th.
	2/Lieut.	E.L.	TURNER	3rd Bn:	'W' and 'M'	22nd.
	T/2.Lieut.	A.W.	BARNARD	-	Killed.	24th.
	T/Capt.	R.	ENGLAND, MC.	9th Bn:	Missing.	22nd.
	T/Lieut.	H.C.	MATHEW, MC.	No. MC.	Missing.	22nd.
	T/Lieut.	G.	HOPKINS	T/2Lt. 9th Bn:	Missing.	22nd.
	T/2.Lieut.	A.J.	WELLS	Reg. Bn:	Missing.	22nd.
	T/2.Lieut.	J.A.	BLANCH	Reg. Bn:	Missing.	22nd.
	2nd.Lieut.	S.E.	CLARKE	Reg. Bn:	Missing.	22nd.
	T/2.Lieut.	G.T.	TAYLOR	Reg. Bn:	Missing.	22nd.
	2/Lieut.(TF)	G.	HALLSMITH DSO.	5th Bn:	Missing.	22nd.
	2/Lieut.(TF)	C.H.	HITCHCOCK	-	Missing.	22nd.
	2nd. Lieut.	G.F.	FRANKLIN	Col: 1016 d	Wounded.	22nd.
12 Suff.att 10/11 HLI.	T/2.Lieut.	R.F.	FRANCIS	-	Missing.	21st.

Cont.

- 4 -

UNIT.	Rank.	Initials.	Name.	Differences in Army List.	Nature of Casualty.	DATE.
13th Bn. Yorks. Rgt.						March
	T/Lt.a/Cpt.	H.H.	SIMPKIN	a/Capt.not shewn.	Killed.	22nd.
	T/2.Lieut.	E.F.	BEAL	-	Killed.	22nd.
	T/Capt.	A.W.	SIMPKIN	-	Wounded.	22nd.
	T/Capt.	H.K.C.	HARE	7th Bn:	Wounded.	22nd.
	T/2.Lieut.	E.E.	WOOD	7th Bn:	Wounded.	22nd.
	2nd. Lieut.	M.P.	HOLGATE	3rd Bn:	Wounded.	22nd.
	T/2.Lieut.	B.G.	BOWEN	-	Wounded.	22nd.
	T/2.Lieut.	F.W.	HUDSON	7th Bn:	Wounded.	22nd.
	2nd. Lieut.	J.	ELLIS	Reg. Bn:	Wounded.	22nd.
20th Bn. Middx.Rgt.	T/Lt.a/Cpt.	H.R.	BOURKE	-	Wounded.	24th.
	T/2.Lieut.	P.H.	FORD	Reg. Bn:	Wounded.	24th.
	T/2.Lieut.	V.J.H.	HALL	Reg. Bn:	Wounded.	23rd.
	T/Lieut.	W.	WELLS	Reg. Bn:	Missing.	26th.
	T/2.Lieut.	E.	SPARKE	-	Missing.	22nd.
	T/2.Lieut.	E.T.	HOOPER	16th Bn:	Missing.	24th.
	T/2.Lieut.	J.	PHILLPOTTS	16th Bn:	Wounded.	22nd.
12th Yorks.R.(P).	Maj.(T/Lt.Col)H W		BECHER,DSO	-	Wounded.	23rd.
	T/Major.	H.F.	SHEPPERD MC.	-	Wounded.	25th.
	T/Lieut.	G.	MACDONALD	-	Wounded.	25th.
178th Bde. RFA.	T/Lieut.	H.W.	MANN	-	Killed.	30th.
	Maj.a/LtCol:	W.P.	PARSONS,DSO	-	Wounded.	29th.
	Lt.a/Maj.	F.W.E.	COOK MC.	a/Capt.	Wounded.	30th.
	2nd.Lieut.	D.	DUNBAR	-	Wounded.	30th.
	2nd Lt.	G.N.	BUSHMAN	-	Wounded at duty.	30th.
	2nd Lt.	G.M.	BROWN	-	Wounded at duty.	30th.
181st Bde.RFA.	Lieut.(TF)	J.D.	MOORE	-	Killed.	22nd.
	2nd Lieut.	J.L.M.	SINNETT	-	Wounded.	28th.
	Lt.a/Capt.	H.	WHITTLES.	-	Wounded.	22nd.
	Lieut.	C.D.	ROBERTSON.	-	Wounded.	25th.
	2nd.Lieut.	D.	HENDERSON	-	Wounded.	25th.

/Contd.

— 5 —

UNIT.	Rank.	Initials.	Name.	Differences in Army List.	Nature of casualty.	Date.
						March.
40th Bn: M.G.Corps.	T/Lt.a/Maj.	J.H.	OLIVER-THOMPSON	-	Killed.	21st.
	T/2nd.Lt.	W.I.	TFAMS.	-	Wounded at duty.	21st.
	T/Lt.a/Cpt.	A.H.	GRAVES. MC.	-	Killed.	22nd.
	T/2.Lieut.	W.J.	WESTWOOD	-	Wounded.	25th.
	T/Lieut.	A.	DUNCAN	-	Killed.	25th.
	a/Major.	S.G.	DAVEY.	Lieut.	'M' bel: 'K'	25th.
	T/2.Lieut.	C.E.	AMOS.	-	'M' bel: 'K'	22nd.
	T/2.Lieut.	J.	GORDON	-	Missing.	22nd.
	T/2.Lieut.	E.	LIGHT	-	Missing.	23rd.
	T/2.Lieut.	B.	HOWARD.	-	Missing.	24th.
	a/Capt.	B.F.	PHILLIPS	-	Wounded (Gas)	25th.
	T/2.Lieut.	C.F.L.D/PELHAM		T/Lieut.	Wounded (Gas)	25th.
	T/Lieut.	G.E.A.	ANDERSON	-	Killed.	22nd.
	T/2.Lieut.	H.W.	SPURRELL	-	Wounded.	22nd.
	T/2.Lieut.	S.G.	WHITAKER	-	Killed.	21st.
	Lieut.	W.F.	AMSDEN	-	Wounded.	22nd.
	T/2.Lieut.	J.G.	THOMAS	-	Wounded.	22nd.
	T/Lieut.	R.R.	FLOOD.	-	Wounded.	26th.
R.A.M.C.att'16th Welsh Regt.	T/Capt.	S.E.	McCIATCHY	-	Killed.	26th.
RAMC att 13 Yks.R.	T/Capt.	W.	BROWNLIE	-	Killed.	26th.
US MC " 13 E.Surr.R.	Lieut.	D.E.	BERIEY	-	Wounded and Missing.	26th.
RAMC att 178 Bde.RFA	T/Capt.	J.W.	BINGHAM	-	Wounded and Missing.	
4th E.Yks.att DHQ	Maj.(TF)	G.J.	INGLEBY		Wounded.	25th.

S E C R E T.

ORDER OF BATTLE.

COMPOSITE BRIGADES - 40TH DIVISION.

No. 1 COMPOSITE BRIGADE.

Headquarters. (121st Inf. Brigade).	A/Commander. A/Bde. Major. Staff Captain.	Lt.-Col. A.C.Baylay, D.S.O., R.E. Capt. R.C.Dickie, M.C., A.& S. Hrs. Captain P.H.Lawless, Genl. List.
'A' Battn. (12th Suffolks)	C.O. A/2nd in Commd. Adjutant.	Lt.-Col. L. Lloyd, D.S.O. Captain A.M. Cross, M.C. Captain A.A. Smee.
'B' Battn. (13/Yorks & 1 Coy.21/Middx.)	C.O. 2nd in Commd. Adjutant.	Lt.-Col. F. Miskin, M.C. Major R.H. Forster, M.C. Captain E.W. Dobinson.
'C' Battn. (20/Middx. & 1 Coy.21/Middx.)	C.O. A/2nd in Cmd. A/Adjutant.	Lt.-Col. C.E.M.Richards, M.C. Captain W.W. Milne, M.C. Captain C. Smee.
121st T.M.Batty.	O.C.	Lieut. T.A.H. Jones.
'D' Coy. 40th Battn. M.G.C.	O.C.	Major M.C. Cooper.
137th Field Ambulance.	C.O.	Lt.-Col.W.McK.H.M.McCullagh, D.S.O., M.C.

No. 2 COMPOSITE BRIGADE.

Headquarters. (119th Inf. Bde.)	Commander. Bde. Major. A/Staff Capt.	Brig.Genl. F.P.Crozier, CMG., DSO. Capt. A.J.Muirhead, M.C., Oxford Yeo. Capt. R.W. May, M.C., Welsh Regt.
'A' Battn. (18th Welsh R.)	C.O. 2nd in Commd. A/Adjutant.	Lt.-Col. W.E. Brown, M.C. Lieut. I.T. Laurence.
'B' Battn. (13th E.Surreys)	C.O. 2nd in Commd. A/Adjt.	Lt.-Col. H.L.Warden, D.S.O. Lieut. E.C. Deacon.

/Over.

No. 2 COMPOSITE BRIGADE (Cont.).

```
'C' Battn.              C.O.              Lt.-Col. A.H. Seagrim.
(H.Q. & 2 Coys.         A/2nd in Comd.    Captain J. Johnston.
10/11th H.L.I.          Adjutant.         Captain J.F. Marshall.
2 Coys./14th HLI.

One Coy. 40th Bn.       C.O.              Captain G. McCree.
  M.G. Corps.

136th Fld.Ambce.        C.O.              Lt.-Col. I.R. Hudleston.
```

27th April, 1918.

SECRET.   40th Division No. 822 (A).

(a) Approximate Strengths of Composite Brigades as follows :-

No. 1. Composite Brigade.

	Officers.	O.R.
H.Qrs. 121st Infantry Brigade.	6	100
"A" Bn. (12th Suffolk Regt.).	29	708
"B" Bn. (13th Yorks. & 1 Coy. 21st Middx.)	14	543
"C" Bn. (20th Middx. and 1 Coy 21st Middx).	19	949
"D" Coy. M.G. Battalion.	10	239.
121st Trench Mortar Battery.	3	61.
224th Field Coy. R.E.	6	201.
No. 4 Coy. Divisional Train.	4	85.
137th Field Ambulance.	8	226.

No. 2 Composite Brigade.

	Officers.	O.R.
H.Qrs. 119th Infantry Brigade.	6	100.
"A" Bn. (18th Welsh Regiment)	15	814.
"B" Bn. (13th E. Surrey Regt.).	7	528.
"C" Bn. (10/11th H.L.I. H.Q. & 2 Coys.) (14th H.L.I. 2 Coys.)	18	600
Coy. 40th Bn. M.G.C.	10	230.
No. 2 Coy. Divisional Train.	4	85.
136th Field Ambulance.	7	176.

(b). Above figures include transport, Headquarters and Signal Sections - i.e. all men actually present with Units.

27th April, 1918.

(WB).

Major,
D. A. A. G.,
40th Division.

Distribution:- VIII Corps "A"
All branches 40th Divnl. Hd.Qrs.
40th Divisional Train, A.S.C.

(7)

UNIT.	RANK.	INITIALS & NAME	Casualty. Nature.	Date.	In Army List.
40th Div: Train.	T/2Lt.	J.P. HOGAN	'W'	April 9th.	
Army Chaplains Dept.	Revd.	J.E.M. WATSON, CF.	'K'	10th.	
	Revd.	J. SHINE. CF.	'W'		
	R-vd.	H. DAVIES, CF.	'M'bel'p'	9th.	
MORC.USA.att 13.E.Surr.	Lieut.	F.B. PEDRICK	'M'	9th.	
RAMC. att 18 Welsh.	T/Capt.	R.D. McGREGOR	'W'&'M'	9th.	
do 21st Mx.	T/Capt.	G.O'MALLEY	'M'	9th.	
do 20th Mx.	T/Capt.	C.A. MEADEN	'M'bel 'p'	9th.	

Div: H.Q.;
23rd April 1918.

CONFIDENTIAL.　　　　　　　　　　　　　　　　　　ORIGINAL.

WAR DIARY.

"A" AND "Q" BRANCH.

40TH DIVISION.

VOL. XXIV.

FROM :-　　1st May, 1918.

TO :-　　31st May, 1918.

28031 W3125/M2250 1000m 6/17 M.R.Co.,Ltd. (1367) Forms W3091   Army Form W.3091.

Cover for Documents.

Nature of Enclosures

Notes, or Letters written.

WAR DIARY
or
INTELLIGENCE SUMMARY

Army Form C. 2118

A & Q
Head Qrs
40 Division

Place	Date MAY 1918	Hour	Summary of Events and Information	Remarks and references to Appendices
STOMER	1		Croix de Guerre (French decoration) awarded to 2/Lt R J Linburn DSO MC, 17 Welch Regt and Capt H G Eady MC RS Bde HQr 120 Bde and 2/Capt LINTON 229 FdCoyRE. 229 Immediate awards granted to be drawn for by lotting between Arras and Bapaume in March 1918. Italian decoration Silver medal for valour awarded to 2/Lt A R MOFFAT 14 A & S Kts Who	Case
	2		121 Camp Bde march from near PROVEN to RYVELD. 119 Bde. from RYVELD to ST MOMEUN. 121 Bde from Ryveld to St Momelin on 3rd May. 120 Bde details attached to 34th Divn from Lumbres to SERQUES. Arrangements made for detached units forming composite btles to rejoin their Brigades.	Case
	3		Personnel & transport of 40 H.G. Bn. 40th Divn ordered to be reduced to training Staff Cadres.	Case
	4		Surplus personnel of 13 E Surrey Pgt., 12 Yorks (Pioneers) 11/9 T M Bay, 18 Welch Pgt, 21 Middx Pgt, returned by Wallon and STOMER for CALAIS. Bvde Commander presented medal ribands Recipients on 4 & 7 May.	Case
	5		Surplus personnel of 10/11 HLI, 14 HLI, 120 T M Bvg, 13 Yorks Pgt, 12 Suffolk Pgt returned at STOMER and WATTEN for CALAIS. Location Units shown on attached appendix A	Appendix A
	6		All transport of above units and 2 Coy A 6 C to be prepared to proceed by march route. Concentrated at St...	Case
	7		MOMELIN. Posn Genl W B GARNETT DSO, R Welch Inno. appts. Br. Bde. 121 Inf Bde. Balance Shuts of all regimental funds to be prepared. Lt Col LLOYD appts. C.O. 12 Suffolk Pgt.	Case
	8		Captain D B WARREN H.L.I. appts. Staff Captain Solange VI Corps. — Instructions received for the preparation of the WINNIZEELE defence line. Each Bde details to prepare a Corps area report for	Case
	9		occupation by a corps. Captains DICKEN & CHAPMAN appts to form staff for preparation of a front Corps area.	Case
	10		Location of units shown in attached appendix B	Appendix B
	11		Col. Lord Henry Scott. Labour Cct. "Y" Corps attached to Divl Head Qrs. for administration of labour units working in Winnizeele line. Major Genl Kenyon C.E. attacks to Divl. HS Divn as adviser on	Case
	12		WINNIZEELE defence. —	
	13		Sample transport of units despatched by march route to CUCQ near ETAPLES — 3 stages.	Case
	14		Reported that no restrictions should be placed on sale of beer to the men. Two police posts established	Case
	15		at STAPLE and OVER ZEELE for policing of WINNIZEELE line — Captain R W MAY MC attempted Staff Captain 119 Inf Bde vice Capt Horne appta O.C. 21 Middx Pgt.	Case

WAR DIARY

Army Form C. 2118

2nd Sheet

INTELLIGENCE SUMMARY A+Q H.d. of 40 Divn

(Erase heading not required.)

Place	Date	Hour	Summary of Events and Information	Remarks and references to Appendices
ST. OMER	MAY 1918 17		Attacked last chess immediate rewards for the 2nd Divn Cup fifth between 21st & 26 March 1918	Appendix C
	18		All Bab Hot John and Staff of A Section located as shown in Appendix D, working on reconnaissance of approach to PEUPLINGUE corps area. The SAA Section & DACC proceed by march route to PEUPLINGUE	Appendix D
	19		Camp 4 miles West of Calais. Standards with recommunity at hospitals. Arrangements made for cases of S.I.W.	
	20		86 Militia medals awarded the Division for operations between 9th & 13th April 1918	
	21		1 Candidate for them. Also sent to England for Temporary Commission from the division	
	22		7 motor ambulances lent to 63rd Division of all personnel of Field Corps Coy likely to become A- are not returned. One Candidate for RE Cadet Unit & furnished each week	
	23		14 days leave granted to Lt/Col Black GSO1 40th Divn	
	24		MC awarded to Lat Rev. J.E.M. Watson attached 21 Middx Regt.	
	25		Decorations awarded in connection with Operations 9th to 13th April - Bar to MC 1. DCM 2 Bar to MC 13.	
	26		Rev. J. Stone posted to III Corps as ACG.	Appendix E
	27		Interrenewation Daily leave allotment of 1 for the division commencing on 1st June.	
	28		Personnel of Transport accompanying 101 Em Tpt of American units may remain for fortnight	
	29		2 Lt. Jones M.C. 18 Welsh Regt awarded a Bar to M.C. Command pay may be drawn by C.Os of Training Cadre Battalions.	
	30		Enemys Air raid on ST.OMER. Casualties Capt. Thatcher DADMS 40 Divn & Lieut O.R. killed	
	31		30 other ranks wounded. Further rewards for Operations 9th to 13th April 1918. Lt.Col Metcalfe 21 Middx Regt. Bar to D.S.O. Lt.Col. Brown. MC. 12 S.W.Borderers also 12 Welsh Regt. DSO. and 6 military crosses to officers. Complete scheme for an army area of 4 Corps and 12 divisions forwarded to 1st Corps. (Warrigate line defences)	

CyMaretHal a.d.c. 40 Divn

SECRET.

40TH DIVISION.

LOCATION OF UNITS - 5TH MAY, 1918.

Map Refs. :- Sheet 27 and Hazebrouck 5.A.

40TH DIVNL. HD.QRS.	17 Rue FAIDHERBE, ST. OMER.

ROYAL ARTILLERY.
  C.R.A.   )
  178th Bde. R.F.A.   )
  181st Bde. R.F.A.   )   Detached.
  40th D.A.C.(less SAA. Sec.))
  S.A.A. Sec., 40th D.A.C.   ZUDROVE.

ROYAL ENGINEERS.

C.R.E.	RYVELD.
224th Field Coy. R.E.	J.25.b.2.8.
229th Field Coy. R.E.	D.14.c.3.7.
231st Field Coy. R.E.	J.19.d.central.

119TH INF. BDE. TRAINING STAFF.

Headquarters.	NIEURLET.
13th E.Surrey Regt.	NIEURLET.
18th Welsh Regt.	S. of BOIS DU HAM.
21st Middlesex Regt.	BONNECHEM.

120TH INF. BRIGADE.

Headquarters.	SERQUES.
10/11th Bn. H.L.I.	Tented Camp vicinity of WATTEN.
14th Bn. H.L.I.	Do. do.

121ST INF. BRIGADE.

Headquarters.	KINDERBELCK.
12th Suffolk Regt. H.Q.	KINDERBELCK.
Personnel	In tented camp W. of KINDERBELCK.
13th Yorks. Regt. H.Q.	KINDERBELCK.
Personnel.	In tented camp W. of KINDERBELCK.
20th Middlesex Regt. H.Q.	KINDERBELCK.
Personnel.	In tented camp W.of KINDERBELCK.

12th Yorks. Regt. (Pnrs).

Battn. Training Staff.	KINDERBELCK.

/Over.

- 2 -

40TH DIVNL. TRAIN, A.S.C.
  Headquarters.   LUMBRES.
  No. 1 Company.   Detached with Divnl. Arty.
  No. 2 Company.   N. of SERQUES.
  No. 3 Company.   BLEUE MAISON.
  No. 4 Company.   S. of KINDERBELCK.

R.A.M.C.
  135th Field Ambulance.   Under canvas near WATTEN.
  136th Field Ambulance.   Under canvas near KINDERBELCK.
  137th Field Ambulance.   Under canvas near KINDERBELCK.

51st Mobile Vet. Section.   ST. MOMELIN.

40th Divnl. Wing.   ST. OMER.

40TH DIVNL. M.T. COY.
  Hd.Qrs. & Park.   BAYENGHEM.
  Workshops.   LUMBRES.

D.A.D.O.S.   WIZERNES.

237th Divnl. Employment Coy.   WIZERNES.

                                                          Captain,
H.Q., 40th Division.   for D.A.A.G.,
5th May, 1918.   40th Division.

Distribution:- H.Q., VII Corps (4 Copies).
                  All Units, 40th Division.
                  All Branches, 40th Divnl. Hd.Qrs.

(RSJ)

SECRET.   40TH DIVISION.

Map Ref:-
Sheet 27.   LOCATION OF UNITS -- 11TH MAY, 1918.
& Hazebrouck 5A.

UNIT.   LOCATION.   TRANSPORT LINES.

40th DIVNL. HD.QRS.   17 Rue Faidherbe, ST.OMER.

ROYAL ARTILLERY.
  C.R.A.   )
  178th Bde. R.F.A.   )
  181st Bde. R.F.A.   )   Detached.
  40th D.A.C. (less   )
     S.A.A. Section)   )
  S.A.A. Sec. 40th D.A.C.   ZUDROVE.

ROYAL ENGINEERS.
  C.R.E.   RYVELD.
  224th Field Coy. R.E.   J.25.b.2.8.
  229th Field Coy. R.E.   D.14.c.3.7.
  231st Field Coy. R.E.   J.19.d.central.

STAFF SUPERVISING 'A' SECTION.   SERQUS, Billet 19.

119TH BRIGADE TRAINING STAFF.
        'B' Section.
  Headquarters.   O.29.a.9.7. Billet 101

  13th E. Surrey Regt.   C.34.d.5.6.   NIEURLET.
  18th Welsh Regt.   P.25.c.7.7.   S. of BOIS DU HAM.
  21st Middx. Regt.   P.20.c.8.6.   BONNEGHEM.

120TH BRIGADE TRAINING STAFF.
        'C' Section.
  Headquarters.   C.2.b.2.7. near
                                  ESQUELBECQUE.
  10/11th H.L.I.   N. of ESQUELBECQUE.   E. of WATTEN.
  14th Bn. H.L.I.   N. of ESQUELBECQUE.   E. of WATTEN.
  12th Yorks. Regt.(Pnrs).   N. of ESQUELBECQUE.   Kinderbelck.

121ST BRIGADE TRAINING STAFF.
        'D' Section.
  Headquarters.   H.36.d.2.5. LE TOM.
  12th Suffolk Regt.   KINDERBELCK, G.33.d.3.0. KINDERBELCK.
  13th Yorks. Regt.   Camp in vicinity of
                                  OUDEZEELE. J.20.a.77 W. of KINDERBELCK.
  20th Middx. Regt.   Camp in vicinity of
                                  TERDEGHEM.   do.   do.
                                  (P.7.b.2.2.)

40TH DIVNL. TRAIN, A.S.C.
  Headquarters.   LUMBRES.
  No. 1 Company.   Det'd with Divnl. Arty.
  No. 2 Company.   HONDEGHEM.
  No. 3 Company.   BLEUE MAISON (WATTEN Area)
  No. 4 Company.   S. of KINDERBELCK.

R.A.M.C.
  135th Fld. Ambulance.   Under canvas nr. WATTEN.
     A.D.S.   O.30.b.4.7.
  136th Fld. Ambulance.   Under canvas nr. KINDERBELCK.
     A.D.S.   P.31.a.3.2.
  137th Fld. Ambulance.   Under canvas nr. KINDERBELCK.
     A.D.S.   J.16.central.

51ST MOBILE VET. SECTION.   NOORDPEENE.

                                                              /Over.

40TH DIVN. M.T. COY.
   Hd.Qrs. and Park.   BAYENGHEM.
   Workshops.   LUMBRES.

D.A.D.O.S.   WIZERNES.

237th Divnl. Employt. Coy.   ST. OMER.

   A.P.M., 40th Division.   17 Rue de Bergues, CASSEL.
   Major HUTH.   With 75 Labour Group.
                                          WINNIZEELE.

C.R.E. No. 1 Sector.
  (Lt.Col. CLOSE).   P.32.c.8.8.

C.R.E. Nos. 2 & 3 Sectors.
  (Lt.Col. HOYSTED).   O.30.b.7.5.

C.R.E. No. 4 Sector.
  (Lt.Col. BAYLAY).   RYVELD

C.R.E. No. 5 Sector.
  (Lt.Col. VESEY).   To be notified later.

ROYAL ENGINEERS.

227th Fld.Coy.R.E.	P.27.a.2.9.	431 Fld.Coy.R.E.	Nr.ST.MARIE CAPPEL.
167th A.T.Coy.R.E.	P.32.c.8.8.		
234th Fld.Coy.R.E.	@	432 Fld.Coy.R.E.	U.8.b.4.9.
245th A.T.Coy.R.E.	@	224 Fld.Coy.R.E.	@
229th Fld.Coy.R.E.	@	231 Fld.Coy.R.E.	@
196 Land Drainage Coy. R.E.)	C.22.c.5.4. (Sheet 36a)		

@ Locations will be notified later.

LABOUR COMPANIES.

No. 31 Labour Group.
  Headquarters.   QUEUE d' OXELAERE.
  12 Labour Coy.   LA CUNEELE. 36a. D.1.b.6.5.
  53 Labour Coy.   ST.MARIE CAPPEL. P.20.cent.
  55 Labour Coy.   QUEUE d' OXELAERE. O.24.d.6.1.
  67 Labour Coy.   TERDEGHEM. P.10.c.5.3.
  133 Labour Coy.   TERDEGHEM. P.15.b.2.6.
  147 Labour Coy.   ST.SILVESTRE-CAPPEL, P.17.c.2.2.
  164 Labour Coy.   ST.MARIE CAPPEL, P.26.d.6.8.
  176 Labour Coy.   ST.SILVESTRE-CAPPEL. P.23.a.5.8.
  188 Labour Coy.   CAMPAGNE DREVE. P.25.b.central.
  Det. 730 Labour Coy.   TERDEGHEM. P.10.c.5.5.
  Det. 172 Labour Coy.   TERDEGHEM. P.10.c.5.5.
  72 Chinese Labour Coy.   STAPLE. U.15.d.4.8.
  116   do.   do.   LONGUE-CROIX. T.5.c.3.2.
  167   do.   do.   STAPLE. U.9.b.2.9.
  179   do.   do.   LE NOIR TROU. U.26.d.7.9.

No. 75 Labour Group.
  Headquarters.   WINNIZEELE.
  61 Labour Coy.   RVELD. J.33.a.3.7.
  93 Labour Coy.   HARDIFOOT. J.19.b.6.4.
  633 Area Employt. Coy.   HARDIFOOT. J.19.b.central.
  58 Chinese Labour Coy.   HERZEELE. D.9.a.2.0.
  66 Chinese Labour Coy.   HERZEELE. D.15.b.central.
  180   do.   do.   BRIEL. D.27.a.6.6.
  181   do.   do.   HARDIFOOT. J.13.d.9.7.
  182   do.   do.   BRIARDE. J.1.b.0.

---

  43 Labour Coy.   P.36.a.8.2.
  132 Labour Coy.   P.36.a.9.2.
  94   do.   do.   V.6.a.8.7.

/Cont.

LABOUR COYS. (Cont).

780 Area Employt. Coy.		U.15.a.8.6.
781 do. do.		U.15.a.8.6.
782 do. do.		C.21.d.9.6. (Sheet 36a).
849 do. do.		C.21.d.9.5. "

INFANTRY.

No. 3 Reinforcement Camp.	U.23.d.3.3.
No. do. do.	C.16.c.4.9. (Sheet 36a).

H.Q., 40th Division.

11th May, 1918.

(RSJ)

[signature]
Captain,
for D.A.A.G.,
40th Division.

40TH DIVISION.
AWARDS.

BAR TO THE DISTINGUISHED SERVICE ORDER.

T/Lt.-Col. H.L. WARDEN, DSO., 13th East Surrey Regt.

THE DISTINGUISHED SERVICE ORDER.

T/Maj.(A/Lt.Col) H.C. METCALFE,	3rd Northants Regt, attd. 21st Middlesex Regiment.
T/Capt. R.D. de QUETTEVILLE, MC.,	13th Yorkshire Regiment.
T/Major F.R. HILL,	20th Middlesex Regiment.

2nd BAR TO THE MILITARY CROSS.

T/Capt. P.F. HONE, MC., General List (Staff Capt. A/Bde. Major, 119th I.B.).

BAR TO THE MILITARY CROSS.

T/Lieut. H. CAMPBELL, MC., DCM.,	40th Div. Signal Coy. R.E. i/c 119th I.B. Sig. Section.
T/2nd Lieut. G.V. JONES, MC.,	18th Welsh Regt. attd. 119th I.B.
T/Capt. F.B. McCARTER, MC.,	RAMC. attd. 14th Bn. H.L.I.

THE MILITARY CROSS.

Lt.(A/Maj.) H.B. BAVISTER,	C/178th Brigade, RFA.
2nd Lieut. L.M. SINNETT,	A/181st Brigade, RFA. (SR).
2nd Lt. McD. CLARK,	C/181st Brigade, RFA. (SR).
2nd Lt. A.N. GRIGG,	C/181st Brigade, RFA. (SR).
Lt. (A/Maj.) H.P. NESHAM,	D/181st Brigade, RFA. (SR).
T/Lt.(A/Capt.) C.A. ROBERTSON,	40th Div. Signal Coy. R.E.
T/Lieut. R.E. WOODHOUSE,	- do -
T/Lieut. G.A. CLARK,	224th Field Coy. R.E.
T/Lt.(A/Capt.) F.S. BEECROFT,	13th East Surrey Regiment.
T/Lieut. J.E.M. CROWTHER,	- do -
Lieut. H.W. ALLASON,	- do -
T/2nd Lieut. G.R. TARRY,	- do -
T/Capt. F.S. AINGER,	- do -
T/Lieut. D. BERNEY,	MORC., USA., attd. 13th East Surrey Regiment.
No. 482, CSM. R. REED,	13th East Surrey Regiment.
Lieut. T.J. GOUGH,	4th R.W.F. attd. 18th Welsh Regt. attd. H.Q., 119th Inf. Bde.
T/Lieut. G.I. TURNBULL,	18th Bn. Welsh Regiment.
T/Lieut. J.J. BOWEN,	- do -
Lt.(T/Capt.) G.F.P. WORTHINGTON,	West India Regt. attd. 21st Bn. Middlesex Regt.
Qr.Mr. & T/Hon.Capt. A.E. STEEL,	21st Middlesex Regiment.
T/2nd Lieut. A.A.T. MORRIS,	- do -
T/2nd Lieut. J. FREEMAN,	- do -
Capt. R.W. LAWSON,	H.L.I. (TF) attd. 10/11th Bn.
T/2nd Lieut. D. MORGAN,	10/11th Bn. H.L.I.
T/Capt. R.C. McCANKIE,	14th Bn. H.L.I.
T/Lieut. C.C. JENNINGS,	- do -
T/Lieut. J.H. SHARP.	14th Argyll & Suth'd Highrs.
2nd Lieut. W. KNOX,	A. & S. Highrs (TF) attd. 14th Battn.
T/2nd Lieut. A. BROWN,	14th Argyll & Suth'd Highrs.
T/2nd Lieut. F.H.B. FRASER,	12th Yorkshire Regt. (Pnrs).
Capt. F.H. GOSS,	RAMC.(SR) attd. 12th Suffolk R.
T/2nd Lieut. C.W. TUNNICLIFFE,	13th Yorkshire Regiment.
T/Capt. E.W. DOBINSON,	- do -
T/Capt. L. PRICE,	20th Middlesex Regiment.
T/2nd Lt. E.C.P. WILLIAMS,	- do -

/Over.

THE MILITARY CROSS (Cont).

T/2nd Lt. H.W. SPURRELL,	40th Battn. M.G. Corps.
Lt.(A/Maj.) M.C. COOPER,	4th Ox.& Bucks Lt.Inf. attd. 40th Bn., M.G.Corps.
T/2nd Lt. J.G. THOMAS,	40th Battn. M.G. Corps.
T/2nd Lt. C.P. DUNN,	40th Battn. M.G. Corps.
T/Lieut. J.B. NORMAN,	- do -
T/2nd Lt. W.I. THAMS,	- do -
2nd Lt.(A/Capt.) E.G. HERBERT,	R.Warwick Regt. attd. 40th Battn. M.G. Corps.
T/2nd Lieut. T. BOWKER,	40th Battn. M.G. Corps.
T/Capt.(A/Maj.) J.W. LINNELL,	137th Field Amb. RAMC.
T/Capt. D. CRELLIN,	136th Field Amb. RAMC.

BAR TO THE DISTINGUISHED CONDUCT MEDAL.

No.F.3055, Cpl.(L/Sgt) J. HICKMAN, DCM., MM.	21st Middlesex Regiment.
No.27544, Sgt.(A/CSM) M. NEWMAN, DCM., MM.	18th Welsh Regiment.

THE DISTINGUISHED CONDUCT MEDAL.

No.34232, Gnr. J. HARDMAN, MM.	A/181st Brigade, RFA.
No.L.25401 Sergt. A.E. KING,	D/181st Brigade, RFA.
No.106867, Sergt. W. ROOKES, MM.	40th Div. Signal Coy. R.E. attd. H.Q., 119th Inf.Bde.
No.11316, Pte. W. WARMAN,	13th East Surrey Regiment.
No.24625, Pte. J. GEARY,	- do -
No.13277, Pte. F. EYLES,	- do -
No. 8514, RSM. J.A. LEE,	- do -
No.25278, Sgt. D.P. O'SULLIVAN, MM.	18th Welsh Regiment.
No.G.15032, CSM. R.C. FISHER,	21st Middlesex Regiment.
No.14231, Cpl.(L/Sgt) J.ROBERTSON,	14th Argyll & Suth'd Highrs.
No.13341, Pte. C. CANT,	- do -
No.50012, Pte. M. HEARNE,	12th Suffolk Regiment.
No. 23404, Pte. W. ROBERTS, MM.	13th Yorkshire Regiment.
No.14979, Pte. W. BEARDMORE,	- do -
No.19763, Pte. R. DAVISON,	- do -
No.12587, L/Cpl. H.C. PEARCE,	40th Battn. M.G. Corps.

THE MILITARY MEDAL.

No.23928, Pte. H. WHITEHEAD,	12th Yorkshire Regt.(Pnrs).
No.75114, Pte.(L/Cpl) F. VASEY,	137th Field Amb., RAMC.

Issued with Divisional Routine Orders dated 15th May, 1918.

S E C R E T.

40TH DIVISION.

Map Ref:-
Sheet 27.
& Hazebrouck 3A.   LOCATION OF UNITS   -   18TH MAY, 1918.

UNIT.	LOCATION.
40TH DIVN'L HD.QRS.	17 Rue Faidherbe, ST OMER.

ROYAL ARTILLERY.
  C.R.A.)
  178th Brigade R.F.A.)
  181st Brigade R.F.A.)   Detached.
  40th D.A.C.)

ROYAL ENGINEERS.
C.R.E.	RYVELD.
224th Field Coy.R.E.	J.25.b.2.8.
229th Field Coy.R.E.	D.14.c.3.7.
231st Field Coy.R.E.	J.19.d.Central.

STAFF SUPERVISING 'A' SECTION.   SERCUS, Billet 19.

119TH BRIGADE TRAINING STAFF
      'B' SECTION.
Headquarters.	O.29.a.9.7. Billet 101.
13th E.Surrey Regt.	C.22.d.Central.
18th Welsh Regt.	O.30.a.3.2.
21st Midd'x Regt.	P.20.c.8.6.

120TH BRIGADE TRAINING STAFF.
      'D' SECTION.
Headquarters.	C.2.b.8.9.
10/11th H.L.I.	N. of ESQUELBECQUE.
14th H.L.I.	N. of ESQUELBECQUE.
12th Yorks.R.(Pnrs).	N. of ESQUELBECQUE.

121ST BRIGADE TRAINING STAFF.
      'C' SECTION.
Headquarters.	H.36.d.2.5. LE TOM.
12th Suffolk Regt.	C.11.a.Central.
13th Yorks Regt.	Camp in vicinity of OUDEZEELE J.20.a.7.7.
20th Midd'x Regt.	Camp in vicinity of TERDEGHEM. P.7.b.2.2.

40TH DIVNL TRAIN.A.S.C.
Headquarters.	No. 2 Rue St Croix, ST OMER.
No. 1 Company.	Detached with Divl.Artillery.
No. 2 Company.	Le Chateau, STAPLE.

R.A.M.C.
135th Field Ambulance. A.D.S.	Under Canvas nr KINDERBELCK. P.30.b.4.7.
136th Field Ambulance. A.D.S.	Under Canvas nr KINDERBELCK. O.30.a.2.2.
137th Field Ambulance. A.D.S.	Under Canvas nr KINDERBELCK. J.16.Central.

51ST MOBILE VET SECTION.   I.31.c.3.3./nr LE TOM.

40TH DIVNL. M.T.COMPANY.
| Headquarters and Workshops. | LUMBRES. |
| Supply Section. | STAPLE, U.3.b.2.8. |

P.T.O.

- 2 -

UNIT.	LOCATION.
D.A.D.O.S.	EBBLINGHEM.
237th Divisional Emplt.Coy.	ST OMER.
A.P.M., 40th Division. Major HUTH.	17 Rue de BURGUES, CASSEL. With 75 Labour Group, WINNEZEELE.

C.R.E., No. 1 Sector.   P.32.c.8.8.
   (Lt-Col) CLOSE).

C.R.E. Nos. 2, 3, & 5 Sectors.   O.30.b.7.5.
   (Lt-Col. HOYSTED).

C.R.E. No. 4 Sector.   RYVELD.
   (Lt-Col. BAYLAY).

ROYAL ENGINEERS.
167 A.T.Coy.R.E.   P.32.c.8.8;   231st Fld.Coy.R.E. J.19.d.central.
224th Fld.Coy.R.E. J.25.b.2.8;   234th Fld.Coy.R.E. U.1.b.6.7.
227th Fld.Coy.R.E. P.27.a.2.9;   431st Fld.Coy.R.E. P.20.d.2.7.
229th Fld.Coy.R.E. D.14.c.3.7.   432nd Fld.Coy.R.E. U.8.b.4.9.
              R.E.Reinfcts.   O.30.b.7.5.

LABOUR COMPANIES.

No. 31 Labour Group.
Headquarters.   QUEUE d'OXELAERE. O.36.b.1.8.
  12 Labour Coy.   36A/C.5.c.7.9.
  13 Labour Coy.   ST MARIE CAPPEL. P.20.Central.
  43 Labour Coy.   P.36.a.2.2.
  55 Labour Coy.   QUEUE d'OXELAERE. O.24.d.6.1.
  67 Labour Coy.   TERDEGHEM. P.10.c.5.3.
  94 Labour Coy.   P.35.a.3.8.
 132 Labour Coy.   P.36.a.9.2.
 133 Labour Coy.   TERDEGHEM. P.15.b.2.6.
 147 Labour Coy.   St.SILVESTRE-CAPPEL. P.17.c.2.2.
 164 Labour Coy.   St.MARIE CAPPEL. P.26.d.6.8.
 Det.172 Labour Coy.   TERDEGHEM. P.10.c.5.5.
 176 Labour Coy.   St.SILVESTRE-CAPPEL. P.23.a.5.8.
 188 Labour Coy.   CAMPAGNE DREVE. P.25.b.central.
 Det.730 Labour Coy.   TERDEGHEM. P.10.c.5.5.
  72 Chinese Labour Coy.   STAPLE. U.15.d.4.8.
 116   do   do   LONGUE CROIX. U.5.c.3.2.
 167   do   do   STAPLE. U.9.b.2.9.
 179   do   do   LE NOIR TROU. U.26.d.7.9.

No. 75 Labour Group
Headquarters.   J.2.a.
  61 Labour Coy.   RYVELD. J.33.a.3.7.
  93 Labour Coy.   HARDIFOOT. J.19.b.6.4.
 833 Area Emplt.Coy.   HARDIFOOT. J.19.b.central.
  58 Chinese Labour Coy.   HERZEELE. D.9.a.2.0.
  66   do   do   HERZEELE. D.15.b.central.
 180   do   do   ERIEL. D.27.a.6.6.
 181   do   do   HARDIFOOT. J.13.d.9.7.
 182   do   do   BRIARDE. J.1.b.central.

18th May, 1918.

(WB).

Major,
D.A.A.G.,
40th Division.

40TH DIVISION.

AWARDS.

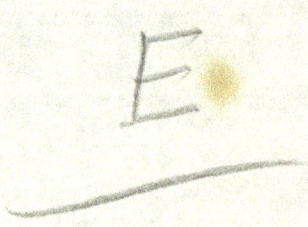

BAR TO THE MILITARY CROSS.

2nd Lieut. G.V. JONES, M.C.,   3rd attached 18th Welsh Regt.

THE MILITARY CROSS.

T/Lieut. F.N. CORBEN,	13th East Surrey Regt., attd. 119th Infy. Bde. H.Q.
2/Lieut. C.F. WILKS,	13th East Surrey Regt.
T/2nd Lt. W.T.H. SEWELL,	- do -
T/Lieut. I.T. LAWRENCE,	18th Welsh Regiment.
Lieut. D.J. DAVIES,	Pembroke Yeo. attd. 18th Welsh Regiment.
The Revd. H.W. JONES,	ACD. attd. 18th Welsh Regiment.
T/Capt. A.G. SYMONS,	21st Middlesex Regiment.
2nd Lt. W. RIDDELL,	3rd attached 2nd Royal Scots Fusiliers.
T/Lt.(a/Capt.) H.S. DAINTREE,	East Surrey Regt., attd. 120th T.M. Battery.
T/Capt. A.A. SMEE,	12th Suffolk. Regt.
2nd Lt. G. DUCKER,	Yorks. Regt.(TF) attd. 13th Bn.
T/2nd Lt. H. STORCH,	13th Yorkshire Regt.
Lieut. J.G. DUNCAN,	9th R. Scots, attd. 40th Bn. Machine Gun Corps.
T/2nd Lt. W.K. WHITSON,	40th Bn. Machine Gun Corps.

THE DISTINGUISHED CONDUCT MEDAL.

No. 99292	C.S.M. C.A. THIRWALL,	229th Field Coy. R.E.
No. 3/10300	Sergt. A.C. SMITH,	12th Suffolk Regiment.
No. 11296	Sergt. F.S. METCALFE,	13th Yorkshire Regt.

Issued with Divisional Routine Orders dated 28th May, 1918.

CONFIDENTIAL.   ORIGINAL.

WAR DIARY.

40TH DIVISION.

"A" & "Q" BRANCH,

FROM :- 1st JUNE, 1918.

TO :- 30th JUNE, 1918.

VOLUME XXV.

CONFIDENTIAL.   ORIGINAL.

28031 W3125/M2250 1000m 6/17 M.R.Co.,Ltd. (1367) Forms W3091. Army Form W. 3091.

Cover for Documents.

Natures of Enclosures.

Notes, or Letters written.

WAR DIARY
INTELLIGENCE SUMMARY

A + Q.
Head Quarters 40th Division

Place	Date 1918 JUNE	Hour	Summary of Events and Information	Remarks and references to Appendices
ST OMER	1		Divisional Cavalry of 1 Sub. Head Qrs; 3 Bde Hd Qrs; 3 A. Coys RE; Tracing Staff of 3 Bns; 2 Coys ASC; 1 Fd Ambulance; Mob. Vet. Section; Employment Coy; RA detached to Guards Division. Victoria Cross awarded to	Appx
	2		Lt. 24. BEAL. 13 Y & L Regt. and Pte (a/Cpl) A.H. Cross. 40th Bn M.G. Corps—	Appendix A
LEDERZEELE	3		Location of units as shown in Appendix A. Recommendation made that 40th to be retrained.	Appx
	4		Amount of drifting returned by the few units sent with the Divn. during month of May. Appendix B.	Appx B
	5		Bde K.M.C. awarded to Capt A.G. Symons 21 Middx Regt and Capt A.A. Somer 12 Suffolk Regt (59k)	Appx
	6		2/Col. A.C. Baylay DSO CRE 40 Divn appointed to command of an Inf Bde. (59 k)	Appx
	7		2/Col. Carlisle DSO MC RE, CRE 17 Yorks Pioneers, appointed to command of 1/7 Bn West Riding Regt. Recommended that a definite announcement be kept afoot for individuals who may have shown initiative	Appx
	8		during during minor operations, but that it should be certain that time is no delay in getting the case	Appx
	9		Captain A.C. JEBB appointed DADMS 40th Division. Vice Capt/Major THATCHER Killed	Appx
	10		The Head Quarters of 6 Garrison Bns. for posting to 40th Divn arrive at WATTEN on 10 June.	Appx
			6 Garrison Coys from First Army & 6 Garrison Coys from Third Army arrive at Watten on 13 June. The Divisional area	Appendix C
	11		4 Garrison Coys from Fourth Army arrive at Watten on 8 June shown in appendix C is allotted for accommodation. Units accommodated on 8 June. Disposition allotted to Units returns by Hd Qrs. Division. Forms an appendix C— Permanent designation of units appendix D	Appx at appendix D
	12		Garrison Bns. of Hd Divn. become 11 Cambrian Hldrs; 13 Numis Yeos; 13 East Lancs; 10 KOSB; 15 KOYLI; 12 M.	Appx
	13		Nos. 6 & 11 Sw. Yeos. Staff Rept.	Appx
	14		G.C.M. sub Lt. Jas. Burnett a/a at ST MOMELIN. For trial of an officer of Labour Corps. Instructions issued concerning precautions to be taken as a military measure.	Appx
	15		Recommended that 7. F. Canteen stores be issued to Division equally according to submitted demands and not indiscriminate, so as to prevent where one Division might obtain all available to the detriment of other divisions	Appx

Secret

Second Page

WAR DIARY
or
INTELLIGENCE SUMMARY
(Erase heading not required.)

Army Form C. 2118

A & Q Head Quarters 40 Divn

Instructions regarding War Diaries and Intelligence Summaries are contained in F.S. Regs., Part II. and the Staff Manual respectively. Title Pages will be prepared in manuscript.

Place	Date	Hour	Summary of Events and Information	Remarks and references to Appendices
LEDERZEELE	JUNE 1918 16		Captain (A/Major) R.P. PAKENHAM-WALSH MC RE appointed CRE 40 Division.	(A)
	17		12 Pnrs (Training Staff) Suffolk Regt to proceed to England.	(A)
	18		Divl. Reception Camp formed at WATTEN. Div. Buss Reserve complete scale of transport.	(B)
	19		Arrangements made to move all units of Division and attached units to occupy & defend the WINNEZEELE – WHAZEBROUCK line in case of necessity.	(C)
	20		Location of units on 17 June as shewn in appendix E. Return forwarded to	appendix E (D)
	21		Intell. Branch units and Cttees & personnel despatched to appropriate fronts.	(E)
	22		8 Garrison Coys at BOLLEZEELE from the division complete 6 battalions.	(E)
			Reinforcements from 59 Divn. Complete to 16 Bns. 121 Inf Bde. to form KATP RHOII Cdrs for one month attached to	(F)
REMESCURE	23		Captain R.C. Matthews M.C. Bde Major 121 Bde to proceed KAT RHO II STOMER on 22 – & took & EBBLINGHEM in	(F) appendix F (G)
			Intelligence duties. Railheads changed. Location of units appendix F. Trains and Blankets during summer months. (C) (M) inspection 24.15 HQ 24.15	(G)
	24		C in C inspection division as an unit. Indents submitted accordingly – SS 4 Section 40 E, A. Cyclist Bn reformed and 16 Division. Purchases from forge by	(G)
	25		Training Staff 18 Welsh Regt. proceed to England with 16 Division. 2 R. Irish Regt 23 Cheshire form 121 Bde.	(G)
	26		Belgium not to be made. I Worcester; 23 Lanc. Fus. 2 R. Irish Regt 23 Cheshire form 121 Bde	(G)
	27		Leave allotment of 1 per diem to division increased by ultimate already joining.	(G)
	28		A Pioneer Bn to be formed 17 Worcester chosen for this purpose applicants made for NCOs	(G)
	29		Barker & Training Staff of 12 Yorks Regt (Pioneers) to be absorbed.	(G)
	30		69 officers & other ranks forming units of division medically examined and amongst found unfit to be sent home. Febrase S.A. Return to be formed of Category A men. to join on 1st July.	(G)
			G HQ have applied to War Office for designation "Garrison" to be eliminated from Infl. Bns. 40 Division. GH Mootly Major	(G)

1875 Wt. W593/826 1,000,000 4/15 J.B.C. & A. A.D.S.S./Forms/C. 2118.

SECRET.

40TH DIVISION.

Map Ref:-
Sheet 27,
& Hazebrouck 5A.   LOCATION OF UNITS.   -   3RD JUNE, 1918.

UNIT.	LOCATION.
40TH DIVN'L HD.QRS.	LEDERZEELE, Sheet 27.

ROYAL ARTILLERY.
C.R.A.)
178th Brigade R.F.A.)   Detached with Guards Division.
181st Brigade R.F.A.)
40th D.A.C.)

ROYAL ENGINEERS.
C.R.E.   DOORNAERT, H.14.3.4.6. (Sheet 27).
224th Field Coy.R.E.   J.25.b.2.8.
229th Field Coy.R.E.   D.14.c.3.7.
231st Field Coy.R.E.   J.19.d.Central.

119TH BRIGADE TRAINING STAFF
'B' SECTION.
Headquarters.   O.29.a.9.7. Billet 101.
18th Welsh Regt.   O.30.a.3.2.

120TH BRIGADE TRAINING STAFF
'D' SECTION.
Headquarters.   C.2.b.8.9.
12th Yorks.Regt. (P).   LES RUES B.25.c.7.8.

121ST BRIGADE TRAINING STAFF
'C' SECTION.
Headquarters.   H.36.d.2.5. LE TOM.
12th Suffolk Regiment.   NOORDPEENE.(Sheet 27 N.6.d.1.3.).

40TH DIVISIONAL TRAIN.A.S.C.
Headquarters.   No. 2 Rue St CROIX, ST OMER.
No. 1 Company.   Detached with Divisional Artillery.
No. 2 Company.   Le Chateau, STAPLE.

R.A.M.C.
A.D.S. (135th Fld.Amblc). C.30.b.4.7.
A.D.S. (136th Fld.Amblc). O.30.a.2.2.
137th Field Ambulance.   Under canvas near KINDERBELCK.
   A.D.S.   J.15.d.0.5.

51ST MOBILE VET.SECTION.   I.31.c.3.3. Nr. LE TOM.

40th DIVNL.M.T.COMPANY.
Headquarters & Workshops. Sheet 27 A.,S.E. X.15.b.8.5.(Longuenesse).
Supply Section.   STAPLE, U.3.b.2.8.

D.A.D.C.S.   EBBLINGHEM.

237th Divnl.Employt.Coy.   BROXEELE.

Divl.Gas Officer.   BROXEELE.
Divl.Claims & Baths Officer.   do.
Divl.Salvage and Burial Offr. do.

A.P.M.,40th Division.   17 Rue de BURGUES, CASSEL.

P.T.O.

UNIT.	LOCATION.
C.R.E., No. 1 Sector. (Lt-Col.CLOSE).	P.32.c.8.8.
C.R.E., No's 2, 3, & 5 Sectors. (Lt-Col.HOYSTED).	O.30.b.7.5.
C.R.E., No. 4 Sector. (Lt-Col. BAYLAY).	RYVELD.

ROYAL ENGINEERS.
H.Qrs. & 2 Sections –
  224th Field Coy.R.E.   H.33.b.6.5.
Remaining 2 Sections.   J.25.b.2.8.
227th Field Coy.R.E.   P.27.a.2.9.
H.Qrs. & 2 Sections –
  229th Field Coy.R.E,   B.25.b.5.2.
Remaining 2 Sections.   D.20.b.
H.Qrs. & 2 Sections –
  231st Field Coy.R.E.   J.19.d.central.
Remaining 2 Sections.   P.24.a.5.2.
234th Field Coy.R.E.   U.1.b.6.7.
236th A.T.Coy.R.E.   P.20.central (Sheet 27).
R.E.Reinfcts.   O.30.b.7.5.

No. 31 Labour Group.
Headquarters.   QUEUE d'OXELAERE. O.36.b.1.8.
  12 Labour Company.   36A/C.5.d.9.5.
  13 Labour Company.   ST.MARIE CAPPEL. P.20.central.
  43 Labour Coy.   P.36.a.2.2.
  55 Labour Coy.   TERDEGHEM. P.10.c.5.3.
  67 Labour Coy.   QUEUE d'OXELAERE. O.24.d.6.1.
  94 Labour Coy.   P.35.a.3.8.
  132 Labour Coy.   P.36.a.9.2.
  133 Labour Coy.   TERDEGHEM. P.15.b.2.6.
  147 Labour Coy.   St.SILVESTRE-CAPPEL. P.17.c.2.2.
  164 Labour Coy.   ST.MARIE-CAPPEL. P.26.d.6.8.
  Det.172 Labour Coy.   TERDEGHEM. P.10.c.5.5.
  176 Labour Coy.   St.SILVESTRE-CAPPEL. P.23.a.5.8.
  188 Labour Coy.   CAMPAGNE DREVE. P.25.b.central.
  Det.730 Labour Coy.   TERDEGHEM. P.10.c.5.5.
  167 Chinese Labour Coy.   STAPLE. U.9.b.2.9.
  179   do.   do.   LE NOIR TROU. U.26.d.7.9.
  111 Labour Coy.   V.15.a.7.3.

No. 75 Labour Group.
  Headquarters.   J.2.a.8.2. LA LOGE.
  61 Labour Coy.   RVELD. J.33.a.3.7.
  93 Labour Coy.   HARDIFOOT. H.16.c.5.7.
  833 Area Employt. Coy.   HARDIFOOT. H.16.c.5.7.
  180 Chinese Labour Coy.   BRIEL. D.27.a.6.6.
  181   do.   do.   HARDIFOOT. J.13.d.9.7.
  182   do.   do.   H.8.b.7.6.

H.Q., 40th Division.

3rd June, 1918.

Capt.
Major,
D.A.A.G.,
40th Division.

40TH DIVISION.

STATEMENT OF DRIPPING HANDED IN BY UNITS DURING MONTH OF MAY, 1918.

	1st to 7th lbs.	8th to 14th lbs.	15th to 21st lbs.	22nd to 31st lbs.	Total lbs.	Amount recd. paid or to be paid to units Francs.
ROYAL ARTILLERY.						
SAA. Sec. 40th DAC.	-	87	-	-	87	30.45
ROYAL ENGINEERS.						
224th Fld.Coy. R.E.	-	-	-	100	100	35.00
231st Fld.Coy. R.E.	45	-	-	-	45	15.75
119TH INF. BRIGADE.						
21st Middx. Regt.	44	-	-	-	44	15.40
120TH INF. BRIGADE.						
14th H.L.I.	-	48	-	-	48	16.80
121ST INF. BRIGADE.						
12th Suffolk Regt.	254	-	-	-	254	88.90
13th Yorks. Regt.	-	-	100	-	100	35.00
20th Middx. Regt.	150	-	-	-	150	52.50
R.A.M.C.						
136th Fld. Amb.	-	40	50	50	140	49.00
40TH DIVNL. TRAIN.						
No. 2 Coy. A.S.C.	-	-	-	108	108	37.80
No. 4 Coy. A.S.C.	40	-	-	-	40	14.00
12th Yorks. Regt.(P).	-	85	-	-	85	29.75
40th Divn. M.T.Coy.	-	-	-	145	145	50.75
31ST LABOUR GROUP.						
13th Labour Coy.	-	-	-	288	288	100.80
67th Labour Coy.	-	-	-	194	194	67.90
94th Labour Coy.	-	-	-	99	99	34.65
133rd Labour Coy.	-	-	135	135	270	94.50
147th Labour Coy.	-	-	-	48	48	16.80
164th Labour Coy.	-	100	100	96	296	103.60
176th Labour Coy.	-	-	-	196	196	68.60
188th Labour Coy.	-	100	53	99	252	88.20
75TH LABOUR GROUP.						
35th Area Emplyt.Co.	-	-	-	144	144	50.40
61st Labour Coy.	-	-	-	96	96	33.60
93rd Labour Coy.	-	-	-	96	96	33.60
TOTAL.	533	460	438	1894	3325	1163.75.

Issued with Divnl. Routine Orders, dated 5th June, 1918.

(RSJ)

SECRET.

40TH DIVISION.

Map Ref.:-
Sheet 27.
& Hazebrouck 5 A.   LOCATION OF UNITS. -   8TH JUNE, 1918.

UNIT.	LOCATION.
40TH DIVN'L HD.QRS.	LEDERZEELE, Sheet 27.
ROYAL ARTILLERY.	
C.R.A.)	
178th Brigade R.F.A.)	
181st Brigade R.F.A.)	Detached with Guards Division.
40th D.A.C.)	
119TH BRIGADE TRAINING STAFF 'B' SECTION.	
Headquarters.	O.29.a.9.7. Billet No. 101.
18th Welsh Regiment.	O.30.a.3.2.
120TH BRIGADE TRAINING STAFF 'D' SECTION.	
Headquarters.	H.3.a.2.5. (Sheet 27).
12th Yorks Regt. (P).	LES RUES B.25.c.7.8.
121ST BRIGADE TRAINING STAFF 'C' SECTION.	
Headquarters.	H.36.d.2.5. LE TOM.
Detachment.	C.2.b.8.9.
12th Suffolk Regiment.	P.7.b.2.2.
40TH DIVISIONAL TRAIN A.S.C.	
Headquarters.	LEDERZEELE.
No. 1 Company.	Detached with Divisional Artillery.
No. 2 Company.	Le Chateau, STAPLE.
R.A.M.C.	
137th Field Ambulance.	Under Canvas near KINDERBELCK.
A.D.S.	J.15.d.0.5.
A.D.S.	O.30.a.2.2.
51ST MOBILE VET. SECTION.	I.31.c.3.3. near LE TOM.
40TH DIVN'L M.T.COMPANY.	
Headquarters & Workshops.	Sheet 27 A.,S.E. X.15.b.8.5. (Longuénésse).
Supply Section.	STAPLE, U.3.b.2.8.
D.A.D.O.S.	EBBLINGHEM.
237th Divnl.Employment Coy.	BROXEELE.
Divnl.Claims and Baths Officer.	do.
Divnl.Salvage and Burial Officer.	do.
A.P.M.,40th Division.	17 Rue de BURGUES, CASSEL.

P. T. O.

- 2 -

UNIT.	LOCATION.
C.R.E., No. 1 Sector. (Lt-Col. CLOSE).	P.32.c.8.8.
C.R.E., No's 2, 3, & 5 Sectors. (Lt-Col. HOYSTED).	O.25.c.2.7.
C.R.E., No. 4 Sector.	DOORNAERT (H.14.b.4.6.) Sheet 27.

ROYAL ENGINEERS.
H.Qrs. and 2 Sections –
224th Field Company R.E.   H.33.b.5.5.
Remaining 2 Sections.   J.25.b.2.8.
H.Qrs., 227th Field Company R.E.   P.27.a.2.9.
Detachment.   N.12.c.8.1.
H.Qrs., and 2 Sections –
229th Field Company R.E.   B.25.b.5.2.
Remaining 2 Sections.   D.20.b.
H.Qrs., and 2 Sections –
231st Field Company R.E.   J.19.d.central.
Remaining 2 Sections.   P.24.a.5.2.
234th Field Company R.E.   U.1.b.6.7.
236th A.T. Company R.E.   P.20.central (Sheet 27).
R.E. Reinforcements.   O.25.c.1.8.

No. 31 Labour Group.
Headquarters.   QUEUE d' OXELAERE. O.36.b.1.8.
  12 Labour Company.   36A/C.5.d.9.5.
  13 Labour Company.   V.13.d.3.0.
  55 Labour Company.   U.25.a.7.2. (Sheet 27).
  61 Labour Company.   V.3.c.8.3.
  67 Labour Company.   TERDEGHEM. P.10.c.5.3.
  94 Labour Company.   C.22.d.6.5. (Sheet 36 A).
  132 Labour Company.   P.36.a.9.2.
  133 Labour Company.   TERDEGHEM. P.15.b.2.6.
  147 Labour Company.   ST SILVESTRE-CAPPEL. P.17.c.2.2.
  164 Labour Company.   ST MARIE-CAPPEL. P.26.d.6.8.
  Det 172 Labour Company.   TERDEGHEM. P.10.c.5.5.
  188 Labour Company.   CAMPAGNE DREVE. P.25.b.central.
  Det 730 Labour Company.   TERDEGHEM. P.10.c.5.5.
  167 Chinese Labour Company.   STAPLE. U.9.b.2.9.
  ~~179 Chinese Labour Company.~~ ~~LE NOIR TROU. U.26.d.7.9.~~
  111 Labour Company.   V.15.a.7.3.

No. 75 Labour Group.
Headquarters.   H.14.d.9.7. (Sheet 27).
  93 Labour Company.   HARDIFOOT. H.16.c.5.7.
  833 Area Employment Coy.   HARDIFOOT. H.16.c.5.7.
  180 Chinese Labour Company.   BRIEL. D.27.a.6.6.
  181 Chinese Labour Company.   HARDIFOOT. J.13.d.9.7.
  182 Chinese Labour Company.   H.2.c.1.9.
  1st Middlesex Labour Coy.   H.26.d.8.0.

179 Chinese Lab. Coy   *LE KOEP. H.8.b.7.6. (Sheet 27)*

                                   [signature]
                                   Captain,
                                   for D. A. A. G.,
                                   40th Division.

H.Q., 40th Division.
8th June, 1918.
(WB).

S E C R E T.

40TH DIVISION.

Map Ref:-
Sheet 27.
& Hazebrouck 5 A.   LOCATION OF UNITS.   10TH JUNE, 1918.

UNIT.	LOCATION.
40TH DIVN'L HD.QRS.	LEDERZEELE, Sheet 27).
ROYAL ARTILLERY.	
C.R.A.)	
178th Brigade R.F.A.)	Detached with Guards Division.
181st Brigade R.F.A.)	
40th D. A. C.)	
119TH BRIGADE TRAINING STAFF	
'B' SECTION.	
Headquarters.	N.12.d.2.3.
18th Bn. Welsh Regiment.	N.17.b.0.1.(Sheet 27).
120TH BRIGADE TRAINING STAFF.	
'D' SECTION.	
Headquarters.	LEDERZEELE.
12th Bn. Yorks Regt.(P).	LES RUES B.25.c.7.8.
No. 6 Garrison Battalion.	LES 5 RUES.
No. 7 do do.	WULVERDINGE.
No. 8 do do.	COPVEL, MIDDEL STRAETE,
	& PELDERHOUCK.
No. 9 do do.	BUYSSCHEURE.
No.10 do do.	BUYSSCHEURE.
No.11 do do.	BROXEELE-RUBROUCK Road.
121ST BRIGADE TRAINING STAFF.	
'C' SECTION.	
Headquarters.	H.36.d.2.5. LE TOM.
Detachment.	C.2.b.8.9.
12th Bn. Suffolk Regiment.	P.7.b.2.2.
40TH DIVISIONAL TRAIN A.S.C.	
Headquarters.	BUYSSCHEURE.
No. 1 Company.	Detached with Divisional Artillery.
No. 2 Company.	Le Chateau, STAPLE.
R. A. M. C.	
137th Field Ambulance.	Under canvas near KINDERBELCK.
51ST MOBILE VET.SECTION.	I.31.c.3.3. near LE TOM.
40TH DIVN'L M.T.COMPANY.	
Headquarters & Workshops.	Sheet 27 A.,S.E. X.15.b.8.5.
	(LONGUENESSE).
Supply Section.	STAPLE, U.3.b.2.8.
D. A. D. O. S.	EBBLINGHEM.
237th Divn'l Employment Coy.	BROXEELE.
Divnl.Claims and Baths Officer.	do.
Divnl.Salvage and Burial Officer.	do.
A.P.M.,40th Division.	17 Rue de BURGUES, CASSEL.

/P.T.O.

- 2 -

UNIT.	LOCATION.
C.R.E., No. 1 Sector. (Lt-Col. CLOSE).	P.32.c.8.8.
C.R.E., No's 2, 3 & 5 Sectors. (Lt-Col HOYSTED).	C.25.c.2.7.
C.R.E., No. 4 Sector.	DOORNAERT (N.14.b.4.6) Sheet 27.

ROYAL ENGINEERS.

224th Field Coy. R.E.	H.33.b.6.5.
H.Qrs., 227th Field Coy. R.E.	P.27.a.2.9.
Detachment.	N.12.c.8.1.
229th Field Coy. R.E.	B.25.b.5.2.
231st Field Coy. R.E.	V.15.a.5.1.
234th Field Coy. R.E.	U.1.b.6.7.
236th A.T. Coy. R.E.	P.20.central (Sheet 27).
R.E., Reinforcements.	C.25.c.1.8.

No. 5 Labour Group.

Headquarters.	Near STAPLE, U.4.d.2.4.
12 Labour Company.	36A/C.5.d.9.5.
13 do do.	V.13.d.3.0.
55 do do.	U.25.a.7.2. (Sheet 27).
61 do do.	V.3.c.8.3.
94 do do.	C.22.d.6.5. (Sheet 36 A).
111 do do.	V.15.a.7.3.
132 do do.	P.36.a.9.2.
164 do do.	ST MARIE-CAPPEL, P.26.c.6.8.
178 do do.	36A/C.5.b.2.8.

No. 31 Labour Group.

Headquarters.	QUEUE d' CXELAERE, C.36.b.1.8.
67 Labour Company.	TERDEGHEM, P.10.c.5.3.
135 do do.	TERDEGHEM, P.15.b.2.6.
147 do do.	ST SILVESTRE-CAPPEL, P.17.c.2.2.
188 do do.	CAMPAGNE DREVE, P.23.a.central.
Det.172 Labour Coy.	TERDEGHEM, P.10.c.5.3.
Det.730 do do.	TERDEGHEM, P.10.c.5.5.
167 Chinese Labour Coy.	STAPLE, U.9.b.2.9.

No. 75 Labour Group.

Headquarters.	H.14.d.9.7. (Sheet 27).
1st Middlesex Labour Coy.	H.26.b.2.3.
93 Labour Company.	HARDIFOOT, H.16.c.5.7.
833 Area Employment Coy.	HARDIFOOT, H.16.c.5.7.
179 Chinese Labour Coy.	LE KOEP, H.8.b.7.6. (Sheet 27).
180 do do.	BRIEF, D.27.a.6.6.
181 do do.	HARDIFOOT, J.13.c.9.7.
182 do do.	H.2.c.1.9.

H.Qrs., 40th Division.
10th June, 1918.
(WB).

[signature]
Captain,
for D.A.A.G.,
40th Division.

S E C R E T.   40TH   DIVISION.

Map Ref :-
Sheet 27.
& Hazebrouck 5 A.   LOCATION OF UNITS.   17TH JUNE, 1918.

UNIT.   LOCATION.

40TH DIVN'L HD.QRS.   LEDERZEELE,

ROYAL ARTILLERY.
  C.R.A.   )
  178th Brigade R.F.A.   )
  181st Brigade R.F.A.   ) Detached with 2nd. Division.
  40th D.A.C.   )

119TH INFANTRY BRIGADE.
  Headquarters,   NIEURLET.
  13th Garr.Bn.R.Innis.Fus.   -do-
  15th   -do- E.Lancs.Regt.   KINDERBELCK.
  12th   -do- N.Staff.Regt.   LE PARADIS.

120TH INFANTRY BRIGADE.
  Headquarters,   LEDERZEELE.
  10th Garr.Bn.K.O.S.Bdrs.   BUYSSCHEURE.
  15th   -do- K.O.Y.L.I.   -do-
  11th   -do- Cameron Hdrs.   LES 5 RUES.
  12th Bn.Yorks Regt. (P).   LES RUES, B.25.e.7.8.

121ST INFANTRY BRIGADE.
  Headquarters,   SALPERWICK, 27a.S.E./R.20.b.7.1.

40TH DIVN'L TRAIN,A.S.C.
  Headquarters,   BUYSSCHEURE.
  No. 1 Company.   Detached with Divisional Artillery.
  No. 2 Company.   LE CHATEAU, STAPLE.
  No. 3 Company.   BUYSSCHEURE.
  No. 4 Company.   ST MARTIN AU LAERT Area.

R.A.M.C.
  137th Field Ambulance.   Under canvas near KINDERBELCK.

51ST MOBILE VET SECTION.   ST MOMELIN.

40TH DIVN'L M.T.COMPANY.
  Headquarters & Workshops.   Sheet 27 A.,S.E. X.15.b.8.5.
                                            (LONGUENESSE).
  Supply Section.   STAPLE, U.3.b.2.8.

D.A.D.O.S.   EBBLINGHEM.

237th Divnl.Employment Coy.   BROXEELE.
Divnl.Claims and Baths Offr.   -do-
Divnl. Salv: and Burial Offr.   -do-
Divnl. Gas Officer.   -do-

A.P.M.,40th Division.   LEDERZEELE.

/P.T.O.

- 2 -

UNIT.	LOCATION.
C.R.E., No.1 Sector. (Lt-Col OLOSE).	P.32.c.8.8.
C.R.E., No's 2, 3 & 5 Sectors. (Lt-Col.HOYSTED)	O.25.c.2.7.
C.R.E., No.4 Sector. (Lt-Col.PAKENHAM-WALSH).	DOORNAERT (N.14.b.4.6.). Sheet 27.

ROYAL ENGINEERS.
```
  224th Field Company.R.E.        H.33.b.6.5.
  H.Q.,227th Field Coy.R.E.       P.27.a.2.9.
    Detachment.                   N.12.c.8.1.
  229th Field Company R.E.        B.25.b.5.2.
  231st Field Company R.E.        V.15.a.5.1.
  234th Field Company.R.E.        U.1.b.6.7.
  236th Field Company R.E.        36A/C.9.SERCUS.
  R.E.Reinforcements.             O.25.c.1.8.
```

No.5 Labour Group.
```
  Headquarters,                   Near STAPLE, U.4.d.2.4.
  12 Labour Company.              36A/C.5.d.9.5.
  13     -do-                     V.13.d.3.0.
  55     -do-                     V.25.a.7.2. (Sheet 27).
  61     -do-                     V.c.3.8.3.
  94     -do-                     C.22.d.6.5. (Sheet 36 A).
  111    -do-                     V.15.a.7.3.
  132    -do-                     P.36.a.9.2.
  164    -do-                     ST MARIE-CAPPEL, P.26.d.6.8.
  178    -do-                     36A/ C.5.b.2.8.
```

No. 31 Labour Group.
```
  Headquarters,                   QUEUE d' OXELAERE, C.36.b.1.8.
  67 Labour Company.              U.5.c.8.9.
  93     -do-                     STAPLE, U.5.c.5.3.
  133    -do-                     U.9.b.2.9.
  147    -do-                     U.10.b.9.1.
  188    -do-                     CAMPAGNE DREVE, P.25.b.central.
  Det.172 Lab.Company.            TERDEGHEM, P.10.c.5.5.
  Det.730   -do-                    do,      do.
  833 Area Employment Coy.        STAPLE, U.10.b.7.8.
```

No. 75 Labour Group.
```
  Headquarters.                   H.14.c.9.7. (Sheet 27).
  1st Middlesex Lab.Coy.          H.26.b.2.3.
  167 Chinese Labour Coy.         H.22.b.4.7. (Sheet 27).
  179     -do-                    LE KOEF, H.3.b.7.5. (Sheet 27).
  180     -do-                    B.19.d.9.2.
  181     -do-                    H.34.c.3.0.
  182     -do-                    H.2.c.1.9.
```

H.Q., 40th Division.

(WB).

W. D. Fitz-Gibbon.
Captain,
for D. A. A. G.,
40th Division.

S E C R E T.

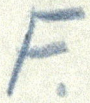

40TH DIVISION.

Map Ref:-
Sheet 27.&
Hazebrouck 5 A.

LOCATION OF UNITS LIST dated 23rd June, 1918.

UNIT.	LOCATION.
40TH DIVN'L Hd.Qrs.	RENESCURE.

ROYAL ARTILLERY.
   C.R.A.   )
   178th Brigade R.F.A.)
   181st Brigade R.F.A.)   Detached with 2nd Division.
   40th D.A.C.   )

119TH INFANTRY BRIGADE.
Headquarters.	27/U.18.d.9.7.
13th Garr.Bn.Innisk. Fus.	27/U.17.d.2.2.
13th do. E.Lancs.Regt.	27/U.18.d.7.5.
12th do. N. Staffs,Regt.	27/U.16.b.7.2.

120TH INFANTRY BRIGADE.
Headquarters.	36A/C.21.d.0.3.
10th Garr.Bn.K.O.S.Bdrs.	36A/C.21.a.2.5.
15th do. K.O.Y.L.I.	36A/C.14.d.6.2.
11th do. Cameron Hldrs.	36A/C.14.c.7.7.
12th Bn. Yorks. Regt.(P).	36A/C.14.c.7.2.

121ST INFANTRY BRIGADE.
Headquarters.	36A/C.3.c.5.3.
23rd Garr.Bn. Lancs. Fus.	27/U.27.b.3.5.
17th do. Worcester Regt.	27/U.26.d.4.7.
23rd do. Cheshire Regt.	27/U.27.a.0.3.
2nd do. R. Irish Regt.	27/U.27.c.3.2.

40TH DIVN'L TRAIN. A.S.C.
Headquarters,	RENESCURE.
No. 1 Company.	Detached with Divnl.Artil'y.
No. 2 Company.	LE CHATEAU, STAPLE.
No. 3 Company.	36A/C.14.c.4.8.
No. 4 Company.	27/U.28.b.0.6.

R.A.M.C.
   137th Field Ambulance.   27/C.8.b.5.7.

51ST MOBILE VET. SECTION.   36A/B.11.a.

40TH DIVN'L M.T. COMPANY.
   Headquarters & Workshops.   Sheet 27 A.,S.E.
                                          X.15.b.8.5.(LONGUENESSE).
   Supply Section.   STAPLE, U.3.b.2.8.

D.A.D.O.S.   EBBLINGHEM.

237th Divnl. Employment Coy.	RENESCURE.
Divnl.Claims & Baths Offr.	do.
Divnl.Salvage & Burial Offr.	do.
Divnl. Gas Officer.	do.

- 2 -

UNIT.	LOCATION.

C.R.E. No. 1 Sector.
  (Lt.Col. CLOSE).
C.R.E. No's 2, 3, & 5 Sectors.
  (Lt.Col. HOYSTED).
C.R.E. No. 4 Sector.
  (Lt.Col. PAKENHAM-WALSH).

DOORNAERT, (27/N.14.b.4.6.).

O.25.c.2.7.

RENESCURE.

ROYAL ENGINEERS.
```
  224th Field Company R.E.          U.18.d.central.
  H.Q., 227th Field Coy. R.E.       P.27.a.2.9.
  Detachment.                       N.12.c.8.1.
  229th Field Coy. R.E.             C.3.d.8.1.
  231st    do.                      V.15.a.5.1.
  234th    do.                      U.1.b.6.7.
  207th    do.                      H.33.b.7.6.
  R.E. Reinforcements.              O.25.c.1.8.
```

No. 5 Labour Group.
```
  Headquarters.               Near STAPLE, U.4.d.2.4.
  12 Labour Company.          36A/C.5.d.9.5.
  13       do.                27/V.14.b.7.5.
  55       do.                27/P.20.central.
  61       do.                V.3.c.8.5.
  94       do.                36A/C.22.d.6.5.
  111      do.                V.15.a.7.3.
  132      do.                V.5.a.7.8.
  164      do.                ST. MARIE-CAPPEL, P.26.d.6.8.
  178      do.                36A/C.5.b.2.8.
```

No. 31 Labour Group.
```
  Headquarters.               QUEUE d'OXELAERE, O.36.b.1.8.
  67 Labour Company.          U.5.c.8.9.
  93       do.                STAPLE, U.5.c.5.3.
  133      do.                U.9.b.2.9.
  147      do.                U.10.b.9.1.
  188      do.                CAMPAGNE DREVE, P.25.b.central.
  Det.172 Labour Coy.         U.5.c.5.3.
  Det.730    do.              P.20.d.8.3.
  833 Area Employment Coy.    STAPLE, U.10.b.7.8.
```

No. 75 Labour Group.
```
  Headquarters.               27/H.14.d.9.7.
  1st Middlesex Lab.Coy.      H.26.b.2.3.
  167 Chinese Labour Coy.     27/H.22.b.4.7.
  179       do.               27/LE KOEP, H.8.b.7.5.
  180       do.               B.19.d.9.2.
  181       do.               H.34.c.3.0.
  182       do.               H.2.c.1.9.
```

23rd June, 1918.
(JM)

Sd/ M.D. FITZ-GIBBON, Captain,
for D.A.A.G., 40th Division.

CONFIDENTIAL. ORIGINAL.

WAR DIARY

OF

"A" AND "Q" BRANCH.

40TH DIVISION.

FROM :- 1st to 31st JULY, 1918.

VOLUME XXVI.

WAR DIARY or **INTELLIGENCE SUMMARY**
(Erase heading not required.)

Army Form C. 2118.

July 1918.
A+Q Head Qrs
Hd Divn

Place	Date	Hour	Summary of Events and Information	Remarks and references to Appendices
RENESCURE	July 1918 1.		Arrangements made for inspection of 3 Inf. Bats & Pioneer Bn. by H.R.H. Duke of Connaught. Programme attached.	Appendix A
	2.		Programme carried out previous to 4 hour late. No staff Officers to meet H.R.H. at Cassel.	Appendix A Copy
	3.		H.R.H. expressed satisfaction of the turnout of the Bdes. finished all ranks to be informed. Major Gen. Pereira Proceeds to Command of the Division & takes over command of the 5th Divn.	Appendix B
	4.		Major Gen. W. H. Peyton K.C.B. etc takes over Command of the Division. Farewell order attached	Appendix B Copy
	5.		S.A.A. Section D.A. Col. forms the Division. 2426 S wagons load temporarily struck to 2nd Army. A.G + Q.M.G. instructions.	Copy
	6.		Reference formation of Pioneer Battalion awaited. Word rec'd as matter is being delayed. L.G.S. wagons have been asked to Divn. of Travelling kitchens but only as a temporary measure. Captain G.P. Lempriere A.E.C.att A. Army [Land Capt.?] S.D.G.A.Q. been lent to army that joined the Divn. on Camps Feb. 14/98.	Copy
	7.		A football match for Princess Caraman-Chimay Cup arranged to take place on the 15th versus 9th Division	Copy
	8.		Schools, machinery plant arrived. Prepared to open factory at Longuenesse. Smithy dump, in case of attack, for superfluous stores to not required at the moment, to be established at Longuenesse - Celighem states as showing profits by Govt. It's intended to S.A. proposed to carry about 3 rounds for gun. Drastic rearrangement with battalion insufficient for this purpose.	Copy
	9.		Approval received to about 16 Ex-Tramway Staff Wireless Ops. into the 40th Divn. Initial points to Officers to be made of newly formed battalion informed.	Copy
	10.		Practical concentration of troops in W. Hazebrouck line.	Copy
	11.		Inspection of Battalion by Divl Commander. Death of purely retable - difficulty of obtaining officers.- Reference to 6th Abbeville	Copy Copy
	12.		I. Cpls Transport	
	13.		17 Members to bring up to scale of Pioneer Bn. arrives on 14th from Abbeville. Question of arrangements for transport concentration - evacuation of aeroplane stores in event of enemy attack. Inspection of Inf. Bns by Divl Gen. completed.	Copy
	14.		Lt. Col. Parkinson V.O.E. C.R.E. 41st Divn intro. to gen. 3 Divn A.C.R.E. Authority received to eliminate Item "Garrison" in designation of Sanit. Bns. H.Q. Divn. Conference of Senrs. at D.H.Q. Permmunton party forwarded to French mission & Constabulary personnel attached to 40 Divn. 1 B.C.H. 1 M.N. & 2 M.S.M. - Arrangements made for inspection of R.E., A.S.C., R.A.M.C. units & Mob. Vet. section by Brig. Gen.	Copy
	15.			Copy
	16.		119 Inf. Bde. ordered to go into the line to be attached 101 Australian Division and relieve 87 Bde. of 29th Divn. relief to be completed on by 6 a.m. on 19 July.	Copy

WAR DIARY or **INTELLIGENCE SUMMARY**

Army Form C. 2118

July 1918
A & Q Head Qts
4th Divn Second Page

Secret

Place	Date 1918	Hour	Summary of Events and Information	Remarks and references to Appendices
RENESCURE	17		1/Capt R. Lawler to assume command of 40 Divn M.T. Coy vice Major J. Gilman Coy. leave sick.	Copy
	18		Revised leave allotment received — much reduced. — Period of officers leave extended to 7 months. 119th Inf Bde relieved 87th Divn Bde in line, attached K10, Aust. Gnr. Regn for Coy, addressed Battalion Coy.	Copy
	19		Admin. & Corps officers on subject of discipline etc. Requisition of Railwaymen for W. Hazebrouck Defences. Major for Polytn assumes temporary command of XI Corps during absence of Corps Cdr. R.G.N.	Copy
	20		Holbrook CB, 126 Fld. as temporary command of 40 Division. 119th Bde in line rel. by B/Ja Brigar.	Copy Appendix C
	21		Location of units as shown on attached Table appendix C.	Copy
	22		Church parade service. 1701, 121 Bdes, & detachment 1 R.E. ASC & RAMC also 2 boys & 7 [Warrants] (Females) Depôt.	G
	23		Church parade service. 1702, 121 Bdes. a concerted in lieu to the UK for one month.	D
			The A.A. & Q.M.G. & Nelinan in consequence at home to the UK for one month. Lt. Col. Wilson. M.C. R.E. appointed C.R.E. 40 Division. Q.S.O. (2) 40 Division appointed to Q.S. O. (2) XVII Corps. Major W. Carter. M.C. G.S.O. (2) 40 Division appointed Q.S. O. (2) 40 Divn Capt. M.H. King M.C. West Riding Regt. appointed R.G.A. (2) (moved 22 July 10)	D
	24		Lt Col H. Mc DOUGALL appointed A.A. & Q.M.G. Divn (moved 22 July 10)	D
	25		Provisional programme of events for proposed Divisional Home Show circulated to units.	D
	26		Nothing of interest remained beyond the normal Routine of the Divn. Capt R. B. KERR Staff Capt 120 Infantry Brigade appointed Staff Capt (Division) 80th Anne 2 Ath Division Comd of Div. W.E. PEYTON. N.O.R. K.C.V.O.	D
	27		Command of the Division, assumed to Major General Sir W.E. PEYTON. N.O.R. K.C.V.O.	D
	28		D.S.O. - resumed Establish from procedure of several for proposed Divn as shown circulated to units Army Head quarters. D.fence Scheme - removed reprimand reported. — Div. Pigeon By K.C. 27th section under orders to 1st -	D
	29		General Gutterton. resumed Reprimand (report) of leave to officers and other ranks.	I
	30		The Divisional Canteen Mangan inferred following orders. and wounded Military Patient. 115 Infantry Brigade in the line under orders at 1-2.	J
	31		121 Inf Brigade relieved 119 Inf Brigade during period 18/7 - 31 July. Total Casualties Killed 2 Offrs 16 Ors Wounded 1 " 64 " Injured — " 75 " Missing	J

3/8/18 [Signature] Major R.B. for G.S.O. 4th Divn

1875 Wt. W593/826 1,000,000 4/15 J.B.C. & A. A.D.S.S./Forms/C.2118.

40th Division No. 866 (A).

PROGRAMME :- Inspection of Infantry Battalions, 40th Division by H.R.H. THE DUKE OF CONNAUGHT, K.G., K.T., K.P., G.C.B., G.C.S.I., G.C.M.G., G.C.I.E., G.C.V.O.,

on the 2nd July, 1918.

His Royal Highness arrives at the Band Stand, CASSEL Square, 3 P.M.

A Staff Officer 40th Divisional Headquarters will be at the band stand, with a motor car, to act as guide.

Inspection of 119th Infantry Brigade at 27/U.17.c.7.8. at 3-15 P.M.

Inspection of 120th Infantry Brigade at 36A/C.10.b.central at 3-40 P.M.
 (Including 17th (G) Bn. Worcester Regt. (Pioneers).

Inspection of 121st Infantry Brigade at 36A/C.3.central at 3-55 P.M.

30th June, 1918.

(WB).

No. 561.

R O U T I N E   O R D E R S
-by-
MAJOR-GENERAL J. PONSONBY, C.B., C.M.G., D.S.O.,
COMMANDING 40TH DIVISION.

Headquarters, 40th Division,
2nd July, 1918.

2085.   FAREWELL ORDER.   2085.

    Major-General J. PONSONBY in handing over the command of the Division directs that all ranks should be informed of his sincere appreciation of their loyal co-operation and of their services rendered.

    He wishes one and all the best of Good Luck in the future.

C. F. MOORES, Lt. Colonel,
A. A. & L. P. G.

SECRET.

40TH DIVISION.

Map Refs:-
Sheet 27 and 36A.   LOCATION OF UNITS.   18TH JULY, 1918.

UNIT.	LOCATION.	REMARKS.
40TH DIVN'L HD.QRS.	RENESCURE.	

ROYAL ARTILLERY.

Complete less S.A.A., Section 40th D.A.C.		Detached with VI Corps.
S.A.A. Section, 40th D.A.C.	27/T.29.a.6.1.	

ROYAL ENGINEERS.

C.R.E.	With Divnl. Hd.Qrs.
224th Field Company R.E.	27/Q.25.d.9.9.
229th Field Company R.E.	36A/C.3.d.8.1.
231st Field Company R.E.	27/V.15.a.5.1.
H.Qrs. 40th Divl. Signal Coy.	With Divnl. Hd.Qrs.

119TH INFANTRY BRIGADE.

Headquarters,	27/W.25.a.5.8.	
13th Bn. R.Innis.Fusrs.)		
13th Bn. E.Lancs.Regt.)		In the Line. Detached to 1st Australian Division.
12th Bn. N.Staffs.Regt.)		
119th Trench Mortar Batty.)		

120TH INFANTRY BRIGADE.

Headquarters,	36A/C.3.c.5.3.
10th Bn. K.O.S.Bdrs.	36A/C.21.a.6.5.
15th Bn. K.O.Y.L.Infy.	36A/C.14.d.6.2.
11th Bn. Cameron Hldrs.	27/U.27.b.3.5.
120th Trench Mortar Batty.	36A/C.20.b.8.8.

121ST INFANTRY BRIGADE.

Headquarters,	27/V.13.c.0.6.
23rd Bn. Lancs.Fusrs.	27/V.13.d.1.1.
23rd Bn. Cheshire Regt.	27/U.17.c.7.8.
8th Bn. R.Irish Regt.	27/U.10.c.2.0.
121st Trench Mortar Batty.	27/V.13.d.1.1.

17TH BN. WORCESTER REGT. (P).   27/U.26.d.4.7.

40TH DIVISIONAL TRAIN A.S.C.

Headquarters,	RENESCURE.
No. 1 Company.	Detached with Divisional Artillery.
No. 2 Company.	Le Chateau, STAPLE.
No. 3 Company.	36A/C.14.c.4.8.
No. 4 Company.	27/T.29.a.2.4.

R.A.M.C.

135th Field Ambulance.	36A/B.18.c.0.0.
136th Field Ambulance.	27/T.18.d.2.7.
137th Field Ambulance.	27/T.22.a.3.4.

/Over.

- 2 -

UNIT.	LOCATION.	REMARKS.
51ST MOB.VET.SECTION.	36A/B.11.a.	
40TH DIVNL.M.T.COY.		
H.Q. & Workshops.	LONGUENESSE.	
Supply Section.	STAPLE (U.3.b.2.8.).	
D.A.D.O.S.	EBBLINGHEM.	
237th Divnl.Empyt Coy.)		
Div.Claims & Baths.Offr.)	RENESCURE.	
Div.Salvage & Burial Offr.)		
Div. Gas Officer.)		
Divl.Reception Camp.	EBBLINGHEM. (27/T.23.b.5.2.).	

19th July, 1918.
(WB).

Major,
D. A. Q. M. G.,
40th Division.

CONFIDENTIAL. ORIGINAL.

WAR DIARY.

40th DIVISION.

A and Q BRANCH.

VOLUME. XXVII.

From :-   1st August, 1918.

To :-   31st August, 1918.

CONFIDENTIAL. ORIGINAL.

SECRET.

Army Form C. 2118

WAR DIARY
or
INTELLIGENCE SUMMARY

"A" & "Q" BRANCH, HEADQUARTERS, 40TH DIVISION.

AUGUST, 1918.

(Erase heading not required.)

Instructions regarding War Diaries and Intelligence Summaries are contained in F.S. Regs., Part II. and the Staff Manual respectively. Title Pages will be prepared in manuscript.

Place	Date Aug. 1918.	Hour	Summary of Events and Information	Remarks and references to Appendices
RENESCURE	1.		One United Board Chaplain and one R.C. Chaplain posted to the Division.	
	2.		5 Officers posted to 15th K.O.Y.L.I. as reinforcements. Capt. J. KNOX-SHAW, M.C., York. & Lancs. Regt. appointed Staff Captain, 120th Infantry Brigade. Administrative Arrangements issued for transfer of 121st Infantry Brigade from 29th Division to 31st Division for duty in the Line. Brig-General F.P. CROZIER, G.O.C. 119th Infantry Brigade assumed temporary Command of the Division during absence on leave of Major-General W.E. PEYTON.	
	3.		Nothing of interest occurred beyond the normal routine of the Division.	
	4.		Instructions received from Corps to prepare estimate for Winter accommodation.	
	5.		Notification of increased leave allotment to United Kingdom to take effect from 9th August, 1918. Location of Units as shewn in attached list - Appendix 'A'. Division provided one Company (composed of all Arms) at Second Army Special Commemoration Parade Service.	Appx A
	6.		Nothing of interest occurred beyond the normal routine of the Division.	
	7.		Nothing of interest occurred beyond the normal routine of the Division.	
	8.		Nothing of interest occurred beyond the normal routine of the Division.	
	9.		Divisional arrangements for carriage of Lewis Guns and Magazines approved pending issue of instructions from Headquarters.	
	10.		Administrative arrangements issued for relief of 121st Infantry Brigade in Line on night 12/13th August, 1918.	
	11.		Division provided 1 Company (composed of all Arms) at Second Army Special Church Parade Service at which His Majesty The KING was present.	

Army Form C. 2118

WAR DIARY or INTELLIGENCE SUMMARY

(Erase heading not required.)

AUGUST, 1918. "A" & "Q" BRANCH, HEADQUARTERS, 40TH DIVISION.

Place	Date Aug. 1918.	Hour	Summary of Events and Information	Remarks and references to Appendices
RENESCURE	12		Sites for Winter Camps to be selected and submitted to Corps. Approval received for transfer of 41 men from Infantry Battalions of the Division to S.A.A. Section, 40th Divnl. Ammunition Column.	
	13.		Nothing of interest occurred beyond the normal routine of the Division.	
	14.		Nothing of interest occurred beyond the normal routine of the Division.	
	15.		Nothing of interest occurred beyond the normal routine of the Division.	
	16.		Nothing of interest occurred beyond the normal routine of the Division.	
	17.		Nothing of interest occurred beyond the normal routine of the Division.	
	18.		Nothing of interest occurred beyond the normal routine of the Division.	
	19.		Major-General Sir W.E. PEYTON resumed Command of the Division on return from leave. Divisional Horse Show held at RENESCURE.	
	20.		Corps Commander and D.D.M.S., XV Corps inspected 136th Field Ambulance.	
WALLON-CAPPEL	21 22		Orders received known his Head Quarter East of Wallon-Cappel. He Div. relieve 31st Division in the line. Divl. Agricultural party formed under 21. Bn. IDF. A.S.C. to cut rolled corn crops east of the Hazebrouck Railway. All baggage wagons of units refitted for this purpose. Fortnightly Corps & laundry returns rendered.	copy copy
	23		31st Divn. Winter Knitting Scheme considered and offered to meet present requirements. Renewed leave allotment received. New scheme for allotting canteen stores to Divnd. not satisfactory owing to reduced allotment being insufficient. Proposal taken Designation of (17) Worcester Regt. to 12 York R. not approved. 104 M.G. Bn. joined Division. This unit furnished information	copy copy
	24		Transport only, consequently horse transport has to be printed from margin Regimental reserves + the S.A.4 Section is diminished from this Unit. 4.6.5. wagon lent by I Corps from 9 Division. Coralie	
	25		list of units on 23rd August - appendix B	Appendix B

Secret.   Army Form C. 2118

WAR DIARY
or
INTELLIGENCE SUMMARY
(Erase heading not required.)

Third page

August 1918   A & Q Head Qrs.
              4to Division

Place	Date	Hour	Summary of Events and Information	Remarks and references to Appendices
WARLON- CAPPEL	Aug 1918 26		No motor cars sent by 31st Div. to Divl. Train; required as 31st Div. artillery is attached to this Divn for supplies. Spared be sent in accordance with G.R.O. 2037. A number of French decorations allotted to the Division for NCOs + the ranks.	Appx A
	27		Owing to the withdrawal of the Germans from our front, arrangements necessary to consider repair of forward roads. The Division is in host with the retiring enemy by means of one brigade acting as advance guard. Means of applying to quartering this brigade are difficult owing to the funnel area having been destroyed.	Appx B
	28		Jubilee medal awarded to 2 men of the 1st KOYLI. Congratulatory telegrams receives from Army + Corps Cdrs. conveyed to the troops, together with a message from the Divl. Cdr. on their good work in a minor operation in pushing the enemy back.	Appx C
	29			Appx C
	30			Appx C
	31st		London Gazetted awards. Appendix B.1. Casualties during the month, including times when one brigade from the Division was always in the line, until present date. The total killed Officers 3 Other ranks 88, Wounded Officers 22 Other ranks 403 missing Offrs 3 OR 10 Sergeant Duffy etc. saved by the Divn during the month in appendix C.	Appx appendix B1. Appx appendix C.

A.Moore Maj Gen
4th Divn -

SECRET.

40TH DIVISION.

Map ref:-
Sheet 27 & 36A.   **LOCATION OF UNITS.**   **5TH AUGUST, 1918.**

UNIT.	LOCATION.	TRANSPORT LINES.
40TH DIVNL. HD. QRS.	RENESCURE.	

ROYAL ARTILLERY.

Complete less S.A.A.Section.   Detached with VI Corps.
   40th D. A. C.

S.A.A.Section, 40th D.A.C.   27/T.29.a.6.1.

ROYAL ENGINEERS.

C. R. E.	With Divnl. Hd.Qrs.
224th Field Coy.R.E.	27/Q.25.d.9.9.
229th Field Coy.R.E.	36A/C.3.d.8.1.
231st Field Coy.R.E.	27/V.15.a.5.1.
H.Qrs., Divl.Sig.Company.	With Divnl.Hd.Qrs.

119TH INFANTRY BRIGADE.

Headquarters.	27/V.13.c.0.6.
13th Bn. R.Innis.Fus.	27/U.17.c.5.7.
13th Bn. East Lancs.Regt.	27/V.13.d.1.1.
12th Bn. North Staffs.Regt.	27/U.10.c.3.1.
119th T.M.Battery.	With 13th Bn.E.Lancs Regt.

120TH INFANTRY BRIGADE.

Headquarters.	36A/C.3.c.5.3.
10th Bn. K.O.S.Bdrs.	36A/C.21.a.6.5.
15th Bn. K.O.Y.L.Infy.	Second Army Musketry Camp. LUMBRES.
11th Bn. Cameron Hldrs.	36A/C.3.a.8.3.
120th T.M.Battery.	36A/C.20.b.8.8.

121ST INFANTRY BRIGADE.

Headquarters.	36A/D.17.a.7.3.	36A/D.8.c.2.3.
8th Bn.R.Irish Regt.)		36A/D.8.c.1.2.
23rd Bn.Lancs Lancs Fus.)	In the Line.	36A/C.12.b.9.9.
23rd Bn.Cheshire Regt.)		36A/C.12.b.9.9.
121st T.M.Battery.)		

17TH BN. WORCESTER REGT (P). 36A/C.14.d.6.2.

40TH DIVISIONAL TRAIN.

Headquarters.	RENESCURE.
No. 1 Company.	Detached with Divisional Artillery.
No. 2 Company.	27/U.9.b.3.2.
No. 3 Company.	36A/C.14.c.4.8.
No. 4 Company.	27/T.29.a.2.4.

R.A.M.C.

135th Field Ambulance.	36A/B.18.c.0.0.
136th Field Ambulance.	27/T.18.d.2.7.
137th Field Ambulance.	27/T.22.a.3.4.

/Over.

- 2 -

UNIT.	LOCATION.	TRANSPORT LINES.
51ST MOBILE VET.SEC.	36A/B.11.a.	
40th DIVNL.M.T.COY.	LONGUENESSE.	
D.A.D.O.S.	EBBLINGHEM,(27/T.16.c.2.8.)	
237th Div.Emplyt.Coy.) Div.Claims & Baths Offr.) Div.Salvage & Burial Offr) Div.Gas Officer.)	RENESCURE.	
Divnl.Reception Camp.	EBBLINGHEM.(27/T.23.b.5.2.).	

----------oOo----------

5th August, 1918.
(WB).

A. L. Costan.
Major,
L. A. A. G.,
40th Division.

SECRET.

40TH DIVISION.

LOCATION OF UNITS LIST — 23RD AUGUST, 1918.

UNIT.	LOCATION.	TRANSPORT LINES.	REMARKS.
40th Divn.H.Qrs.	27/U.30.c.0.7.		
A.D.M.S.	WALLON CAPPEL.		
D.A.D.V.S. @	)		Those marked @ move to WALLON CAPPEL on 24th August,1918. Div. Burial Officer moves on 24th Aug to destination to be notified. Chaplains mov forward on 24th Aug. Destinations will be notified.
D.A.P.M. @	)		
French Mission. @	)		
Div.Empyt Coy. @	) RENESCURE.		
Div.Clms & Baths Offr.@	)		
Div.Sal.& Burial Offr.	)		
Div. Gas Officer. @	)		
D.A.D.O.S. @	EBBLINGHEM.		
S.C.F.(D.C.G's Dept).	) RENESCURE.		
S.C.F.(P.C's Dept).	)		
Divnl. Agricultural Officer.	36A/D.1.d.1.2.		

ROYAL ARTILLERY.

UNIT.	LOCATION.	TRANSPORT LINES.	REMARKS.
40th Divnl.Arty.complete less S.A.A.Sec.D.A.C.	Detached to VI Corps.		
S.A.A.Section, 40th D.A.C.	27/U.21.b.6.5.		
31st Divnl Arty.H.Qrs.	27/U.23.c/8/1.		
165th Bgde. R.F.A.	36A/D.23.d.2.8.	36A/C.23.b.1.9.	
170th Bgde. R.F.A.	36A/D.18.a.0.7.	36A/D.13.b.4.8.	
28th A.F.A.Brigade.	36A/D.10.d.3.5.	36A/C.6.d.2.6.	
31st D.A.C.	36A/C.3.d.1.6.		
X/31 T.M.Battery.	36A/E.27.a.2.0.		
Y/31 T.M.Battery.	36A/E.20.d.9.9.		

ROYAL ENGINEERS.

UNIT.	LOCATION.	TRANSPORT LINES.	REMARKS.
C.R.E.	With D.H.Qrs.		
224th Field Coy.R.E.	36A/D.5.c.9.1.	27/V.25.d.0.7.	(Moves to this (location on 24t (Aug.from presen (location.
229th Field Coy R.E.	36A/D.9.b.5.4.	36A/D.1.d.8.8.	
231st Field Coy R.E.	36A/D.9.c.6.3.	36A/D.7.b.1.9.	
40th Divnl.Sig.Coy.R.E.	With Divisional Headquarters.		

/Over.

- 2 -

UNIT.	LOCATION.	TRANSPORT LINES.	REMARKS.
119TH INFANTRY BRIGADE.			
Brigade Headquarters.	Sediment House. (36A/D.11.d.5.7)	D.15.c.4.7.	(Left Sector (Divnl Front.
13th Bn. Innis. Fusrs.)		27/U.17.c.5.7.)	
13th Bn. E.Lancs.Regt.)	In the Line,	27/V.13.d.2.1.)	These Transport
12th Bn. N.Staffs.Regt.)	Left Sector.	27/U.10.c.3.1.)	Lines move on
119th T.M.Battery.)			24th Aug. to D/10.
120TH INFANTRY BRIGADE.			
Brigade Headquarters.	36A/D.24.a.7.1.)		
10th Bn. K.O.S.Bdrs.)			Right Sector
15th Bn. K.O.Y.L.Infy.)	In the Line	36A/D.16.d.1.1.	Divnl Front.
11th Bn. Cameron Hldrs.)			
120th T.M.Battery.			
121ST INFANTRY BRIGADE.			
Brigade Headquarters.	27/V.27.c.3.2.	36A/D.13.b.2.8.)	
8th Bn. R.Irish Regt.	36A/D.19.a.5.6.	36A/C.5.a.8.8.)	In Divisional
23rd Lancs. Fusrs.	36A/D.9.a.5.8.	36A/C.5.d.5.8.)	Reserve.
23rd Bn. Cheshire Regt.	36A/D.21.a.0.8.	36A/C.6.b.2.5.)	
121st T.M.Battery.	36A/D.3.c.5.3.	----)	
17th Bn. Worcester R.(P).	36A/C.21.a.6.5.		Moves on 25th Aug. to 36A/D.2.c.9.1.
40TH DIVISIONAL TRAIN.			
Headquarters.	With Div.H.Qrs.		(Move to this (location on (24th Aug/18.
No. 1 Company.	Detached with 40th Divnl.Artillery.		
No. 2 Company.	27/U.28.b.4.6.		(Move to this (location on 24th (August.
No. 3 Company.	36A/C.14.c.4.8.		
No. 4 Company.	27/T.29.a.2.4.		Move to U.28.b.8.0. on 25th August.
31ST DIVISIONAL TRAIN.			
No. 1 Company.	36A/C.8.b.5.6.		(Attached with (31st Div.Arty.
R.A.M.C.			
135th Field Amblce.	27/U.24.c.2.0.		
136th Field Amblce.	27/T.18.c.8.7.		
137th Field Amblce.	36A/C.5.a.5.9.		
51ST MOB.VET.SECTION.	36A/C.2.d.3.3.		(Move to this location on 24th August, 1918.
40TH DIV.M.T.COMPANY.			
Headquarters.	LONGUENESSE.		
Divisional Reception Camp.	EBBLINGHEM (27/T.23.b.5.2.)		

/OVER.

- 3 -

ATTACHED UNITS.

UNIT.	LOCATION.	TRANSPORT LINES.	REMARKS.
31st M.G.Battn.	27/V.25.d.6.1.		
104th M.G.Battn.	RACQUINGHEM.		Moving in relief of 31st M.G. Bn. between 23rd and 28th August.
1 Coy. XV Corps Cyclist Battn.	Attached 119th Inf.Bde.		

NOTE.   Any discrepancies in this Location List should be notified at once by Units concerned direct to this Office.

23rd August; 1918.
(WB).

A. L. Grootan.
Major,
D. A. A. G.,
40th Division.

S E C R E T.

B.1.

40TH DIVISION.

LOCATION OF UNITS LIST - - 31ST AUGUST, 1918.

UNIT.	LOCATION.	Transport Lines.
40th DIVNL.H.QRS., ("G" "A & Q", A.D.M.S., and Camp Commandant).	27/U.30.c.0.7.	
Remainder, 40th Divnl. Headquarters.	WALLON CAPPEL.	
D.A.D.O.S.	D.9.a.5.5.	
Divn. Agricultural Offr.	D.1.d.1.2.	

ROYAL ARTILLERY.

31st Divnl. Artillery.

Headquarters.	27/U.23.c.8.1.	
165th Brigade R.F.A.	SEDIMENT HOUSE) D.11.d.5.7.)	C.23.b. & d.
170th Brigade R.F.A.	D.18.a.0.7.	D.13. D.12. D.24. and D.1.
28th A.F.A.Brigade.	GLIM FARM, E.20.c.2.8.	D.2, D.6, 7 and 8.
31st D.A.C.	36A/C.3.d.1.6.	
X/31. T.M.Battery.	36A/E.27.a.2.0.	
Y/31 T.M.Battery.	36A/E.20.d.9.9.	

40th Divisional Artillery,
complete less S.A.A.Sect.,   ) Detached to VI Corps.
40th D.A.C.   )

| S.A.A.Section, 40th D.A.C. | D.1.b.8.3. | |

ROYAL ENGINEERS.

C.R.E.	With Divnl.Hd.Qrs.	
224th Field Compy.R.E.	36A/E.15.a.7.6.	36A/D.5.c.9.1.
229th Field Compy.R.E.	36A/D.30.d.1.4.	36A/D.9.b.5.4.
231st Field Compy.R.E.	36A/D.16.b.4.9.	36A/D.16.b.4.9.
40th Divl.Sig.Coy.R.E.	With Divl.Hd.Qrs.	

119TH INFANTRY BRIGADE.

Headquarters.	27/V.27.c.3.2.	D.8.d.3.2.
13th Bn. R.Innis.Fus.	D.21.a.6.8.)	
13th Bn. E.Lancs.Regt.	LE TIR ANGLAIS,) (D.17.c.6.9).)	D.16.d.1.1.
12th Bn. N.Staffs.Regt.	"Z" Line with H.Qrs.,) in SWARTENBROUCK.)	
119th T.M.Battery.	D.9.a.7.8.	

120TH INFANTRY BRIGADE.

Headquarters.	WALLON CAPPEL.	
10th Bn. K.O.S.Bdrs.	36A/C.5.d.8.8.	C.5.c.8.8.
15th Bn. K.O.Y.L.Infy.	27/U.24.c.2.4.	C.5.d.5.8.
11th Bn. Cameron Hdrs.	27/U.30.a.8.8.	C.6.b.2.4.
120th T.M.Battery.	WALLON CAPPEL.	

/Over.

- 2 -

121ST INFANTRY BRIGADE.		
Headquarters.	E.20.b.7.0.	D.11.d.5.7.
8th Bn. R. Irish Regt.)		E.7.b.7.7.
23rd Bn. Lancs. Fusrs.)	In the line.	E.7.a.2.9.
23rd Bn. Cheshire Regt.)		E.7.b.0.7.
121st T.M. Battery.)		
Details Camp.	---	D.19.a.5.6.

17th Bn. Worcester Regt (P).
- Headquarters.   36A/D.2.c.9.1.
- No.1 Company.   E.14.d.5.2.
- No.2 Company.   D.30.d.3.3.
- No.3 Company.   E.9.a.4.3.

104th Bn. Machine Gun Corps.
- Advanced Headquarters.   36A/D.24.a.7.1.
- Rear Headquarters.   27/V.25.d.6.1.
- Horse Transport.   36A/E.13.a.2.4. (Spearmint Corner).
- Motor Transport.   36A/D.17.a.7.3. (Senator House).

1 Coy. XV Corps Cyclist Bn.   Attached 121st Inf. Bgde.

40th DIVNL TRAIN. A.S.C.
- Headquarters.   With Divnl. Hd. Qrs.
- No. 1 Company.   Detached with 40th Divl. Artillery.
- No. 2 Company.   27/U.28.b.4.6.
- No. 3 Company.   36A/D.1.d.1.2.
- No. 4 Company.   36A/D.7.a.5.8.

31st DIVISIONAL TRAIN. A.S.C.
- No. 1 Company.   27/V.25.c.2.3.
- Attached with 31st Divnl. Artillery.

R.A.M.C.
- 135th Field Ambulance.   D.18.c.7.7.
- 136th Field Ambulance. H.Q.,   27/T.18.c.8.7.
- Detachment.   36A/C.5.a.5.9.
- 137th Field Ambulance.   LA MOTTE.

51ST MOBILE VET. Sect.   27/U.30.b.2.2.

40TH DIV. M.T. COY.   LONGUENESSE.

DIVNL. RECEPTION CAMP.   EBBLINGHEM. 27/T.23.b.5.2.

------o0o------

31st August, 1918.

(WB).

A. L. Croton.
Major,
D.A.A.G.,
40th Division.

40th Division No. 28 (Q).

40TH DIVISION.

The following is circulated for information :-

HORSES EVACUATED DURING JULY, 1918.

Average weekly strength,- 1421.   Evacuated - 31ˣ

    ˣIncludes 1 wounds.

DRIPPING.

Amount (including Labour Companies attached) handed in to Railhead during July, 1918.   22,491 lbs.

WASTE-PAPER.

Quantity returned to Railhead during July, 1918.   78 Bags

JAM CARTONS.

Amount (including Labour Companies attached), despatched to Base during July, 1918.   2,882 lbs.

SOLDER.

Quantity recovered during July, 1918.   26 lbs.

4th August, 1918.

(WB).

                                        Major,
                                  D. A. Q. M. G.,
                                  40th Division.

CONFIDENTIAL.   ORIGINAL.

WAR DIARY.

40TH DIVISION.

"A" AND "Q" BRANCH.

VOL. XXVIII.

FROM :-   1st September, 1918.
TO:-   30th September, 1918.

Secret

A & Q
Head Quarters
40 Divn

Army Form C. 2118

WAR DIARY
or
INTELLIGENCE SUMMARY
(Erase heading not required.)

Instructions regarding War Diaries and Intelligence Summaries are contained in F. S. Regs., Part II. and the Staff Manual respectively. Title Pages will be prepared in manuscript.

September 1918

Place	Date	Hour	Summary of Events and Information	Remarks and references to Appendices
Sept WALLON= CAPPELL LA MOTTE	Sept 1.1918 1		Inspection of Transport lines 119 Bde by Divl Commander. Preparations for parade at LA MOTTE there.	copy
	2		To move the Divl. Head Quarters. Divl Hd Qrs. moved to La Motte. Divl. Find advanced to CRoix du BAC. Northn Regt funds handed to Divl Fund – Supply railhead of the rear Haybrouck to the 3 Sept. Personnel	copy
	3		location of transport lines – Supply railhead to the rear Haybrouck to the 3 Sept. Personnel at Haybrouck – reception camp formed there. Approval given for interning into the issues of Blankets	copy
	4		to find of their equipment. Inspection by Divl Cdr. of 120th Bde. Presentation of 2 military medals. Hantsprot entrance in Revo othon	copy
	5		Relief of 121st Bde by 119 Bde. 104 NCO. Bn. being with out divn transport suffers serious demobilities. Transport and	copy
	6		by S Inspection & turtle work of A.S.C.	copy
	7		Amount of shipping etc returned during month August. Appendix A.	appendix A copy
			120 Inf Bde Sports. 66th Divl Artillery to from be attached to the Divn. – Arrive at CAESTRE. Ste.	copy
	8		accommodated in fort support area near DOULIEU. 2 military medals awarded 23 Cheshire Regt. Bar to M. Medal awarded to 1 pte of NOS Borthner. 17 Mil. medals awarded to NCOs & men of the Divn. for Operation.	copy
	9		On 23rd August. 120th Bde will probably relieve 121 Bde on 11th Sept. Arrangements to move them by rail to train. 120 to relieve 121 Bde move by Larry during 11th & 12th Sept. 121 move to Grand BECEOIS area – Instruction	copy
	10		about enemy prevention of Trench Fact. Difficulty obtaining difficient stokes. Trench Fact. Ovry & continued met weather, difficulty of unit about S. of Steenwerk. – Troof traction established there. – Ovry & continued met weather, difficulty of obtaining other referencing intelligence knows on area vacated by Germans which owing to posibility of delay action	copy
	11		104 H. Sw. Bn. leaves division by 15th Sept. 39 M.G.Bn. joins divn. 28th AFA Bde leaves	copy
	12		the divn. 2 men of 13th Lancs Reg awarded militymedal. Scheme for incoming sale of war-savings Centificates. 3rd & 4th.	copy
	13		Bathe maybe word formed. Supplishion & ordering Stopes in recent battle area.	copy
	14		Location of units: appendix B. Application made for a second blanket for men on 10th October – Vacancies allotted	appendix B copy
	15		for officers at Hardicourt Plage Officers hostel. Manchfaast. Presentation of Killets Hpf lines by Bried Cdr. Manxymonto mado men	copy
			on leave to STOMETSLYNGHAL. Inspection of immediate award by Brd Cdr of 119 Bde	copy
	16		10 military medals awarded to the divn.	copy

1875 W. W593/826 1,000,000 4/15 J.B.C. & A. A.D.S.S./Forms/C. 2118.

WAR DIARY
INTELLIGENCE SUMMARY

A. & Q. Branch, Scrap page
Head Qrs 40 Division

Army Form C. 2118

Place	Date Sept 1918	Hour	Summary of Events and Information	Remarks and references to Appendices
LAMOTTE	18/19		Corpl Lawless Staff Capt 121 Bde transferred as Staff Capt to H.S.D. Prov. awarded period our H.S.D. Br. General G.C. Stubbs apptd. for 121 Inf Bde vice Lt Col Lawrett to 8 Inf Lewis 136 Ft. Capt. D.B. Warren apptd. Staff Capt 121 Bde vice Capt Lawless to 31st Divn. as Staff Capt.	Copy Copy
	19		Ambulance honoured to North of Proven. 8 cases.	Copy
	20		Bar to MC awarded to Capt. W.E.E. JAFFREY 13 Yorks L.I. Military Cross awarded to 2/Lt S. SCARR KOYLI. Ramer of	Copy
	21		Mr C.Os. & 2/i/CO for 3 months leave & substitutes. Precautions against Transferred onbrd.	Copy
	22		Arrangements to move Divl. Htd. Qrs forward to near Steenwerck. Allotment & Davn. for 4 yards	Copy
	23		awards: Officers 1 ribbon. 21 months & Sergeants + 4 months & 74 months militia index under Pte Parker 17 R. Inn Davn	Copy
	24		German MGuns allotted for instructional purposes - Advanced Divl Hd Qrs prepared west of STEENWERCK	Copy
	25		Military Cross awarded to officers & 180CH to a N.C.O. for employing gallantry and devotion to duty. Lt Col Munro	Copy
	26		DSO. OC 13 EYL Amba obtained command of a Casualty Clearing Station - Hence the Division. Merry Brid Ireland	Copy
	27		Canteen & Divl clean clothing establishment up to Steenwerck. Question of supply a motion lorry for supply Officer & Divl. Arty. when detailed from division. In no case has any park been sent to this division for its attached artillery.	Copy
	28		Consequently not possible to send one lorry for the detached no Brit. Arty. Winds. Clothing Steamed - as there are surplus Davison officers they may be used for lending continuity battling who are short of officers.	Copy
	29		120 Front andean still attached under charge of 40 Divl. Agricultural Officer	Copy
	30		A. Divl Ht. Qrs. move to West of STEENWERCK. Near echelon the moment as accommodation can be provided.	Copy

30/9/18

C.Moore-McCrea
ADDn
HqDn

40th Division No. 28 (Q).

40TH DIVISION.

STATEMENT OF HORSES EVACUATED, AND MEASURES TAKEN FOR PREVENTION OF WASTE DURING MONTH OF AUGUST, 1918.

1. Average strength of horses during month — 1521
   Number of evacuations. — 15

2. Amount of Dripping returned to Railhead. — 11,999 lbs

3. Jam Cartons returned to Ordnance. — 1,536 lbs.

4. Waste paper collected and sent to Base — 66 Bags.

5. Solder recovered — 108 lbs.
   Zinc recovered. — 28 lbs.

4th September, 1918.
(WB).

J. Lawson.
Major,
D. A. Q. M. G.,
40th Division.

SECRET.

40TH DIVISION.

"LOCATION OF UNITS"   17th September, 1918.

UNIT.	LOCATION.	TRANSPORT LINES.
40TH DIVNL.HD.QRS. (Complete).	LA MOTTE.	
D.A.P.M.	F.22.d.6.3.	
D.A.D.O.S.) Div.Burial & Salv.Offr.)	A.15.b.5.3.	
Divl. Agricultural Offr.	LOCUST FARM. (E.7.c.).	
ROYAL ARTILLERY.		
40TH DIVNL.ARTILLERY. Complete less S.A.A., Section 40th D.A.C.	Detached.	
S.A.A.Section, 40th D.A.C.	A.22.a.5.5.	
66TH DIVNL.ARTILLERY. Headquarters.	LA MOTTE.	D.30.d.1.4.
330th Brigade R.F.A. Headquarters.	A.23.b.1.1.	A.25.d.0.9.
A/330 Battery		A.25.d.2.7.
B/330 do		L.5.a.2.2.
C/330 do		A.25.b.8.2.
D/330 do		F.23.d.5.8.
331st Brigade R.F.A. Headquarters.	A.23.b.1.3.	F.24.c.8.6.
A/331 Battery.		F.24.d.1.7.
B/331 do		F.30.a.7.9.
C/331 do		F.30.a.5.9.
D/331 do		F.30.c.5.5.
66th D.A.C.	F.23.a.5.6.	
ROYAL ENGINEERS.		
C.R.E.	With Divl.Hd.Qrs.	
224th Field Coy.R.E.	A.18.d.2.3.	A.22.central.
229th Field Coy.R.E.	A.28.b.2.8.	
231st Field Coy.R.E., complete less 2 Sections.	A.27.c.2.2.	
1 Section.	L.5.a.6.1.	
1 Section.	D.16.b.4.9.	
40th Divl.Sig.Coy.	With Divl.Hd.Qrs.	
119TH INFANTRY BRIGADE.		
Headquarters.	A.20.b.3.3.	A.20.b.3.5.
13th Bn. R.Innis.Fusrs.	A.21.d.4.3.	F.30.a.2.5.
13th Bn. E.Lancs.Regt.	F.22.d.9.3.	F.23.d.1.2.
12th Bn. N.Staffs.Regt.	A.16.c.6.5.	A.19.d.1.1.
119th T.M.Battery.	A.20.b.5.6.	

/P.T.O.

UNIT.	LOCATION.	Transport Lines.
120TH INFANTRY BRIGADE.		
Headquarters.	A.24.c.7.7.	A.23.a.2.8.
10th Bn.K.O.S.Bdrs.)		A.22.b.8.6.
15th Bn. K.O.Y.L.Infy.)		A.22.d.5.9.
11th Bn. Cameron Hdrs.)	In the Line.	A.23.a.8.3.
120th T.M.Battery.)		
121ST INFANTRY BRIGADE.		
Headquarters.	V.27.c.3.2.	D.9.b.4.4.
8th Bn. R.Irish Regt.	D.3.b.3.3.	D.10.d.9.9.
23rd Bn. Lancs.Fusrs.	D.4.c.2.9.	D.10.d.9.1.
23rd Bn.Cheshire Regt.	D.3.b.9.2.	D.10.d.9.7.
121st T.M.Battery.	D.18.d..7.7.	
17TH BN.WORCESTER REGT (P).		
Headquarters and Transport.	A.16.d.9.2.	A.22.a.2.7.
No. 1 Company.	F.21.b.1.8.	
No. 2 Company.	F.30.c.6.8.	
No. 3 Company.	A.21.c.4.5.	
39TH BN.Machine Gun.Cps.	F.24.a.10.75.	
1 Company XV Corps Cyclists Bn.	Attached to 119th Infantry Brigade.	
40TH DIVNL.TRAIN.A.S.C.		
Headquarters.	With Divnl.Hd.Qrs.	
No. 1 Company.	Detached with 40th Div.Arty.	
No. 2 Company.	A.16.a.1.5.	
No. 3 Company.	A.15.d.central.	
No. 4 Company.	E.7.c.6.3.	
66TH DIVNL.TRAIN.A.S.C.		
No. 1 Company.	F.23.c.9.4.	
R.A.M.C.		
135th Field Ambulance.	E.21.a.9.4.	
136th Field Ambulance.	F.29.b.6.9. (Main Dressing Station).	
137th Field Ambulance.	A.21.b.2.8.	
51ST MOBILE VET SECTION.	VIEUX BERQUIN(E.11.a.2.4).	
40TH DIV.M.T.COMPANY.	HAZEBROUCK.	
DIVL.RECEPTION CAMP.	F.5.d.5.5.	

17th September, 1918.

(WB).

Lieut.,
for D. A. A. G.,
40th Division.

CONFIDENTIAL.   ORIGINAL.

WAR DIARY.

40TH DIVISION.

"A" AND "Q" BRANCH.

VOL. XXIX.

From :- 1st October, 1918.
To :- 31st October, 1918.

WAR DIARY / INTELLIGENCE SUMMARY

Army Form C. 2118

A ✓ Q
Head Qtrs
40 Division

Place	Date	Hour	Summary of Events and Information	Remarks and references to Appendices
STEENWERCK	Oct 1918 1		Location of units — Appendix A. Major W. Cowan Roe, R. Inniskilling, now appointed G.S.O.2. to join later.	Appendix A
	2		Moving up 2 Scholen Brit Hd. Qtrs. forw. Steenwerck — 135 Fd Ambce to open a rest station at Chateau La Motte.	Copy
	3		Boais reported Huns withdrawn from Armentières. Patrol out of bounds & all Tel. Reinforcements 2 officers & 150 other ranks reported to have been despatched from base. Capt. Jarvis 23 Cheshires Rgt. awarded M.C. 1 German Officer and 11 other ranks captured. Return called for showing number of women available to employ and number of agricultural labourers in Division — telling at what % the agricultural labourers are withdrawn the division will be reduced to a non-fighting capacity.	Copy
	4		112 officers — reinforcements —	Copy
	5		Church parade by 121 Bde. immediate rewards presented — Bde marched past.	Copy
	6		Supply Personnel Falkhed changed to STEENWERCK on 8. Division with one brigade in line, in support and in reserve. Place Artheus armed stations command of 119 E. Lanes Regt. — 1 Chinese labour Coy quartered in Steenwerck between the town	Copy
	7			Copy
	8		Reinforcements 5 officers 91 other ranks — Inspection of Reception Camp.	
	9		employed for purpose of a "Hostile" in Steenwerck. Inspection of the works carried out by R.E.	
	10		4 Horsely Coys + 1 Indy Coy developed 4, 119 Bde.	Copy
	11		Railway nearly up to Armentières. Preparation of accommodation, ammunition for Div. Hd. Qtrs —	Copy
	12		RA 40" Div. joining by rail on the 16th. Soup kitchen + baths in Erquinghem.	Copy
	13		Major Harding Steenwerck 135 Fd Ambce now M.Col Hunt. Ted 1 A.C.C.S. Major WALES joined	Copy
	14			Copy
	15		O.C. G.S.O.2. Arrangements for accommodating artillery during relief of 66 D. Div by 40 D. Div.	Copy
	16		Appendix B — Major J. Crawford RAMC awarded bar to military Cross.	Appendix B
	17		Enemy evacuating area in front of Division, which is moving forward towards ROUBAIX.	
ARMENTIERES	18		Divisional Hd. Qrs moved Armentières. Relief of 66 D. Arty by 40 D. Arty. 66 Div. now on 29 at Battalion	Copy
	19		STRAZEELE — 121 Bde have moved forward to near ROUBAIX — orders to lay bridges across the river BASSE DEULE and bridges over safes on roads near PREVOTE the delivery of supplies etc. being difficult. Bridges near Prévote will not carry lorries — Bridges made fit 119 Bde at Prévote	Copy
MOUVAUX	20		St Andre. J.B.C. & A. '121 Bde at Croix (Roubaix) M.C. awarded Major E. O'Connor Inniskilling. Brit Hd. Qrs moved — Capt. Chapman G.SS. acting Bde. Major 121 vice Capt. Matthews on Cambridge Course.	Copy

WAR DIARY or INTELLIGENCE SUMMARY

Army Form C. 2118

6 October 1918
A+Q Head Qrs
40th Division

Place	Date 1918 Oct	Hour	Summary of Events and Information	Remarks and references to Appendices
MOUVAUX	21		Ref Gen. Hon. W. Hon. Rathbone assumed command of 121 Inf Bde on 18th – vice Br. General Hughes for 6 months. Units quartered as shown in Location List appendix "C".	Copy appendix Copy
near	22		Captain Hughes Bde Major 119 Bde – Did Bond Play in R.O.V.B/AK daily & please individuals.	Copy
ROUBAIX	23		119 Bde & Div HQ BONDUES Captain Chapman G.S.O 3 acting Bde Major 121 Bde –	Copy
	24		Inspection & survey held of bicycles. Each bicycle numbered. List kept with each unit and	Copy
	25		police instructed to make monthly check on roads – Capt N.S. Hart to act as Bde Major 120 Bde any arrangements for relief (31 Divis.) by 4th Army Div to be complete by 1/600 on 27th	Copy
LENNOY	26		Div. Find necessary a Battalion in HOUPLINES.	
	27		Divn. boots as in appendix D.	appendix D
	28		Arrangements made for baths in LENNOY & LEERS front & LENNOY.	Copy
	29		Recommendations for 35 Hard Decorations (Australia Issue) submitted from Divisions. Inspection of 39 N.G. Bn. & 17 Hordston Pioneers by the Genl. Commanding	Copy
	30		Inspection of No. 1 Cay Divl. Train by Divl Car. Croutiers & Leers Wambrechies, Leers Nord returned by 40 Divn.	Copy
	31		Casualties month of October : Killed Officers — O.R. 231 Wnded Officers 25 O.R. 53 Wnded Officers 5 O.R. 29 Missing Officer 1 O.R. 29	Copy
			Bn.Hd. changes from Armentières to Madeleine	

C Moorehead Colonel
A+Q
40 Divn

SECRET.   40TH DIVISION.

"LOCATION OF UNITS" 1st October, 1918.

A

UNIT.	LOCATION.	TRANSPORT LINES.
40TH DIVL.HD.QRS.	A.21.b.2.7.	
D.A.P.M.	F.22.d.6.3.	
D.A.D.D.S.)		
Div.Burial & Salv.Offr)	A.16.b.5.3.	
40th Div.Empyt.Coy	F.30.c.3.6.	
40TH DIVL.ARTILLERY.		
Complete less S.A.A., Section,40th D.A.C.	Detached.	
S.A.A.Section, 40th D.A.C.	A.22.a.5.5.	
66TH DIVNL.ARTILLERY.		
Headquarters.	With Divl.Hd.Qrs.	
330TH BRIGADE R.F.A.		
Headquarters.	T.16.d.5.5.	A.5.d.1.9.
A/330th Battery.	T.23.b.5.5.	A.4.c.5.5.
B/330th do.	T.17.d.5.1.	A.5.a.5.0.
C/330th do.	T.17.d.5.4.	A.5.b.3.0.
D/330th do.	T.17.b.5.1.	A.5.b.5.1.
331ST BRIGADE R.F.A.		
Headquarters.	A.23.b.1.0.	A.21.d.6.8.
A/331st Battery.	B.14.a.25.60.	A.21.d.6.8.
B/331st do.	(B.13.c.2.5.65.	A.27.d.4.8.
	(B.13.c.40.10.	
C/331st do.	(B.19.b.35.26.	A.27.d.9.6.
	(B.25.a.75.40.	
D/331st do.	(B.25.a.51.05.	A.21.d.5.9.
	(B.25.a.42.42.	
66TH D.A.C.		
Headquarters.	F.23.a.5.4.	
No. 1 Section.	A.3.a.5.5.	
No. 2 Section.	F.23.a.5.4.	
ROYAL ENGINEERS.		
C.R.E.	With Divl.Hd.Qrs.	
224th Field Company.R.E.	A.18.d.2.3.	A.22.central.
229th Field Company.R.E.	A.28.b.2.8.	
231st Field Company.R.E.	B.7.c.3.1.	A.27.c.2.2.
40th Div.Sig.Coy.R.E.	With Div.Hd.Qrs.	
119TH INFANTRY BRIGADE.		
Headquarters.	B.8.a.4.2.	A.10.d.8.6.
13th R.Innis.Fus.)		A.10.b.1.3.
13th E.Lancs Regt.)	In the Line.	A.10.b.2.2.
12th N.Staffs Regt.)		A.10.d.1.6.
119th T.M.Battery.)		

P.T.O.

UNIT.	LOCATION.	Transport Lines.
120TH INFANTRY BRIGADE.		
Headquarters.	B.21.a.9.5.	A.23.a.2.8.
	(moves to this location on 2nd Oct).	
10th K.O.S.Bdrs.)		A.22.b.8.7.
15th K.O.Y.L.Infy.)		A.22.d.5.8.
11th Cameron Hldrs.)		A.23.a.5.8.
120th T.M.Battery.)		
121ST INFANTRY BRIGADE.		
Headquarters.	LOWER FARM.	
	(A.24.c.7.7.)	A.28.b.7.2.
8th R.Irish Regt.	A.27.b.5.8.	-do-
23rd Lancs Fusrs.	A.11.a.3.3.	A.28.b.1.9.
23rd Cheshire Regt.	A.22.a.7.9.	-do-
121st T.M.Battery.	A.21.b.5.7.	
17TH WORCESTER REGT (P).		
Headquarters & Tpt.	A.16.d.9.2.	A.22.a.2.7.
No. 1 Company.	A.28.b.9.5.	
No. 2 do.	A.29.c.5.1.	
No. 3 do.	A.21.c.4.5.	
39TH BN. MACHINE GUN CPS.	F.24.a.10.75.	
1 Coy.XV Corps Cyclist Bn.	Attached to 120th Inf.Bde.	
40TH DIVL.TRAIN A.S.C.		
Headquarters.	A.15.c.central.	
No. 1 Company.	Detached with 40th Div.Artillery.	
No. 2 do.	A.9.a.7.4.	
No. 3 do.	A.15.d.central.	
No. 4 do.	A.16.a.1.5.	
66TH DIVNL.TRAIN A.S.C.		
No. 1 Company.	F.23.c.9.4.	
R.A.M.C.		
135th Field Ambulance.	E.21.a.9.4.	
136th Field Ambulance.	Detached to II Corps.	
137th Field Ambulance.	L.5.a.6.0.(Main Dressing Station).	
51ST MOB.VET.SECTION.	VIEUX BERQUIN(E.11.a.2.4).	
40th Div.M.T.Coy.	HAZEBROUCK.	
Divl.Reception Camp.	F.5.d.5.5.	

1st October, 1918.

WE.

A. S. Corotan
Major,
D.A.A.G.,
40th Division.

B/

ALLOTMENT OF ACCOMMODATION.

UNIT.	Night 16/17th.	Night 17/18th.	Night 18/19th.	Night 19/20th.
40th Div.Arty.H.Q.	Chateau, LA MOTTE.	Chateau, LA MOTTE.	Chateau, LA MOTTE.	A.21.b.2.7. (Present 66/Div.Arty H.Q.)
1 Bde.40/Div.Arty.	MORBECQUE.	Staging Area 'X' Camp in F.24.a.with H.Q. at F.21.a.3.9.	Wagon Lines and Gun positions of 331/Bde 66th Div.Arty.	No move.
1 Bde.40/Div.Arty.	P.POTE (D/16/d) & TIR ANGLAIS (D.17.c).	Staging Area 'Z'. Bde.H.Q. in DOULIEU. Camp in vicinity.	Wagon Lines and Gun positions of 330/Bde RFA., taking with them tents from Stag.Area Z.	No move.
40th Div.Ammn.Col.	I.18.a and c.	Remain D.18.a and c.	Lines of 66th D.A.C.	No move.
No.1 Co.40/Div.Train.	LA MOTTE.	Remain LA MOTTE.	Lines of No.1 Coy.66th Divnl.Train.	No move.
Med.T.Ms.40th Div.	LA MOTTE.	Remain LA MOTTE.	To be located under orders of H.Q.40/Div.Arty.	To be located under orders of HQ.40/D.Arty.
66th Div.Arty.H.Q.			No move.	Chateau LA MOTTE.
331/Bde.66th D.Arty.	N O	N O	Staging Area 'X'.	No move.
330/Bde.66th D.Arty.			Remains in Wagon Lines.	Remains in Wagon Lines.
66th Div.Ammn.Col.	M O V E.	M O V E.	1 Sec.to Stag.Area 'X'. Balance to remain in wagon lines "doubled up" with 40/D.A.C.	No move.
No.1 Co.66/Div.Train			No move. To remain in wagon lines "doubled up" with No. 1 Coy. 40th Div.Train.	Staging Area 'X' or in present wag.lines doubled up with No.1Co.

NOTES. — 1. The Bde. of 40th Div.Arty.detraining THIENNES will be billeted in MORBECQUE.
2. Tents for staging areas will be delivered as follows on morning 17th October and will be taken over by representative 40th Div.Arty :- (a). 75 tents DOULIEU Church for 'Z' Staging Area.
(b). 75 tents ORB HOUSE (F.24.a.3.9.) for 'X' Staging Area,
3. Of the 75 tents brought up from Staging Area 'Z', a proportion will be made available by 40th Div. Arty. for use of D.A.C. and No.1 Coy. Divnl.Train.

SECRET.

40TH DIVISION.

"LOCATION OF UNITS LIST"   21st October, 1918.

```
UNIT.                          LOCATION.

40th Divl.Hd.Qrs.              F.21.d.5.7.

Divl.Emplyt Coy.      )
Divl.Gas Officer.     )
Divl.Claims Offr.     )        WAMBRECHIES.
Wholesale Canteens.   )

D. A. P. M.                    CROIX (L.10) joins Div.H.Qrs at early date.

D. A. D. O. S.                 ) ARMENTIERES.
Divl.Salv.Offr & Burial Offr)  ( C.26.d.2.7.).
```

40TH DIVL ARTILLERY.
```
   Headquarters.              With Divl.Hd.Qrs.
   178th Brigade R.F.A. )
   181st Brigade R.F.A. )    Moving.
   40th D.A.C., less    )    Will be notified later.
   S.A.A.Section.       )
   S.A.A.Section.             E.25.d.2.8.
```

ROYAL ENGINEERS.
```
   C. R. E.                   With Divl.Hd.Qrs.
   224th Field Coy (less 1 Section) J.8.d.6.0.
      1 Section.                    B.30.c.4.1.
   229th Field Coy.           K.2.b.8.9.
   231st Field Coy.           F.27.b.9.9.
   40th Div.Signal Coy.       With Divl.Hd.Qrs.
```

119TH INFANTRY BRIGADE.
```
   Headquarters.       )
   13th R.Innis Fus.   )      J.1.a.9.1.
   18th E.Lancs Regt.         J.1.b.
   12th N.Staffs Regt.        L.12.b.6.3.
```

120TH INFANTRY BRIGADE.
```
   Headquarters.       )
   10th K.O.S.Bdrs.    )
   15th K.O.Y.L.I.     )      ST ANDRE (K.14.a.
   11th Cameron Hdrs.  )
   120th T.M.Battery.  )
```

121ST INFANTRY BRIGADE.
```
   Headquarters.              CROIX (L.10.a.2.1.).
   8th R.Irish Regt.   )
   23rd Lancs.Fus.     )      CROIX.
   23rd Cheshire Regt. )
   121st T.M.Battery.  )
```

17TH BN.WORCESTER REGT (P).   D.29.b.5.5.

/ P.T.O.

- 2 -

UNIT.	LOCATION.
39TH BN. MACHINE GUN CORPS.	WAMBRECHIES.

40TH DIVL.TRAIN.A.S.C.
   Headquarters.   MOUVAUX. (101 Rue de Lille).
   No. 1 Company.   NOUVEL HOUPLINES (C.26.b).
   No. 2 Company.   J.1.central.
   No. 3 Company.)
   No. 4 Company.)   WAMBRECHIES.

R.A.M.C.
   135th Field Amblce.   WAMBRECHIES.
   1 Section.   CROIX.
   136th Field Amblce.   Civil Hospital, ARMENTIERES.
   137th Field Ambulance.   WAMBRECHIES.

51ST MOB.VET.SECTION.   WAMBRECHIES.

40TH DIV.M.T.COMPANY.   STEENWERCK.

40TH DIV.RECEPTION CAMP.   ARMENTIERES.(B.30.b.9.1.).

21st October, 1918.
WB.

                              Major,
                              D.A.A.G.,
                              40th Division.

SECRET.

40TH DIVISION.

LOCATION OF UNITS. 28th October, 1918.

UNIT.	LOCATION.	Transport Lines.
40th Div. Hd. Qrs.)		
Div. Emplyt Coy.)		
Div. Gas Officer.)		
Div. Claims Offr.)	LANNOY.	
Wholesale Canteens.)		
D. A. D. O. S.)		

40TH DIVL. ARTILLERY.
  Headquarters. — With Divl. Hd. Qrs.
  178th Brigade R.F.A. — WAMBRECHIES.
  181st Brigade R.F.A. — 37/A. 29 & 30.

  40th D. A. C., H. Qrs &
    No. 1 Section. — WAMBRECHIES.
    No. 2 Section. — LANNOY.

  S.A.A. Section. — G.9.c.1.4.

ROYAL ENGINEERS.
  C. R. E. — With Divl. Hd. Qrs.
  224th Field Coy. R.E. — G.5.c.0.0.
  229th Field Coy. R.E. — 37/H.14.c.6.8.
  231st Field Coy. R.E. — 37/H.8. central.
  Div. Signal Coy. — With Div. Hd. Qrs.

119TH INFANTRY BRIGADE.
  Headquarters. — 37/A.21.a.4.9.
  13th R. Innis. Fus. — 37/A.22.a.6.3.
  13th E. Lancs Regt. — WATTRELOS.
  12th N. Staffs Regt. — 37/A.14.d.0.5.
  119th T.M. Battery. — 37/A.14.d.7.5.

120TH INFANTRY BRIGADE.
  Headquarters.)
  10th K.O.S.Bdrs.)
  15th K.O.K.L. Infy.) LANNOY.
  11th Cameron Hdrs.)
  120th T.M. Battery.)

121ST INFANTRY BRIGADE.
  Headquarters. — H.11.a.9.9.
  8th Bn. R. Irish Regt.)
  23rd Lancs. Fus.)
  23rd Cheshire Regt.) In the Line.
  121st T.M. Battery.)

<u>17th Worcester Regt (P).</u> — LANNOY.

<u>39th Bn. Machine Gun Corps.</u> — LEERS.
  1 Company. — In the Line.

/Over.

- 2 -

UNIT.	LOCATION.	TRANSPORT LINES.

40TH DIVL.TRAIN A.S.C.
  Headquarters.   LANNOY.
  No. 1 Company.   36/F.17.b.2.2.
  No. 2 Company.   36/F.17.d.3.5
  No. 3 Company.   37/G.8.b.5.1.
  No. 4 Company.   37/G.8.b.5.4.

R.A.M.C.
  135th Field Amblce.   Rue de la Sagasse, ROUBAIX.
  136th Field Amblce.   37/G.19.b.4.4.
  137th Field Amblce.   WAMBRECHIES.

51st Mov.Vet.Sect.   36/F.17.b.central.

40th Div.M.T.Coy.   36/K.6.central.

40th Div.Reception Camp.   ARMENTIERES (B.30.b.3.1).

28th October, 1918.
WB.

A.L.Cooton.
Major,
D.A.A.G.,
40th Division.

CONFIDENTIAL.

WAR DIARY.

"A" AND "Q" BRANCH.

40TH DIVISION.

VOLUME XXX

FROM :- 1st NOVEMBER, 1918.
To :-   30th NOVEMBER, 1918.

WAR DIARY / INTELLIGENCE SUMMARY

Army Form C. 2118

A & Q
Head Qrs
H⁰ Division

Secret
November 1918

Place	Date	Hour	Summary of Events and Information	Remarks and references to Appendices
LANNOY	Nov 1918 1		One bar & 3 M.M's awarded personnel of ASC & RAMC for bravery in saving civil inhabitants from influenza. All church services cancelled. Lectures indoors put a stop to owing to necessity for checking spread of influenza. Band plays for civilian inhabitants. Fried potato to take place in the Division to issue of appointed.	Copy
	2		Proposed scarcity 6" Newton medium Trench mortar beds on a rear carriage attached to forecarriage of L.G. Six wheelers.	Copy
	3			Copy
	4		Militia medal awarded 2 men ASC Mech. Trpt. attached to RAMC.	Copy
	5		40 Belgian Crois de Guerre offered Captain M. HAY Staff Capt. R.A. XIII Corps. He attached to A & Q for Report on his suitability for advancement on the Staff.	Copy
	6		Report on homes of the 'B'n by Corps Horsemasters. Call satisfactory except 175 Bde R.F.A. Captain Dawson BARNES proceeds on leave of absence. Captain Warren Staff Captain 121 Bde acts in his place.	Copy
	7		21 prs. saddles to 119 Bde for infantry operation in addition & those on establishment.	Copy
	8		Militia crosses 12 Bde. awarded of thefts from a French woman.	Copy
	9		Sergeant, relinquishing command of 10. K.O.Y. Borderers - Major H.F. Wailes G.S.O. 2 to command 1 Bn. E. Yorks pigs, when relieved in this appointment. Enemy have withdrawn from our front. 119 Bde cross the R. Scaut. 120 Bde move forward & the river. All ammunition needles amphious & rattle reserves.	Copy
	10		No civilians allowed across the river. Ceremonial Church Parade 121 Bde. But Cdr. presents medal ribbons.	Copy
	11		Major H.R.S. MASSY D.S.O. MCRA appts G.S.O.2 110 Div. Turns to the location of the 119 Bde.	Copy
	12		120 Bde near HERRINES and no Bde return to NECHIN Area. Conference at XIII Corps Head Qrs.	Copy
	13		Division means of amusement for the troops - Capt. Ruffles Borie applied G.S.O.3 4th Divn. and Capts.	Copy
	14		Chapman Bde Major 121 Bde.	Copy
	15		39 M.G. Bn. to come on establishment of the division. Arrangements for Thanksgiving Service at Roubaix on 17 Nov. Rev. H. Gibson the BACG XIII Corps - Rev. Grice Hutchinson to the S.C.F. to do same.	Copy
	16		Thanksgiving Service March past of Representatives of units of 2 Army before Lt General Jacob - Wambrechies Ave. 119 Bde Crois - 120 Bde Roubaix and	Copy
	17		Refurned. 120 Bde Ceremonial. R.A. 110 Divn. London	Copy
	18		121 Bde at LANNOY inspection Ceremonial parade 120 Bde by IX Corps Commander. Schofields images. Labour of help the local farmers in fifth Army - arrangements made to provide horses to plough & harvest potatoes & crops -	Copy
	19		IX Corps near in fifth Army.	Copy
	20		local farmers to plough & prepare lands for crops. Arrangements for a grant of £10,000. 119 Bde to 2 Army Cdr. on	Copy
	21		application. Rev. Grice - Hutchinson as S.C.F. cancelled. Arrangements for production of Play by Major of Roubaix. Occasion of production of Play by Major of Roubaix	Copy

1875 Wt. W593/826 1,000,000 4/15 J.B.C. & A. A.D.S.S./Forms/C. 2118.

Army Form C. 2118

WAR DIARY or INTELLIGENCE SUMMARY

A + Q Section
Head Qrs. / HQ Divn.

November 1918

Place	Date 1918	Hour	Summary of Events and Information	Remarks and references to Appendices
LANNOY	Nov 22		Guard of Honour formed by 2/Officers & 50 O.R. 13 R.Innisk.Fus. at ROUBAIX Square on account of exchange of flags – 3 Army Chr. & Mayor of Roubaix. 23 November anniversary of the fall of Roubaix.	Copy
	23		BOUELON WOOD. When HQ Divn. Schrs conspicuously & took hero-gram specially printed for the occasion, as a part of the ceremonial. Instructions received to inform certain classes	Copy Copy
	24		of Miners. Divl. Head Qrts. moved ROUBAIX. Recommendations made to discontinue service	Copy
ROUBAIX	25		120 Bde HQ to move to LANNOY. Preparations for Xmas Pantomime within the Divsn. of disabled alcohol.	Copy
	26		Ferry Chr. to see Divl. Chr. & Edu. today. – Recommendation to be submitted for Belgian decoration.	Copy
	27		Ceremonial parade 121 Bde postponed on account of bad weather. – Arrangements to re-open Casino Theatre	Copy
	28		at ROUBAIX for Bde. Concert party. – Office hours in the Divsn. normally to be 9 to 1 & 2 to 7.	
	29		Large reserve stock required for transportation – Arrangements made to assist French farmers	Copy
	30		with horses & labour to return to work at their farms.	

J. Elliott Wood
Br. Genl.
HQ Divn.

SECRET.

WAR DIARY

of

'A' and 'Q' BRANCH, 40TH DIVISION.

PERIOD --- 1st to 31st DECEMBER, 1918.

VOLUME XXXI.

WAR DIARY

Army Form C. 2118

INTELLIGENCE SUMMARY

A & Q

Head Qrts Ho'Dun

December 1918

Place	Date 1918	Hour	Summary of Events and Information	Remarks and references to Appendices
ROUBAIX	DEC 1		55000 Div Christmas cards received. Arrangements being made for Divl Pantomime, and purchase of Turkeys through the canteen. Theatre "CIRQUE" been informed of Roubaix. Demobilization of Coalminers proceeds. 30 Officers and other ranks warned to French Groside mine. Representations frequently made to Corps re the inadequacy of Canteen supplies. Nothing happens up to date to increase amounts allotted to this Division. Capt. Wilburn apptd. Adjutant Re Div Capt Baybetone K.G.S.O.3. Arrangements made for visit of H.M. the King on the 7th December.	Copy Copy Copy Copy
	2			
	3			
	4			
	5			
	6			
	7		Gun near Belcaut Mun[?] the recognised view of parties. 2 or 3 divisions visit this.	Copy
	8		Divl. S. Lloyd Spicer apptd K.S.O. apptd MA to Relief in Salary scheme – Capt Cowan A.S.C. asst Divl. Mun and K.S. Craffin Rest Supbs Russel in Quffis VIth Corps. Coalminers & Pivotal men being despatched home.	Copy
	9		Frequent cases of loss of Govt. Bicycles by theft. Captain Ray de Bries GSO3 left to take up appt under AMG GHQ. Li Eyeing. Divl. Intelligence Officer for duty with 2nd Army.	Copy Copy
	10			
	11		Arrangements made for Xmas dinners. GFC sketched a certain quantity will be available. Boxing and cross country running competition. Ceremonial parade of 3 Inf Bdes and MGBn + Pioneer Bn near Wattrelos. 252 War Bounty Certificates sold during month of December. Ceremonial parade of Division which includes 3 Inf. Bdes 210 MG Bn and Pioneer Battalion. also 3 Bdes RFA postponed owing to bad weather. Lt.Col. Moores AA&QMG appointed AA&QMG the ROUEN Division. 15.	Copy Copy Copy
	12			
	13			
	14			
	15			
	16			
	17		Col. Moores departed.	Copy
	18		Batches of Pivotal men & Miners have been despatched daily up to 18th to despatch of miners from 19. on. Multitudes hitherto lists of cycles from units reveniloieur. Capt. Warren took over duties as D.A.A.G. during absence of Maj. Contan on leave. 7th Hayling attached B.A. + Q. office, from 20th The arrangements being made for 6600 children of CROIX & ROUBAIX to visit the Gameeords performance in Roubaix "Cirque" about new year.	Copy White White White White White
	19			
	20			
	21			
	22			

Army Form C. 2118

WAR DIARY
or
INTELLIGENCE SUMMARY

A. & Q.

December 1918.

Hd. Qrs. 40th Division (Erase heading not required.)

Instructions regarding War Diaries and Intelligence Summaries are contained in F. S. Regs., Part II. and the Staff Manual respectively. Title Pages will be prepared in manuscript.

Place	Date Dec 1918	Hour	Summary of Events and Information	Remarks and references to Appendices
ROUBAIX	23		Christmas tree ordered some weeks ago from E.F.C. has not yet turned up.	Initialled
	24		Small allotment of Turkeys, geese & pork arrived in hulk & was distributed to units by the evening.	Initialled
	25		Kept as a holiday as far as possible, + men detached from their units were returned wherever it could be arranged.	Initialled
	26			
	27		Allotments of vacancies to various slip men, etc. for dispersal continue to be received daily; labour allotment remains solid.	Initialled
	28			
	29		Many returns etc. required for demobilization purposes.	Initialled
	30			
	31		Inspection of horses + classification into groups for dispersal commenced by R.A.V.C.	Initialled

ORIGINAL.

40TH DIVISION

WAR DIARY.

"A. & Q" BRANCH.

VOL. XXXII.

1st January, 1919 to
31st January, 1919.

WAR DIARY or INTELLIGENCE SUMMARY

Army Form C. 2118

A + Q Branch
H.Q. 40th Division.
January 1919.

Place	Date JAN.	Hour	Summary of Events and Information	Remarks and references to Appendices
ROUBAIX	1	14.00	Matinée of Pantomime "ALI BABA" given to the children of CROIX, and another on	AHH
	2	14.00	to children of ROUBAIX. Confidential reports on all officers being prepared	AHH
	3		for submission to the War Office. Demobilization also proceeding +	
	4		nearly fifty men per day being despatched.	
	5		Orders received to clean all "War of Details" (men completing colour service between	
	6		1.4.19 + 14.20 by the end of the week. Major A.L. COUTAN MC. DAAG returned	AHH
	7		from leave.	
	8		Orders received to prepare personnel for staff of 4 horse collecting station at KAIN.	AHH
	9		Considerable amount of work entailed by Confidential Reports on officers.	AHH
	10		Demobilization + arranging entertainments with other Divisions. XI Corps	AHH
	11		Entertainments officer, + I Army Recreation Officer; "The Gamecocks"	AHH
	12		performing in Pantomime at COURTRAI. No men for demobilization	AHH
	13		to be sent to Concentration Camps on Thursdays or Fridays in future.	AHH
	14		Allotments received for about 1000 men to go on 20th, 21st + 22nd, making	AHH
	15		a total of 3150 demobilized from the Division since 11.12.18.	AHH
	16		Some trouble with men at LA TOMBE Animal Collecting Camp, Nott of TOURNAI, which had	
	17		been formed with 300 men + 5 officers of the Division under command Major HART	
	18		C/64 Army Bde. RFA, to deal with horses from III Corps	AHH
	19		Major A.L. COUTAN MC. → to XV Corps as DAAG.	AHH
	20			
	21			
	22			
	23			
	24		Horses starting to go to Kinvelles + Courtrai Collecting Camps	AHH
	25			

WAR DIARY or INTELLIGENCE SUMMARY

Army Form C. 2118

A + Q Branch H.Q. 40th Division.

January 1919

Place	Date 1919 Jan.	Hour	Summary of Events and Information	Remarks and references to Appendices
ROUBAIX	26, 27, 28, 29, 30, 31		Demobilisation proceeding at the rate of about 250 men per day five days per week. Some 50 Officers per week have to be found, so that by the end of January practically all Officers desirous of + eligible for Demob. have been sent, + draft conducting Officers have to be substituted. By the end of the month 4600 men have been demobilised, in addition to an unknown number getting released whilst on leave in England. Daily Leave allotment is 2 Officers + 40 Other Ranks per day; but trains have been uncertain owing to trouble at Calais.	BHH BHH BHH BHH BHH

CONFIDENTIAL.   ORIGINAL.

WAR   DIARY.

- 40TH DIVISION. -

"A" AND "Q"   BRANCH.

VOL : XXVIII.

From :-   1st February, 1919.
To :-   28th February, 1919.

(6392) Wt. W6192/P875 1,500,000 4/18 McA & W Ltd (E 2815) Forms W3091/4.   Army Form W.3091.

Cover for Documents.

Nature of Enclosures.

Notes, or Letters written.

Secret.

40th Divnl. Hd.Qrs Army Form C.2118
"A & Q" Branch
February 1919.

WAR DIARY
or
INTELLIGENCE SUMMARY
(Erase heading not required.)

Instructions regarding War Diaries and Intelligence Summaries are contained in F. S. Regs., Part II. and the Staff Manual respectively. Title Pages will be prepared in manuscript.

Place	Date	Hour	Summary of Events and Information	Remarks and references to Appendices
ROUBAIX	1st		Arrangements made for visit of Royal Artillery Band on 18/2/19.	A
"	2nd		Instructions issued regarding reconnaissance of railroads in area available for entraining troops.	B
"	3rd		Instructions issued regarding selection of personnel for demobilisation after 10/2/19.	
"			Instructions issued regarding control of traffic in the event of troop precautions being raised.	C
"	6th		Instructions issued regarding provision of reinforcements for armies in Germany.	D
"	7th		Major A.T. Miller, M.C. Notts and Derby Regt. appointed S.O.2 40th Division.	E
"	12th		Orders issued for transfer of 2 Officers and 100 O.R. to be posted from 39th Bn. M.G.C. to 34th Bn. M.G.C.	F
"	15th		Military Medal awarded to 14 O.R. of 40th Divnl. Artillery and other units of Division	G
"	18th		New scheme for drawing supplies inaugurated.	
"	27th		Capt. C.F. Chute, M.C. R.E. Roster to command of 40th Divnl. Signal Coy.	L
"	28th		The work of demobilisation has proceeded satisfactorily during the month.	

11/3/15 W.Crossman Major for Col.
C.R.A. 40th Division.

Not for visitors

EXTRACT from DIARY

of

MAJOR GENERAL PONSONBY.

LIST OF COMMANDS HELD BY

MAJOR-GENERAL J. PONSONBY MENTIONED IN THIS DIARY.

---

1 9 1 6.

    28th December.   1st Thames & Medway Reserve Bde - CHATHAM.

1 9 1 7.

    8th March.   21st Inf. Bde, 30th Div. VII Corps - FRANCE.

    21st March.   2nd Guards Brigade.   "

    18th August.   40th Division, IV Corps.   "

1916/1917.

At the end of December I was appointed to command the 1st Thames and Medway Reserve Brigade at Chatham and to relieve General Lumley who had been in command of this particular brigade since the war was started.

Arrived at Chatham on 28th December and motored round with General Lumley to the various barracks, camps and forts where the battalions are stationed:-

The battalions I now command are as follows:-

3/Northamptonshire Regt.

    C.O.   Lieut.-Colonel de Crespigny;
    S/C   Major Grant Thorold
    Adj.   Captain Coldwell

5/Middlesex Regiment:

    C.O.   Lieut.-Colonel C. Collison;
    s/c   Major Swainson;
    Adj.   Capt. Appleby.

6/Middlesex Regiment:

    C.O.   Lieut.-Colonel G. Barker;
    s/c   Major Shee;
    Adj.   Capt. Belfield.

3/West Kent Regiment:

    C.O.   Lieut.-Col. Barron;
    s/c   Major Allfrey;
    Adj.   Capt. Westmacott.

1/Home Service (Garrison) Middlesex Regiment.
    C.O.   Lieut.-Col. C. Chesney;
    s/c   Major Lennox Cunningham;
    Adj.   Lieut. Hill.

1/Home Service (Garrison) West Kent. Regt.

    C.O.   Lieut.-Col. Warden;
    s/c   Major Wake;
    Adj.   Lieut. Dew.

The Brigade is nearly 10,000 strong, most battalions of an average of 1,600 strong, but this includes crocks and all.

I am now in Thames and Medway Garrison, which includes Gravesend, Maidstone, Sheppey and Chatham. The whole garrison is commanded by Major-General Mullaly with staff.

My brigade is what they call a draft finding brigade, that is to say, recruits for the above regiments are sent here and after being trained for about 10 weeks are sent out as drafts to France. The remainder of the battalions are made up of returned Expeditionary Force men. The majority of these men have been wounded, and having been discharged from Hospital are sent to their Reserve Battalions to be got fit or what is termed "hardening up." These men stay about a month with their Reserve Battalions and are then sent out to France in drafts to rejoin their regiments.

Everybody therefore keeps changing over with the exception perhaps of the permanent staff and Commanding Officers, etc., but although these remain longer, eventually something happens and away they go. The officers and men are classified as follows:-

    A 1   Those that are trained fit and ready to go out;
    A 2   Recruits still training;
    A 3   Returned Expeditionary Force men
    B 4   Under age, i.e. boys under 18 years old.
    B   Men not likely to be fit for some time;
    C   Men never likely to be fit for service abroad.

There is no reason, and in fact it is generally the case that men keep moving from B and C categories into A category.

My work here consists chiefly of inspecting drafts just before they leave for the front. It generaly takes either the whole morning or afternoon to see a draft of any particular regiment; the principal points being drill, handling of arms gas helmet drill, bombing and musketry. The curious point is that I find these drafts vary very much inefficiency although trained under the same instructors. The recruits we are now getting are, of course, for the most part conscripts, and vary much in age and physique. But I find the Commanding Officers are always right when they announce on my arrival A2 real good draft to-day" or, on the other hand, Say, "a batch of crocks and stumers."

In each battalion they have officers specially selected to look after the training of the actual recruits. These officers are generally former Sergeant Majors who have been promoted and who know the job thoroughly.

There are lots of restrictions about leave and it is not easy to get away even for a night. Apparently a good number of our new officers in this large army of ours are unable to behave themselves properly when they do go up to London, and there have been so many complaints of bad behaviour at restaurants and theatres that leave has practically been stopped everywhere. An order came down from the Field-Marshal (Lord French) commanding Home Forces that all officers should only be allowed leave on very urgent affairs and that should be granted very sparingly, so there is nothing more to be said.

Women at Chatham are very much to the fore and they are fairly doing their bit. . . .There are some 2,000 women employed in the Pay Department and also in the Dockyards and everywhere one sees women working in the fields or doing some war job of sorts.

To go back to the soldiering side of the place, I find that the finest type of man comes from the Northamptonshire. Most of their recruits were formerly boys in shoe trade, which apparently is a healthier trade than I imagined it to be, as they arrive in the pink of conditions. The Middlesex Regt. is not quite so good as regards physique. The discipline in these two Middlesex battalions is very high, consequently the turn out and drill are good. Unfortunately there is a good deal of absence especially in the 5th battalion, and Court Martials are a daily affair.

When not inspecting drafts my time has been occupied in inspecting the coast defences in the Isle of Sheppey. Here General Mullaly has dug about 30 miles of trenches with support and communication trenches. The object of these trenches is to hold up any landing or raid that might take place. The idea is that if the Germans did land they could not bring any very heavy guns with them and these trenches are consequently made to resist an infantry attack and field guns only. On the other

1917

days I have visited the ranges and seen recruits doing their part I. of Musketry. The standard of shooting is not high and very few marksmen are to be found now-a-days. Metcalfe runs the brigade musketry and is a first-rate officer

On 3rd March I received a telegram ordering me to return to France and report to G.H.Q. but a further telegram arrived the same day saying I was to take up the command of the 21st Infantry Brigade in France on 8th March. This is a great blow I had hoped very much to have returned to my old brigade and had been practically promised that this should be the case. I am told that every brigadier who came home for three months has been treated in the same way. Geoffrey Feilding writes however, that he and Fatty Cavan are doing their best to get me back, so I can only hope for the best. The following is a letter I wrote on "Recruits training at Home," which was asked for by Home Forces and which may be interesting afterwards in seeing whether any of my suggestions ever came to pass:

G.H.Q. Home Forces.

In reply to your Home Forces No. 10098/TB dated 18th December 1916, I have the honour to make the following remarks:
I have now been in command of the 1st Thames and Medway Special Reserve Bde. for a month and have been much struck with the excellent training carried our by all 4 battns. namely:-
The 3/Northamptonshire Regt.;
3/Royal West Kent Regt;
5/ and 6/Middlesex Regt.

I have already experienced represented to the Garrison Command that in my opinion the period of training undergone by recruits, namely about 9 weeks is too short, and it is impossible to turn out a thoroughly trained man in that time.

I understand that further training is given to drafts on their arrival in France, but I do not think this is a satisfactory method. There is always a tendency for new instructors to emphasize the fact that the men learnt nothing under their former instructors and that what they have learnt has been taught in the wrong manner.

The responsibility of sending out good or bad drafts to battalions, that is to say well trained men or badly trained men, cannot with any fairness be brought home to the training centre either at home or abroad when the training is divided between them.

In my experience when in command of a battalion and in command of the 2nd Guards Bde. in France, the conditions at the time were somewhat different as recruits then had more training at home than they have now, but I noticed certain failings and my attention to others was drawn by officers commanding battalions. The points chiefly noticeable were:-

1) The inferior march discipline and the inability of young recruits to carry a pack for a long march;
2) Fire discipline in some cases not as good as one would wish it to be;
3) Inability of men to act for themselves when deprived of their commander.

In regard to (1) very little can be done in the way of route marching owing to the shortened course of training being now carried out by special reserve battalions at home.

The route marching carried out in my brigade consists chiefly in marching with full packs to and from the Ranges, a distance of 10 miles in all. This is good practice as far as it goes. The men also wear a full pack at drill after their third week's training, but there is some considerable difference between this and having to march some 12 miles perhaps on end.

I do not see myself any way of increasing the marching except at the expense of more important training, such as

Musketry or Physical Training.

March discipline is of course a matter for officers and N.C.O's to be trained in and to take in hand.

As regards Fire control, I am of opinion that recruits should be trained to fire at more objects outside the Barrack Square than is at present done.

Their powers of observation would then be increased.

The landscape target is good practice, but I consider more realistic practices could be carried out say by firing at dummies in an actual trench at an unknown range. I have arranged for this to be carried out in future.

As regards the last point, that is to say, the inability of men to act for themselves, I think this comes about through recruits being generally under the same instructor for the same subject. I am in favour of a change of instructors in the teaching of a particular subject so that recruits should not become too dependent upon the individuality of a particular instructor.

I have on an occasion asked a recruit to simply march some men say out of a Gymansium in any way he likes. I have told him not to mind the right word of command but just to get them out, but I have found in a good many cases a man loses his head and does nothing. In fact recruits become rather like a flock of sheep and lose all individuality.

In order to counteract this tendency I would suggest men being taken out into the country early during the training and placed in positions where they must act for themselves with no instructor to help them. If the period of training could be increased to what it was before, I would advocate that Saturday afternoon be given up to such games as football bomb-ball, hockey, paper chases, etc. As it is at present, the instructors hardly get any rest and go on week after week with their work, and consequently are apt to get stale, and the men work much better if they have Saturday afternoon to look forward to.

When I talk about football for the men, I don't mean 22 men playing and 5,000 looking on, but more after the fashion of one platoon playing another. It teaches men to charge about and not to mind getting knocked over and there is no better training for the men

The question of training officers and N.C.O's is also a subject which I think could be improved upon. A good many officers have already been to the front in my battalions and have gained most excellent experience, but I think there is still room for them to acquire more military knowledge during the time they are at home Officers attend various courses while they are at home, which is excellent in its way, but I would be in favour of Garrison Classes which could teach subjects such as tactics and outposts, etc., being instituted as they were before and some capable instructors being appointed

It is difficult for a commanding officer to see to all the instruction in his battalion when his battalion sometimes numbers over 2,000 men with a large number of officers and a vast amount of correspondence to deal with.

The Second in Command may be, or may not be, a capable instructor and trainer. It is, in my opinion, essential to get good instructors for this kind of work and I do not think there would be much difficulty in getting qualified officers without interfering with officers going through special courses. These officers might be drawn from retired officers of any age who have acted as Crammers in their day. They would only instruct in general subjects and the "Art of War," which does not change, and leave special subjects to be taught at schools now formed for that purpose.

I must again repeat how impressed I have been with the zealous and keen manner in which officers and N.C.O's of all battalions in this brigade are carrying out their duties and on the other hand how eager and keen the recruits are to learn their duties as soldiers. I have seen many drafts from all four regiments and have not seen any that would not be a credit to the Regiment they are to join.

John Ponsonby.

1917

8th March: Left London to command 21st Inf. Brigade 30th Div. stationed near Arras. My Brigade is in VII. Corps, commanded by General Snow, and in 30th Division, commanded by Major-General Shea:

 GSO 1 Colonel Webber;
 GSOs 2 Major Wood and Capt. Brockholes.
 DAQMG Col. Stanley Clarke (Scots Gds.).

Division consists of 21st, 89th and 90th Bde., commanded by Derdy Stanley and Gen. Lloyd.

   21st Brigade:

 G.O.C. J. Ponsonby
 Bde. Major Capt. Hobson (1/West Yorks).
 Staff Capt. Cpt. Torrance (2/Manchester)
 Asst. do. Lieut. Whiting (2/Yorkshire Regt.)
 A.D.C. " Higgins (19/Manchester)
 Intelligence Cpt. Clayton (2/Wiltshire)
 Machine Gun: Capt. Delbos M.G. Corps
 Signalling Lieut. Hepburne R.E.
 Bombing " Higson (19/King's)
 Art. Group Cdr. Col. Jelf

18/King's (Col. Pinwell); 2/Yorkshire (Col. Edwardes); 2/Wiltshire (Col. Gillson) 19/Manchester (Col. White).

March 16th: Raid carried out last night by 18/King's was a success. The party numbered all told about 100 all ranks. They entered German trench at 10.40 p.m. cutting their way through the wire just in front of Agny which is just south of Arras. They got into German support trench and bombed all the dugouts but did not reach the third German trench. There was some maxim fire on the flanks, but not much and the curious part was that the Germans did not put any barrage down on our front line till nearly half an hour afterwards. German line must have been very thinly held as our casualties were only 1 man killed and 5 wounded no missing. ... I think Shea's plan of seeing and talking to the men immediately after they return from a raid a very good one. Men were all in the highest spirits and each man was most anxious to tell one his own experiences. Forwarded Pinwell's report of the raid with the following letter:

> "I forward Col. Pinwell's report on the raid undertaken by the battalion under his command, namely the 18/King's on the night of 15th-16th March. I consider the success of the enterprise is due to a large extent to the careful preparation and organization carried out personally by Col. Pinwell. The co-operation of the artillery and trench mortars was very satisfactory. The raiding party were well led by Capt. Jones and the excellent spirit and dash that animated the men gives good promise that this battalion will more than maintain their high reputation in future operations."

18th March: To hospital near St. Pol with bronchitis

20th " Received telegram that I was to command 2nd Guards Bde. and that D. Goodman (comdg. 52nd Brigade) was appointed to command 21st Inf. Bde.

21st March Left No. 12 Stationery Hospital at St. Pol, and arrived at 21st Brigade Hqrs. Found that Goodman had already taken over. Left soon after luncheon and arrived at Billon Camp about 8 p.m., between Bray and Maricourt, where I joined Hqrs. of 2nd Gds. Bde. Loyd is now brigade major.

24th March: Battalions are now all employed in road making and in the construction of railways. The Scots Guards are at Clery The Coldstream at Combles, Irish Gds. at Montauban and 3rd Grenadiers at Ginchy.

27th March:

    Bulgy Thorne commands 2/Grenadiers;
    Byng Hopwood　　" 　1/Coldstream;
    Sherard Godman　" 　1/Scots;
    Eric Greer　　　 " 　2/Irish

I find the Pioneer Company has practically ceased to exist. I propose reestablishing it as I am convinced that it is most important and useful. Commanding officers are not in favour of bombers being kept together in one section in the platoon. This is the new order - A platoon is now divided into four sections as follows: Lewis Gun Section, one section of expert bombers, two sections of riflemen with a proportion of rifle grenadiers. The proportion of the latter is not clearly laid down, and I am asking the division for a decision. I myself think bombers should be kept together in a section and have laid this down, but I agree that there must be at least two sections of riflemen

* * *

11th April: Geoffrey Feilding has gone home on leave, so I find myself in command of the Guards Division. Eric Greer commands my brigade pro tem.

12th April. Guffin says that when the war started there were so very few officers who had been through the Staff College that it was essential to make a rule that an officer with a Staff College record should remain on the staff whether he liked it or not. Now they have got Staff College courses going on out here and also at home, and the supply of budding or what is called sucking Staff Officers is plentiful, but these are all of course for Junior Staff appointments and the higher appointments are naturally still in the hands of regular Staff College graduates.

18th April. Divisional Hqrs. moved from Maurepas to Curlu, which is on the banks of the Somme.

20th April. The question of leave is still rather a troublesome one, as it always has been. The question of leave is apt to bring out the best or the worst qualities of individuals. It is the old question or rather the old grievance, as there is no doubt that the Staff get more leave than the Regimental officer. At the present moment we are told by the corps that leave is stopped except under the most exceptional conditions yet we know that most of the corps have been able to get their leave all right. It ought to be laid down clearer who can and who cannot get away. Byng Hopwood has written to me a brochure on the subject, but I don't see what can be done until the whole system is better regulated.

22nd April. Geoffrey Feilding returned so I am back with brigade. Now camped at Omnicourt.
30th April. Moved camp today to Le Mesnil, where we are next door to 3/Grenadiers. The Scots Gds. are at Rocquigny; Coldstream at Le Transloy and Irish Gds. at Les Boeufs. All battalions working on the railway and roads.

8th May: Orders to move. At first only the Coldstream and Irish Guards, who are to go to Curlu. Am moving my hqrs. on 10th to Curlu.

9th May

Guards Division:

G.O.C.	Major-General G. Feilding CB DSO
A.D.C.	Capt. G. Lane, Coldstream;
	Lieut. Lord Holmesdale Coldstream.
G.S.O. 1	Lieut.-Col. C.P. Heywood Coldstream
2	Capt. E. Seymour, Gren.
3	Capt. O. Hambro, Scots.
AAQMG	Lt.-Col. F. Alston Scots.
DAQMG	Major R. Hermon Hodge, Gren.
DAAG	Capt. B. Dykes, Scots.
APM.	Capt. Earl of Clanwilliam, RHG.
CRE	Col. Brough, DSO RE
CRA	Br.-Gen. Evans, CMG
ADVS	Major O'Rorke, CMG
ADMS	Lt.-Col. Fawcus, RAMC
S Chaplain	Major Rev. P. McCormack.
Intell.	Lieut. Laing, Coldstream
Salvage	Capt. Viscount Castlerosse, Irish
OC Div.Trn.	Col. Davies.

1st Brigade.

GOC.	Br.-Gen. G.D. Jeffries, DSO Gren.
Bde. Major	Capt. M. Beckwith Smith, DSO Coldstream.
Staff Cpt.	Capt. Evans, MC Welsh Gds.
Bombing	Lieut. C. Hambro, Coldstream
Signalling	Lieut. Barnard

2/Grenadier Guards:
C.O.	Lieut. Col. C. de Crespigny, DSO
2nd in-C	Major Hon W.D. Bailey;
Adj.	Capt. A. Penn.

2/Coldstream Guards:
C.O.	Lieut.-Col. G. Follett, DSO
2nd-in-C	Major J. Brand, MC
Adj.	Lieut. J. Coates.

3/Coldstream Guards:
C.O.	Lieut.-Col. R. Crawford;
2nd-in-C	Major F. Longueville, DSO
Adj.	Lieut. J. Gascoigne.

1/Irish Gds.
C.O.	Lieut.-Col. A. Alexander, DSO MC
Adj.	Lieut. Gordon

2nd Guards Brigade

GOC	Br.-Gen. J. Ponsonby, CMG DSO Coldstream Gds.
Bde. Major	Capt. Loyd, MC Coldstream
Staff Cpt.	Capt. Sir John Dyer, Bart. MC Scots Guards.
Asst. Staff Capt.	Capt. O. Lyttelton DSO Gren. Gds.
Bombing	Lieut. H. Dundas Scots Gds.
Vet.	Capt. M. Mitchell AVC
Signalling	Lieut. A. Turnbull R. Scots Fus.

1917

3/Grenadier Guards:

```
C.O.       Lieut.-Colonel A. Thorne, DSO
2nd-in-C.  Major G. Rasch, DSO
Adj.       Lieut. A. Mildmay
Transport  Lieut. Duquenoy;
QM.        Capt. Wall;
Chaplain   Rev. F. Head.
```

Company Commanders: Capts. J. Craigie, R.W. Parker, W.C. Neville; Hon. F. Eaton.

1/Coldstream Guards:

```
C.O.       Lieut.-Col. D. Gregge Hopwood, DSO.
2nd-in-C   Major S. Burton;
Adj.       Capt. Hon. K. Digby, MC.
Transport  Lieut. Lord Hugh Kennedy;
QM         Capt. J. Boyd.
Chaplain   Rev. A. Secker.
```

Company Commanders; Capts. A. Selfe, J. Barnsley, Trelcar, W. Bosanquet.

1/Scots Guards:

```
C.O.       Lieut.-Col. Romilly DSO
2nd-in-C   Major M. Barne, DSO
Adj.       Capt. Eric Mackenzie, DSO
Transport  Lieut. Trafford;
QM         Capt. D. Kinley
Chaplain   Rev. J. Thompson
```

Company Commanders: Capts. Hugh Rose, F. Ward, I. Cobbold, C. Gordon Ives.

2/Irish Guards:

```
C.O.       Lieut.-Col. E. Greer, MC.
2nd-in-C   Major Pollock
Adj.       Lieut. Hely Hutchinson
Transport
QM         Capt. Brennan
Chaplain   Rev. Father Knapp MC
```

Company Comdrs.: Capts. Witts, Ferguson, Hon. A. Alexander; Synge, MC.

3rd Guards Brigade:

```
G.O.C.      Br.-General Lord Henry Seymour, DSO  Grenadier Gds.
Bde. Major  Capt. Aubrey Fletcher, Grenadier Gds.
Staff Cpt.  Capt. C. Bewicke, Scots Gds.
Signals     Lieut. J. Balfour, Scots Gds.
Bombing     Lieut. Heneage, Grenadier Gds.
```

1/Grenadier Gds.

```
C.O.       Lieut.-Col. Mark Maitland;
2nd-in-C   Major N. Vaughn
Adj.       Capt. C. Pearson Gregory
QM.        Lieut. T. Teece.
```

4/Grenadier Gds.

```
C.O.       Lieut.-Colonel Viscount Gort.
2nd-in-C   Major W. Pilcher, DSO
Adj.       Capt. R.S. Lambert.
```

2/Scots Guards:
- C.O.   Lieut.-Col. Norman Orr Ewing.
- 2nd-in-C   Major T. Stirling.
- Adj.   Lieut. P. McDougall.
- QM   Capt. Ross.

1/Welch Gds.
- C.O.   Lieut.-Col. Douglas Gordon
- 2nd-in-C   Major H. Dene, DSO
- Adj.   Capt. Perrings.

13th May: We have just had orders that "Le Roi des Belges" is to come here on the 15th to inspect us. Another ceremonial affair, which is a great nuisance, as it interferes with training

15th May The inspection went off all right this afternoon. King Albert arrived in the uniform of a British Colonel and with him were a host of generals and staff officers.

17th May We moved to day to Bronfey

18th May Marched to-day to Ville sur ancre

30th May To-day we left the valley of the Somme and the Ancre on our way to northern France. We went by train - a journey of about ten hours. Detrained at Arques. The whole brigade is billeted in or near the village of Wardecques

15th June Returned from leave to Hqrs. at Elverdinghe Chateau, just behind the Canal bank and within easy reach of Ypres.

5th July: The 1st Brigade carried out a raid the night before last and apparently both the officers and a sergeant and a man got separated from the others in the dark and have not been heard of since. There were sounds of firing and bombing and it looks very much as if they had been killed. . I liked Basis Blackwood very much indeed.

6th July The King paid us a visit to-day. He was accompanied by a brilliant Staff. Gough, Cavan, Feilding and his Staff.

23rd July I have pointed out strongly to Geoffrey Feilding that unless we get reinforcements up we shall go in too weak to be of any use. We want at this moment about 200 men as reinforcements for each battalion, with a proportion of officers There are two things absolutely necessary if the show is to be a success. The German guns must be got well under by our counter battery work and our battalions must go in with a strength at least of 130 men per company.

25th July 2/Scots Gds. on the left opposite Boesinghe and 1/Coldstream on the right below railway raided the hun trenches at 1 a.m. this morning.
The Scots Guards party, about 50 men under Esmond Elliot, crossed the Canal without difficulty, although they got wet up to their arm pits. They met with no Germans, but two Germans came over later and surrendered. The Coldstream party, also fifty strong, met however, with opposition and were only successful in getting over in two places. They lost a man killed, and 7 wounded and had to retire back.

31st July. 3.50 a.m. ZERO The terrific roar of the guns have started. I looked at it from the parapet just outside the dugout Our shells are screaming over in thousands. It is still dark. German rockets and Very lights are going up everywhere. There seems to be very little counter shelling from the Hun side.

5 a.m. News in that the French have reached their first objective.

5.30 a.m. Scots Gds. and Irish Gds. report having reached the "Blue Line," their first objective. Ivan Cobbold, Scots Gds. reported wounded.

6.30 a.m. Battn. hqrs. 1/Scots Guards established at Thatched House. Reports from wounded men that our troops are passing over Caribou Trench. Flares seen in Wood 15.

6.40 a.m. Eric Greer comdg. 2/Irish Guards reported killed. A terrible loss.

7.15 a.m. Digny reports attack going splendidly. The 1/Coldstream are moving hqrs. to Hey Wood. Irish Guards report unable to move hqrs. from Canal Bank owing to heavy bombardment

7.15 a.m. Reports in that Black Line or 2nd objective carried also that XVIII. and XIX. corps doing Well. II. Corps report capture of Stirling Castle.

8.30 a.m. Aeroplane reports part of Green line, 3rd objective to be taken. On right there is temporary check owing to some Germans holding out in some fortified houses.

9.30 a.m. "Germans fought well and were big fine young men."

10.30 a.m. 3/Grenadiers in touch with 113th Bde. on their right in Green Line. Coldstream not in touch yet with our 3rd Brigade. 2/Scots Gds. are for moment held up with the French in front of a strong German post.

Noon. Noise slackening off. We are now trying to get guns forward over the Canal, but Pontoons have to be brought up, which takes time.

1 p.m. Five German officers taken prisoner brought to my dugout One Hauptmann or Captain says he was in command of his battalion. The others seemed very young, one officer said he was just 18. They all belonged to an Hanoverian Regt. and had "Gibraltar" embroidered on their right sleeve.

2 p.m. Casualties in Brigade estimated to be between 6 and 700. 1st Bde. have gone through the Green dotted line, our 4th Objective, and have called on one company 3/Grenadiers to support them

4 p.m. Jack Dyer has been killed, one of the very best friends I ever had. Can't write any more to-day, as this seems a sort of break to some of my happiest days in my life when Jack was with me

1st August. Went up round the line. The whole battlefield is now just like the Somme. Nothing but a mass of shell holes and mud up to one's knees.

Poor Father Knapp has been killed. He is a terrible loss to all of us. He had been out practically all the war and was, I think, one of the most wonderful men I have ever met.

2nd August. Poured with rain the whole day. Ma Jeffries reports the conditions in the front line to be worse than anything that he could imagine.

3rd August. Poured with rain last night and it is still raining. Owing to the terrible condition of mud many men of the 2/Grenadier Guards had to be taken out of the line completely exhausted

4th August. Rained all night, in fact it has now rained for three days and two nights without ceasing.

5th August. The rain has stopped, but there is a thick mist everywhere.

6th August. We are in a camp about a mile outside the town of Proven.

18th August: Have just heard that I have been promoted temporary Major-General and am to command the 40th Division

23rd August. To Sorel le Grand, which is my new Headquarters.

1917.
                                        (40th)
    August 24th.   The officers in my Division/are as follows:-

    G.S.O.   Lt.Colonel Charles,   Essex Regiment.
    G.S.O.2.   Major Burbury,   Yorkshire Regiment.
    G.S.O.3.   Captain Chapman,   General list.
    A.A.& Q.M.G.   Lt.Col.Moores,   A.S.C.
    D.A.Q.M.G.   Major Gordon.   Royal Irish Regiment.
    D.A.A.G.   Captain Cowtam,   London Regiment.
    A.P.M.   Captain Baden Powell.
    A.D.M.S.   Col.Luther.
    D.A.D.M.S.   Captain Thatcher.
    Divisional Signal Co. Major Kidner,R.E.
    D.A.D.O.S.   Captain Lawrence.
    S.C.F.   Revd.F.Stone.
    Liaison Officer.
    Divisional Artillery, Brigadier General G.Nicholson.
    C.R.E.   Lt. Colonel Baylay.

    There are other appointments but I have just written down the principal ones.

    September 6th.   Two men of the American Railway Company, who are employed here in making a permanent way, were wounded yesterday at Gouzicourt.   These are, I think, the very first American casualties in the war.

    November 22nd.   Last night I got orders that we were to join the 4th Corps under General Woolcombe.   We seem rather to shift from one Corps to another.   Personally I wish we had stayed in our original Corps under Putty.   However I suppose these things can't be helped as nobody knows how things will develop.   I and Charles went off to a 4th Corps Conference this morning, those present were: The Corps Commander Sir F.Woolcombe, General "Uncle" Harper commanding the 51st Division, General Braithwaite commanding the 62nd Division, myself, General Nicholson, General Geddes, Charles, Dupres who is B.G.G.S. and some others.   I gathered that reinforcements had come from Russia and that the Germans were stiffening up their defence. They, the Germans had counter attacked strongly yesterday, especially the 3rd Corps at Nirvilles and Rumilly.   Fontaine just south of Bourlon Wood had been occupied last night by troops of the 51st Div.   The Cavalry have been unable to push forward from Cantaine.

    My Division the 40th is to take Bourlon Wood and the Village North of it to-morrow.   Two other Divisions move on each flank. The 51st on our right and the 36th under Nugent on our left. A conference at 1.30 at my Head Quarters.   I have decided to send two Brigades forward to take the wood and village, namely the 119th under Crozier and the 121st under Campbell. Campbell's Brigade pushes forward to the West of the Wood keeping in touch with the 36th Division and with the object of trying to get round the West side of the village.

    There are a good many Hun trenches running practically North and South but these can be enfiladed by our guns.   I have been given 6 extra Batteries.   The 119th are to push through the wood behind the tanks.   The Corps Commander has given me 50 Tanks which I propose to divide equally between the leading Brigades. Burbery is just off to try and get hold of the O.C.Tanks who seems to be rather an elusive gent as it is indefinite where his Head Quarters are.   Willoughby's Brigade I keep in reserve, Pioneers and Sappers go to Havrincourt tonight, they are still working on the roads.   Thisis just the rough plan as far as it goes, no time to write down details.

Nov.22nd Contd.

Left Beaumetz with Charles about 3.30 and went to 36th Division Head Quarters, and 51st Division Head Quarters to get all the information we could. Uncle Harper who commands the 51st Div. had just heard that his Division had been counter-attacked heavily and that they had lost Fontaine, so he was not in the best of spiritts. Having got as much news as we could and having given them a rough idea of what my Division are to do to-morrow, we motored on to Havrincourt. The roads were in a terrible order and quite blocked with traffic. Finally we had to walk and reached the Chateau in the dark about 8 p.m. only a few walls standing and the ground a mass of shell holes. However we got to work to write the detailed orders. Brigadier General Elles, Colonel Baker, Carr and his Tank Commanders arrived and we had to go through carefully all the orders for the tanks and the orders for the Artillery Barrage. This was finally completed soon after midnight but none of our wagons or the rest of the Head Quarters arrived. We decided to move to the south edge of the town in a park as communications by road seemed hopeless. I turned in eventually about 3 a.m. hungry and tired as no food had come up.

November 23rd. The baggage and Mess eventually arrived about 7 a.m. this morning having been stuck on the road all night. Water is now the difficulty here as there is only a small well by the Chateau which is a mile off.

Nicholson turned up late last night, he tells me it is impossible to get up the smoke ammunition which has been asked for by the Tanks. There also seems to be a difficulty about Petrol for the Tanks but I think we shall get this up in time.

Zero hour is to be at 10.30 p.m. Leverson in the 18th Hussars has arrived as Cavalry Liaison officer.

The attack started at 10.30 a.m.; as usual for about 2 hours there was no news, then it came in in rushes. First reports good, everything going well, then a check, then better news and a good advance forward. In the meantime Staff Officers of every grade blew in from the road, from G.H.Q. including Wal Grigg, from the Army, from the Corps, from the Tanks, from the Cavalry, and finally Bubbles himself who came to get the latest. Messages were for a time somewhat contradictory; about tea-time the news was depressing, 9 different German Battalions had been identified on our actual front including the 3rd Guards Corps.

The Germans were counter-attacking heavily on both our flanks. Brigadiers were shouting for reinforcements, and the 9th Cavalry Brigade consisting of the 15th Hussars, 19th Hussars and the Bedfordshire Yeomanry were put at my disposal.

I have ordered the dismounted Cavalry up, to stiffen up the front line and told Brigadiers they must hang on to what they have captured.

Two battalions of the 120th.I have moved up in readiness to meet a serious attack. About 7 p.m. the situation improved, Brigadiers report that their front line is further up than they thought. Matters are quiet and Battalions are consolidating.

I think the danger is that the enemy will counter-attack on both flanks and try and get the village of Bourlon back. At present only half the village is in our possession. Both Divisions on our right and left are tired. My Division has been fighting all day and casualties are said to be heavy especially as regards officers.

Nov. 23rd. Contd.

The Guards Division relieved the 51st Division tonight on our right. A very tiring day after a sleepless night, Charles is a first rate G.S.O. and I have great faith in him.

November 24th. This battle is like an erratic Barometer which goes up and down, it was high last night, all was reported well and the night was fairly quiet.

Soon after 6 a.m. Charles and I went up to the 120th Brigade to talk over the attack on the remaining part of Bourlon village. Have decided to send up the Highland Light Infantry and to send the 14th Batt. Argyll and Sutherland Highlanders to attack in conjunction with the 12th Suffolk Regiment. Campbell who is on the spot to take command of the force, no sooner arranged, than a severe counter-attack took place at 10 a.m. with the result that Crozier's line has been driven back to the centre of the wood. The 19th Hussars and the 14th Argyll and Sutherland Highlanders have been put in to restore the situation. At 12.30 p.m. the barometer again rose, a message in to say that the Germans have been driven back and we are back in our original position. Villiers, Harry Graham's brother-in-law, has I regret to say been reported killed. A very good officer 2nd in command to the Machine Gun Company. Kennedy who commands the 17th Welsh Regiment reported killed. Andrews who commands the 18th Welsh reported wounded. Reports in of estimated casualties said to be about 1,500. This may I think be considered to be over estimated, but the Division has had to stand three separate strong counter-attacks probably from nine different German Battalions.

The Corps Commander Woolcombe came up about 1 p.m. and said he was very pleased with the work done by the Division. The second attack on the village is to take place to-morrow morning and not this afternoon. Baker Carr came to see me and said he would raise 25 tanks for the show. Another Cavalry Brigade has been sent to me dismounted as a reserve, namely, the 18th Hussars, the 4th Dragoon Guards and the 9th Lancers. A dismounted Cavalry Brigade musters only about 600 men, equal to an Infantry Battalion as they have to leave a good many men to look after their horses.

Another counter-attack was repulsed about 2 p.m. by the South Wales Borderers. But about 6 p.m. the Barometer fell; a fourth strong counter-attack was made which drove in the troops on the right flank and casualties were reported to be heavy. The 2nd Batt. Scots Guards on our right was called upon to help and fighting in the wood still continues. In the meantime for some unknown reason we have been cut off by telephone from Brigade Head Quarters and can hear nothing. Communication by runners has been established but by the time one gets a message through the situation has completely changed in front. Campbell not hearing that the attack was postponed till to-morrow attacked at 3 p.m. The 14th Highland Light Infantry got through the right of the village, but the East Surrey on the left were held up. The whole position seemed very obscure, but on the whole favourable. About midnight the barometer rose again as a message came in to say that although the centre of the village was held in pockets, the whole front of the village was in our hands. The 119th Brigade on our right report that the situation there is easier and that although wood fighting still continues we are holding our own. Rained heavily in the night, very cold in a tent, but it must be much worse for the men in the open.

November 25th.   The Cavalry Corps are anxious now to put the Cavalry through. Greenly who commands the 1st Cavalry Division came up with his staff. We talked over the situation, we both agree that to shove the Cavalry through against the enemy's organised Infantry is a mistake.   Personally I could promise him little assistance as the men are "all out" after 3 days hard fighting. He has gone off again to see Kavanagh who commands the Cavalry Corps.

Last evening Harry Graham found a dead Hun tied by a chain round his leg to a tree, shot through the head just in the wood by our Camp.   He was no doubt a machine gunner who had been chained to his post to prevent him running away. A bitterly cold North East Wind is blowing. It is very cold, but no rain. It is difficult to keep warm.

Mullins who commands the 1st Cavalry Division came up to see me about 11 a.m. He also is very doubtful as to the possibility of pushing the Cavalry through, but he tells me the Cavalry Corps Commander has decided to try it. Then soon afterwards Kavanagh who commands the Cavalry Corps put in an appearance and told me the whole Cavalry attack was off. The Barometer fell badly about 4 p.m. Campbell reports the Huns have recaptured the village and are now in occupation of it and our line runs along south edge of the village. The fact is the village is full of cellars and dug outs and it has been very difficult for the Battalions to mop it up properly and also to hold the first line.

At 7 p.m. the barometer rose slightly, the Welsh Fusiliers under Plunkett attacked the enemy and drove him to the East end of the Wood. They were counter-attacked by the enemy, but repulsed the counter-attack and have maintained their position. We are to be relieved to-night by the 62nd Division. Braithwaite and his Staff arrived about 6 p.m.

November 26th.   Very cold night.   Brigades were relieved last night and early this morning, still no news of H.L.I. or the two companies of the East Surrey. They may still be fighting and may get out. I have asked particularly that the village shall not be bombarded till more is known.

Bourlon is to be attacked at daybreak to-morrow morning. The Guards Division is to attack Fontaine. There was a great conference this morning at Havringcourt. The Army Commander, Corps Commander, and finally the Commander-in-Chief. I have just received the following letter from the Army Commander:-

"My dear Ponsonby,

"Whatever may be the final result of the operations as "a whole, I cannot let this particular period of it pass "without sending you a line to convey my most sincere con-"gratulations on your feat of arms.
"The capture of Bourlon Wood to my mind stands out "amongst all the other splendid actions of our Infantry since "the attack started on the 20th. and in years to come I shall "remember with unqualified satisfaction that it was performed "by the splendid Division with which I have now been associated "for some time.
"My sincerest wishes for the continued success and my "best congratulations.
             Yours sincerely.

                  J. BYNG."

Nov. 26th.Contd.

The Division moved to Neuville this afternoon. Sir Douglas Haig, the Commander-in-Chief, arrived at my Hd.Quarters, he said he had come expressly to congratulate the 40th Division. He seemed very pleased.

Novemeber 27th. Last night the Barometer rose and we received the news that the East Surrey Regiment were holding on in Bourlon village. There is now great hopes in my mind that the H.L.I. will be able to do the same although they are at the North end of the village and completely cut off. The difficulty is that they must come under our own barrage unless they are clear of the village. The Gunners have arranged to lift the Barage off the edge of the village some 200 yards.

We suddenly received orders late that we have got to clear out and go by tactical trains to the Basseux area. I protested strongly down the telephone as this means that tonight will be the fifth night the men will have been without sleep. Telephone kept going till past midnight. However in the end it was arranged that the 119th. and 120th Brigades will not entrain till early this morning.

I had luncheon with the 5th Corps. Charles and Burbery went back to Havrincourt to see about East Surrey and H.L.I. Reports came in during the afternoon that practically all the East Surrey had withdrawn from the village. They had been hanging on the South edge of the village under their commanding officer Col.Warden who refused to move without a direct order. A 100 or so of the Highland Light Infantry were with them. The remainder it was presumed were still fighting in the North Edge of the village. The 62nd Division attacked at dawn and were not particularly successful. They now hold the North edge of the wood but were unable to take the whole village. The Guards Division attacked at the same time and reached their objective, but also were unable to take the whole village of Fontaine which now remains partly in our hands and partly in the Bosch hands. I hear they have a good many casualties from machine gun fire directed from "La Folie" Wood and the 59th Division have been moved up to support them.

Fontaine seems to be the most difficult place of all to hold as it is surrounded on three sides by the enemy guns.

We are now in Basseux, in a poor looking unfinished Chateau with most of the windows broken. Dined tonight with Nicholson and his R.A.Staff at the Officers Club at Arras.

November 28th. Gordon my D.A.Q.M.G. has done splendidly. He got everything ready for the men. Blankets, Shelters,etc., etc., when they got in last night. During the fighting he managed to get up over a million rounds of ammunition by pack animals to the various Battalions and also large quantities of bombs and trench mortar ammunition. We are now in the 6th Corps under Haldane.

It is a bore always changing one's Corps Commander. During the last month we have been in the 3rd Corps, the 5th Corps, the 4th Corps and now we are in the 6th Corps. Haldane came to see me. He tells me we shall probably be put in the trenches in the Arras sector, probably near Bullicourt.

November 29th. A long conference at my Hd.Quarters to discuss lessons to be learnt from the recent fighting. Rode over with Fitzgibbon to see the Highland Light Infantry and East Surrey Battalions. I am afraid now that there is no hope of getting the 3 companies of H.L.I. back and I see in the German Communique

Nov. 29th Contd.

that they claim 300 prisoners which looks as if the Companies had been obliged to surrender, probably having no food left. Col. Warden told me in Bourlon village the German machine guns sprang up everywhere in the night. He thinks they were brought up from the cellars. There were also a large number in the top storeys of the houses, which of course were impossible to knock out by tanks. In fact the general conclusion I have come to is that the village should have been more heavily bombarded before we attempted to take it. Altogether the Division took over 500 prisoners. It is a curious thing that 3 officers and 3 men committed suicide when they were taken prisoners. Two German officers poisoned themselves and one officer committed "Harikari" by plunging a knife into his stomach.

As far as the returns go at present our casualties have been in the Division, 78 officers killed and wounded and about 2,500 men killed, wounded and missing.

November 30th. Went over to Neuville to see Geoffrey Feilding to ask him whether he would allow Kenny Digby or Gillilan to come and command one of my battalions. I found everybody very "distrait" and was told that they were in the middle of a Battle. It appeared that the huns had attacked in strength during the morning and had taken the village of Gonnelieu, Villiers Guislain and even Gouzecourt and the Guards Division had been ordered to retake the villages. Geoffrey himself was at Metz and Sandy Ruthven G.S.O.1 and Becky Smith were just going up to join him. They told me the 1st Guards Brigade were at that moment in action and the other two Guards Brigades were moving up in support.

Finding myself very much "de trop" I snatched a hasty luncheon and went off. On my way through the village I met my old Brigade marching out, they told me that they had attacked La Fontaine about 2 days ago and had had a good many casualties, I believe 1,200 in the Brigade. . . . .
Orders received to-night that we are to go back to Achit-le-Petit.

December 1st. Orders and counter-orders going on. The last order is that we are to relieve the 16th Division in the trenches at Bullicourt. Our total casualties in the fighting at Bourlon amount to a total of 172 officers killed, wounded and missing, and 3,171 men ditto.

Haldane the Corps Commander came to see me. He told me of his various hobbies which on the whole seem sensible enough, but I think for a Corps Commander he enters too much into detail. He seems however very well disposed towards us.

December 2nd. 121st Brigade and 119th Brigade move into the trenches to-day. Baylay goes as Commandant to the R.E. School at G.H.Q. for two months. He has been perfectly excellent, the best C.R.E. in France, and I trust I shan't lose him.

December 3rd. To-day we moved to Behagnies not far from Bapaume and relieved the 16th Division under Hickie. The 16th Division have devoted a lot of trouble to their Head Quarters, most comfortable huts and fireplaces everywhere, good stables. I hear however that things up on the line are not so good, no soup kitchens and no gum boot stores. However, having advanced their line some 3 or 4 hundred yards and having occupied the Hindenburg line, it is of course to be expected that the trenches are in a very primitive condition.

December 3rd. Contd.

Hickie told me that he was far from well, but was full of talk. He had apparently fallen out with Jules Pereira who commanded one of his Brigades. The result of course is that Jules Pereira is reported to be 'very tired' and has now been sent home. Deverell who commands the 3rd Division on our right came over to see me. He brought very sinister rumours about the 55th Division, also that the Huns had taken a good many prisoners and guns, but it is not confirmed at present. The situation as they say is a bit obscure, but all subsequent German attacks have been repulsed. Very cold, freezing hard.

December 4th. Neuralgia most of the day. I think the cold East wind is responsible, no more news. The Corps Commander came to see me and says at present everything is quiet down the line. Apparently it was the 55th Division who got it in the neck and who lost so many men taken prisoners.

December 5th. Charles and I went round the trenches, it was fairly quiet in the front trenches, but a little difficult walking about, as the trenches had been badly knocked about. On the way back the Huns started shelling Croisilles but luckily their shells were falling all in one place by the ruins of the church, so we made a detour and eventually returned hungry and safe.

News has come in that we have given up Bourlon Wood and gone back to Flecquieres ridge. I, myself think this was the only thing to be done under the circumstances, as Bourlon position was bound to go sooner or later unless we were able to get the high ground on each flank.

In the German Communique this evening I read that the Germans claim to have annihilated several British Divisions including the 40th. I believe they have taken a great many prisoners, but I believe these chiefly belong to the 55th Division, but I have heard nothing very definite. In the meantime the Corps has become rather windy and anticipate an attack on our front. Everybody therefore has been warned to be on the alert especially against Gas shells and Charlie Willoughby's Brigade goes out at dawn to dig fresh trenches and put up more wire. It is freezing hard and bitterly cold.

December 7th. Lt. Col. Baxendale commanding Hants Yeomanry has been appointed to command the 14th Batt. Highland Light Infantry vice Battye killed in action. Major Coulson, K.O.S.B. whom I knew in Egypt has been appointed to command the 17th Batt. Welsh Regiment vice Andrews wounded.

December 11th. A certain amount of wind last night and Army reported great movements going on in German lines. Artillery Cavalry and infantry reported to be moving north. A prisoner was captured with a letter on him saying there was to be an attack near Arras. Enemy's Aeroplanes also very active all day; the result was that everybody was warned to be very much on the "qui vive". Brigade in reserve stood to arms for two hours. Reserve Machine Gun Company moved up in support line. However, the night passed quietly and so far nothing untoward has happened.

News in the evening that Allenby has captured Jerusalem. Persistent and heavy shelling continues all day but it is not intense on our actual front. A conference this morning at the 119th Brigade Head Quarters. We discussed various ways and means for the capture of the Juno Trench on our right flank.

December 12th. The Huns attacked about 6 a.m. this morning

December 12th Contd.

just before dawn. The attack was chiefly directed on the 3rd Division on our right. We all nipped out of bed and hung about waiting for news. About 7 a.m. the S.O.S. went everywhere and every gun in the place was hard at work. In fact, as the Germans put it, it was a case of intense drum fire all down the line, but after a time it quieted down. Apparently the Hun attacked in force the 3rd Division and succeeded in occupying Apex Trench. Their attack on our front with a barrage of artillery and a smoke barrage was only a feint but was successful in a way, in that we thought they were going to try and break through our line. Gun fire went on nearly all day, but our casualties were very slight, about 27 all told. Some prisoners have been captured who announce that the attack is to be resumed at daybreak tomorrow morning.

I have moved up the Brigade in reserve to St Ledger and all our machine gun companies are in theline. Our own Artillery rejoin us tonight which means that we shall have 72 guns ready on our front.

Went round this evening to see Charlie Willoughby and Campbell and discussed the question of counter attacks in case our line should be broken.

December 13th. Nothing happened. Everybody up at dawn waiting for it, but beyond a small attack on our right the Hun apparently has postponed his attack. The question is now whether he will attack tomorrow morning instead. In order to be on the safe side I have given out that the same precautions as last night are to be carried out.

Went round with Nicholson to all the gun positions and saw most of the Battery Commanders also Col.Palmer who commands the group (40th Div.Artillery). I told him that they had all done very well and that I had received many letters from other Divisional Commanders cracking them all up. Our Gunners have only just left Havrincourt and have been fighting hard for the last fortnight. They claim to have exterminated a large number of Huns. We had a good many casualties last night and today from Gas shells.

Metcalfe from the base who was on my Staff at Chatham has joined me. I wrote for him to come out and command a Battalion I hope he will be able to stick it. He is a hard nut, but as he is now well over 50, it will be a bit of a trial for him, but he is just the right sort that I want.

1918.

March 21st.   The battle has begun, heavy firing from big guns started about 5 a.m. all back areas are also being shelled. Beaumetz, which is the village next door is catching it with 15 inch shells.

10 a.m.   Enemy's Infantry reported to be attacking in masses on our actual front.

11.a.m.   Message from Corps Commander asking me to come over and see him.   On arrival he told me the Huns had penetrated into our front line on a long front but the exact places were still unknown.   Bullecourt had fallen; the shelling has been very intense all the morning, our casualties are probably high Received orders to move up the 120th to the trenches in the third system south of St Ledger.

The 121st Brigade to move to Hamlincourt.   The Division Artillery to move south of Mory.

Went off with Black to see Forbes who is now in command of the 120th Brigade and explain the orders.   Forbes tells me he has had 50 casualties chiefly in the 10th, 11th Highland Light Infantry.   Both Brigades move after their dinner about 1 p.m.

2 p.m.   News is that Ecoust and Noreilles have fallen.
Divisional Head Quarters are to remain at Basseux but to be ready to move at any moment.

2.30 p.m.   Orders just received that I am to move up to Battle Head Quarters at Behagnies.

At 3 p.m. I was again sent for by the Corps Commander.   He told me the situation was very serious.   The Battle seems to be going in favour of the enemy.   It is reported that he has broken through our front line in several places and that our troops are now holding the third line of defence.   The Division is to move up at once and occupy the trenches.   The 120th Brigade now under Forbes to get into touch with the 6th Division, the 121st to move into the trenches on the left of the 120th.

I then went myself to Behagnies, which I propose to make my Head Quarters, and saw Romer who commands the 59th Division.   He told me that the shelling had been so terrific that most of his Division had been blotted out.   His right had been turned and he was moving his Head Quarters.   Shells were falling into Ervilliers and the Arras Bapaume road was becoming most unhealthy.   The road was a bit congested with Gun limbers, etc.

I then went off to see Nicholson who commands the 34th Division.   He was in his dug out at Gommecourt.   He was very anxious that my Division should come up in time to retrieve the situation which he described as critical.   Croziers Brigade, the 119th, has been placed at his disposal to hold Henin Hill.

At 6.30 p.m. I heard that the two Brigades were in position.

From all accounts the shelling this morning must have been terrific.   It was what the Germans describe as annihilating fire.   I have moved my Head Quarters to Hamlincourt.   The shelling still continues and there is also a great roar of musketry and machine gun fires going on.   A mist is getting up now about midnight things are a bit quieter; a few bombs fell near our camp but no damage done.

22nd March. Fighting started again early and it is reported that the enemy has reached the outskirts of St Ledger.

Croziers Brigade has rejoined me. I have put them in the Army line about 500 yards behind the other two Brigades. I have also moved the two Field Companies R.E. and the Pioneer Battalion into this line.

9 a.m. Reported that enemy is massing in the neighbourhood of Croisilles; all our guns are concentrating on the spot.

10 a.m. About 300 of the enemy have formed a pocket or wedge in our front line. I have ordered Campbell to attack them at once on both flanks. In the meantime I hear that the Yorkshire Regiment in Campbell's Brigade has been heavily attacked and has now fallen back to the Army line. Reports are coming in every moment not of a very reassuring type.

It is reported continually that troops on our right are being driven back.

12 noon. About 30 prisoners have been brought in, including a Doctor who was armed to the teeth with a revolver and a big dagger. They are being interviewed by Nason my intelligence officer, but I hear they refuse to give any information of any value.

A few shells fell into Hamlincourt in the afternoon, but on the whole it has been quieter than I expected. It warmed up about 7 p.m. and a great bombardment took place. All our guns are heavily engaged, a strong attack on St ledger is taking place.

Pot Ardee has arrived with Oliver Lyttleton, his Brigade Major. Pot commands the 4th Guards Brigade, who are now in the 31st Division. The Division is to be put in on our left. The Brigade Staff of one of the Brigades of the 34th Division has also arrived at Hamlincourt having had to abandon their forward Head Quarters, so the place is being crowded out.

I am moving my Head Quarters back to Bucquoy.

9 p.m. It is quieter now, and I am moving back, having sent most of the Staff back a few hours ago. Haldane came up about midnight and told me that the Germans had taken Mory. I tried to get in touch with Crozier to find out what had happened but the wires were cut. Spent a very anxious night. Campbell sent in about 3 a.m. that he had been obliged to move his Head Quarters.

March 23rd. 177th Brigade under James has been put under my orders. All Brigade Head Quarters have moved back to Gommecourt

It is very hot. I rode over to see Brigadiers at Gommecourt; everything seems quieter. Crozier is arranging a counter-attack on Mory to be carried out by the 21st Middlesex under Metcalfe and the 13th East Surrey under Warden.

Fighting began about 5 p.m. and went on all night. The Germans seem to be pressing hard with fresh Divisions. The counter-attack came off and we drove the enemy out of Mory. It would have I think, been more successful if I could have got the 120th Brigade to co-operate; but Crozier started the counter-attack straight off, as he had come to the conclusion that there was not a moment to lose.

Our guns have been got away just in time and Palmer has got both Brigades north of Gommecourt. The 119th Brigade are now

March 23rd Contd.

holding part of Mory Village and Mory Copse. The Yorkshire are on their left in touch with the 31st Division. Our right apparently in the air. Heavy firing is going on, and things look decidedly rocky. Solly Flood's Division the 42nd are coming up.

March 24th. Very hot. Solly Flood and his Staff have arrived His Division is at Adinfer Wood.

Rode off to Gommecourt with Solly Flood. The place was becoming unhealthy and was being shelled. Told Campbell he had better move his Head Quarters behind the Railway Embankment. Haldane came up in the afternoon; he was very pleased with the stand we have made at Mory. The weather is perfectly extraordinary, it might be midsummer it is so hot. Unfortunately there is a bit of Haze on, which prevents our aeroplanes doing any decent observations.

In the evening after another bombardment the Germans again attacked and are reported to be right round us; we are told Bapaume has fallen. It is therefore imperative that the 42nd Division should be pushed off to the right to hold the enemy.

The Argyll and Sutherland Highlander are reported to be heavily enegaged. Orders have now been sent to fall back on some old trenches at Gommecourt and to hold on for all we are worth. Fighting went on all night and there is that uncomfortable and worrying feeling that the Germans are doing their utmost to surround us.

March 25th. My birthday. The Germans have, according to reports, taken Behagnies. They are now advancing in great numbers towards Achit le Grand and Achit le Petit. My Division is to be withdrawn as they are too exhausted to go on any more. The command now falls on Solly Flood and we are consulting together. He is sending out the Tanks towards Achit le Petit to do what they can. "Uncle Harper" who commands the 4th Corps has just ridden up. He is sending up the 62nd Division to help the 42nd Division. The 41st which came up a few days ago on our right and the 25th Division seem to have been knocked badly and are falling back. My Brigades are to be withdrawn at once and I go to Monchy aux Bois.

Bucquoy is now being shelled and the congestion on the roads is terrific but the various transports are being gradually got away.
Established my Head Quarters to-night at Monchy aux Bois: feel desperately tired which is the case with everybody. It has now turned very cold.

March 26th. Spent the night in some wooden huts at Monchy aux Bois. During the morning I attempted to go in my motor to Pas to see the Corps Commander but the roads were blocked everywhere with traffic. I got as far as Fontevillers where the utmost confusion reigned, as it was reported that the Bosch was entering the far end of the town. Almost a panic existed but there was no reason at all for this canard. However, to be on the safe side against any attacks, I told the 119th and 120th Brigades to move up on the high ground at Adinfer road and to hold the ground in case of a sudden attack.

March 26th Contd.

In the afternoon I moved my Head Quarters to Baiellmont, which is nearer Adinfer Wood. Here I found all the details of the 4th Guards Brigade and also some of the Guards Division. I saw Pritchard Quartermaster 3rd Batt Coldstream, who told me the most sinister rumours were afloat. I also saw an old friend in Quartermaster Sergt. Jones of the 3rd Coldstreams. As far as I could gather the Guards Division itself has not so far suffered to any great extent, but the 31st Division have lost pretty heavily. I also met an Australian Division moving up towards Hebuterne. Orders received to-night that the Division is to move to Habarg.

March 27th. Our Quarters last night were in a very large Chateaux next to a church in the village of Habarg. It used to be a Hospital some months ago but has now been given up. No sooner did we arrive and finish a somewhat sketchy meal than orders were received for the Division to go to Warluzel. Staff Officers had to fly off in various directions to divert the various Brigades. This they succeeded in doing with the exception of two Battalions.

Moved to Warluzel area where I saw nearly all the Battalions and the Brigade Head Quarters. The men had their tails well up, and although they had been marching all night looked very cheerful and fit. Our casualties are something over 3000 in the Division but at present, owing to all these moves, it is difficult to get a very accurate return.

Warluzel was so full of troops that I have moved my Head Quarters into the neighbouring village of Lucheux where we have been before. My old friend the Mator was most depressed. The newspapers say that the Germans claim 50,000 prisoners and 1000 guns.

March 28th. Went to 6th Corps Headquarters at Noyelle Vion. I saw the Corps Commander and thanked him for his letter. The contents of his letter, after a few personal remarks, were:- "As regards your fighting troops, Infantry, Artillery, and Royal Engineers I cannot speak too highly. They have made a magnificent defence and tired as they must be with so prolonged a struggle, they have stood like a stone wall between my right and the Germans. All I can say is that I am deeply grateful and feel that they have nobly upheld the great fighting traditions of the British Army"

Haldane told me we were going to be moved N at once to form part of the 1st Army and would join the 13th Corps under De Lisle. We are to move to-morrow. He told me our line is not broken and fighting has been continuous. The Australians and New Zealanders have repulsed a strong attack near Hebuterne.

The 31st and Guards Division have also been attacked and driven the enemy back. In fact, the news is better all round.

March 29th. We moved today to Chelers; poured with rain all day. As usual orders came in to say we were to move again at once - We are to join the 15th Corps and are to go by bus and lorries to Merville.

March 30th De Lisle came to see me and immediately afterwards the King came in his motor accompanied by Lord Stamfordham, Derick Keppel, Clive Wigram and the Army Commander, Sir H. Horne and his A.D.C. Philip Hundlocke. The King was very cordial and I gave him the best account I could of the fighting. He

March 30th Contd.

told me to let the men know of his great appreciation of their gallant behaviour and how much he deplored the heavy casualties. He was very sorry to miss the men but they had just gone off in busses to Merville. He has been in France three days and has been round to see most of the men in the Divisions that have been fighting.

I think the King coming at once to France was a splendid idea and has really done good. It is a great thing to do a thing like this at once and not wait a week or two.

Dined with the Army Commander (Horne)

March 31st. Moved to Merville; stopped on the way at the 1st Corps Head Quarters which are at La Bussiere and had a talk with Teddy Seymour. The latest news is that the Huns are only about 12 miles from Amiens and it is believed that their object is to take the town and destroy the railway. French troops are reported to be arriving in that vicinity in large numbers.

After luncheon at Merville, went up to the Head Quarters of the 57th Division who are commanded by Barnes late of the 10th Hussars. He is own brother to Violet and Irene Vanbrugh the famous actresses. I found George Paynter here also; he is commanding one of the Brigades in the 57th. We take over from the 57th on April 2nd. The Portuguese is on the right at Laventie and La Gorgue.

April 1st. Went up to Brigade Head Quarters in the line. A conference was held today by our Corps Commander General Du Cane (15th Corps). I was much struck by the way he talked and the way in which he told us what should be done in this part of the line. I have always heard he is about the best General we have got in France. He is a bit nervous that the Portuguese will not stand a very heavy bombardment and that the Bosch may make an attack down the La Bassee road. The whole country is very much cut up with big ditches which will make the Bosch keep to the road.

There are now only two Divisions in this Corps, ourselves and the 34th, who were next to us in the Bullecourt Sector; and we are holding a pretty long bit of the line some 16,000 yards with no Division in reserve or support.

Each Division therefore has to have one Brigade in reserve which is to be used by the Corps Commander as circumstances permit. Heavy fighting continues in the South and our Cavalry are said to have done splendidly.

April 2nd. Relieved the 57th Division today in the line. Barnes tells me he has orders to go to Luchex and that his Division will be with the 6th Corps under Haldane. Our Head Quarters are now at Croix du Bac. We have been refitted with Machine and Lewis Guns; reinforcements, I am told, will be with us in a few days time.

There are now of course several vacancies for commands of Battalions. Eardley Wilmot commanding the 12th Suffolk was, I believe killed, and Lloyd second in command has taken over command. Long in the Yorkshire was wounded. Baxendale commanding the 14th H.L.I. wounded and is succeeded by Seagrim. The command of the Argyll and Sutherland Highlanders is vacant, as Benzie was wounded and there is no one to take his place, so I have applied to the Corps. Becher who commanded the Pioneers

April 2nd Contd.

was hit in the head and there is also no one to replace him.

This afternoon I held a Conference and later on went with Black to Lestrem to call on General Gomez da Costa who commands the Portuguese on the right. A fine big man who talks English well. He told me he was arranging a raid for to-night on the Bosch trenches in front of Laventie. I wonder how the Bosch enjoys being raided by Portuguese.

April 3rd. The Portuguese raid went off all right but they found the Bosch Trenches unoccupied. It was I hear, with great difficulty that they were persuaded to return to their own lines, as they were much elated by their occupation of the enemy's trench.

Went round the front line this morning with Black and Barebones (Fitzgibbon): extraordinarily quiet. The line is held in posts behind breast works, the line is exactly like the line I was in two years ago at Laventie which, in fact, is next door.
I came across a good number of Portuguese: they seemed very cheery when I wished them "Bon Jour" which they understand. Kilgour in the Argylls tells me they sing all night in the trenches which is rather trying for the Highlanders who are next to them.
The Corps Commander came up to see me. There has just come in an order to say the 14th Argyll and Sutherland Highlanders are to be disbanded and sent off as various reinforcements to their other Battalions. I have sent in a strong protest as this Battalion has done particularly well and it is a great shame to break them up after they have been so highly commended by the Commander in Chief.

I received to-night the following letter from General Sir Julian Byng:-
"I cannot allow the 40th Division to leave the Third Army "without expressing my appreciation of their splendid conduct "during the stage of the great Battle which has just completed. " By their devotion and courage they have broken up overwhelm- "ingattacks and prevented the enemy gaining his object, namely "a decisive victory. I wish them every possible good luck,"
(signed) J.Byng. General.

April 4th. Twinges of lumbago and a cold coming, which is a nuisance. Baylay is now back as my C.R.E., which is a great thing, although I was very sorry to part with Goodwin. Baylay tells me that when he was down at G.H.Q. he met the chief Paymaster, who showed him some extraordinary letters he had received from wives of soldiers out here. ....

The Hun was a bit truculent to-day and sent over many shells than usual.

April 5th. Cold rather troublesome, kept indoors. Corps Commander came to see me with regard to work in the line. He tells me the news South is on the whole satisfactory. The Bosch attacked yesterday with 11 Divisions but was checked by the French. He tells me the 50th Division is coming up behind us as a reserve.

April 6th. Walked round the Battle Zone with Baylay, Campbell and Hobkirke. The wire looks pretty moderate. We selected 4 new positions for Battalion Headquarters. The Bosch has increased his shelling very much the last few days especially in the roads and emergency tracks.

April 7th. The 14th Battalion Argyll and Sutherland Highlanders has been disbanded and are to be broken up and sent off in

April 7th Contd.

detachments to form other Battalions. The 2nd Battalion Royal Scots Fusiliers come to the Division in their place.

It seems a great pity to have broken the Argylls up. They were the finest Battalion in the Division and they had distinguished themselves on every occasion.

I went down to say goodbye to the Headquarters. I should have liked to have seen the whole Battalion but they had to go off at odd times in buses to different locations.

There is considerable movement going on on our front. The Corps Commander spent about three hours with me this morning. It looks rather as if the Bosch intended to do something in this direction. One never can tell what he is up to, but the Aeroplanes report abnormal traffic, and mysterious looking dumps and wire being sent out for passage of troops.

April 8th. Round the Bridge heads and the Army line with Forbes and Barebones. Enemy shelling Fleurbaix as usual.

In the afternoon saw the 20th Middlesex rehearsing a raid which is to take place to-morrow morning. I rather feel that the artillery preparation is not quite enough and that we shall be stopped by the enemy's wire, but Richards, who commands the 20th Middlesex, is very confident and says his scouts who have been out the last two nights have discovered two distinct lanes or paths through the wires and he does not think there will be any trouble.

Probably the front trenches of the enemy will be either unoccupied or the posts withdrawn when we cross over. The difficulty I think will be in taking on the support trenches in rear.

April 9th. About 4 a.m. a great roar of guns and rifle fire took place. At first I thought it was our raid but I soon realised it was something very much bigger.

Patterson (Carter) told me about 4.30 a.m. that the whole of our front line was being heavily shelled. Soon after 5 a.m. a message was received that the Portuguese on our right had been driven back. I sent orders for the 120th Brigade under Hobkirke in reserve to move up to Laventie Station. I sent Harry Graham to Lestrem in a motor at 5.30 a.m. to the Portuguese Head Quarters to find out the situation. Soon afterwards a report came in that the Bosch was in our front trenches and that Crozier was organizing a counter-attack to drive them out. Harry Graham had great difficulty in getting to Lestrem as the roads were being heavily shelled. He could not get through Estaires as the streets were blocked with debris of the houses that had been knocked down by shells.

On arrival at Lestrem he found General da Costa at his Head Quarters but the upper floor of the Chateau had been blown in by a shell and everything was more or less in a state of confusion. The British Mission was still working under Glover but the general idea seemed to be that most of the Portuguese troops had been driven out of their trenches.

Reports came in about 7 a.m. that our right was being completely turned but that the 120th Brigade were moving up to the Battle Zone in front of Laventie. Nevertheless the Bosch was reported to have got right round on our right as far as Chard Post and Windy Corner. Fleurbaie Defences were holding out and

April 9th Contd.

our left was secure.

The Corps Commander Du Cane came to see me about 9 a.m. He told me the enemy were attacking Givenchy on our right. He was of opinion that the attack, although a strong one, was a local one and probably delivered with the object of making us withdraw Divisions from the South. As the morning went on reports came streaming in that the Bosch was penetrating everywhere. Both Brigade Head Quarters near Fleurbaix were obliged to evacuate their Quarters about mid-day.

Enemy reported to have reached the South Banks of the Lys about 1 p.m. Bayley my C.R.E. has blown up the main bridges across the River, leaving foot bridges for the Infantry. It then became necessary to move as many troops as possible to cover the crossings of the River.

The difficulty then became the evacuation of the civil population, who by now were becoming panic striken as shells were beginning to fall in the village.

After a hasty luncheon, I was told that the Bosch had crossed the River and was advancing on our Head Quarters and matters became uncommonly unpleasant as bullets began coming in by the door and through the windows. Incriminating documents Maps etc. were burnt and I decided to move my headquarters to Doulieu. I went first to Steenwerck and saw Nicholson and gave him the situation. It appears that 8 German Divisions attacked our front this morning. The roads were crowded with unfortunate refugees flying for their lives - very old women carrying their beds on their shoulders - babies being wheeled along three in a perambulator. The roads were full of wounded in fact it was the days of 1914 over again, only rather worse, as these people have lived in comparative safety here for over 3 years.

At doulieu a deputation of Priests came to see me and asked me to tell them what was going on. I told them all I could, but am afraid I pictured the situation as more hopeful than I knew it was. Campbell's Brigade, having got completely mixed up with the 34th Division on our left, has been put under their orders.

4 p.m. Crozier's Brigade is still fighting at Croix de Bac. I am told the 50th Division is coming up on our right and probably the 29th Division will be coming tomorrow. The question is, can we hold the Bosch who seems to be pushing forward everywhere.

During the night the situation became a little easier and the shelling died down. Have moved to Vielle Berquin.

April 10th. Corps Commander (Du Cane) came up early. He tells me the enemy are attacking hard on our left and are going for the Messines Ridge. It has been discovered that his objective yesterday was the Lys River. The report, that he had crossed the river in large numbers, seems unfounded. There is heavy fighting going on everywhere, and I have now ordered Crozier to hold the line of the Steenbeck Switch. We don't seem to be really in touch, either with the 50th Division on our right, or with the 34th Division, who have now withdrawn from the Lys. The 74th and 88th Brigade are on our left, but are now very weak. There is a constant flow of unfortunate refugees passing through the village. Priests are administering the Last Sacrament on the roads to many of the wounded. I am told the sights now in the village are very terrible. Dead women and dead children are lying about

April 10th Contd.

everywhere.

All villages are being shelled and fighting is going on hard everywhere. Fresh German Divisions are appearing against us.

About 5 p.m. the 14th H.L.I., the 2nd Royal Scots Fusiliers and the 21st Middlesex made a desperate counter attack against the enemy and drove them back some 1000 yards. When dark came everything became quieter and the shelling ceased.

April 11th. I went to Doulieu this morning with Bayley and Chapman. Campbell has got his Head Quarters here and is collecting all the men together that he can, to defend the village. The village was being shelled rather heavily. I went on then to the Petite Ferme de Bois, which is North of Doulieu, where I found Crozier and Hobkirke; they both seemed tired out. All I could tell them was that Divisions were coming up behind us and that we must all hang on as long as possible and stop the Bosch.

I saw the Yorkshire digging and some of the 20th Middlesex and spoke to them. They were alright but pretty nearly all out with fatigue.

Shelling seems to be increasing. Soon after my return to my Head Quarters the Corps Commander came round to see me. He told me 26 German Divisions are now in front of us and he thinks the object is Hazebrouk and the Railway. He told me he was very much pleased with the way the Division had fought and stuck it out. We are to be relieved to-night and are to be wihtdrawn right behind. Our casualties I believe have been high but it is impossible to say how many. The rough estimate is that there are about 500 men left in each Brigade.

The Corps Commander told me he had just received orders to join General Foch and that the command of the Corps would be taken by General de L'isle.

I moved my Head Quarters at 5 p.m. to La Motte which is nearer to Hazebrouk where the Division is to assemble. The place however was choc a bloc, Head Quarters of the 31st Division arrived here at the same time, and I came across the 4th Guards Brigade who are now under Leslie Butler.

About 7 p.m. a report came in that the Germans having taken Merville were now pushing on to La Motte and that there were now no troops between us and the enemy as the 50th Division had been unable to stop the rush. Being away from the remnants of my Division, I decided to move to a farm called "La Souveraine" where I could get into easier touch with them.

Old Metcalfe who commands the 21st Middlesex having commanded his battalion splendidly for the last 3 days has now been hit, leg broken I believe. Watson the Chaplain of the 119th Brigade died this evening of wounds, an extraordinary brave Padre. He was killed trying to help the wounded along.

It was much quieter this evening. The 31st Division carried out a good counter attack about 7 p.m. and the situation is now a bit easier.

April 12th. Much quieter during the night although small local attacks were taking place. I am remaining at La Souveraine Farm as orders from Corps have arrived that no troops at all can be relieved. The place is being shelled. The weather has cleared and today is almost a hot summer's day.

This afternoon a strong attack was made on Mellis but the

enemy were held.

Received orders to take up a defensive position round Strazeele in case of a break through, also to take up positions for the defence of Hazebrouk.

Orders sent to Crozier to take up a position with the Brigade on high ground East of Strazeele. The 120th Brigade to be in close support. Trenches to be dug and constant patrols to be pushed forward towards Mellis and Meteren. I estimate both these Brigades will number about a thousand Rifles. I have sent 16 machine guns to be put under Crozier. Roberts goes down to select positions. The defences of Hazebrouk I have entrusted to Campbell. He has not got many troops but I have told him to collect all stragglers he can; I have told him to hold the roads strongly, and have sent 16 machine guns to support him. The Australian Division has come up. Our casualties in this second Battle amount to 4,300 all ranks.

April 13th. Heavy firing went on all night and increased in volume early this morning. A very misty morning. The roads are being shelled and it seems only a question of time when we shall get a direct hit on Head Quarters.

About 11 a.m. the Bosch made a very strong attack in large numbers on Mellis but I hear we have pushed him back. Meterin is being very heavily shelled.

At 4 p.m. I received orders to withdraw my Division and to concentrate in the Eblingham Area. Left Le Souverain Farm soon after 5 p.m. and passed through Hazebrouk. The whole town is completely deserted, like a city of the dead. A good many houses have been destroyed by shell fire.

Reports are just in that the 4th Guards Brigade is heavily engaged but they are holding their ground well. The second Cavalry Division are now moving up and an Australian Division is supporting the 31st Division.

On looking back on these last few days of hard fighting, the following points seem to have impressed themselves on me. Although there were a few signs of unusual movement behind the German lines but no indications of an attack on a large scale, it seemed to be the general impression that the Germans would attack somewhere North after their success in the South, but their main attack would go on in the South: also that they would probably chose a place for the secondary attack where we might imagine we were secure. The front we have just been holding was always considered to be the "cushiest" part of the line. We ought therefore to have been stronger and to have had more Divisions in reserve.

The Corps Commander at the Conference told us that he thought it possible that they would make an attack on Laventie, but he thought it would be more or less of an attack to make us bring reserves up from the South and would not be the real thing. He had however asked for another Division to come up as a reserve, but there seems to have been a delay over this.

The danger as far as we personally were concerned was of course our right flank. The Portuguese had never come in for a very strong bombardment or either a strong attack and having been so long in one place were xxxfxxxxx perhaps over confident.

I went over myself to see our right defences and came to

April 13th Contd.

the conclusion that the reserve Brigade was rather too far back. However the 50th had been ordered up and the 120th were to be brought up closer immediately it could be arranged. The difficulty was that they were reorganizing at the time as the 14th Argylls had been broken up and a new battalion the 2nd Royal Scots Fusiliers had only just arrived after having had very severe fighting with the 5th Army. It was therefore imperative to give them 24 hours rest.

The bombardment was very intense and our front and support lines were completely blotted out. Of course the same, if not worse, bombardment took place on the Portuguese front and may have extended down to their reserve line, but as far as I can gather when they started retiring they seemed to have cleared away altogether which enabled the Bosch to completely turn our front. Our left Brigade were not attacked till several hours later.

I can't help feeling if more concrete emplacements for machine guns had been made, we could have held out longer. There were concrete Pillboxes but only half of them had been completed with loopholes. As it was the defences at Fleurbaix and at Canteen Farm which were held up by the 12th Suffolks held out for some eight hours although surrounded.

The question of the River Lys is a difficult one. Would it perhaps have been better policy for the army to have taken up a line North of the river and made the river a strong obstacle. The difficulty of course was that so many villages and towns like Bac St Maur, Estaires, La Gorgue were really for the most part on the South side of the river and would have had to have been evacuated. Personally I think we ought to have done this but this is a question for higher commands.

It was impossible to blow up the bridges till the very last moment, as our men were all on the South side and fighting hard. The big bridges were of course blown up earlier, although the bridge at Estaires was not destroyed as the leads were destroyed by hostile shelling.

The Lys is practically a canal and is only about 20 yards wide, so there was no difficulty in bridging it, especially when the enemy crossed over at Estaires and took the Bridge head defences in rear.

The Bosch very cleverly occupied the top stories in the houses at Bac St Maur and used their machine guns to sweep down all the trenches on the North side of the River, which made the defences difficult to hold.

The worst part of the whole battle was the evacuation of the French Civil Population. This was left in the hands of the French Mission who apparently were helpless and did nothing. The people refused to leave their houses, as they refused to believe after three years of comparative safety that the Bosch would ever attack in these parts. The results was that the casualties among the poor women and children must have been very terrible. I think the French ought never to have allowed the civil population to have been so close up to the front line.

As regards the German tactics they undoubtedly know how to exploit a success. They push their light machine guns well forward, taking advantage of any folds in the ground and invariably try to push their guns up on any exposed flank with a view of bringing enfilade fire to bear on our troops.

April 13th Contd.

Communications worked well during the whole battle, but it was a soldier's battle and almost impossible to direct matters from Head Quarters, as the situation kept changing every minute.

The essential thing is the leadership and it is only the officers on the spot who can personally direct matters. Big gaps kept on occurring and perpetual messages came through to say "we are not in touch with the Brigades on our right or on our left", "The Brigade on our right has fallen back", "The enemy are now moving in large numbers round our right rear" and so on. The Divisions that came up in support were used/chiefly to fill the gaps or what was called at the time "to plug the holes". They became involved in the fighting before they knew where they were. It perhaps would have been better for these new Divisions to have established themselves on some definite line of defence in rear instead of being rushed up. The difficulty in this case was that the troops in front were not only dead beat but were completely outnumbered, and in order to check a bad break through it was necessary to support the troops who were fighting well in front and give them confidence.

When men begin to retire the danger is that the rot will set in all down the line. From what I hear and saw myself I came to the conclusion that the only way to stop the rush of the enemy was to immediately counter-attack him. This of course takes some organising but whenever it was carried out it was immediately successful.

April 14th. Orders received for the Division to go to Longuenesse just west of St Omer. As I passed through St Omer I noticed many signs that the civil population had been alarmed by recent events; most of the shops were shut and a good many people were packing up and leaving the town. I think that the chief reason for this was that the town was badly bombed the night before last and they expected still more raids. Several houses had been completely demolished and there had been over 30 people killed in the last raid.

We are billetted in a small chateau near a hospital. The Duchess of Sutherland is running a hospital next door. She moved her hospital up from Calais and I believe it is now to be a casualty clearing station. Harry Graham and I went to tea with her. She has been doing great work evacuating people from the Eblingham area in her motor ambulances. The news from the front is decidedly better. The Bosch has apparently been brought to a standstill and is now making no headway.

April 15th The news still continues good, but I am rather suspicious as to what the Hun is up to. Everybody resting and sleeping; weather cold.

April 16th We move today to Wisherne just a few miles away in order to get better accommodation.

April 17th. Bailleul has fallen into the hands of the Hun but as they were all round it this was only to be expected, but on other sides the news is quite good.

We are now in the 8th Corps and under the command of Hunter Weston, generally known as Hunter Bunter. He came to see me today and talked a lot. We have been ordered to form one composite Brigade out of the Division which is to be ready for any emergency.

April 17th Contd.

I have arranged for Campbell to take command of the Brigade It is to consist of the 13th Batt. Yorkshire, 12th Suffolks and 20th Middlesex. All Battalions to be made up to full strength from men of the 13th East Surreys, 18th Welsh Regiments and ~~xix~~ 21st Middlesex.

Ruggles Brise who formerly commanded the Division came to see me this evening. He is now Military Secretary at G.H.Q.

April 18th. Frank Mildmay came over with Guise Moores to luncheon. They are both with the Head Quarters of the 2nd Army.

Today I went round to inspect the Field Companies R.E., they all looked exceedingly well and fit and were well turned out which was very creditable, and later I inspected the 135, 136 and 137 Field Ambulances. I spoke a few words to the men and congratulated them on having carried out their duties so splendidly during the Battle.

April 19th. A conference with the three Brigadiers chiefly concerning lessons to be learnt for the future. The weather remains cold and dreary.

April 20th. 400 men of the Yorkshires and 200 men of the Highland Light Infantry have been ordered to join other Divisions. I went down to the station to see them off. We have been ordered to reconnoitre a defensive line East of Cassel. Baylay and Black went round in the morning and Chapman and myself went round in the afternoon to look at the ground.

There are now a large number of French troops in the district they really look a very fine lot of men mostly young soldiers.

April 21st The Deputy Chaplain General (Dr.Gwynne, Bishop of Khartoum) preached to various Battalions of the Division to-day. I went to one of the services, it turned out to be a Noncomformist one, but the Noncomformist Chaplain asked me to stay; the Bishop preached to the men and we all became Noncomformist for the time being owing to the fervent prayers of Mr Davis, the Welsh Chaplain. The Bishop himself got quite carried away and gave the blessing with an unorthodox prayer that we might all be given strength to "stick it out" to the end.

In the afternoon the Bishop took me over in his motor to see the 3rd Battalion Coldstream who are near the Forest of Nieppe. Longueville who commands tells me they had a very hard time of it, only 2 officers and 40 men came through out of it, and the Battalion did magnificently. They are now about 500 strong, having got their details back and also a strong draft from home.

April 22nd. I had luncheon today with the Corps Commander Hunter Bunter at Cassell. From what he tells me I am afraid the Division is to be practically broken up and the men sent off to other Divisions. The Staff and Headquarters are to remain, as is hoped to reform the Division in the next three months. This news has caused much consternation and grief throughout the whole Division. It seems a great pity, just as the Division has got a great esprit de corps and has done very well in the last two battles to go and do away with it.

April 23rd. Went over with Black to G.H.Q. to see Guy Dawnay and to find out our ultimate fate. It appears there is no help for it and we are to be broken up, but all Headquarters, that is to say Divisional, Brigade and Battalion, are to remain with

April 23rd Contd.

their staffs as it is hoped to fill up the Division later on. In the meantime it seems more than probable that we shall be employed in training Americans.

April 24th. Bayley and I went to Cassel to walk round the new line which is being dug a few miles east of Cassel. The trenches are being carefully concealed behind the hedges and immediately they are dug they are at once camouflaged over with branches and green turf.

April 25th. The 2nd Batt. Royal Scots Fusiliers left us to-day to join the 9th Division. I went to the Station at St Omer to see them off.

It is very worrying seeing all these fine troops leaving my command. Guy Dawnay told me that in order to keep our present line good and up to strength, it has been necessary to deplete 10 Divisions and other may follow.

April 26th. Frank came over this afternoon: he says the news is not over good and that Mount Kemmel has fallen. Foch laid great stress on holding this high ground and sent several French Divisions up to help but apparently they havn't been able to do it.

April 27th. John Campbell, who commands the 121st Brigade, has been promoted Major General and leaves today to command the 32nd Division. An order has just come in to say that no more troops are to leave the Division and that a second composite Brigade is to be formed and that we shall probably be moved up into the Popperinghe area.

April 29th. Enemy attacked this morning the French and our 2nd Army, but apparently gained very little, if anything at all.

April 30th. We have been ordered to move into St Omer as our present quarters are required for the French troops.

May 1st. I went up today to Proven to see the 121st Brigade they are digging the Popperinghe line, they are digging under orders of the 2nd Corps and are administered by the 8th Corps which is not very satisfactory.

The 119th Composite Brigade moved up East of Cassel today.

May 2nd. French troops are pouring up, Gunners, Cavalry and Infantry. Aspinall the B.G.G.S VIII told me how difficult it is at present to send definite orders as we are practically all under Foch who wants to get most of his troops up in the area. He apologised for sending so many different orders and I quite understand under these circumstances that it can't be helped. Aspinall seems a particularly clear headed man and it seems a pity that he should not take the command of the VIII Corps instead of H.B.

Orders received tonight that the 121st Brigade is to move back to Ryweld and the 119th Brigade to march back to St Momelin and that the process of disbandment is to be carried out.

It is rumoured that the Division is to be filled up with B.1 men, that is to say with old soldiers who are not fit for very active operations.

May 3rd. Frank came over to see me but did not have any fresh news. Sandy Ruthven B.G.G.S. 7th Corps arrived later at my Headquarters. He tells me we are now in the 7th Corps under Whigham, that we are to have 7 Garrison Battalions attached to us after all, my own battalions have been broken up and that we

May 3rd Contd.

are to continue making the Winnezeekl line into a strong line of defence. This perpetual shifting from one Corps to another seems to me to be a bad plan, as no sooner does one begin to know the staff than off one goes to another Corps. During the last 6 months my Division has formed part of the following Army Corps: The 3rd Army Corps under Pulteney, the 5th Army Corps under Fanshaw, the 4th Army Corps under Woolcombe, the 6th Army Corps under Haldane, the 15th Army Corps under Du Cane, the 8th Army Corps under Hunter Weston, the 7th Army Corps under Whigham.

Not knowing quite what order will come next, I decided to spend the day at Dunkirke with Black and Harry Graham. When I returned to St Omer I found orders that we are not to be filled up with Garrison Battalions but are to proceed South, to come under the 1st Army and to train Americans. I fully expect to hear tomorrow morning that this has been cancelled.

Patterson Carter my G.S.O.2 tells me that from what he heard at 2nd Army Headquarters they expect a strong attack from the Bosch almost at once, and they think the place of attack will be Mont des Cats and the high ground just west of Mount Kemmel.

Garnett from the Royal Welsh Fusiliers has been appointed Brigadier General in succession to Campbell and to command the 121st Brigade.

May 4th. Presented medal ribbons to the 119th and 121st Brigades. These decorations were earned for the first battle. Out of the 100 awarded there are about 30 on parade, all the rest are practically casualties or have been transferred.

May 5th. The last order received states we are to remain in the 7th Corps and in the 2nd Army.

Presented medal ribbons on a Brigade Ceremonial Parade to the 120th Scottish Brigade. Went to Wanneton and St Omer Railway Station to see the 119th Brigade and the 121st Brigade off to Calais.

I have now only got the skeletons of the Battalions left, that is to say the Commanding Officers, Adjutants, Sergeant Majors left and the Brigade Staffs. What is going to happen to us seems still undecided. There is a rumour that we are to superintend Chinese labour companies. I have applied for 3 weeks leave.

May 6th. Saw the last of the Division, the 120th Brigade, off by rail to Calais.

July 5th. My new Division is constituted as follows:-

G. O. C.   J.P.

General Staff.

G.S.O.1.   Lt.Col.Hall.
G.S.O.2.   Major Broughton.
G.S.O.3.   Captain Pepler.

Administrative Staff.

A.A.& Q.M.G.   Lt.Col.White.
D.A.A.G.   Major Inman,
D.A.Q.M.G.   Major Hawes.
A.D.M.S.   Col.Hewetson.

Administrative Staaf Contd.

D.A.D.M.S.	Major Kelly.
D.A.D.V.S.	Major Holmes.
D.A.D.O.S.	Major Shortt.
A.P.M.	Captain Coates.
O.C.Train.	Lt.Col. Wood.
S.S.O.	Major Clare.

Divisional Artillery.

Brig.General A.Hussey.

Divisional Engineers.

Lt.Col.Homer.

Pioneers Batt.

Lt.Col.Coates.

Machine Gun Battery.

Lt.Col.Cutting.

13th Infantry Brigade.

Commander.	Brig.General I. Jones, DSO.
Brigade Major.	Captain Lake.

14th Royal Warwickshire Regiment,
        commanded by Lt.Col.Wilberforce.
15th Bn.Royal Warwickshire Regiment,
        commanded by Lt.Col.Miller.
2nd Bn.King's Own Scottish Borderers
        commanded by Lt.Col.Furber.
1st Bn.Royal West Kents
        commanded by Lt.Col.Johnstone

15th Infantry Brigade.

Commanded by	Brig.General R.Oldman,CMG.
Brigade Major.	Major Gent.

16th Bn.Royal Warwickshire Regiment
        commanded by Lt.Col.Deakin.
1st Bn.Norfolk Regiment
        commanded by Lt.Col.Humphries.
1st Batt Bedfordshire Regiment
        commanded by Major Courtenay.
1st Batt Cheshire Regiment
        commanded by Lt.Col.Roddy.

95th Infantry Brigade.

Commanded by	Brig.General C.Norton,DSO.
Brigade Major	Captain Gotto.

1st Bn.Devonshire Regiment
        commanded by Lt.Colonel Halford.
12th Bn.Gloucestershire Regiment
        commanded by Lt.Col.Colt.
1st Bn.East Surrey Regiment
        commanded by Lt Col.Minogue.
1st Bn.Duke of Cornwall's Light Infantry
        commanded by Lt.Col.Kirk.

July 5th Contd.

White my A.A. and Q.M.G. took me round the Reserve Battalions. We walked through the Forest of Nieppe. It was a case of having to carry a Gas bag and a tin hat, although it was not necessary to use them. However, the whole Wood stank of gas, and it was the most fetid atmosphere I have breathed for a long time. There were over thirty casualties last night in the Division, chiefly owing to Gas poisoning, otherwise the casualties from shell and rifle fire are slight.

Dined with Haking my Corps Commander to-night. He goes on leave tomorrow, and I take over the command of the Corps in his absence as apparently I am the Senior Divisional Commander in the Corps.

July 6th. Round the front line with Gordon Hall my G.S.O.1. There were a good many Bosch Aeroplanes flying about over the wood. As we passed through the forest to go up to the front line, they started shelling the edge of the forest, but we got clear and in the trenches everything was quiet. I met a Lieut. Wheeler up the line who told me he had been a Sergeant in the 1st Batt.Coldstream during the early part of this war, he is now a Lieutenant in the Devonshire Regiment. I had a long talk with him and he seems to be getting on very well.

This afternoon I had a Divisional Conference. The worst part of this Sector is that one has to walk about a mile through the Forest before one can get anywhere and as it reeks with gas, I don't dare take my dog "Sandy" with me as I feel certain he would be gassed in no time.

General Oldham who was gassed about a week ago has had to go home today on leave. His eyes are very bad and he is so hoarse he can't talk at all.

July 7th. Felt rather cheap to-day. Black came over from the 40th. In the afternoon after tea Barebones and I rode into Aire, the place has been knocked about by bombs. A lot of houses have been destroyed, but the big Church is intact. I visited this town about two years ago when it was in a very prosperous condition

The string band of the Division played to-night. They are not anywhere near up to the form of Mr Parks and the band of the 40th Division which I shall always think was quite the best band in France. However it is a great thing having a band at all.

August 18th. When I got back to my Headquarters at Rebreuve I found that I had been sent for both by the 6th Corps and by the 4th Corps, that we were to move at once. At 6 p.m. I went to a conference at 4th Corps. The Corps Commander is Sir G.Harper generally known as Uncle Harper. Braithwaite 62nd Division, Williams 37th Division, Russell New Zealand Division and many others including Parker B.G.G.3 who was with me at Chatham. Tolly (Tollemache) now G.S.O.2, Bisset (Charlie Willoughby's late Brigade Major) and David Sherlock acting C.R.A. 62nd Division.

The whole plans seem to be terribly rushed, continually being altered and very little time to get down to it; at any rate we are in for a show almost at once.

August 19th. A conference late last night. The Brigades marched during the night. We moved to Authie, where I was two years ago before the Somme battle. Hard at it all day with conferences, went round to see 37th Division, New Zealand Division and 62nd

August 20th.

Went up the line to see ~~attack~~ the country we are going over, very quiet, country very much devastated. All the Staff very hard at it. Went over to see General Lawrie who commands the 63rd Naval Division. Zero is to be at 4.55 a.m. tomorrow morning. Moved my Headquarters tonight after dinner to some dugouts at Fonquevillers where also the Headquarters of the 63rd Division and New Zealand Divisions have taken up their residence for the Battle. The place is generally known as Funk Villas.

August 21st. The general plan of the attack is as follows: the 6th Corps on our left are to advance as far as the Arras Albert Railway and are to take Moyenville en route, 3rd Division on the right, the Guards Division on the left. The objective of the 4th Corps to which we now belong is a line east of the railway including the villages of Achit le Petit and Achit le Grand.

To carry this out the orders are that the 37th Division are to take the first objective Ablainasville and a line about 700 yards from their front trenches. Then we are to push through them, the 5th Division on our left, the New Zealanders then to advance and capture Erles. It is practically an advance on a three Corps frontage. The ultimate object is to drive the enemy out of Bapaume and to secure the Arras Bapaume Road. We are to be supported by Tanks and Whippets (small Tanks)

The barrage started at zero 4.55 a.m. There is a thick mist and it is difficult to see more than 50 yards in front of one. Everything seems to be going well. The 37th Division gained their objective without much opposition and with little loss. The 63rd Division and my Division passed through the 37th Division about 6.35 a.m., strong opposition is reported by the 63rd Division at Logeast Wood.

Both my Brigades Report doing well. The 95th Brigade under Norton are advancing on a two Battalion frontage. The 1st Devons on the right, the 1st East Surrey on the left. The 1st Batt.Duke of Cornwall Light Infantry in support and the 12th Battalion Gloucester Regiment in reserve.

They are advancing behind the Tanks but report that the mist is so thick that it is difficult to keep proper direction. Their casualties are slight and they are moving well forward to the railway cutting. (The Albert Arras Railway). On their left Oldman's Brigade the 15th has met with some opposition at Achit le Petit. They also are moving on a two Battalion frontage.

The 16th Batt.Warwick's on the right, the 1st Cheshires on the left. The 1st Battalion Bedfords are in support and the 1st Batt Norfolks in reserve.

About 8.30 a.m. I received the news that we had taken Achit le Petit and that several hundred prisoners had been taken. The advance across the railway was strongly opposed by the Bosch who laid his guns on all the crossings and consequently they were able to knock out all the tanks, chiefly however the small fast tanks (known as whippets) immediately they attempted to pass over.

The 63rd Division at Logeast Wood were counter-attacked and had to fall back. This left our left rather in the air, and the 15th Brigade had to form a defensive flank.

August 21st Contd.

It has been terribly hot all day, in the evening the situation was as follows: The right Brigade was on the hill overlooking the railway cutting. The left Brigade was on the hill overlooking the railway cutting. The left Brigade was in a trench slightly in rear with their left thrown right back.

The 63rd Division were on the Eastern edge of Logeast Wood, and apparently there was a gap between them and the 3rd Division on their left. On our right the New Zealanders and the 42nd Division were on the West side of Miraumont and apparently waiting for us to take Irles. However as we are now far in advance of where they are, a combined attack to capture both Miraumont and Irles is the only solution.

The Corps Commander Uncle Harper arrived at my Dug out about 7 p.m. It was then decided that as tanks were unable to co-operate the attack would have to be postponed until a concentration of Guns could be obtained.

August 22nd.
Fairly quiet night although the enemy started shelling early this morning. Went up to Buquoy Trench about 6.30 a.m. with Gordon Hall and Homer my C.R.E.

The Bosch attacked our right flank about 7 a.m. but were thrown back and the 1st Devons counter attacking took 240 prisoners, a very good bit of work. The Bosch then made a determined attack on the 63rd Division on our left but here also they have been driven back. There has been heavy shelling this afternoon along our whole front. The Norfolks are reported to have had many casualties including their commanding officer Col.Humphries and their Adjutant. The number of prisoners taken by the 4th and 6th Corps are estimated to be about 2,000.

Good reports are coming in ~~regarding~~ concerning the progress of the French 10th Army and also splendid reports from our 4th Army.

It is baking hot, one of the hottest days I have struck; in the dug out however it is damp and chilly so one goes from one extreme to the other.

Uncle Harper our Corps Commander came up about 8 p.m. and says we are to attack again tomorrow morning. The 63rd are to be relieved by the 37th. We are to take Irles and the Ridge east of the Railway. On our left Northwards I understand the 3rd Division has taken Gomiecourt (This was my old Headquarters last January). Heavy shelling most of the night.

I think myself the great difficulty for us will be the crossing of the railway, as I believe the ridge East of this is full of hostile machine Guns. I have asked for some smoke shells but it appears these are difficult to obtain as the transport for H.E. 106 Fuze shell is of course more important.

August 23rd.
Zero was at 11 a.m. this morning. Again the 95th and 15th Brigades attacked as it was impossible to get the reserve Brigade up in time.

Both the Brigades "went over the top" with gret elan. The 12th Gloucesters on the right, the 1st Bedfords on the left. The Railway was crossed under a creeping Barrage carried out by 6 Brigades of Artillery on our Divisional front. The 37th Division advanced on our left. All objectives were taken, but

August 23rd Contd.

I am told we had many casualties including Coutenay who commands the Bedfords, I hear he has been badly hit. The trouble is now on our right.

1 p.m. Irles still remains in the enemy's hands. The Norfolks and East Surreys who were left and right battalions, in fact the centre battalions of the Division have now pushed on and are level with the Battalions on the flanks.

3 p.m. Report in to say that 6th Corps are progressing well in the North.

4 p.m. A large number of prisoners are coming down. We have been ordered to exploit our success and push on the Greyvillers.
Have ordered the 13th Brigade under Jones to push through the leading Brigades and if possible to gain the outskirts of Lupart Wood. Tanks tonight have rather failed me, I ordered them to co-operate with the 13th Brigade in their advance and to be ready at 5 p.m. but I have since received a message that they will not be able to get across the railway till after 7 p.m. I therefore postponed the attack of the 13th Brigade till 7.30 p.m. I have doubts that they will get there even then in time. I have therefore arranged with Hussy my C.R.A. for a creeping barrage.

7 p.m. The Commander in Chief Sir Douglas Haig arrived at my dug out. He told me he was very pleased with the action of the Division and that the whole battle was going spendidly.
He urged me to push on as much as possible as the Hun was showing signs of breaking. I am not quite happy at the attack at 7.30 p.m. It is too late as it is dark at 6.30 p.m. and I am afraid the Battalions will lose themselves.

7.30 p.m. The Corps Commander arrived. He was anxious to know the result of the attack, but I told him that it would be probably hopeless to find out anything before midnight. In the meantime the New Zealanders have orders to pass through us at Dawn.

August 24th. The 13th Brigade under Jones in spite of many difficulties owing to darkness and lack of tanks scored a great success. They pushed on towards Lupart Wood, they took over 300 prisoners and a battery of guns.

This morning the New Zealanders advanced through us at an early hour. They took Greyvillers and Biefvillers about 9 a.m. They report many prisoners captured. Gordon Hall and I went up to Achit le Petit and then on to the 3 Brigade Headquarters. The whole country is like the Somme Battle fields, a vast mass of Shell holes. We apparently have taken a large quantity of Hun War material and machine guns; I saw stacks and dumps of German ammunition everywhere. I also saw a good many prisoners being marched down.

The 42nd Division under Solly Flood on our right report that they have captured Miraumont and crossed the Ancre River. Oldham told me his Brigade has captured over 700 prisoners the last 3 days and I think the other two Brigades have accounted for another 800 altogether making a total of 1500 prisoners captured by the Division. Our casualties are about 90 officers and about 2000 other ranks killed and wounded. I have not received the actual returns so far.

I am very sorry to hear that Colt who commands the 12th

August 24th Contd.

Gloucesters has been badly wounded. Courtenay who commands the Bedfords is badly wounded in the stomach and they don't hold out much hope, but he is still alive according to reports from the Field Ambulance. The Division is in great spirits and they certainly have done splendidly.

A conference this evening as Uncle Harper appeared with Williams and Russell outside our dug outs. We are to remain where we are and to collect Battalions together near the Railway Embankment with a view of pushing or rather "leap frogging" over the New Zealanders or perhaps the 37th Division. Russell who commands the New Zealanders impresses me very much as a strong and capable man.

August 25th. Have just received the following message from the Corps Commander.

"The Corps Commander wishes to convey to all ranks under your command his thanks for their work during the last three days and to congratulate them on their success which could only have been attained by great fighting capacity and endurance".

After practically only 24 hours rest we are for it again and orders have been received that we are to take over tonight from the 37th Division after they have attacked the enemy North of Bapaume. Bapaume is to be attacked tonight on the North by the 37th on the South by the New Zealanders with the object of pinching the place and avoiding a frontal attack.

I moved my Head Quarters today to some German dug outs east of Achiet le Petit and east of the railway.

This place has just been vacated by the Bosch. It is in a filthy condition and there are a good many dead bodies British and German lying about unburied. However it is the only place we can find at present as it is away from observation and has some dug outs where one can escape from bombing. Communications are good but it is a beastly dirty place taking it as a whole.

August 26th. We have had to move our Headquarters back to Buquoy by orders of the Corps Commander as he wishes to keep all the Divisional Headquarters together. The 13th Brigade attacked Favreil at 6.30 p.m. and took place. The 2nd Kings Own Scottish Borderers leading the attack and capturing about 60 prisoners.

August 27th. This morning the 2nd Battalion K.O.S.Bs. advanced as far as Beunatre (the men call this Bug Nature) the New Zealanders have been held up South of Bapaume. They report the place chock full of machine guns. They are giving the place a miss and are established just north of Bapaume on the Fremicourt Road.

I hear the division on our right is held up at Thilloy. All the Divisions north of us are doing well but are not meeting with so much opposition.

A report in to say that the Guards Division has taken Monchy East of Arras. The idea now I believe is to swoop down from the North clearing up the Hindenburg Line "en pasaant".

August 27th Contd.

Dudgeon commanding the 2nd Batt. K.O.S.B. has been wounded. I sent Lake up (Brigade Major 13th Brigade) to take over the command but he hadn't been there long before he himself was shot through both legs. I have asked the Corps for the services of Luss Colquhoun, but whether I shall get him or not is very doubtful. I have got a very heavy cold which is a nuisance, I think caught by sleeping in damp dug outs.

August 28th. The situation remains unchanged, both Bapaume and Thilloy remain in the hands of the enemy and by now they may have been reinforced. I believe the Army Commander intends to make a great combined attack along the whole front as isolated attacks by Divisions only cause casualties.

Sam Pepler my G.S.O.3 has been rather badly wounded this afternoon through the lung. I sent him up yesterday to act as Brigade Major to the 13th Brigade. I hear he was hit by a chance rifle bullet. He will be a great loss to the Division as he was a most promising fellow. My cold is still very heavy.

August 29th. The enemy evacuated Bapaume probably during the night as the New Zealand patrols went through the place without opposition. About 9 a.m. Uncle Harper held a conference the gist of which was that we are to push on but to conserve our strength and not to attack places that are held on strength. Thilloy has fallen into the hands of the 42nd Division who are pushing forward to get level with the New Zealanders.

Whigham has been appointed to command the 62nd Division on our left vice Braithwaite who has got a Corps; he came over to see me this morning and tells me the Bosche is still in Vaulx Vraucourt and is showing determined resistance to his patrols.

Tommy Pitman who commands the Cavalry Division came over to see me, his cavalry are now rather split up. Pinto came over to luncheon, his Division (the 2nd Div.) are in reserve to the 62nd, the third Division are in reserve to the Guards Division.

August 30th. Last night about 9 p.m. I received orders from the Corps that a general advance was to be made. My Division was ordered to advance and take Beugny, Lebucquiere, and Velu. On our left the 62nd Division were to go for Vaulx Vraucourt, Morcnies and Meaumetz. On our right the New Zealanders to go for Remicourt and Bertincourt. How much we shall be able to carry out this rather ambitious programme is to my mind rather doubtful. I wish we could get the warning orders earlier. It is a great business getting the orders through to the various Battalions on a dark wet night when the attack has to start at 5 a.m.

I ordered the 95th Brigade to carry out the attack. We have got three Brigades of Artillery forming a creeping barrage also we have got 12 tanks attached to the Division.

All four Divisions attacked at 5 a.m. under a barrage.

The 1st Devons and 1st Duke of Cornwall's Light Infantry leading the attack for the 5th Division; strong opposition was met with everywhere. My Division however went forward splendidly and carried their first objective which was a line of trenches running North and South of Beugny. The D.C.L.I. suffered from Machine Guns on the right and had to form a defensive flank. The Devons pushing on reached the village and took 7 officers and 250 men prisoners including a Battalion Commander.

The New Zealanders took Fremicourt but were unable to take

the high ground South East of the Village. The 42nd Division were hung up at Reincourt, but on our left the 62nd pushed through Vaulx Vraucourt and got into touch with the 1st Norfolks who were sent up in support of the 95th Brigade to hold the trenches on their left flank.

The 27th Field Artillery Brigade did a very smart bit of work, they galloped forward about a mile and a half immediately the first objective was taken and got into action within half an hour.

Our casualties were chiefly in the D.C.L.I. but I don't know how many, probably about 200.

Uncle Harper came up in the afternoon and seemed to think we ought not to have pushed on against opposition. I pointed out that the orders he sent were clear enough on the subject and there it was in black and white that our objective was Beugny.

I moved my Head Quarters this evening to Behucourt.

We are in a German concrete building, probably used as a Bath house. It is made of concrete with dugouts outside the house but I am rather nervous that the place may be full of booby traps and go up in the air any moment. It has been quite impossible to sleep to-night as there is one of our 6 inch guns just outside which is firing every five minutes.

August 31st. Spent rather a rotten night owing to the noise. This evening we were counter attacked from the north of Beugny and also from the south: both attacks were beaten off with heavy loss to the enemy. In conjunction with the New Zealanders we took about 50 prisoners.

Conference at 11 a.m. at Sapnignies with the Brigadiers.
Corps Conference at Bucquoy in the afternoon. Enemy reported to be shelling Fremicourt heavily this evening.

I am told Torquhil Mattheson has got the Guards Division vice Geoffrey who goes home to command the London District. I had hoped that it might have come my way as I am senior to Torquhil although junior to Pinto. Torquhil however is quite excellent and is thought most highly of by everyone.

September 1st. A minor operation this morning in conjunction with the New Zealanders. We advanced our line a few hundred yards South of Beugny and the new Zealanders went for the high ground running south west. They took 100 prisoners and we bagged about 20.

Conference with Brigadiers at 11 a.m. then conference with Corps Commander, then back to Sapignies for final conference with G.O.C. 15th Brigade. We attack again to-morrow morning.

September 2nd. The general plan was as follows: The 1st Army and part of the 3rd Army are to attack this morning and to drive the enemy South. The remainder of the 3rd Army including the 6th, 4th and 5th Corps are to press forward in an easterly direction
As regards our actual front the 62nd Division are to go for Morchies on our immediate left, our objectives are beugny, Lebuquiere and Velu. On our right the New Zealanders and 42nd Division are to go for Villers au Flos and Haplincourt and to exploit their success.

At 8 a.m. we heard that Beugny had been taken and that 250 prisoners had been taken by the Norfolks. About 10 a.m. heavy fighting was reported to have taken place in the village and apparently Beugny was still held by the enemy. The 1st Cheshire are reported to have had a good many casualties, the New Zealanders are not up level with us, but the Norfolks report our right flank to be secure. On our left the 62nd are reported to be making good progress.

We started the attack with 4 tanks but it seems very indefinite as to what happened to them. One is reported by the Aeroplane to be in flames: probably the other have broken down, as Baker Carr told me last night they were pretty well worn out.

2 p.m. The New Zealanders are now well up, and the situation on our right is much better. Oldman tells me he hopes to get the high ground East of Beugny to-night, as the village itself is reported to be clear of the enemy. The enemy counter-attacked in the afternoon but was driven off leaving a few prisoners in our hands.

5.30 p.m. Conference with Corps Commander: we are to clear up Beugny to-morrow morning and consolidate our position.

September 3rd. A barrage was arranged for 5.20 a.m. this morning, but on following the barrage through the village of Beugny the Bedfords found the place evacuated. It was then realized the the Bosch had retired all down the line. The Guards Division, the 2nd Division, ourselves and the New Zealanders found that the Bosch had gone right back. Our patrols pushed on as far as Hermies but the New Zealanders met with opposition when trying to cross the railway at Bertincourt.

A Corps conference at 12: we go into reserve and are relieved by the 37th Division. The Brigades are to assemble either to-night or to-morrow in the Behucourt, Grey Villiers areas. It is a desolate place and there are very few huts but it will be a rest.

I went up to Lebucquiere this afternoon and passed through Beugny where we had all the severe fighting yesterday. There is hardly anything left except a few walls in the village. The ridge east of Beugny looked a very difficult place to take and there were signs everywhere of heavy fighting. I hear 10,000 Germans have been taken prisoner by the 1st Army; the Germans are reported to be in Havrincourt Wood. I expect they will take up a position round Bourlon Wood, but our first Army should then be able to deal with that situation.

September 4th. Brigades marched back to the Grey Villiers and Behucourt areas. Conference at Corps Head Quarters. A Brochure from the Army Commander was read out to say that troops were to be rested as much as possible. Advanced Guards were to feel their way forward, but if the enemy were in strength they were not to be attacked.

September 5th. A quiet day. The 37th Division and New Zealanders are pushing their way to the Northern part of Havrincourt Wood.
The 42nd Division are attacking Neuville. Rode round the various battalions xxxxx with Barebones. The men are resting and washing and are all in good spirits.

September 6th. Rode round the Battalions again with Barebones. It is always most depressing to see the terrible changes in each Battalion after a battle. New commanding officers, new adjutants, etc., etc., and such a small proportion of officers left. Our casualties, I believe, have been about 4,000 during the last ten days fighting.

Conference to-night with Brigadiers. We went thoroughly into every subject: Artillery support, Machine Guns, action of Tanks, etc.,etc.

I have heard that I have been given 5 days leave in France, am off early to-morrow with Parsons and Barebones to Deauville.

We may go on to Paris if we are bored stiff at the sea side.

September 16th. A very hot day: I went up to the front line, a very long tiring walk, extraordinarily quiet. In the afternoon Uncle Harper and Staff came up for a long conference. We are in for a small show.

The trouble is as always that the Division on the flank always want one to push right out and hold the ground on their flank, but it doesn't seem to be realized that unless the whole Corps move forward together, the flank Division covering the next one will always in its turn have its flank in the air, and therefore will be subject to the danger of being enfiladed.

September 17th. A tremendous thunderstorm last night. I have never seen such vivid lightening. The Bosch shelled Villiers au Flos early this morning with "Percy" This is the name given to the long range Naval Gun.

Conference at 13th Brigade Head Quarters to talk over the attack to-morrow morning.

Col. Kirk, D.C.L.I. is now commanding the Brigade: he is a good officer and capable so there is no fear of his making a mess of it.

The Bosch started shelling the roads with Percy about 5 p.m. Some shells fell unpleasantly close, and splinters were flying about in all directions. Uncle Harper came up with Geddis, his chief Gunner, about 5.30 p.m. His great hobby now appears to be the use of Rifle grenades.

September 18th. Bombing and shelling went on during the night. I am rather wondering whether the Bosch has spotted our head Quarters. The Battle started at 5.20 a.m. this morning. We were on the extreme left of the attack and had a small part to play as the 5th Corps and 4th Army were pushing up in a N.E. direction and were practically pivoted on Gozeaucourt.

It is curious getting back to all these well known villages where I was this time last year with the 40th Division.

Our role was to protect the left flank of the 38th Division. One battalion of the 13th Brigade at present commanded by Kirk in the D.C.L.I. started under a creeping barrage to occupy "African Trench" and to form a defensive flank to the larger operation. Unfortunately the Battalion on the left of the 38th Division were held up by machine gun fire and consequently when the K.O.S.Bs. got to African Trench, they were unable to hold it as they were enfiladed from both flanks and eventually were obliged to withdraw to the trench they started from. The battalion on their right were in the same predicament and likewise had to fall back. The right of the 38th Division, however, secured their objectives without much opposition. On our left the 37th Division were counter-attacked about 5 p.m. but the Bosch were driven off. Our batteries on the South of Havrincourt Wood had rather a bad time of it, principally through Gas shelling but stuck to it well all day, in spite of a good many casualties.

September 19th. Gore Browne and I walked up to the 13th Brigade Head Quarters: the hostile shelling was rather disagreeable. A lot of stuff going into the ruined village of Metz. We stuck to Havrincourt Wood most of the way. I told Kirk and Furber that the K.O.S.B. had done all they could and that it was certainly not their fault in any way that they finally had been compelled to withdraw.

Our communications are bad and I am sure we want to get down to the question more thoroughly. I held forth on the subject rather strongly when I was at the advanced Brigade Head Quarters and I hope it may improve.

Yesterday's operations accounted for about 7,000 prisoners, 6000 from the 4th Army and 1000 from the 5th Corps on our right. A conference this afternoon at Corps Head Quarters. We are for it again in about a week's time.

September 20th. A cold day, conferences going on most of the day. Gerry Ruthven arrived in the middle of the night. I understand he is to be attached to my Division until he gets a Brigade.
Beckwith has been appointed to command the 13th Brigade vice Jones. Uncle Harper tells me he is very good.

September 21st. Went up with G.B. to see the Artillery Group commanders Hawke and Berkeley. The Bosche are shelling the villages and roads everywhere and are becoming highly offensive. Burnett Stewart came over to see me from G.H.Q.

September 22nd. Col. Bradley R.A.M.C. and Major McCormick R.A.M.C. both of the 15th Field Ambulance, were killed last night in their dug out by a high velocity shell. I went to their funeral at Barastre in the afternoon. Rained all the afternoon, Parker B.G.G.S. IV Corps came up after dinner with orders from the Corps

September 23rd A Divisional conference this morning. Beckwith my new Brigadier General seems very much all there and I think he will be a very good commander. The Army commander Sir Julien Byng came up to see me about 11 a.m.: he was in great spirits and very complimentary. He thinks it very probable that the war may be over this year, but we have so often heard the same story that I doubt myself that this most desired ending will be accomplished. The news from Palestine is good: Allenby has reached Nazareth and has taken 18,000 prisoners.

September 24th. A very long walk this morning with Gordon Hall and Barebones to the front trenches.

I found everybody in good spirits and Wheeler in the Devons, who was in my battalion at the beginning of the war, showed me round the sector. I saw a Bosch on sentry through the periscope, but he seemed to be "very idle on sentry" and not paying much attention to his duties. Counter battery work by the Bosch went on all the morning. Our villages were also shelled by their H.V. guns. The Corps commander came up for a conference. I wish we could get the plan of the next battle more definitely fixed: at present there is too much argument going on between Corps and Divisions. Dined with Solly Flood at Velu.

September 25th. Conference with my Brigadiers this morning. The creeping barrage time table is getting more complicated than ever. There is also great difficulty experienced in getting the Trench Mortar ammunition up. These shells are of enormous weight and have to be carried up from the Dumps, to the front trenches by fatigue parties from the Infantry.

Last night we had over 30 casualties doing this job. It may have been just bad luck, but the question is whether the game is worth the candle. However, as our artillery barrage is none too strong, I think we must make more effort to get it up and so have ordered the fatigue parties to be continued.

Davis Campbell, generaly known as Soarer Campbell because he won the Grand National on a horse called Soarer, came up to see me. He commands the 21st Division which is on our right.
His Division is to attack or rather get round Gouzeaucourt village moving north eastwards on Z 1 day. He is going to make a night show of it and wants me to cooperate by moving a Brigade down in a South easterly direction on to Gonnelieu.

This will be a difficult operation and will have to be most carefully worked out, as in the dark I foresee there may be considerable danger of one Division attacking the other if they are converging towards each other from different directions. However, if worked out well and distinctive features of the ground marked as Boundaries from which troops should not push forward, the fall of Gozeaucourt will be a "fait accompli" and on the whole I am in favour of the scheme.

Pinney who commands the 33rd Division, which will be on the right of the 21st Division, also came over to see me but his movements will not effect me. Dined with Russell who commands the New Zealanders and went to his Concert Party. A musical Comedy given by the "Kiwis" a very good show. Several very pretty camouflaged ladies dancing and singing. This troupe consists of over 50 performers and the show is run by Irene Vanbrugh's head man from London, who is now a Sergeant in the New Zealanders. I believe Irene Vanbrugh has given the troupe all her best gowns and frocks, which are now worn by the New Zealand Private soldiers who take the female parts. Wonderful scenery and lights, in fact it was like being back at the Gaiety in London. The New Zealanders have built the Theatre out of the remains of an old farm cow house.

After dinner Russell and I had a long talk concerning the imminent battle which is to come off at once. He is rather Napoleonic in his ideas and has great ideas on pushing right forward beyond Cambrai.

September 26th Final preparations for the attack; as far as I am concerned there is not much to be done. It is now for the Brigades to complete their arrangements.

Moved up to Ytres this evening and have taken up our residence in some dug outs. My dug out feels damp and cold, what with the electric light and the earth having fallen in in places, it resembles a grotto.

September 27th. Zero at 5.20 a.m. this morning (the time was officially called General Ponsonby 20, which reads, of course 5.20).

It is a big battle and most of the 1st and 3rd Army are engaged. On our left the Canadians are going for Bourlon. The Guards and 3rd Division are going for Flecquieres Ridge and Ribecourt. The 42nd Division on our immediate left move from Trescault along the low ground to the trenches North of

Beaucamp. We go for the high ground running northwards from the north of Gozeaucourt to Beaucamp and then push eastwards to Welsh Ridge.

The 5th Corps on our right consisting of the 21st Division and 33rd go for Gonnelieu to-night and try in this way to envelope the enemy holding Gouzeaucourt. As regards the 5th Division, the 13th Brigade under Beckwith are attacking, 1st West Kents on the Right, 15th Warwicks on the left, 14th Warwicks in support, 2nd K.O.S.Bs. in reserve.

Their first objective is African Trench which I believe is strongly held by the Bosch. They move under a creeping barrage and with Mark V tanks to protect their left. The 15th Brigade under Oldham move on Beaucamp and the high ground south of it.

In this Brigade the 1stBatt.Bedfords are on the right supported by the 16th Warwicks, the 1st Cheshires on the left, rather echeloned to the rear. The two right Battalions are to move N.Eastwards and the Cheshires behind them over the low ground with orders to mop up Beaucamp when the Bedfords have passed through it to the high ground beyond. The 6th Corps and the 1st Army advanced at zero hour and it was arranged that the 4th Corps should move at zero. 150: in other words two and a half hours later, which made it ten minutes to 8.

First reports state the 13th Brigade were heavily engaged and were unable to make any progress. African Trench is strongly held and the machine gun fire very severe. The 15th Warwicks have pushed on towards Beaucamp ridge. The 15th Brigade report good progress and slight casualties on our left, the 42nd Division in the low ground is experiencing strong resistance.

About 1 p.m. I heard that Flecquieres had been taken by the 3rd Division. The Guards Division I am told has had some very hard fighting, and on the other hand the Canadians on the left have met with slight opposition and are pushing on. At 5 p.m. the 42nd Division had made some progress, but were still some way behind us. Corps Commander sent orders for me to meet him at Valu to discuss future plans. The original plan was for the 42nd to advance at 6.30 p.m. and for ourselves to push off at 7 p.m. under a barrage and with the object of reaching the brown dotted line. This line includes the Northern edge of Beaucamp ridge and the village of Villiers Pluish. Oldman telephones down to say that he would be unable to start till 7.30 p.m. The 42nd said this would be too late, so it was finally decided to move forward at 1.30 a.m. in the moonlight.

Just as the conference was ending G.B. told me that a message had arrived from Gordon Hill at Ytres to say that we were being heavily counter-attacked. We had been forced to retire from Beaucamp village and our right was back in our original trench.

The 21st Division had also been obliged to fall back on to their original lines. In fact, the whole position was obscure and looked rather bad.

G.B. and I hurried back to our Head Quarters at Ytres and I gathered from Oldham that he was holding his own and had only been forced back a few hundred yards by Bosch bombing parties.

The amount of casualties was unknown and the position of the 15th Warwicks was very indefinite. I decided that the only thing to do was to stick to our original plan, but that the 95th

Brigade should carry out the job and push through the 15th
Brigade, counter-attack the enemy and drive him off Beaucamp
ridge. The advance to take place at 2.30 a.m. Gore Brown
went up to both Brigade Head Quarters to see that everything
was thoroughly understood.

September 28th. The moonlight advance was successful. A rear
Guard left by the Bosch of over 100 men surrendered to the 42nd
Division. On our front the Bosch Jaegers put up a good fight
in fact up to 10 a.m. this morning pockets of Bosch were still
holding out opposite the 15th Brigade.

11.30 a.m. 42nd Division reported to have gained Wesh ridge.
The 95th Brigade report they are in touch with them. The 21st
Division in my opinion ought to go straight for Gonnelieu.
This is the time to push everywhere. The New Zealanders behind
us are champing at their bits and want to push straight on:
I hope the Corps will let them go.

Went up to our advanced Report Centre at 2 p.m. where I
remained all the afternoon. Conflicting reports continually
being received from various sources as to our exact position.
I think there is no doubt that by this evening we shall be
east of the main railway that runs North and South and just East
of Gouzeaucourt and Villiers Pluish. Orders have arrived that
we are to move on eastwards at 3.30 a.m. to-morrow morning.

The New Zealanders on our left, the 21st Division on our right.

September 29th. The Division pushed on as ordered. The 15th
Brigade were unable to push through the 95th Brigade owing to
machine gun fire from Gonnelieu and did not get much beyond
"Holly" Trench. The New Zealanders pushed on Northwards and
reached the Canal but it appears doubtful whether they thoroughly
mopped up La Vacherie en route.

I went up to advanced Head Quarters and then took a walk
with Gerry Ruthven as far as African Trench. I am afraid most
of the dead we saw on the Battle field were our men, men of the
West Kent who had made such a gallant attack two days ago to
capture African Trench. It is a painful and melancholy business walking over a battle field strewn chiefly with our own
dead before they have had time to bury them. The Bosch was
shelling the valleys and his machine guns were very active.

Corps commander came up and discussed the situation with
Russell and myself. We are to make another effort to reach
the Canal to-night. I have sent orders to the 15th Brigade to
advance on Barrack Trench at 4 a.m. this morning as his first
objective and then to press on to the Gonnelieu ridge keeping
his left in touch with the New Zealanders and his right thrown
back on Bleak trench. I asked the 21st Division to co-operate
by moving from their present position on to Bleak Trench: but
I am told this is impossible as the Bosch has counter-attacked
the 33rd Division and have re-captured Villers Guisland. This
makes it awkward for us and gives us a very long flank to hold
on our right, I feel convinced however that the Bosch will
clear out of Gonnelieu to-night and have told Oldham he must
carry on with the attack. It is very cold and raining hard.

September 30th. Oldman's Brigade attacked at 4 a.m. They
took Gonnelieu which was practically evacuated except by a small
party of the enemy about 30 strong.

They then pushed on towards Santeux where they established

themselves on the high ground and pushed patrols into the village. They took nearly 300 prisoners. The attack was chiefly carried out by the 1st Batt. Norfolk Regiment.

Gordon Hall, Gerry Ruthven and I walked up to Oldham's Head Quarters which are now established by the Gouzeaucourt Cambrai main railway line.

We passed several young Bosch officers who looked quite a decent lot and heard that a British officer in the Lincolns who had been taken prisoner by the Bosch had been found on the road. He stated he had received very kind treatment and had been well looked after. He had been wounded and his wounds were well dressed, he was kept warm in blankets and given coffee. As one rarely hears any good concerning the Bosch I record this benevolent deed.

Corps Conference/at Metz. this evening The total captures by the British Army for the last three days amount to 25,000 and 400 guns. Les braves Belges also have accounted for another 6,000, and over 100 guns. We are to be relieved this evening by the 37th Division.

October 1st. In reserve, we remain at Ytres. I have now got to set to work to reorganize the Division into 9 Battalions instead of 12. G.H.Q. have decided to send out Pioneer Batt. The Argyles, to the 51st Division as fighting troops. The 14th Warwicks to be disbanded and to be absorbed as reinforcements in the Division. The New Zealanders have pushed forward and taken 60 prisoners, otherwise there seems to be a lull.

October 2nd. In the afternoon Gerry Ruthven and I went over to Lagnicourt to see the Guards Division. We found Torquhil Cook Alston, Guy Darell, Hely Hutchinson, who has become G.S.O. 3, and Cavalry Bewicke.

I heard news about Gilly Follett, he was killed a few days ago by a machine gun bullet. He was in command of the 3rd Guards Brigade, he was a great friend and I have known him now for many years. He had been wounded 3 times already in this war. Poor Henry Dundas is also killed, another great friend, he was brilliantly clever and very amusing. He was on my Staff in the 2nd Guards Brigade, and was only just 20 and must have had a great future before him. I shall miss him very much as he always made me laugh enormously at all his stories and imitations. He was Captain of the Oppidans at Eton when he was just 17 and was in the Eton XI.

I hear fat boy Gort did splendidly and that he has been recommended for the V.C.

The Guards Division Head Quarters are in a wonderful place. The dugs outs are large, well made, panelled and decorated. There is a large hall festooned with Laurel wreaths where it is said the Kaiser took up his abode some months ago, and some wonderful stables also I suppose made for the Kaiser's chargers.

October 20th. The 3rd Army attacked at 2 a.m. this morning, 6th Corps on the left, 4th Corps in the centre, 5th Corps on the right. As regards our Corps the 42nd Division were on the left, My division on the right, on our right were the 17th Division. The objectives were Solesmes on the left and the high ground between the village and Amerval.

The attack was carried out by the 13th Brigade under Beckwith. A very strong barage was put down on the Road railway by four Brigades of Artillery.

The attack started at 2 a.m. it was raining hard and there was a thick mist. This Brigade captured these objectives and took over a hundred prisoners. The 95th Brigade passed through them about 7 a.m. The 1st East Surreys on the right the Devons on the left with the Duke of Cornwall's Light Infantry in support. They reached the "Green Line" without much opposition, when there was a halt for about 3 hours, during which time the 17th Division came up on our right.

On leaving the "Green Line" to get back to their first objective, a line some 2000 yards in front of the railway towards Beaurain they met with determined opposition and were strongly counter attacked.

I went up with Harry Graham to Clermont Chateau our forward Head Quarters at 9 a.m. It was then decided that as the 17th Division on our right and the 42nd Division on our left were held up, another effort under a creeping barage should be carried out at 4 p.m. I spent the day at Clermont Chateau to be in close touch with the Brigadiers. It was the most dismal day I have seen for a long time. A thick mist and heavy rain continuing all day. At 4 p.m. the 2nd attack took place and eventually the final objectives were gained. In the meantime I had moved up the 15th Infantry Brigade in close support and had withdrawn the 13th Brigade to the Reserve area at Bethencourt as they were completely tired out. Both Brigades on our right and left went forward with the 95th with the result that the enemy were driven back with great loss. The 95th Brigade took 150 prisoners making our total captures nearly 300 all told. Our casualties on the whole had been slight and amount to about 250 all ranks, but probably this is a low estimate.

Solly Field reports that at Solermes he has taken 550 prisoners so our total bag must be in the Corps about 1000 and of course in the Army considerably more. Fryers my intelligence officer, generally known as Slab, and who talks German like a native tells me the morale of the Prisoners is very low. They belong chiefly to the 5th, 25th and 2nd Guards Reserve Division and have been bucketed about all over the country. The 25th Division is I believe Princess Alice of Hesse's own, and they wear on their shoulder straps an embroidered crown with the letter "A".

Corps conference late this evening, another push is on the tapes almost at once.

October 21st. A quiet day. I hear the total number of prisoners taken by the 3rd Army exceeds 3,000. The difficulty is now supplies, the Rail head has only just reached Caudry.

October 22nd. Mostyn has just arrived from the War Office to act as G.S.O.2 vice G.B. Evans and I rode up to Briastre very wet and very misty. The Bosch were shelling the ridges just beyond the railway pretty heavily all the morning.

October 23rd. The third Army continued their attack this morning. The only difference was that the 3rd Division were on the left of the 42nd and the 21st Division were on our right. The 15th Brigade under Oldham carried out the attack. The 95th Brigade in support and the 13th Brigade in reserve.

The objective given to us was the high ground east of Beaurain and the capture of the village.

Zero hour for the 5th Corps had been fixed for 2 a.m. and we were ordered to advance at 3.20 a.m. There is no doubt that the enemy expected an attack, soon after 1 a.m. they put down a protective barrage and at 2 p.m. they put down an intense barrage on our front line.

The order of battle was as follows: The 1st Bedfords on the right, the 1st Cheshires on the left, the Norfolks in close support and one battalion namely The Duke of Cornwall's Light Infantry on the railway line. The remaining Battalions of the 95th had been withdrawn to Behucourt to allow the 37th Division to pass through to the final objective.

Two Tanks were employed for the capture of the village.
The intense barrage on the troops forming up for the attack rather threw them out of their stride. There were a good many casualties including Spearman who commands the 1st Bedfords which at first caused considerable delay especially so when it was found that the 21st Division had been hung up by intense machine gun fire from Orvillers and Duke's Wood.

The leading Battalions having been reformed pushed forward and were able to gain their objective up to schedule time: the 21st Division pushing on at the same time and gradually overcoming the machine Gun fire. Oldham decided to push the Norfolks straight through the village, leap frogging the leading battalions. This was entirely successful and the village was in our hands about 8.30 a.m. over 200 prisoners were taken including a Battalion commander and the action ended in a great success.

Soon after 10 a.m. the 37th Division went through and meeting I believe with little opposition reached their objective.

Our casualties, I believe, considering the heavy barrage that was put down are not heavy. Something like 300 all told or may be a little more. I believe the total captures by the Army amount to some 3000.

I have sent the following message:-

TO G.O.C. 15th BRIGADE.

" The Major General would like you to convey to all Battalions under your command his sincere congratulations on their capture of Beaurain this morning in spite of the very determined resistance offered by the enemy.

The Major General would also like you to express to all ranks his admiration for their gallant conduct throughout the battle".

Baker Carr commanding the Tank Brigade and his Staff Captain came to dinner tonight. His Tanks did real good work today. New Zealanders report good progress and the 37th Division have also reached their final objective.

October 24th. Walked round to all Battalions in the 13th and 15th Brigades who are now in the town of Caudry. The men are delighted to get a rest after the severe fighting. Conference this evening, the question to be decided in future is to what is the best thing to be done when a Division on the right or left have their zero hour one hour and a half before we start our attack. It means that the enemy's counter barrage comes down on the line and causes loss and confusion before the flag drops. This is what happened to the 15th Brigade who had about 350 casualties entirely due from shell fire.

If Brigades are formed up in front of their original position, this may give the attack away. One must form up at least 2 or 300 yards in front and the danger is that the Division may be committed to an attack before the Divisions on their flanks can come up. If on the other hand you form up in rear: You must be some 1000 yards in rear to be any good and eventually you will have to go through the barage some time or another. However we decided that this second alternative was the best of two evils. Young Trelawny in the D.C.L.I. was killed yesterday also the Chaplain The Rev.Dugdale. Two very good fellows.

We asked the proprietor of one house and his two daughters to dinner to-night. They were full of stories of the German occupation of the town.

The local barber came to cut my hair in the afternoon.
He struck so many atitudes of revenge when he spoke of the Germans that the operation lasted over an hour.

www.ingramcontent.com/pod-product-compliance
Lightning Source LLC
Chambersburg PA
CBHW081045020526
44114CB00044B/2347